P9-EDN-490

To DIE in CHICAGO

To DIE in CHICAGO

Confederate Prisoners at Camp Douglas 1862-65

GEORGE LEVY

PELICAN PUBLISHING COMPANY
Gretna 1999

Published by Evanston Publishing, Inc., 1994
Extensively revised and published by arrangement with the author by
Pelican Publishing Company, Inc., 1999

Library of Congress Cataloging-in-Publication Data

Levy, George
To Die in Chicago : Confederate prisoners at Camp Douglas, 1862-65 / by George Levy. — 2nd ed.
p. cm.
Includes bibliographical references and index.
ISBN 1-56554-331-9 (hc : alk. paper)
1. United States—History—Civil War, 1861-1865—Prisoners and prisons. 2. Camp Douglas (Ill.)—History. 3. Prisoners of war—United States—History—19th century.
E616.D7L48 1998
973.7'72—dc21 98-21807
CIP

Manufactured in the United States of America

Published by Pelican Publishing Company, Inc.
1000 Burmaster, Gretna, Louisiana 70053

Twas a Pleasant Home of Ours Sister

Dedicated to Our Lady Friends
By Joseph H. Dunavan, Co. D, 2nd Kentucky Cavalry.

"Composed and Arranged in Camp Douglas"

1. Just a pleasant home of ours sister, in the springtime of our life.
   In those happy days when bright and gay we knew no sorrow or strife. . . .
   But time has sadly changed dearest. Those happy days are gone.
   And the playground of our childhood Ah its sad to look up-on.

2. That dear old home I've left sister. I've obeyed my country's call.
   To defend the land we so love and win our freedom or fall.
   Though not a joyous lot is mine. All dark with clouds is my sky.
   And within a prison's close embrace the hours pass sadly by.

3. Yet despair not of success sister which will bless our cause so grand.
   All we ask from god above is a great free southern land.
   Oh heaven may grant that prayer to us and victory and peace may come.
   Then joyfull shall be my glad return to that dear old happy home.

Contents

Illustrations

Tables

Acknowledgments

The staffs of following archives and libraries graciously made their material available:

Interlibrary Loan, Roosevelt University
Library of Congress-Prints & Photos-Manuscripts
U S. Army Military History Institute
Chicago Historical Society
Newberry Library, Chicago
Chicago Park District
Chicago Public Library
Louisiana State University, Middleton Library
American Philatelic Society
Duke University, Perkins Library
St. James Catholic Church
Museum of the Confederacy
Rush-Presbyterian-St. Luke's Medical Center
Moody Bible Institute
University of Kentucky Library
North Carolina State Archives
Tennessee State Archives
Illinois State Historical Library
The Filson Club, Louisville

Persons responsible:

Eileen Flanagan-Chicago Historical Society
Sara Schwartz-Illinois Regional Archives Depository
Soubretta Skyles-Oak Woods Cemetery
Charlotte Wells-Hebrew Benevolent Cemetery
Michael Musick-National Archives
Richard Popp-Special Collections, University of Chicago
Mary Michals-Illinois State Historical Library
Dr. Wayne C. Temple-Illinois State Archives
Mark W. Sorensen-Illinois State Archives
Paul Brockman-Indiana Historical Society
Dr. Richard J. Sommers and Michael Winey-U.S. Army Military History Institute

Introduction

Much has happened since this book was first published on July 1, 1994. Newly found hospital records in the National Archives verify the enormous death toll between January and May 1863, revealing that more Union dead were mixed up with the Confederate prisoners than was previously believed.

Court-martial records conclude the story of Pvt. P. K. Thornhill, the only Camp Douglas prisoner under a death sentence. More prison journals, such as that of Sgt. Oscar Cliett, 55th Georgia Infantry, complete the picture of what it was like to be a Confederate prisoner, or a Union soldier, in Chicago.

I had no preconceptions when I set out to write the Camp Douglas story. I had no ax to grind because the book does not spring out of my own character or experience. Any case to be made is not mine, but comes from the camp's records and documents left by those who lived and died there. My history professor at the University of Chicago is responsible for my undertaking this task. His sly remarks about the school concealing its Civil War heritage next to a prison camp made me curious. However, the university's alleged coverup proved only a minor ripple compared with more critical questions about Camp Douglas.

Why is there no simple explanation for the human misery that flowed in and out of it? For example, why did prison officials build a modern sanitary system and prison hospital years ahead of their time, while deliberately creating conditions that caused more deaths? What was it about the American experience that caused officers to shrug when guards killed prisoners on the streets of Camp Douglas for no reason? Many historians ridicule the idea that we Americans belonged to two different countries when the Civil War started. Does Camp Douglas prove them wrong? Why did prisoners never attempt to burn the camp down, although they had plenty of matches? Federal soldiers tried it. How did it happen that with approximately four hundred escapes, prisoners never harmed civilians? I have been left to try to explain these matters by myself because my old professor is now beyond criticism.

Nevertheless, I have not taken on the job of prosecutor or defense counsel. The facts are eloquent enough. The United Daughters of the Confederacy came to rededicate the Confederate monument at Oak Woods Cemetery in Chicago on May 30, 1995. Captain Ernest Griffin, descendent of a black recruit at Camp Douglas, was the instrumental force in bringing about a meeting with these ladies, and a feeling of reconciliation extended on all sides, or did it? Griffin, too, has answered the long roll near the camp about which he loved to talk.

In the beginning, Camp Douglas was not meant to be a prison. Construction for a recruiting and training depot began in September 1861. Barracks and stables were prepared for about eight thousand troops and two thousand horses. Suddenly, in that bitter winter of 1861-62, some strangers appeared at the edge of the city. With their odd accents and thin clothing, they were almost like foreigners. What sort of place had they come to? Was there any plan to care for them? What chance did they have of surviving in the near arctic climate? Due to their presence, Chicago would become the largest Confederate burial site outside the South.

To Die in Chicago describes the reaction of the citizens and Confederates as thousands of prisoners of war were dumped here after Union victories in the West. In this book, I try to go beyond statistics and probe the feelings and experiences of these men in an alien climate, often without sufficient food, clothing, shelter, or medical care.

Extensive research in archives, libraries, and historical societies has revealed information not readily available when the war ended, such as:

The Henry Morton Stanley Hoax: Historians relied upon his harrowing account as a Confederate prisoner at Camp Douglas before he became a famous explorer. According to the records he was never there.

The Black Prisoners of War: Black Confederates were held illegally at Camp Douglas until late in the war, according to prison rolls.

The University of Chicago: Inadvertently placed in the line of fire by Sen. Stephen A. Douglas's generosity, only a country lane separated it from Camp Douglas. Disease and death at the camp threatened its life throughout the war.

The Religion Issue: Conflicts arose between Chicago clergymen and commanding officers over a chapel, preaching, and evangelistic work.

The Fate of the Confederate Dead: Historical detective work tracked the remains of prisoners to five cemeteries in and around Chicago and revealed the indifference and mismanagement attending the burials.

The Commanders: Biographical sketches of the nine men who served as commandants from 1862-1865 showed widely different abilities and personalities. They revealed how their goals vitally affected the prisoners.

The Parolees: Union prisoners of war captured by the South in the disaster at Harper's Ferry found themselves prisoners at Camp Douglas, treated no better than Confederates.

Other areas of interest: Great escapes and near misses—a quartet of vicious guards who occupied prisoners' thoughts well into the 20th century—running water toilets—the beef scandal, involving President Abraham Lincoln's brother-in-law, and the coverup at the highest levels of government to protect him—a judicious examination of the famous "Chicago Conspiracy" of 1864 to free the prisoners.

GEORGE LEVY
April 10, 1998

Chronology of Events

1861

12 Apr ......Fort Sumter fired upon.
15 Apr ......Huge war meetings held in Chicago.
3 Jun ......Death of Sen. Stephen A. Douglas.
30 Sep ......Camp Douglas opens for recruiting and training.
7 Oct ......Col. William Hoffman named to manage prison camps.
1 Nov ......First barracks completed at Camp Douglas.
18 Dec ......Troops mutiny.

1862

16 Feb ......Fort Donelson falls to Union army.
20 Feb ......First group of prisoners arrive at Camp Douglas.
21 Feb ......Col. Joseph H. Tucker takes command of camp.
24 Feb ......Mayor of Chicago warns that city is in danger.
25 Feb ......Rebel officers and their slaves leave Camp Douglas.
26 Feb ......Col. Tucker replaced by Col. James A. Mulligan.
6-7 Apr ......Battle of Shiloh.
10 Apr ......Island No. 10 captured by Union army.
16 Apr ......Prisoners arrive from Shiloh and Island No. 10.
21 Apr ......Camp Douglas holds 8,962 prisoners.
25 Apr ......Col. Mulligan blocks an escape.
19 May ......Chicago investigates sanitary conditions at camp.
14 Jun ......Col. Daniel Cameron replaces Mulligan.
19 Jun ......Col. Tucker relieves Col. Cameron.
30 Jun ......U.S. Sanitary Commission condemns Camp Douglas.
8 Jul ......Martial law declared around camp.
9 Jul ......Col. Mulligan accused of mismanagement.
15 Jul ......Five women and a child found among prisoners.
22 Jul ......Dix-Hill Cartel: Agreement made to exchange prisoners.
23 Jul ......Prisoners launch major escape attempt.
4 Aug ......Col. Tucker arrests former mayor for aiding escapes.
12 Aug ......Col. Mulligan called to account for missing funds.
28 Aug ......Col. Tucker sends prisoners South for exchange.
9 Sep ......Union defeat at Harpers Ferry, Virginia.

27 Sep ......Camp emptied of prisoners, except for some sick.
28 Sep ......Paroled Union prisoners arrive from Harpers Ferry.
30 Sep ......Gen. Daniel Tyler takes command of Camp Douglas.
1 Oct ......Parolees mutiny and burn barracks and fences.
11 Nov ......Smallpox strikes camp.
23 Nov ......Gen. Tyler calls in regular army to crush mutiny.
13 Dec ......Col. Cameron replaces Gen. Tyler.
15 Dec ......Most parolees have left Camp Douglas.
30 Dec ......Col. Cameron relieved of command.

1863

1 Jan ......Col. Tucker resigns his commission.
5 Jan ......Battle of Stones River, Tennessee.
6 Jan ......Gen. Joseph Ammen assigned to run Camp Douglas.
11 Jan ......Battle of Arkansas Post.
30 Jan ......About 3,800 sick and freezing prisoners in barracks.
23 Feb ......Smallpox cemetery opens across from camp.
31 Mar ......Smallpox epidemic rages at camp.
7 Apr ......Infected prisoners sent to Baltimore for exchange.
13 Apr ......Col. Cameron replaces Gen. Ammen as commander.
19 Apr ......Capt. John C. Phillips succeeds Cameron.
4 May ......Camp emptied of prisoners.
12 May ......Capt. J. S. Putnam takes command.
17 Aug ......Prisoners from Morgan's raid arrive.
18 Aug ......Col. Charles V. De Land ordered to take command.
26 Sep ......309 members of Invalid Corps arrive for guard duty.
22 Oct ......Morgan's men make daring escape from dungeon.
6 Nov ......Running water sewers and toilets start operating.
16 Nov ......Retaliation against prisoners begins.
3 Dec ......About 100 prisoners tunnel out in worst escape ever.
16 Dec ......Gen. William W. Orme replaces De Land.
19 Dec ......Gen. Orme investigates food contractors.
30 Dec ......Blizzard and sub-zero cold strike.

1864

1 Jan ......Gen. Orme appeals on behalf of black prisoners.
3 Jan ......Gen. Orme places new restrictions.
18 Jan ......Prison population reaches 5,616.
28 Jan ......A new "Prisoner's Square" opens.
16 Feb ......Col. Hoffman requests court-martial for De Land.

19 Feb ......All black prisoners at Camp Douglas released.
1 Mar ......Col. James C. Strong assigned to run garrison.
17 Apr ......Gen. Ulysses Grant cancels talks on prisoner exchanges.
29 Apr ......Gen. Orme resigns as camp commander.
2 May ......Col. Benjamin J. Sweet succeeds Orme.
1 Jun ......Prisoner's Square rearranged to improve security.
11 Jun ......Plot to attack Camp Douglas rumored.
4 Jul ......Attack on camp reset to 20 July.
20 Jul ......Conspirators postpone attack to 29 August.
10 Aug ......Sutlers barred from selling food to prisoners.
18 Aug ......Gen. Hoffman orders cooking stoves removed.
28 Aug ......Alleged conspiracy to attack Camp Douglas collapses.
28 Sep ......Col. Sweet warns that escaping prisoners will be shot.
8 Oct ......Prison count reaches 7,402.
28 Oct ......Massive escape attempt smashed.
6 Nov ......Col. Sweet begins arresting "conspirators."
5 Dec ......Remnants of Gen. Hood's army crowd into Camp Douglas.
31 Dec ......Number of prisoners rises to 12,082.

1865

12 Jan ......Inquiries ordered into shooting of prisoners.
31 Jan ......Guards go on drunken rampage.
1 Feb ......Prison count remains at 11,711.
13 Feb ......First prisoner exchange since April 1, 1863, begins.
5 Jul ......Only 30 prisoners remain, and guards are withdrawn.
29 Jul ......University connects to Camp Douglas sewers.
2 Aug ......Officials begin to close camp.
29 Sep ......Gen. Sweet resigns.
1 Dec ......Army searches for over 4,000 dead prisoners.
11 Dec ......Bodies moved from smallpox cemetery to Oak Woods.
24 Dec ......Remaining buildings at camp sold.

1866

8 Jan ......Camp Douglas land returned to owners.
20 Mar ......Camp Douglas officially closed.
1 Dec ......Only 1,402 Confederate graves counted.
17 Dec ......Mayor demands that the army remove them.

1867

Apr 13-27 ..Dead moved to Oak Woods.

1882

25 Jan ......More bodies found at former smallpox cemetery.
3 May ......Army sends 13 bodies to Oak Woods.

1895

30 May ......Ex-Confederates dedicate monument at Oak Woods.

1899

20 May ......Confederate graves sinking into swampy ground.

1903

......Oak Woods fills in burial plot to save remains.

1992

......Furor erupts over proposed landmark status for Confederate monument.

1995

......United Daughters of the Confederacy rededicate monument.

CHAPTER 1

The War Capital of the West

Lincoln blames the war on Chicago—Enthusiasm of the people—Railroads converge on the city—Deadly illnesses—Primitive medicine—Camp Douglas is built—Workers mutiny—Recruits arrive.

Chicago, more than any other city in the North, was responsible for the Civil War, according to President Lincoln. When Joseph Medill, editor of the *Chicago Tribune*, requested the president to lower Chicago's draft quota, Lincoln turned to him with a "black and frowning face."

"After Boston, Chicago has been the chief instrument in bringing this war on the country," Lincoln said. "The Northwest has opposed the South as New England has opposed the South. It is you who are largely responsible for making the blood flow as it has. You called for war until we had it. You called for emancipation and I have given it to you. Now you come here begging to be let off from the call for men which I have made to carry out the war you have demanded."[1]

Surely, the president exaggerated. However, it was true that most Chicagoans supported the war enthusiastically, and per capita the city supplied more volunteers than any other in the Union. Chicago Republicans had masterminded Lincoln's nomination by bringing the convention to their city, and the Fort Dearborn settlement had become the power broker of 1860. Medill went home and raised six thousand more men. In all the city of 156,000 had now contributed 28,000 soldiers.[2]

Only ten years earlier, it required seven days to go from New York to Chicago. The town had no sewers or sidewalks. Streets were impassable in bad weather, and the city was deprived of its mail for weeks. Gas and water did not exist, and a mile from the courthouse was considered out of town, "where wolves were yet occasionally seen prowling about. Residents lived in true country fashion."[3]

Completion of the Illinois and Michigan Canal in April of 1848 brought in thousands of tons of freight. This event set off a building boom from 1851 to 1853, including the combined courthouse and city hall. The former village soon had 145 stores, several hundred homes, and five hotels. Telegraph service was opened in 1848, and some gas works in 1850, with service to two thousand customers by 1855.[4]

Railroads coming into Chicago caused a rapid transition from an agricultural to an industrial and commercial economy. Slaughterhouses, meat packing industries, textiles, and storage silos could feed and clothe many troops. Some 2,933 miles of railroad track touched Chicago, also ten trunk lines and 11 branches. The Michigan Central hauled 3,400 immigrants into town on a single day.[5] Rails of the Galena & Chicago Railroad replaced plank roads as the war began, and the Illinois Central Railroad became the longest railroad in America. It was the main reason for building Camp Douglas.

The growth of lake traffic was almost as spectacular as railroad expansion. Lumber, iron, and goods from the east moved to wharves on the Chicago River, while ships carried farm crops to mills in New York and New England. The city built a water tower in 1853, with a tank out in Lake Michigan, and water started flowing in 1854.[6]

Meanwhile, streets, alleys, and vacant lots reeked with filth. Trash and slops from houses landed in the streets, and the city drank water polluted by manure. Chicago had the highest death rate of any American city in 1855. This affected Camp Douglas when the city supplied it with water free of charge. Chicago had another major problem; it was sinking into the mud because it rested only four to six feet above the river.[7]

While engineering feats greatly improved the city's underpinning, medicine remained primitive. Chicago doctors subscribed to the "miasma" theory that vapors rising from decomposing matter carried diseases through the air. The army hired at least six Chicago doctors to treat Camp Douglas prisoners.

One prescribed roasted onions when a railroad mechanic sought treatment for his wife's earache. Her husband did not say whether she was supposed to eat them. A newspaper asked, "Why do so many children die in Chicago? Nine out of ten quarts of milk came from cows fed on whiskey slops, with their bodies covered with sores and tails all eaten off."[8] People began seeking help elsewhere.

Besides the commercial and industrial forces in the city, a religious movement, revived by the Depression of 1857, gripped the city.

"During the pitiless winter of 1857-58 men of the cloth spoke in daily meetings and by mid-March 1858, recorded over 250 conversions," one historian noted. "Morning and noon prayer meetings brought about striking manifestations of the Spirit's power. Testimonials from gamblers, drunkards, and degenerates of all stripes added to the gatherings, something wholly new in the annals of Chicago."[9] This movement carried over to intense Fundamentalist activity among the Confederate prisoners.

Economic conditions improved by 1860, and membership in the Chicago Board of Trade rose sharply. The population stood at 109,206, and Chicago real estate came to $37,053,512, amounting to one-quarter billion dollars in today's money. This produced $373,515 yearly in real estate taxes. Citizens boasted of a dozen newspapers, a fire department, four district schools, a mechanics trade school, a medical college, and 15 churches.[10] Chicago had the infrastructure for a war capital, with roads, power plants, transportation, and communications. Moreover, a supply of skilled labor, tools, and construction materials were readily available.

In 1860 five streets contained buildings as far out as two miles from downtown. Otherwise, nothing reached farther than a mile and a half from the courthouse. However, the new city was raised, drained, and connected to every part of the country. Streets consisted of planks, cobblestones, and wooden blocks. Swing bridges spanned the river, and horse-drawn street railways began to operate. Gas, water, coal, and stone were plentiful.[11]

Voters had much more power than they do today, electing every city department head including the city attorney, city physician, police board, fire chief, mayor, and 32 aldermen. Political warfare between Republicans and Democrats far exceeded today's animosity. It was the nature and the character of the people that had made the Civil War inevitable, the president thought, and he appears to have been right. The attack on Fort Sumter ignited a giant meeting in downtown Chicago.[12]

"The speech of Mr. Lovejoy was followed by the star-spangled Banner sung in splendid style by Frank Lumbard, the vast audience swelling the chorus with an intensity of feeling and effect we have never seen equaled," the newspapers boasted.[13]

Chicago held a double war meeting a few days later. "It would be impossible to describe the wild enthusiasm of the double meeting at Bryan and Metropolitan Halls last evening, called to procure subscriptions for the immediate expenses of our volunteers," a reporter marveled. "The money came down like rain, and the people rushed forward in unprecedented numbers at the various military headquarters to enroll in defense of the flag."[14]

Even the Wigwam convention center became the "National Hall." More than ten thousand people occupied all available space at a meeting there on April 20, and many were turned away. A judge administered the oath of allegiance to them because of rumors about traitors being present. This war fervor had special significance for Chicago, where some 27,000 Confederate prisoners would arrive.[15] How the city reacted to them is an essential part of the Camp Douglas story.

Senator Stephen A. Douglas was only 48 when he and his wife reached the Tremont Hotel in Chicago on May 1, 1861. He became ill the next day. On June 3, he was dead. He worked too hard, ate too much, drank too heavily, and chewed tobacco.[16]

Ironically, Illinois gave his name to the camp destined to become notorious in the South, although he was no enemy of slavery. He wrote to an autograph seeker in 1859 "that this Union can exist forever divided into free and slave states, as our fathers made it, if the Constitution be preserved inviolate." However, he supported the North in the war, and his "Save the Flag" speech to the Illinois General Assembly on April 15, 1861, made him popular.[17]

Charleston, South Carolina, was even more anxious than Chicago to get the ball rolling. "The most intense excitement prevailed in Charleston, when fire was opened upon Fort Sumter," wrote one reporter who thought the war long overdue. "Ambulances for the wounded were prepared; surgeons were ordered to their posts, and every preparation made for a regular battle."[18]

One war between Athens and Sparta had lasted 27 years, and a protracted war between the American North and the South seemed just as inevitable. "Honor, fear, and interest motivated the North and the South, just as they did the Greeks." Prestige was at stake here. Southern militarists and politicians feared what might happen if President Lincoln was allowed to supply Fort Sumter. Northern leaders worried about the consequences of not responding to the attack.

"But one sentiment prevails, and that is for war on traitors," the *Chicago Tribune* ranted. Women were also intent on fighting. "Sharp eyes detected a girl dressed as a man among them," as a regiment left for the front, the paper reported. "She was taken from the ranks against her protest; her name was Olson."[19]

James A. Mulligan, a leader in the Chicago Irish community, and a future commander of Camp Douglas, was most ferocious. He recruited 1,200 men for his local militia unit called the Irish Brigade. Unfortunately, Federal quotas were full, but he pestered the dying Senator Douglas for a letter to the War Department. Mulligan then traveled to Washington and obtained acceptance of the Irish Brigade as the 23rd Illinois Infantry.[20]

A local merchant contributed more than $120,000 for raising a company named after himself, the Sturgis Rifles.[21] Ethnic groups such as Germans, Jews, and the Irish rushed in to recruit and equip their own regiments. The army housed troops in breweries, public buildings, and even the former Wigwam where Republicans had nominated Abraham Lincoln. They soon spilled onto the prairies adjoining the southeast edge of the city, creating several makeshift camps that became Camp Douglas.

Governor Richard Yates had his hands full, and the Illinois legislature authorized him to establish a military district in Chicago. It covered the northern 25 counties of the state and was administered from Chicago and Camp Douglas.

Yates assigned Judge Allen C. Fuller to select the site for a permanent camp. He inspected the area already in use bordering the city on the southeast. He then chose this location for a permanent camp because of the prairie extending around it and because downtown Chicago was only four miles away. Nearby Lake Michigan offered an abundant water supply, and the Illinois Central railroad ran close by.[22] A more qualified person, such as an engineer, would have made a better choice of location. The ground was so bad that there was talk throughout the war about closing the place.

The governor ordered Col. Joseph H. Tucker, commanding the 60th Regiment, Illinois State Militia, to build the camp. Tucker was born in 1819 and arrived in Chicago in 1858 from Cumberland, Maryland, where he had headed a bank. He became successful in different types of speculative trading with a commodities firm and sat on the Chicago Board of Trade by 1861. He enjoyed part-time military life to relieve the stress of business.[23] The reason for the choice of Tucker cannot be found. Possibly, Yates felt that as a banker and businessman Tucker could best deal with contractors.

Tucker placed the camp's main entrance at the east end, fronting on Cottage Grove. A gate in the south fence allowed access to Douglas

Henry Graves. (Image courtesy of the Chicago Public Library.)

property where the University of Chicago stood. The camp used Douglas land for its smallpox hospital, and about four rows of garrison barracks occupied space there.[24] Illinois Central railroad tracks ran two hundred yards east of Cottage Grove, and the camp soon had its own railway station.

The state built barracks there in October and November 1861, mainly with troops called the Mechanic Fusileers, who were carpenter apprentices and journeymen from the Mechanics Institute in Chicago. These were wooden structures, designed after the customary army barracks. They were one-story, 105 feet long, and 24 feet wide. Interior walls were nine feet high and divided into three rooms, each containing two stoves. Each barrack housed 180 men and cost eight hundred dollars to build. These structures offered little protection against the fierce Chicago winters, with only a single thickness of pine boards, without plastering or ceiling.[25] Outside, the Fusileers covered the seams with narrow wooden strips and layered the roofs with tar paper. The camp held about eight thousand troops and two thousand horses.

The camp's stockade, only a low fence really, enclosed about 300 acres of land, 30.5 acres of which belonged to Henry Graves. Officials named the area Cottage Grove after the Graves's cottage and the grove in which it stood. Only two other houses stood nearby in 1851, but the war caused a local building boom, such as the Cottage Grove Hotel across from camp. However, Graves did not consent to the taking of his land, and he and his wife refused to budge.[26] Camp officials built the fence around the Graves's house so that it was enclosed on all sides except Cottage Grove Avenue.

The height of the camp's fence is a matter of controversy, but it was less than six feet at first. Henry Graves and others met on June 4, 1878, in an attempt to find the former site, but it had been built over.[27] They only found the camp's wooden sewer and the main entrance post.

Drawings in the National Archives show that the camp ran west four blocks from Cottage Grove to present-day Martin Luther King Drive. It was bounded on the north by what is now East 31st Street, and on the south by East 33rd Place, called College Place during the war, after the University of Chicago. The Olivet Baptist Church at East 31st Street and King Drive stands today in the northwest corner of the former camp.

Camp Douglas changed constantly but usually had three divisions.

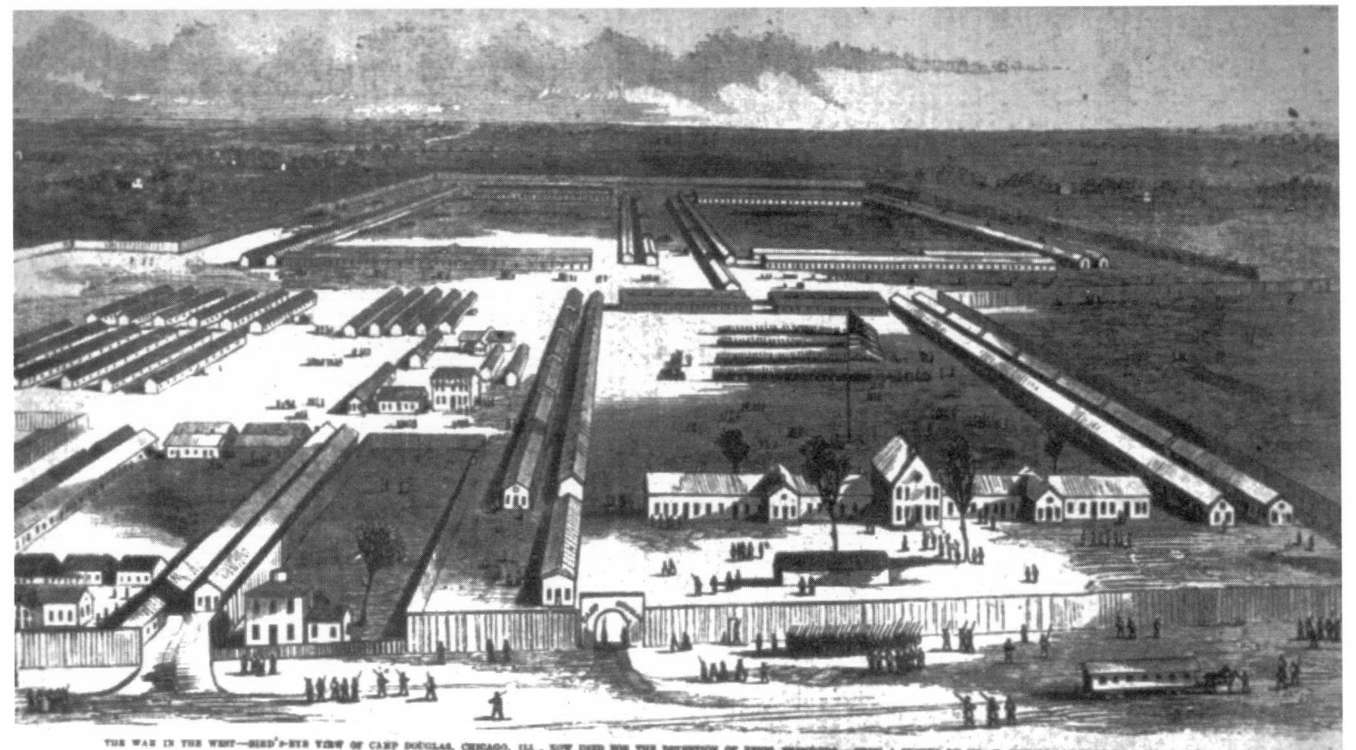

Lithograph of Camp Douglas, April 1862. (Image courtesy of the Chicago Historical Society.)

The eastern division was "Garrison Square," containing officers' quarters, post office, post headquarters, and a parade ground. Adjoining it to the south was the Graves's house and "White Oak Square," which held the infamous White Oak dungeon.

White Oak Square housed both troops and prisoners, until the army built "Prisoner's Square" in the western division of the camp two years later. Prison hospitals and a morgue adjoined White Oak Square. The western division held the post hospital, warehouses, and the surgeon's quarters.[28] Two roadways intersected the camp from north to south and east to west. Water entered through a hydrant in the northeast corner of camp.

However, this was not the extent of Camp Douglas. Troops camped outside as far as four blocks west. Public transportation to the area began in 1860, due to the influence of Senator Douglas, who invested heavily there. His land faced the camp on the east side of Cottage Grove and then crossed to the west where it abutted the camp's south fence. He had donated this western tract to build the University of Chicago, and it was prospering before Camp Douglas came along.

September 30, 1861, was the date reported by the *Tribune* for opening Camp Douglas, but construction was far from complete. "Arrangements have been made with the Illinois Central to give a new crossing and secure ready access to the lake shore," the *Tribune* reported prematurely. "The water in the camp will be supplied direct from city hydrants on the grounds. The City Railway Company are to carry, free, officers and soldiers on the business of the camps." The railroad ran on a single track with horse-drawn cars that came out from downtown Chicago.[29]

Despite the *Tribune*'s optimism, the camp lacked sewers, power, and gas, and the prairie could not absorb the human and animal waste generated by thousands of men and horses.

Governor Yates appointed Colonel Tucker as the first commander, although Tucker had no experience in managing a military depot. Worse, Camp Douglas was under the jurisdiction of the Post of Chicago, which included responsibilities such as recruitment, transportation, and oversight of downstate prisons. While the War Department intended the camp for recruiting and training, it was destined to become a prisoner of war camp and a camp for paroled prisoners of war. Colonel Tucker also lacked any experience in these areas. Regardless, his life became woven into the Camp Douglas experience, and not always for the best.

Private Benjamin J. Smith arrived by streetcar on October 11, 1861, to find "long lines of barracks newly constructed, and clean and comfortable."[30] Double bunks stood on each side of the room, with privies out back. A separate building in the rear contained a kitchen with a long table and benches for a hundred men. These were probably the "cook houses" often mentioned in reports.

Illinois tried to press the Mechanic Fusileers into service as infantry after they had finished constructing the camp, so they mutinied on December 18, 1861. Private Smith saw action sooner than expected and described it to the folks at home.

"A regiment called the Mechanics Fusileers mutinied last night and our boys were ordered out to put the laws in force. They had torn down about 40 yards of fence and burned it, and altogether it was quite a rebellion, but the sight of our bayonets had a very soothing influence on them, and they went to work and built the fence up again."[31]

The story had a good ending when the Fusileers paraded in Chicago and stopped at a saloon for a fill of lager beer before going home. However, their chaplain was not as happy. He had left his congregation to join the regiment and was now out of a job. He wrote to President Lincoln, requesting a chaplain's position at Camp Douglas. "I therefore feel that I have some claim to an appointment which many other clergymen have not," he argued with some merit.[32] He did not succeed because the camp already had a post chaplain named Edmund B. Tuttle.

About 4,222 troops from 11 regiments were at camp by November 15, 1861. Serious cases of measles occurred the following month. A recruit wrote from the hospital, "The provisions that they furnish is nothing extra Betty. I am very weak. It is all that I can do to hold my pencil." Measles remained a threat as late as October 21, 1863, when a prisoner told his mother that his health was good but expressed fear of measles for himself and his brother, also a prisoner.[33]

Regimental reports from Camp Douglas show an astonishing death rate for troops who were in excellent condition, especially compared with the prisoners.[34] Private Smith's bunk mate caught a cold and died on January 18, 1862. The recruits suffered 42 deaths from disease by February, a bad omen for the future prison camp.

CHAPTER 2

Troubles at Camp

A victory in Tennessee—Turmoil at Army Command—Prisoners sent to Camp Douglas—Colonel Joseph H. Tucker in command—Lack of security—Excitement in Chicago—Black prisoners of war.

A rumor was flying about that prison officials had received orders to put Camp Douglas in readiness for the accommodation of five thousand Rebel prisoners. In a classic case of bad timing the *Chicago Tribune* lampooned it as the joke of the season but made an amazing prediction.

"The idea of keeping five thousand prisoners in a camp, where the strongest guard couldn't keep in a drunken corporal is rich. The whole population would have to mount guard and Chicago would find herself in possession of an elephant of the largest description."[1]

Camp Douglas could not keep its own troops. The poor quality of some men exasperated Colonel Tucker. He complained that "recruits are being brought into the camp who for various causes are utterly unfit to be sworn into the service." Tucker charged that "the lack of discipline on the part of the men is due to the utter incompetence and entire negligence of the company officers."[2]

Many officers dressed like enlisted men and lived in their barracks. Colonel Tucker filed charges against 1,037 enlisted men for drunkenness, insubordination, fighting, playing cards with the prisoners, and shooting an officer. Theft, destruction of property, and desertion were widespread. A member of the Irish Brigade had to be bound hand and foot to get him back to camp.[3]

The garrison endangered citizens more than the prisoners did. "Careless handling of guns had wounded one citizen while he was sitting in his home," cited one report. A bullet smashed into a schoolhouse and would have killed any children who happened to be present. "Hen houses around camp were rifled, soldiers robbed citizens of watches, and Union deserters were on the prowl." An officer of the Irish Brigade menaced passengers with his pistol on the State Street car going to Cottage Grove. Several soldiers on the car seized a police officer who attempted to interfere and locked him in White Oak dungeon.[4]

Military police in Chicago, mistakenly believing that the city was under army rule, arrested several citizens and brought them to Camp Douglas. One drunk was doubly confused to see White Oak dungeon looming before him. Fortunately, he was only "reproved and sent out of camp."[5]

One marvels that the North ever gained the final victory. Surprisingly, these rowdies compiled impressive combat records, not the least of whom was the Irish Brigade. Meanwhile, troublemakers created serious security problems at camp, although they were a minority of the 40,000 recruits who arrived for outfitting and training.

A schoolteacher named William H. Tebbets wrote to his parents that he enlisted because his fellow townsmen had given up everything to go to war, "and we staying at home like cowards until those rebels tear down and destroy the best government that ever was; a government for which our forefathers fought bled and died. I have left a loving & beloved wife and five little children."[6] Private Tebbets saw action at Fort Donelson on February 16, 1862, and died at the Battle of Shiloh.

The victory at Fort Donelson set Gen. Ulysses S. Grant on the road to the White House and caused Camp Douglas to fill narratives and reminiscences into the next century. Confederates built the fort on the Cumberland River near the town of Dover, Tennessee. Holding Nashville would be impossible if it fell.[7] They wasted a good deal of time and energy in building Fort Henry on the wrong side of the Tennessee River, 12 miles away. Union forces took it on February 6, 1862.

Fort Donelson was another matter. It could have held, but the Confederate generals decided not to go down fighting. A probe by Grant had not shown any Confederate weaknesses, but plenty of Union weaknesses. Rain, sleet, frigid temperatures, and snow struck on February 14, matching the worst trench warfare of World War I.

Confederates inside the fort had no overcoats, and those outside had left coats, blankets, and knapsacks at Fort Henry. "Many a stout fellow felt that the wind was about to turn his blood into icicles," wrote a survivor.[8] The prisoners were poor candidates for a trek to the frozen prairies of Illinois. The road to Camp Douglas was the graveyard of an uneasy alliance. Americans who had once banded together to fight the British now turned their guns on each other. Neither government would lose any sleep over prisoners of war during the next four years.

Word of the surrender of Fort Donelson excited the North as its first major victory. General Grant gave no thought to what to do with the 12,000 to 15,000 prisoners of war. It was his duty only to collect them. General Henry W. Halleck in St. Louis, who commanded the Department of Missouri, was responsible for them, Grant thought.

The Union army had no experience in collecting and transporting so many other Americans to prison camps, and the War Department was surprised by the situation. Decisions about what to do had to be made on the spot. Officers hastily scribbled prisoner rolls on soiled and tattered scraps of paper, which survive today in the National Archives. Later the army issued printed forms for enrolling prisoners. Messages sent for the next six days were overwhelming despite the primitive telegraph.[9]

Colonel Tucker was on duty in Springfield, Illinois, when he wired General Halleck that Chicago could hold "8,000 or 9,000 prisoners." It was a serious miscalculation. Camp Douglas seemed a logical choice because the Illinois Central Railroad had a terminal at Cairo, Illinois, three hundred miles south of Chicago. Other reasons may be that the camp was well known, and the captor usually selects a distant prison to discourage escape attempts. Governor Yates did not want the prisoners in Springfield. "There are so many secessionists at that place," he warned.[10] Fort Donelson meant more than just the end of a Confederate outpost. A deep-seated animosity was emerging.

Confederate general Simon B. Buckner angrily wired Grant that the "ignorance" of some Federal executive officers caused his men to stand nearly all day in mud and cold without food. Buckner believed that the code of chivalry still lived, and he may have been right. Governor Oliver P. Morton of Indiana telegraphed that he could take three thousand prisoners. The governor of Iowa offered to handle three thousand at 16¢ each per day. Halleck decided that five hundred sick and wounded would go to Cincinnati. Grant advised Halleck that he "was truly glad to get clear of them. It is much less a job to take than to keep them," Grant wrote prophetically. Meanwhile, many escaped in the confusion.

General Henry W. Halleck. (Image courtesy of the USAMHI.)

A heavy burden fell on Brig. Gen. George W. Cullum, Halleck's chief of staff at the scene.[11] He wired Halleck on February 19, 1862, "Eight steamers with 5,000 prisoners here. Shall I send 3,000 to Indiana as proposed yesterday? Telegraph Reply immediately."

A second telegram followed: "About 9,000 prisoners had gone to Saint Louis before receiving your dispatch. One thousand left for Chicago this evening and 500 follow tomorrow morning." Cullum sent a third wire advising that none of Halleck's telegrams had reached him until after he had made disposition of the prisoners. "I am completely fagged out," he confessed, "and being among the little hours of the morning I must say good night."

The code of chivalry added to Cullum's problems. Confederate officers arrived at Cairo wearing swords. General Grant had agreed to this provision in the surrender terms. The United States had collapsed, but some men still cherished ancient ideas of courtesy between foes. Regarding the sick and wounded prisoners, Halleck ordered: "Treat friend and foe alike. It is simply a question of humanity!" General Cullum disarmed the officers, but guards did not search enlisted men thoroughly, and Camp Douglas soon collected a small arsenal.[12]

The War Department attempted to take control and directed the Illinois Central Railroad to move seven thousand prisoners to Chicago. It could move passengers up from Cairo in eight hours, much better time than today. However, the Confederates numbered far fewer than seven thousand, but no one was aware of this fact for days.

Andrew Jackson Campbell, an officer in the 48th Tennessee Infantry, described steamboats carrying the prisoners to Cairo, Illinois, as "filthy." The trip was also dangerous, as guerrillas fired from the shore and wounded several prisoners. Some compensations occurred, however, when sympathizers met the Confederates with great enthusiasm at St. Louis. Women, especially, defied the guards and showered the prisoners with food and tobacco.[13] Confederate officers were gratified to learn that General Halleck would honor the code of chivalry by returning their swords.

One prisoner wrote that memories of the boat trip "made his hair stand on end." He spent a week aboard a "rickety old craft" that was in constant danger of catching fire. Prisoners used a wood stove in the engine room to cook their meat, and the blaze from the drippings reached the underside of the upper deck. Another reluctant passenger described the craft as "old hulks of steamboats that appeared to be rotten from top to bottom, and the men had to eat and sleep on piles of coal."[14]

Halleck realized that the situation was out of control and wired desperately to General Allen C. Fuller in Springfield, Illinois, that the prisoners were traveling without enough security. He ordered Fuller to obtain temporary guards to meet the trains at Chicago and Indianapolis. He did not know when they would arrive, but ordered: "Be ready for them!"[15] Fuller, who selected the site of Camp Douglas, was now adjutant general of the state of Illinois.

Fuller was not "ready for them" because he also needed men and requested time to raise a citizen guard. The Confederates would welcome more protection. A drunken detachment of Union cavalry attacked one train near Chicago. Bricks thrown through the windows injured several prisoners. Two Confederates who went searching for water were left behind. They ran after the train, shouting and waving their hats until taken aboard.[16] The frozen prairies of Illinois were more frightening than any prison.

Union officers did not consult the commissary general of prisoners about moving POWs to Camp Douglas. Otherwise, fewer may have gone. The War Department created the office in 1861 and appointed Lt. Col. William Hoffman to this critical post. His immediate superior was Montgomery C. Meigs, quartermaster general of the Union Army. This office soon became an agency of the War Department, and Hoffman often had to deal with Edwin Stanton, secretary of war.[17]

Colonel Hoffman had spent his life in the army. Born in New York City in 1807, he graduated from West Point in 1829 at age 22. His father was in the War of 1812. Hoffman fought in every major battle of the Mexican War and in most of the Indian uprisings that followed. "Hard bitten" was too mild a term to describe him. He had one son, William, and may have been a widower.[18]

Surprisingly, the colonel was a paroled prisoner. Confederates had wrongfully taken him captive in Texas before the war. Montgomery C. Meigs appointed him commissary general of prisoners after he furnished a detailed report for a prison camp on Johnson's Island in Lake Erie. Unfortunately, the old soldier's initial planning provided for only a thousand prisoners.[19] He must have expected a short war.

Johnson's Island reflected the attitude of the government toward the prisoners at Camp Douglas and elsewhere. "In all that is done, the strictest economy consistent with security and proper welfare of the prisoners must be observed," Meigs told Hoffman on October 26, 1861. As far as practicable the prisoners would have to furnish their own clothing. Meigs closed with, "Trusting much to your discretion and knowledge, and believing that your appointment will alleviate the hardship and confinement of these erring men." It turned out otherwise. Meigs designed Fort Jefferson, which was to hold some famous prisoners of the Civil War.[20] He made no mistake about Hoffman, who proved an obedient, intelligent, and tireless official.

Colonel Hoffman was responsible for the supervision of prisoners, both military and civilian, and supervised correspondence and other business relating to Union prisoners of war confined in the South. The peculiar system of paroling prisoners of war to their respective sides required that parole camps be designated. Such camps also fell into Hoffman's jurisdiction. He had two assistants, Captains Henry M. Lazelle and Henry W. Freedley, who made inspections and reported to him.[21] The South did not develop a central prisoner of war authority until November 21, 1864, by which time it was too late.

Hoffman had yet to visit Camp Douglas, soon to be the largest prison camp in the North. The first prisoners from Fort Donelson arrived on February 20, 1862, and found to their surprise that there was no prison. Officers housed them with Union troops in White Oak Square. A few had managed to save their cooking utensils, such as "camp kettles, skillets, ovens, frying pans, coffee pots, tin pans, tin cups and plates."

Sergeant Charles Edwin Taylor, 20th Mississippi Infantry, had no complaints as he rode up to Chicago in style. "We were very well provided for having good passenger cars to ride in which was a good stove and plenty of fuel." He described his rations as "Crackers, Bakers bread, chip beef—fresh beef, Coffee already ground, sugar, beans, cheese & very good barracks."[22]

Private Milton A. Ryan of the 14th Mississippi Infantry retained bitter memories of parading through the frigid streets of Chicago. "Some would curse us and call us poor ignorant devils; some would curse Jeff Davis for getting us poor ignorant creatures into such a trap."[23]

Federal troops vacated White Oak Square on February 23, except for one regiment left to guard prisoners. The newcomers had upset the camp's tempo. A recruit wrote home, "There is 4,500 secesh here

Lieutenant Colonel William Hoffman (right front) outside his Washington Headquarters. The two men behind him are probably his assistants, Capt. Henry W. Freedley and Capt. Henry M. Lazelle. (Image courtesy of the Library of Congress.)

they have full liberty here in camp and are more numerous than the blue coats." Camp officials established a guard line between the barracks and the fence, but prisoners usually escaped if they could run past the sentinels. They called this exercise "running the guard." It would take years to develop a secure prison. Union prisoners in the South languished in factories and warehouses or went without shelter.[24]

Only one water hydrant in the northeast corner of the camp was working, and a severe shortage of latrines and medical facilities caused hardship to the blue and the gray alike. Colonel Arno Voss, who commanded a cavalry regiment leaving for the front, had taken charge of Camp Douglas on February 18 and attempted to prepare for the prisoners.[25]

G. L. Wells of the Seventh Texas Infantry liked his accommodations after a rough trip by boat and train. "I well remember the disembarking at Chicago before daylight on the morning of February twentieth. I recall how we stood shivering in the cold, crisp atmosphere waiting for the command to take up the march to the quarters that had been prepared for us. Colonel Mulligan was in command of the camp. With a foresight that does credit to the heart of him who suggested it, the stoves in the barracks into which we were ushered had been heated red hot and the barracks had been fitted with new hay. A more comfortable place under the circumstances I never saw."[26]

It is ironic that Wells credited Colonel Mulligan, who successfully avoided responsibility for the camp. The flamboyant Mulligan was Chicago's war hero who had declined to take command of Camp Douglas on February 14, 1862. The burden fell on Colonel Tucker, who had never seen action. Springfield ordered Tucker to return and take temporary charge on February 21. He still acted under authority of Governor Yates, not the Federal government. Adjutant General Fuller instructed him to see that the army quartermaster at Camp Douglas issued food and supplies to the prisoners and guards.[27] The former judge should have known that he could not give orders to the government.

Fuller should have been more concerned about who was guarding the prisoners. Many felt that they were there only because of poor leadership and quickly tested the shaky security as their guards rushed back to the front. There were no rules for providing food, shelter, medical care, or clothing for the prisoners who were organized into companies with their own senior sergeants. Colonel Tucker warned them to "use the sinks and not commit nuisances about the barracks."[28] Tucker faced a vastly different situation than when the camp was used for rendezvous and training of volunteers. He immediately appointed officers to new posts. Mulligan became the censor of prison mail.

Bureaucracies take on a life of their own, and mail service between Camp Douglas and the Confederacy continued without a blink. It was only a matter of postage. Mail within the Union lines could come and go directly, and mail traffic beyond that went through "Flag of Truce" exchange points in enemy territory. Aiken's Landing behind the Confederate lines was designated as such in March 1862.[29] Prisoners attached three cents in Federal stamps and ten cents Confederate, if they had them; otherwise, they had to enclose cash in an outer envelope.

The Federal post office at Fort Monroe, Virginia, was well stocked with Confederate stamps. Officials removed money from the outer envelope and attached postage before the mail went to Aiken's Landing.[30] The Confederate post office collected from the addressee if a prisoner had no money. Neither side provided free mail for prisoners of war, and families frequently sent Confederate stamps to Camp Douglas. This flow of letters sometimes had comic results. Most paper and envelopes at Camp Douglas carried patriotic markings, and prison mail going South often flaunted the Federal shield.

Mail was the most important line of communication for prisoners' families. "Tom Flemming will soon be well," George Pope of Tennessee wrote home. "Jim Booker is in better health than I ever saw him. Where is Buck Burnett, and what Company was cousin William Pope in?" John. W. Robison told about "two deaths here lately young Allen & Ben Godwin." Camp Douglas failed to record Allen Godwin's death.[31]

The war also caused disruption in Northern families, and Tucker received some wrenching letters. Catherine Lahey wrote from Boston about her son, Dennis: "It may be that he is in Chicago," she advised Tucker. "If you should see him, you will be kind enough to say to him that he is very unkind to keep me so long in suspense, and if anything has happened I should like to know." Tucker did not respond but filed her letter with the camp's records. Today this mother's anguish is carefully preserved in the National Archives.

Tucker was too occupied to answer Mrs. Lahey because no one

had said who was responsible for the prisoners, the Federal government or the state of Illinois. He notified Halleck that he lacked sufficient guards to prevent escapes. "The prisoners are being made comfortable in barracks, but they arrive in much confusion—parts of regiments and companies together—and many are thinly clothed and some sick and no surgeons with them," Tucker reported.[32] Camp Douglas was not supposed to receive sick prisoners.

Fuller turned to General Halleck for guidance. "Will you please advise me what character of discipline shall be enforced upon prisoners in our camps? The mayor telegraphs me this evening that there is much indignation that the rebel officers have been feasted at the principal hotels. Shall I order a strong enclosure about the barracks?" Loyalists in Chicago need not have been so indignant. Union officers could leave Libby prison at Richmond, Virginia, until some violated the code of chivalry and escaped.[33] Halleck ordered Fuller to confine all prisoners. "It was contrary to my orders to send officers either to Springfield or Chicago," he grumbled.

Fuller's order to supply clothing and equipment to the prisoners confused Capt. Joseph A. Potter, the assistant army quartermaster at Camp Douglas. "Shall I do it?" he wired the War Department. Fuller advised Halleck that there was only one Confederate surgeon among the prisoners and asked whether he should employ more medical officers. Halleck was furious and promised immediately to send more Confederate surgeons. "Their separation was made by the stupidity of subordinates and contrary to my orders," Halleck complained.[34] Fuller should have directed his question to Colonel Hoffman, not Halleck. This event began a long running dispute.

General Meigs settled the question of authority in a thundering telegram to Potter on February 22. "The prisoners are the prisoners of the United States! The supplies to be issued are the property of the United States. You are an officer of the United States. The State of Illinois has no more right to give you orders than the State of Massachusetts. State authorities have no right to give orders to an officer of the United States."[35] Meigs forgot that the United States was no more.

Chicago's mayor was more worried about the turmoil at camp. He complained to Halleck on February 24 that seven thousand prisoners endangered the city, with no stockade about their barracks and only a skeleton guard force. "I have seen two men guarding 300 feet with no other arms than a stick," he warned. "The secession officers

General Montgomery C. Meigs. (Image courtesy of the Library of Congress.)

are not kept separate from the men, and our best citizens are in great alarm for fear that the prisoners will break through and burn the city." Only 4,459 prisoners had arrived from Fort Donelson, but no one knew this fact.[36]

Fear of Union prisoners breaking out of Libby Prison and burning the city also worried citizens of Richmond. It did not happen there either. Halleck peevishly told Mayor Julian Rumsey to guard the prisoners himself. "Raise a special police force if necessary," he lectured. "I have taken these Confederates in arms behind their entrenchments; it is a great pity if Chicago cannot guard them unarmed for a few days. No troops can be spared from here for that purpose at present!" Halleck was claiming the victory at Donelson, which Grant had won while Halleck was in St. Louis. Mayor Rumsey took Halleck seriously and swore in "fifty good, strong, able-bodied men" to patrol the vicinity of Camp Douglas.[37]

G. L. Wells of the Seventh Texas Infantry believed that Rumsey's fears were groundless. "The enclosure was surrounded by a high board fence, which was well guarded by sentinels day and night," he claimed.[38] Mayor Rumsey sent a large force to watch the camp "so that they may not get loose and come down into the city," according to one homemaker. Her husband, Enoch, had been there every night for the past week on special duty. Nevertheless, about 77 escapes occurred by June, so the mayor had a point.[39]

However, it was not likely that many prisoners cared to escape at the moment. Drummer boy DuPree, 13 years of age, lost most of his clothing at Fort Donelson and recalled what it was like to arrive as a prisoner. "When we reached Chicago, it was below zero. I stood in the crisp snow from 4 til 9 a.m. That first night was bitter cold, and from then until the end of winter, scores of men died daily of pneumonia." He was stretching it a bit. Men died daily, but not by the scores. When a reporter dismissed another young prisoner, only three feet six inches tall, as a drummer boy, he responded with an oath. "I shoulder a musket, by G____!" The youngest prisoner was J. Graves, Company E, First Alabama Infantry, listed as a "child 12 years of age."[40]

The city felt as though aliens had come from some foreign country. "Camp Douglas was at an early hour besieged by thousands of citizens anxious to obtain a sight of the secessionists," the *Tribune* reported. Officials barred all visitors, except "those with business at camp." The exception became the rule as reporters, friends, family, and Southern sympathizers roamed about freely. A tearful reunion attracted attention when the parents of a Chicago lad found him among the prisoners. "Oh, my dear boy!" his mother sobbed. "Thank God we have found you!" Her "dear boy" claimed that he had been forced into the Rebel army while seeking work. This was a frequent excuse. It seemed that half the Rebel enlistments were shotgun weddings.[41]

Prisoners had the run of the camp, according to Frank Tupper, a recruit in training.[42] Camp Douglas was barely a minimum security prison. "Escapes are common," Tupper wrote. "Several have been shot in trying it and numbers have also got away and not been caught." He described the prisoners as "a motley looking crowd." One Mississippian told him that "this was the coldest country he had ever been in." Tupper agreed. "A good share of them won't go to war again once they get home. Others were stubborn and say they will fight again," according to him.

A reporter also saw the Southerners as a "motley assemblage of humanity" because of their ragged and mismatched uniforms. However, another newspaper praised men of the Seventh Texas Infantry and 20th Mississippi as a "dare-devil set of fellows and still full of fight." Two-thirds of the others were glad to be out of the war, according to this reporter, while many were sullen and could not conceal their hatred. They believed that everyone in the North was an abolitionist. "Let us alone and the war will cease!" Confederate officers insisted.

The Mississippians wished to fight on, while many Tennesseans did not, the *Tribune* claimed. However, this did not mean that the North had won any hearts. Private John W. Robison confessed to his wife that her father had been right in advising him to stay home in Tennessee but that taking the oath of allegiance at Camp Douglas would be dishonorable. She kept a stony silence, and John soon complained that "he had not even received the scratch of a pen" from her.[43]

One prisoner had personal reasons for not wanting to be in Chicago. The *Tribune* revealed that "Rev. W. G. Howard, the sermon stealer who formerly presided over the First Baptist Church of this city, is among the number of prisoners in the capacity of a chaplain of one of the Louisiana regiments. Sundry small creditors will be rejoiced at his coming if he has lately been paid off," the paper snickered.[44]

Prison officials furnished soap and water, and the men were "washing and scouring themselves while stripped to the waist in frigid temperatures." A Texan "profanely" remarked that the treatment was "a ——— sight better than we had a right to expect."[45]

Religion made an early appearance when Dr. James Pratt of Trinity Church in Chicago preached the first sermon to prisoners on February 23, and many gathered in the chapel. The minister assured them that he had not come to talk politics but to point out the fearful day of final reckoning. "What would they do then if they still had doubts about religion?"[46]

An army recruiter claimed that he could enlist at least five hundred prisoners at Camp Douglas. "Four out of every five are perfectly willing to take up arms for the Union and anxious thus to testify their loyalty." Hoffman was at his New York City headquarters when he received a telegram from General Meigs on February 24, setting out the first regulations for the care of prisoners. The government would furnish blankets, cooking utensils, and clothing, but only enough to prevent real suffering. "Much clothing not good enough for troops has by fraud of inspectors and dealers been forced into our depots. This will be used."[47]

The question of what to do about black prisoners arose on February 25 when Halleck ordered Tucker to move Confederate officers to Camp Chase at Columbus, Ohio. He said nothing about taking slaves, and six of them went to Camp Chase with their owners. This practice of returning slaves caught the attention of President Lincoln and Congress. Lincoln quickly ordered it stopped, but many believed that his order did not apply to servants captured with their owners. A Senate investigating committee soon discovered more than 70 slaves serving Confederate officers at Camp Chase.[48] Camp Douglas records show much confusion in listing seven blacks on prisoner rolls.

TABLE I

BLACK PRISONERS CAPTURED AT FORT DONELSON[49]

James, black. Co. H, 7th Texas Infantry. Property of W. D. Powell. Captured February 16 1862 at Fort Donelson. Remarks: Enlisted [in Federal service].

Sam [Samuel Hill], contraband. Co. H, 7th Texas Infantry. Property of J. S. Crawford. Captured February 16 1862 at Fort Donelson. Remarks: Exchanged via Cairo.

Nathan, contraband. Co. H, 7th Texas Infantry. Property of T. H. Cray. Captured February 16 1862 at Fort Donelson. Remarks: Enlisted [in Federal service].

Peter Calloway, negro. Co. D, 7th Texas Infantry. Captured February 16 1862 at Fort Donelson. Remarks: Released unconditionally September 10, 1862.

Joseph Matthews, negro. Co. C, 20th Mississippi Infantry. Captured February 16 1862 at Fort Donelson. Remarks: Released unconditionally September 10, 1862.

G. Blackwood, colored. Co. C, 3rd Tennessee Infantry. Captured February 16 1862 at Fort Donelson. Remarks: none.

Isaac Wood, negro. Co. E, 20th Mississippi Infantry. Captured February 16 1862 at Fort Donelson. Remarks: Exchanged Sept/29 62 via Cairo.

Three of these men were undoubtedly servants, and four appeared to be soldiers. The army was not reluctant to jail black prisoners. Racism in the North was widespread, and society discriminated against blacks in education, employment, and civil rights.[50] Black children attended segregated schools in Chicago, for example. Tucker did not even list slaves owned by Confederate officers.

Taking servants to the war was hazardous, however. One *Tribune* reporter overheard a slave say to his owner sarcastically, as he labored under a heavy bag, "Golly, Massa Richards, who'd a thunk that we's comin' to this here Northern water hole to spend the summer!" His owner, wrapped in a yellow blanket, looked around and shivered. Another servant said just as bitingly to his master: "Pears we're takin' our vacation early this year."[51]

The seven blacks remained at Camp Douglas because three belonged to enlisted men, and the rest were either free men or slaves without masters. Some claimed to be soldiers. Others denied it.[52] "One thing is certain," the *Tribune* noted, "that many of them are as well dressed as the commissioned officers we have seen."

The garrison numbered only 469 enlisted men and about 40 officers to hold back 4,022 Rebel privates and 350 noncommissioned officers on February 26, 1862. General Halleck ordered Colonel Tucker to Springfield, despite the danger. The *Tribune* reported that Mulligan assumed command of Camp Douglas on February 26. This was accurate, because Tucker wrote to Mulligan from Springfield on the 22nd again requesting him to take charge of the camp and relieve Illinois of the expense.[53]

Mulligan was a Federal officer, making Camp Douglas the government's responsibility. Tucker would return as commandant on June 19, 1862. Governor Yates, a powerful ally of President Lincoln, was still calling the shots despite General Meigs. Mulligan had much with which to contend. Some problems were of his own making, but the prairie camp site suffered severe deterioration, and sickness and death among the prisoners reached epidemic proportions.

Contrary to Civil War romanticism, the blue and the gray did not feel as though they were brothers or even fellow citizens. Reverend Edmund B. Tuttle, post chaplain, called Confederates "poor white trash, who claimed to be a foreign foe from another country that the North had invaded." Tuttle, unlike some counterfeit army chaplains, was an ordained Episcopal priest and rector of a church.[54]

Colonel Tucker encountered this "foreign foe" argument when he ordered the prisoners to work and improve their own conditions. Nine sergeants of the Tenth Tennessee Infantry vehemently protested, "as we cannot conscientiously nor consistently with our duty to our government while prisoners of war do work for the United States!" Almost identical letters come from the 15th Arkansas Infantry, the Third, 46th and 50th Tennessee, the Seventh Texas, and Second Kentucky Infantry.[55] They had a different view of the war, and no compromise was possible for them.

Tucker backed down, as he had no specific authority to force prisoners to work. Hoffman stated that "all duties connected with the police of the camp and the good condition of the barracks are legitimate duties for them to perform without compensation."[56] He included roof repair, garbage removal, and cleaning sewage as part of normal prison work but drew the line regarding the stockade. The army should pay prisoners for working to keep themselves in if they built one. Still, he gave no orders to use force, and it would be years before prisoners had the choice of working or looking down the barrel of a gun. Confederate surgeons were the exception. They either helped care for prisoners or went to White Oak dungeon.

Meanwhile, Union recruits took up the burden of maintaining the camp, some of whom agreed with Tuttle's low opinion of the prisoners. "The secesh prisoners are as motley a looking set as you ever saw," one man wrote to his hometown paper. "There are of course among so large a number many intelligent faces to be seen," he said smugly, "but their uniform (!) causes them to appear far worse than our common day laborers, when dressed in their every day working suit."[57]

Prisoners jeered at the guards as "stay at home soldiers," not knowing that they were soon going into combat. Many despised the bluecoats as abolitionists who were fighting to put Southern whites under black rule, which was not true. "The more we see of the Yankees the more we hate them," George Pope wrote home on June 21, 1862.[58] Nevertheless, cataclysmic events would lessen their differences.

A nun who lived on the road to camp reported mournfully, "During the greater part of this year, companies of Federal troops, shoeless, hatless, coatless very often, with squads of rebel prisoners, handcuffed singly or in pairs, in the same destitute condition, were crowding into Chicago from the different depots, marching to Camp Douglas. All the glory and panoramas of war had departed from these processions."[59]

CHAPTER 3

Creating a Prison System

Colonel James A. Mulligan replaces Tucker—Poor condition of prisoners—The dying begins—Regulations issued for their care—Colonel William Hoffman visits the camp—A religious dispute—A murder in the barracks—More interference by General Henry Halleck.

James A. Mulligan was born in 1830 at Ithica, New York, and grew up in Chicago. He was a well-educated lawyer and, like Colonel Tucker, enjoyed military life in a local militia company while working at his profession. The young attorney visited Central America on a railroad project, was a clerk in the State Department in Washington, and returned to Chicago to edit a Catholic newspaper.[1]

He helped raise the Irish Brigade, officially known as the 23rd Illinois Infantry Regiment, with himself in command. The unit was not strictly Irish since a recruit named Israel Solomon joined it on June 15, 1861.[2]

Mulligan ended up at Camp Douglas in January 1862 because of some difficulties. He had called the hand of Confederate general Sterling Price at Lexington, Missouri, on September 19, 1861, with only 2,700 men.[3] The Confederate force numbered 18,000. Mulligan refused to retreat and fought for 52 hours before surrendering. This battle cost the North about one hundred killed and wounded. General Price captured the entire army, including Mulligan and five more colonels.

Price also took 118 other officers, five pieces of artillery, two mortars, three thousand rifles, many sabers, 750 horses, wagons, teams, and ammunition. His troops gathered more than $100,000 worth of stores, and $900,000 in cash that Mulligan had confiscated from a Confederate bank. The army exchanged Colonel Mulligan on October 30, 1861, and he enjoyed great popularity in Chicago. One businessman requested Mulligan's autograph for his sister living in Boston. In a

Colonel James A. Mulligan. (Image courtesy of the Library of Congress.)

letter to another admirer Mulligan claimed that General Price had 28,000 men.[4]

The South paroled Mulligan's troops upon their word not to take up arms again until exchanged. The North had to trade many Confederate prisoners or honor the parole. A recaptured soldier who had not been exchanged was subject to summary execution. The army discharged the Irish Brigade on October 8, 1861, as no prisoner exchange was taking place.[5] The South escaped the burden of maintaining prison camps this way, and the North lost many veteran troops. Union general George B. McClellan declared the regiment exchanged two months later, and it reorganized at Camp Douglas.

The War Department placed the Irish Brigade on guard duty when Mulligan took command of Camp Douglas. About five thousand prisoners were on hand, with more arriving almost daily. Schoolchildren sent to taunt prisoners marching to camp from the depot became "still as death at the sight." One child remembered how "we were filled with pity for the poor fellows when we saw their feet peeping out through their poor shoes on the day in February with a slight fall of snow on the ground—about two inches—and some with pieces of carpet and a pillow to keep them warm."[6]

Mary Livermore, a famous feminist and army nurse, took a less sympathetic view. "They seemed a poorly nourished and uncared for company of men," she reported, "and their hopeless and indescribable ignorance intensified their general forlornness. It was pitiful to see how easily they gave up all struggle for life, and how readily they adjusted themselves to the inevitable. Not less uncomplainingly than the camel, which silently succumbs to the heavy load, did these ignorant, unfed and unclad fellows turn their faces to the wall, and breathe out their lives, without a regret, or a murmur."[7]

It is unlikely that prisoners gave up so easily, but their condition was not surprising given the recent winter campaign. The Union army sent three tons of corn meal around March 1, 1862. Included were large quantities of blankets, clothing, shoes, and eating utensils. Cornmeal allowed for the difference in diet, being a Southern staple, while Northerners ate white bread.[8] Worse conditions prevailed in Southern prisons, and Richmond claimed that it could not feed and clothe prisoners. The Federal quartermaster shipped thousands of blankets and shoes and huge quantities of clothing and food to Union prisoners in November 1862.

Mulligan probably continued the guard schedule established by

Colonel Tucker in December 1861. Three squads stood watch with two hours on duty and four hours of rest, with the first guard mount at 9:00 A.M. They lived in tents on the "Old Fair Grounds," a two-block area touching the west side of camp.[9] Sergeants were responsible for ensuring that each squad was ready for duty. They prohibited talking between guards and prisoners, but it never stopped. The men were curious about each other.

Colonel Hoffman was at his headquarters in New York when he received a telegram from Quartermaster General M. C. Meigs, on February 24, 1861. His boss set out the first regulations for care of prisoners. Hoffman was to provide only what was "absolutely necessary" to prevent their suffering. "Besides the rations allowed by regulations without regard to rank the United States will supply such blankets, cooking utensils and clothing as are necessary to prevent real suffering," Meigs added.[10]

The order was inconsistent. Prisoners would receive the same rations as Federal soldiers if Hoffman provided what army regulations called for. This went beyond doing only "what was absolutely necessary." One prisoner soon told his wife, "I am as fat as I ever was. My weight is 163 lbs."[11] Hoffman then came up with a scheme to reduce rations and had problems with Mulligan over it.

Hoffman inspected the camp on March 1, 1862, and commended Mulligan. "The hospitals are well organized and the sick are having the best possible care taken of them," Hoffman wrote to Meigs. Chicago physicians also stopped in. They praised Colonel Mulligan but found many sick prisoners in barracks for lack of hospital space. Mulligan seemed unaware of the need for a quarantine, and Hoffman ordered him to stop admitting visitors. Friends could send packages, and provisions for the sick should go to the hospital. Prisoners could receive small amounts of money.[12]

Mulligan disobeyed Hoffman's order of no visitors, and sympathizers made the camp a social Mecca. A Dr. Walder brought tobacco to Sgt. Charles E. Taylor of the 20th Mississippi on March 6 and introduced him to a Mrs. Morrison [Mary Morris] "who by the way is a fine lady and a good secesh I think," Taylor judged correctly. She became famous in the Camp Douglas Conspiracy of 1864. He also met Howard Priestly who visited an old schoolmate in the 20th Mississippi. Priestly "is a good Union man," Taylor said without malice.

Taylor had a full day on March 8. Priestly came with his wife and sister, bringing "fruit cake, oranges, Biscuits and Milk." Taylor was a musician, and Priestly gave him a violin. He found something special in this teenage sergeant. Following them was a Mr. Clark, "a wealthy gent who lives on the interest of his money," Taylor recorded with amazement. A Mr. Howard and Charles Pope, "nephew of General Pope of the U.S. Army," also arrived.

Visiting continued as late as March 20 when Taylor met with "Mrs. Waller (Mother of Young Waller whom I became acquainted with on our first arrival here)." The Camp Douglas Conspiracy involved Mrs. Waller, and the military arrested young Waller. Colonel Mulligan finally closed the faucet around April 12. The Reverend Thilman Hendrick of Tennessee soon wrote home that coming to Camp Douglas without authority from Governor Andrew Johnson was useless.[13] Only physicians and ministers were admitted.

Captain John Christopher, the army commissary of subsistence, awarded the food contract to a Chicago contractor named John W. Sullivan. His price of $10.85 per ration was reasonable. Hoffman told Mulligan that the ration was "larger than necessary for men living quietly in camp, and by judiciously withholding some part of it to be sold to the commissary a fund may be created with which many articles needful to the prisoners may be purchased and thus save expense to the government."[14] Hoffman suffered much heartburn trying to get the prison fund going.

A ration consisted of 3/4 of a pound of bacon or one and 1/4 pounds of beef, one and 1/3 pounds of white bread or one and 1/4 pounds of corn bread, 1/10 of a pound of coffee, one and 1/2 ounces of rice or hominy, 1/6 of a pound of sugar, a gill [1/4 pint] of vinegar, one candle, one tablespoon of salt, and beans, potatoes, and molasses in small amounts.[15] The ration changed continuously, including the number of days it had to last.

Prison officials sold unissued rations back to the contractor or the army commissary. Prisoners might eat well or go hungry, depending on the number present and the size of the reduction. The commissary of subsistence controlled the prison fund, made disbursements on order of the commandant, and filed a monthly report with Hoffman's office showing expenditures.

This fund paid for tables, cooking utensils, mops, brooms, and other cleaning equipment. Bedticks, straw, repair of barracks, lantern oil, and even stoves, or any other item that could benefit the prisoners came out of it.[16] Extra pay for the clerks who handled prisoner's mail or their money was justified. Some disbursements were to their detriment when, for example, the fund was used to pay detectives, spies, and informants. Business taxes went into it, as did money confiscated from prisoners and money belonging to the deceased.

The post surgeon drew on a hospital fund, in much the same manner, and purchased food supplements, underclothing, laundry, cleaning equipment, and other sanitary items. This fund never amounted to much because the sick needed all of the rations they could get during the severe winters when little food was sold to the contractor.

Prisoners struggled through ice, snow, and the agonizing winds howling off the ice-covered lake during the winter of 1861-62. Frozen hydrants caused a water shortage, and soon two to three hundred prisoners were in the hospital. The number reached 325 on March 4, 1862. "A large barn in the camp has been comfortably fitted up, and yet there is not hospital room enough," the *Tribune* reported. Colonel Hoffman told General Meigs three days later that the camp held more than five thousand prisoners, about four hundred of whom were hospitalized. "There have been comparatively few deaths," Hoffman understated, "and the attending surgeon thinks that now that the sick can be well taken care of the number of patients will rapidly diminish."[17]

Miscalculations continuously plagued Camp Douglas. The toll of Fort Donelson prisoners was severe, contrary to Hoffman's report. They had been in camp the longest and suffered the worst weather. One in eight died of pneumonia, pleurisy, colds, and bowel disorders. Measles even claimed a Union soldier.

Mulligan planned to drain the swampy land by a series of ditches and trenches and to build a stockade 12 feet high with a guard mount on top. These projects had to wait for the ground to thaw. Colonel Hoffman naively reported that prisoners "generally express themselves very well contented with their position and gratified for the kind treatment they have received, and there does not seem to be the least desire on their part to violate any restrictions placed upon them."[18]

Hoffman left camp around March 7, writing Mulligan to requisition all articles "absolutely necessary" for the health and comfort of the prisoners. As usual, economy was the watchword. The ban on visitors continued, and prisoners could receive "non objectionable" material. Nevertheless, Hoffman gave no instructions to reorganize the camp for better security.

Camp Douglas soon earned the reputation that today compares it with Andersonville. Conditions aroused sympathy in Chicago, and Reverend Tuttle became chairman of a relief committee. "Collections were taken up in the churches; and we supplied medicines by the wagon load, and employed careful apothecaries to aid the post surgeon, Dr. Winer," Tuttle reported. "I suppose I distributed clothing from Kentucky, the first year, to the amount of $100,000. It was mainly among the sick and dying."[19]

Colonel Mulligan had "received every possible courtesy from Confederate General Price and his staff" while he was a prisoner. He reciprocated by giving Tuttle's committee some space in his quarters, and he permitted the post surgeon to bring in volunteer doctors from Chicago. Meanwhile, three of the Rebel surgeons sent by General Halleck refused to work because "they would not take orders from a Federal officer," and two resigned.[20] Mulligan told them that prisoners could not resign. A threat to send the trio to White Oak dungeon in irons quickly settled the matter.

The garrison resented the attention given prisoners. "Have the good people of Chicago forgotten that there are such beings as Union soldiers in camp here!" they complained.[21] The committee furnished prisoners with clothing, books, wine, and sweets. Donations even included washtubs and wooden pails, but the garrison received nothing. This was not surprising, considering the fact that some soldiers were getting drunk and committing crimes in the city.

However, the committee's resources were meager in comparison to needs. Survival at Camp Douglas depended upon many factors. Time and place of capture decided how much equipment and clothing a prisoner might save.[22] Finding friends and forming groups for mutual aid, protection, and conversation was important.

The approaching summer would be intolerable without adequate sewage, drainage, and fresh water. Winters were extra severe, and prisoners required warm clothing and a good deal of fuel for their stoves. Colonel Hoffman had proposed two-story barracks, with weather stripping and a ceiling on the second floor. The army rejected this plan in favor of one-story buildings made of a single thickness of pine boards without insulation or shingles and with no plastering or ceilings.[23]

Lack of housing caused a dispute over the chapel. Colonel Mulligan made it a barrack, according to one group dedicated to bringing Christ to the prisoners. Dwight L. Moody had come to Chicago in

1856 from Boston, with a heritage of Puritanism and antislavery zeal. He soon became part of the evangelical church movement through the Young Men's Christian Association. The YMCA built a chapel in Garrison Square in 1861 with Colonel Tucker's permission. Moody went there to preach a week after the first prisoners arrived. "These meetings were kept up two or three weeks, and many were converted," his biographer claimed.[24]

John V. Farwell, president of the YMCA, complained directly to Edwin M. Stanton, secretary of war, on March 7, 1862. "While Providence has permitted our soldiers to fill this camp with our enemies we cannot but believe that we should preach the same gospel to them that we did to the brave fellows who in the march of events have turned the tide of battle in our favor," Farwell griped.[25]

He was careful to exonerate Mulligan from any deliberate wrongdoing. Stanton ordered Colonel Hoffman to return the chapel. It seemed that Mulligan had turned it into a prison hospital, not a barrack. Regardless, Hoffman directed Mulligan to remove the sick.[26]

The chapel dispute was the first time that a religious question arose, and it would not be the last. Colonel Hoffman placed restrictions, however. He denied Farwell's request for undisturbed use of the chapel. Prisoners could attend services when any minister offered to preach to them, not just YMCA clergymen, "but the prisoners only must attend the service on such occasions; there must be no mingling of our troops or visitors with them," Hoffman warned. "The association cannot be permitted to hold meetings with the prisoners."[27]

Mulligan made peace with the clergymen, and the Chicago Bible Society distributed three thousand Testaments, stating "thus we hope that these strangers among us may find their imprisonment the greatest blessing of their lives."[28] Unfortunately, these lives were short term.

The diary of James Taswell Mackey, 48th Tennessee Infantry, echoes even now like the mournful tolling of a church bell counting off the dead each day. "To-day I have to chronicle the death of Mr. James S. Hodge, the most beloved member of our company," Mackey sadly noted. "His manners were unexceptionable, his conversation mild and gentle, and his deportment toward his comrades unchangeably affectionate."[29]

Enlisting prisoners in the Union army came up again as one way of easing conditions at Camp Douglas. Colonel Mulligan wrote to General Halleck that many were in the Rebel army by compulsion, and judging by conversations with them, many were loyal. "One Tennessee regiment, the Tenth, is composed almost exclusively of Irishmen, and they desire to enlist in some of the companies in my regiment," Mulligan added proudly.[30]

Halleck, without authority, gave Colonel Mulligan the go-ahead. However, he advised Mulligan "to be careful as to the character of these recruits, and to make himself personally acquainted with each one."[31] The War Department vetoed the idea when it learned of it, but Mulligan continued to recruit prisoners anyway. He moved these newly converted Yankees to separate barracks.

Colonel Mulligan's determination to fill the regiments reflected his uncertain position. Should he get ready for action or concentrate on Camp Douglas? His primary responsibility was never made officially clear. Yet, Washington held him strictly accountable for his administration.

Another problem was the constant change of command. Colonel Arno Voss had taken over on the eve of his departure for the front. Illinois officials had ordered Colonel Tucker to Springfield in the midst of this turmoil. Now the camp was under the command of an officer who had lost his entire army.

Lack of professionalism was common in the prison system because the Lincoln administration allowed governors to appoint camp commanders. The reason was strictly political. Colonel Hoffman pleaded with the governor of Ohio to stop his frequent changes at Camp Chase. "It required a suitable officer to remain permanently in charge," Hoffman advised.

Meanwhile, by March 17, 1862, 5,500 prisoners were being held at Camp Douglas. No one knew how large the guard force should be. General Halleck planned to send 1,847 more prisoners. The garrison numbered only 510 men in the Irish Brigade and 451 in the 65th Illinois Infantry. Mulligan protested against more prisoners, but Governor Yates thought that his garrison was sufficient.[32]

Bureaucratic infighting placed Colonel Mulligan in the center of a power struggle. General Halleck interfered at Camp Douglas and weakened Colonel Hoffman. He had no authority to order prisoners to Camp Chase or to send Tucker to Springfield. Then Halleck countermanded Colonel Hoffman's order of no visitors. Hoffman complained to General Meigs. "General Halleck has given orders in relation to the prisoners taken at Fort Donelson, even when they were beyond the limits of his department." Hoffman claimed that his office was unknown to the army, and "he only knows what he reads in the papers." Meigs ordered appropriate instructions issued regarding Colonel Hoffman's authority.[33]

Halleck chose to ignore them and ordered Colonel Mulligan to place recaptured prisoners in solitary confinement. This order remained in effect at Camp Douglas for the duration of the war.[34]

Prisoners became belligerent, sensing the lack of command and suffering from Chicago's near arctic cold, the open latrines, sickness, death, boredom, and constraints. A prisoner in the Fifth Tennessee Infantry was knifed on March 19, and two companies of the Tenth Tennessee engaged in a savage fist fight, most likely caused by enlistments in Mulligan's Irish Brigade.[35]

More of Halleck's meddling brought Stanton's wrath down hard, though Halleck's new idea made sense. He sent a commission to explain the oath of allegiance to the prisoners and "the conditions upon which their discharge depended." The *Tribune* reported his activities at Camp Douglas on March 21, 1862, and Stanton had a fit when he saw the article. The War Department ordered Halleck to recall his commission, and Stanton bluntly warned that only the president could order prisoners discharged. Halleck responded evasively that "no commissioners have been empowered by me to release prisoners of war."[36]

Nonetheless, the commission claimed that 1,640 prisoners at Camp Butler were ready to desert the Confederate army. Most came from Tennessee, and others belonged to regiments from Kentucky, Arkansas, Alabama, and Mississippi. Many of these prisoners ended up at Camp Douglas, which was so deep in mud from rain and thaw that neither prisoners nor soldiers ventured out.[37]

Meanwhile, a murder intrigued Chicago. Manslaughter would be a better term for the killing on March 30, 1862. William H. Kilpatrick of Company E, Third Tennessee Infantry, had fatally struck Thomas M. Golden of Company E on the head after Golden forced his way into the kitchen when Kilpatrick was on duty.

One prisoner claimed that Colonel Mulligan chained Kilpatrick outside in sub-zero weather for ten days before the trial. James T. Mackey confirmed the story, but it was not that cold according to him. "In the evening a large crowd gathered around Col. Mulligan's quarters to witness the spectacle of two men sitting astride a wooden horse for intoxication, and a Tennessean bound to a tree awaiting his trial for murder," he recorded.[38]

Corruption added greatly to Mulligan's problems. One of his officers in the 23rd Illinois named Patrick Higgins did more than just take bribes. He organized an escape ring. Higgins could have been shot, or sent to prison, and Hoffman personally filed charges against him. However, Mulligan only drummed him out of the army.

In other bribery cases, five Fort Donelson prisoners in the Third Tennessee Infantry gave a guard ten dollars, almost a month's pay, to let them cross his patrol area. Another guard saw them and opened fire. Only two prisoners escaped. Mulligan marched the corrupt guard out of camp with his head shaved. Later, another guard sold civilian clothes for $7.50.[39] Security was not a priority for Mulligan.

Yet, public officials shielded him. The Cook County Board sent up a hymn of praise for his "excellent hospital management and care of prisoners." The city of Chicago was less assured and requested the Board of Public Works "to examine the privies and drains of Camp Douglas and if found to be in such a state as to endanger the health of citizens or disreputable to the city to notify the County of Cook for abatement."

E. G. Chesbrough, the public works engineer, reported that Colonel Mulligan personally took him on a tour of inspection and that he found conditions much improved. "The measures the Colonel was carrying out will make the camp neater and less offensive than it is practicable to keep many of the streets and alleys of the city," he said with a straight face.[40]

Thawing snow and heavy rains plunged the camp deeper into mud by March 31. Colonel Mulligan set prisoners to work in a futile attempt to drain the ground, and the relief committee furnished dried fruit and much cough syrup to the garrison and prison. Civil War cough syrup had more than medicinal value and was deeply appreciated. Fortunately, only 40 more prisoners arrived. Camp Douglas was not prepared to receive more, but the army did not care about what the camp could manage.

In a masterful understatement, the *Tribune* stated that "the sanitary conditions of the camp notwithstanding, the pleasant weather for the past few days is not so good as might be expected under the circumstances" and revealed that four more prisoners had just died.[41]

Mortality was high despite orders to feed the prisoners the same rations as Federal troops and to issue blankets, cooking utensils, and clothing. "Much clothing not good enough for troops has by fraud of inspectors and dealers been forced into our depots," Meigs told Hoffman candidly. "This will be used." He did not seem to realize that such clothing would further undermine the shaky security at Camp Douglas.

CHAPTER 4

The Confederacy in Chicago

"His Excellency" dispenses justice—Prisoners plead to take the oath of allegiance—Southern sympathizers aid escapes—Henry Morton Stanley a prisoner?—Mulligan disobeys orders.

Cold winds swept across the camp on April 1, 1862. Strong gusts blew down a section of the fence, and two prisoners escaped. Colonel Mulligan caught the pair the following day and had them tied to a tree. He required that eight others parade with boards lashed to their backs reading, "Escaped prisoners recaptured." James T. Mackey sarcastically called Mulligan "His Excellency."[1]

Yet, Mulligan dished out punishment evenly, and one of the Irish Brigade walked around with 70 pounds strapped to his back. Five more Illinois soldiers carried a 200-pound piece of timber. On May 22, 1862, officers charged a prisoner with "defying a guard and drawing a knife on him," but he only served 14 days on a work detail.[2] A few years later guards would kill prisoners for much less.

General Halleck instructed Mulligan to place recaptured prisoners in "close confinement," which meant the dungeon. The army did not define the rights of those who escaped or attempted to do so until 1864. It ruled that "an attempt on the part of prisoners to escape is not regarded as a crime, but it justifies any measures necessary to prevent its recurrence."[3] This double-talk meant that an escapee was not a criminal but was to be treated like one.

A petition from some Tennessee regiments on April 10 requested permission to take the oath of allegiance and go home as "true and loyal citizens of the Union." These Tennesseans appealed to Mulligan, "In view of your personal and political influence with the Federal Government." They knew how to address "His Excellency." The oath of allegiance once brought amnesty, meaning release. Early in the war, prisoners could gain their freedom by exchange in the field or by taking the oath of allegiance.[4]

Fort Donelson prisoners at Camp Douglas. (Image courtesy of the Chicago Historical Society.)

Other Tennesseans were inflexible. "I am a soldier so long as the war continues," George Pope assured his mother. He added menacingly that "it is the intention and dedication of all prisoners that no man whether he is Northern or Southern shall live on confiscated land in his neighborhood."[5]

Governor Andrew Johnson of Tennessee took a personal interest in what was happening at Camp Douglas and intervened for 29 men in a Tennessee artillery battery who claimed that they were only a "home guard" pressed into the army against their will.

President Lincoln was willing to give Johnson, his 1864 running mate, control over releasing Confederate prisoners in Northern prison camps "so far as they may be Tennesseans." Johnson's answer "was not to be made public." Lincoln was justifiably worried, since many Tennessee prisoners fought hard.[6] The offer was soon withdrawn, but only temporarily, "whenever the period arrives that it can properly be exercised."

Commanders at Camp Douglas were cautious about amnesty and looked to Hoffman for instructions. The oath differed from parole, by which the prisoner was free to fight again upon being exchanged. Taking the oath made joining the Confederate army a capital offense if the prisoner was recaptured.

A parole of honor was different from the oath and a parole pending exchange. It was based on the code of chivalry and could mean temporary release for a specific purpose. Going to Chicago on a parole of honor was usual for Confederate surgeons at Camp Douglas. They purchased medical supplies and enjoyed a few hours of relaxation. It could also mean outright release without exchange. The White House often gave a parole of honor to Confederates with influence. A promise not to fight again was sufficient for the privileged.

It was the parole of honor that caused three Rebel doctors to quit work. Mulligan granted it while they were at Camp Douglas, but the commanding officer at Camp Randall, Wisconsin, refused to recognize it after they were transferred there. Hoffman ordered the men returned to Chicago and wrote Mulligan to make the alternative to working "as little agreeable as possible."[7] Mulligan thought the matter was overblown and recommended that the doctors "be restored to their positions and paroled."

Records do not show any clergymen obtaining releases for prisoners, but they continued to give comfort, once with amusing results. "One Sunday Dr. Eddy was reading a verse to them: Show pity, Lord,

O Lord, forgive; the next line was, Let a repenting rebel live. He quickly read it, Let a repenting sinner live, but the verse was well known to the prisoners. There was a roar of laughter and all serious attention vanished."[8]

One preacher came to talk politics, and Mulligan had the prisoners assembled around the flag platform in Garrison Square. Parson William Gannaway Brownlow, a Southern minister of Union persuasion, told them that "they were the dupes of designing leaders." James T. Mackey wrote in his diary that "in the evening parson Brownlow of Knoxville, Tenn. visited Camp Douglas. He was followed by General Cary of Cincinnati, O., who violently denounced the leading secessionists, but like his friend Brownlow expressed sympathy for we poor misguided prisoners who could neither read nor write."[9]

Meanwhile, Mulligan fell behind with his paper work. This was not for lack of workers, as many prisoners were capable, but employing them meant giving them access to confidential records. Adjutant General Fuller was nagging Mulligan on April 14 about his failure to file prison rolls in Springfield for three weeks. Many more prisoners were coming because of General Grant's campaigns in Tennessee.

Small, old, and rickety, Shiloh church became an icon of the Civil War when Southern forces surprised and routed the Union army near Savannah, Tennessee, on April 6, 1862. One sticking point named the "Hornets' Nest" ruined an otherwise perfect day. About a thousand Federal troops held a wood flanked by open fields, and here the attackers broke their hearts. The nest finally crumbled about five o'clock at night, and the Confederate army pressed forward to certain victory, but it was late. They had fought too long and died too much.[10]

The bluecoats defeated and routed them the next day. The South did not realize it then, but it was all behind them now. This abiding determination was the shoal upon which Confederate dreams would take on water and sink.

Camp Douglas received 736 prisoners from Shiloh; about 1,709 more came from Island No. 10, a Confederate stronghold guarding the Mississippi River below Columbus, Kentucky. An additional seven hundred sick and wounded Confederates arrived from various hospitals. The prison held 8,962 prisoners by April 15, 1862. Barracks barely housed eight thousand men, including the garrison, causing stables to become "temporary" barracks. These were collapsing and not fit for habitation. Some 219 prisoners died by April 18.[11]

Picket lines in White Oak Square remained the only barrier to escape, as there was no way to fortify the fence. One young prisoner climbed over it with the help of a bribed guard. He then walked to Cottage Grove and boarded a streetcar leaving for downtown. With the help of sympathizers, he was soon enjoying the comforts of a good hotel. Another escapee simply looked for his brother who was studying at Rush Medical College in the city. The future Dr. R. F. Stone took his brother to an excellent hotel and restaurant and then put him aboard a train headed South.[12]

The presence of Southerners in Chicago benefitted prisoners throughout the war. Southerners had invested in Chicago real estate and visited there often. General Simon Buckner, who surrendered to Grant at Fort Donelson, had been in Chicago managing his wife's real estate when the war started. She was a Chicago heiress with properties on Michigan Avenue. Others had migrated to the city and become part of the legal, medical, industrial, and commercial community. Cyrus McCormick came from Virginia to build his farm tools and was most sentimental at a banquet given for exiles from his native state.[13]

Carter Harrison I, an attorney who served four terms as mayor of Chicago, was from Kentucky. Famous names in Chicago history, such as Honore, Winchester, Waller, and Rogers, were all Kentuckians. Harrison's son, the first Chicago-born mayor, later asserted that his mother never forgave the North for its defeat of her homeland. Camp Douglas commandants jailed two prewar Chicago mayors from Kentucky on conspiracy charges.[14] Riverboat gamblers, criminals, and deserters from the South flocked to Chicago to escape military service and to share in the wartime prosperity of the city.

The army once arrested three editors of the *Chicago Times* because of alleged Southern bias and later seized the paper for a short time.[15]

Most people in the northern Illinois counties were antislavery. However, many others from downstate did not feel that way, and men from the southern part often joined the Confederate army. This caused Chicago businessmen to form the Union League of America in 1862 to guard against alleged dissident groups such as the "Knights of the Golden Circle."[16]

However, sympathizers did not overstate conditions at camp. A prisoner in the 46th Tennessee wrote to a Union army colonel who knew his father.[17] "I take the liberty of addressing you and requesting you to use your influence to get me out of this place," the young man begged, "as I suppose that a faithful observance of a Parole of Honor would be all that would be required by the Federal Government." He added, "Col. please remember the grief of a kind Father and Mother for an absent son."

The young man's attitude, that it was all just a game and that he could pick up his marbles and go home, may have angered the colonel. He was correct in one respect, however. Political influence, if not corruption, was the ticket out of Camp Douglas.

The prison was a killing ground of pestilence under Colonel Mulligan, according to Henry Morton Stanley. Stanley's famous "Doctor Livingstone, I presume" was ten years in the future when he allegedly joined the Confederate army and became a prisoner at Camp Douglas. Stanley claimed that he enlisted in Company E of the Sixth Arkansas Infantry Regiment, although Camp Douglas records do not list a Henry Stanley from this company, nor a John Rowlands, which was his real name.[18]

Maintaining that he was captured at Shiloh, Stanley described his alleged arrival on April 15, 1862. "Our prison-pen was a square and spacious enclosure, like a bleak cattle yard, walled high with planking, on the top of which, at every sixty yards or so, were sentry boxes. About fifty feet from its base, and running parallel with it, was a line of lime wash. That was the dead line, and any prisoner who crossed it was liable to be shot." Stanley charged that "the authorities rigidly excluded every medical, pious, musical, or literary charity that might have alleviated our sufferings."[19] The facts were otherwise.

The fence had no sentry boxes until December 10, 1863. It did not even have a platform until long after Stanley left camp around June 13, 1862. As far as medical care, Confederate surgeons went to the city daily for supplies, and their government channeled money to them through a Chicago law firm. The funds must have been substantial, for the doctors ordered new uniforms from a tailor downtown. Organized religion was active at camp through the YMCA, just one group that reached out to the prisoners.[20]

Stanley's famous chronicle of suffering was as vivid as his tales of exploration, and perhaps just as fanciful: "Exhumed corpses could not have presented anything more hideous than these dead-and-alive men, who oblivious to the weather, hung over the latrines, or lay extended along the open sewer, with only a few gasps intervening between them and death and one insanely damned his vitals and his constitution, because his agonies were so protracted."[21] His story is a hoax.

The only Stanley in Company E of the Sixth Arkansas Infantry was William H. who joined in 1861. He was 18, two years younger than Henry Stanley, and enlisted two hundred miles to the north of where Stanley said he lived.[22] Confederate records in the National Archives show William H. missing at Shiloh but not a prisoner at Camp Douglas.

Stanley may have written this account to explain why he enlisted in the Illinois artillery on June 4, 1862. However, a British subject did not have to join the Union side to escape the camp. Colonel Mulligan, without authority, was releasing Englishmen by order of the British Consul in Chicago. In addition, there was no Henry Stanley, or H. Stanley, in Battery L, 1st Illinois Light Artillery, which he supposedly joined.[23]

Old Confederates expressed their views in later years about the famous explorer. One claimed that Stanley escaped at Shiloh by swimming the river. Another branded him as a thief and a deserter. A third affirmed that "the great African explorer and newspaper correspondent was captured at Shiloh and taken to prison at Camp Douglas." However, he referred to a Stanley in the 13th Arkansas Infantry. A fourth man, writing 67 years later, believed that Henry Morton Stanley was a prisoner at Camp Chase, not Camp Douglas. It is difficult to tell whether these ancient veterans were reshaping the truth or revealing it.[24] There is no doubt that Stanley fought at Shiloh and was captured. He either escaped or, what is more likely, the British Consul obtained his release when the prisoners reached St. Louis.

William Micajah Barrow, Company C, Fourth Louisiana Infantry, gave a contrary account. Barrow suffered severely after his capture at Shiloh, sitting on wet ground for three days, exposed to cold rain, and with little to eat. "Lord deliver me from such hardships," Barrow pleaded.[25]

He was a literate and ardent Southerner who read Dante and the Bible. Major hazards at Camp Douglas for him were boredom and overeating. "We are well fixed off for prisoners," he found to his surprise. "Our quarters are plenty large enough and we are permitted to go out and walk in the enclosure." He probably was referring to White Oak Square. "To day I read and slept the day away. I took a dose of medicine before going to bed.they treat us as if we were their own soldiers give us the same rations and everything that is necessary."[26]

He recovered by May 1 when he did the cooking. "My imprisonment is beginning to pass away a little better than when I was sick," he reported. For dinner he had beans, fried beef, and Irish potatoes.

"May 14th 1862. This morning after breakfast I read Travels in Denmark & Sweden; we got some books through the kind ladies in St. Louis, and we got books at this place through a parson (Presby) by the name of Tutle," his diary reads. "Our dinner today was very good for prisoners of war; we had beefsteak, mashed-irish-potatoes, and a bread pudding with a nice sauce. the beef steak and potatoes was the ration but the sauce was not."[27] Chicago's weather was his major complaint. "How people can live in such a climate I cannot conceive!"

It was not likely that Corporal Barrow calmly read the Bible and several novels while his comrades suffocated in their own waste. The truth is difficult to learn as prisoners failed to keep records or deliberately distorted and exaggerated their experiences. An example is a letter from a prisoner to his beloved niece. He reassured her that "this is as pleasing a prison as there is."[28] Chicago police who searched the barracks enraged Barrow, on the other hand, by the theft of money and valuables. Newspapers were often so partisan that they blew up or played down stories about the camp.

James T. Mackey continued to record many deaths, despite Barrow's pleasant picture. It was almost as though they were in different camps. This probably resulted from different views of prison life. Barrow was intent on recording sights and smells, while Mackey felt that he had to be a voice for the dead.

"Mr. George D. Armstrong, a man loved by his friends and respected by his enemies, today closed his eyes upon the pleasures and pains of this world," Mackey recorded. "Thomas J. Johnson breathed his last to-day. The King of Day had just commenced his course across the azure sky when his gentle spirit took its flight to him who gave it."

"Last night Joseph C. Nichols breathed his last. He was a prepossessing youth, beloved by all his company and his acquaintances. Peace to his ashes. Flowers must wither."[29]

The high mortality may have caused Colonel Mulligan to keep a low profile and not bring William Kilpatrick to trial for killing

Thomas Golden. The "U.S." attorney also washed his hands of the matter but had to make some show of enforcing the law. Accordingly, the army ordered Mulligan to deliver Kilpatrick to civil authorities for trial on April 28, 1862, in the circuit court of Cook County.[30] Chicago was keenly interested because the trial opened a window on how prisoners lived at camp.

A surgeon testified that "if Golden would have had an ordinarily thick skull there would have been no injury." Loss of the body of the victim for a time created more sensation. The jury convicted Kilpatrick on a lesser charge of manslaughter, and he received one year in the former state prison at Alton, Illinois, now housing prisoners of war.[31]

Vaccination of prisoners began that same day, but this did not prevent smallpox from ravaging the camp. Indications are that the vaccine was defective, and the 49th Tennessee apparently planned to escape on April 25, when deaths reached 230. Colonel Mulligan learned of the planned attempt and blocked it by a show of force, with the leaders being sent to White Oak dungeon.[32]

On May 2, Colonel Hoffman rescinded the order permitting prisoners to have money in their possession, because they pooled funds to bribe guards. A bank to hold their money was established at headquarters. They could spend it at the prison sutler who paid a tax of $75 per month, as did the sutler for the garrison.[33]

Camp Douglas sutlers were not the fabled characters appointed to a regiment, sometimes by bribery, and who accompanied Union troops to the war front. Their wagons, loaded with good things to eat, drink, smoke, and chew, were often deep in enemy territory. These larcenous peddlers sometimes became battle casualties or prisoners of war in their relentless pursuit of free enterprise. The drab sutlers at Camp Douglas resembled them only in their high prices. Colonel Tucker appointed regimental officers to a council of administration in 1861 to control them.[34]

Other businesses paid fewer taxes monthly: a photo studio, $5, a barber shop, $1, a newsstand, $4, a shoe maker, $5, a grocery store in Garrison Square, $10. Milk and butter peddlers with wagons paid $5, while vendors who hand-carried milk and vegetables into camp were tax free. Laundresses charged 50¢ for twelve items of enlisted men's wear. Officers had to pay 75¢ because their clothes required ironing.[35]

Talk of exchange was the favorite rumor as the men settled into a prison routine. Families pressured their leaders to exchange prisoners.

The Lincoln administration was reluctant to do so because such a treaty amounted to recognition of the Confederacy. Up to now the two sides had allowed special exchanges between commanders in the field or for specific individuals.[36]

Colonel Mulligan and Colonel Hoffman were examples. The idea of trading prisoners in the middle of a war seems odd today. POWs do not usually go home until the war is over or peace negotiations are in progress. Many months passed before the Union and the Confederacy began a general exchange. Meanwhile, conditions at Camp Douglas deteriorated, and the depressing record of disease and death escalated.

Hoffman added to the misery by ordering Mulligan to close the prison bakery on May 17, 1862, because of fuel costs. He submitted a formula to Mulligan by which outside contractors "can with great profit to themselves take twenty ounces of flour and return twenty-two ounces of bread."[37] Profits would be even greater by substituting cornbread for wheat bread. Hoffman soon discovered that there was no prison fund because Mulligan had ignored his orders to sell rations. He now bypassed Mulligan and sent Camp Morton's scale of rations to Captain Christopher, advising that "they have a fund of $2,400."

Christopher apparently told Mulligan, who directed an angry and impertinent letter to his superior: "Have you issued any orders in regard to shortening the rations of the prisoners in this camp further that [than] myself?" Mulligan was unwise in offending an influential officer such as Colonel Hoffman.

However, he was wise in not reducing rations, because his garrison numbered only one-tenth of the 8,962 prisoners in camp on June 1, 1862.[38] They equaled one-half the army Mulligan faced at the battle of Lexington, Missouri. The colonel was destined to be hopelessly outnumbered by Confederates until the day he died.

CHAPTER 5

Charges of Mismanagement

An objective opinion: Burn Camp Douglas—Colonel Joseph H. Tucker replaces Mulligan—Colonel Hoffman returns—Officials refuse to make improvements—Charges of neglect—Shortage in prison accounts.

The "kind treatment" described by Colonel Hoffman in March 1862 vanished. A drunken soldier fired into a group of prisoners, on June 14, 1862, wounding three seriously and one fatally. The same day a guard killed a delirious prisoner as he ran from the hospital and crossed the deadline. This brought the number of dead to 499.[1] The death rate was a little more than 5 percent and becoming worse.

Describing Mulligan, one newspaper said that "he allowed the prisoners to go the full length of their privileges, and promptly and fully punished the slightest infraction thereof. A showing of teeth was out of the question." For example, he sent a prisoner to the guard-house "for speaking his true sentiments in regard to the U.S. Government." He had 50 men in Company A, 49th Tennessee, sit on the ground all day without food or water for throwing stones at a sentinel. "It will probably teach them better," the *Tribune* muttered.[2]

Nevertheless, Capt. William H. Harder of Co. D, 23rd Tennessee Infantry, captured in April 1862, claimed that "the Confederates liked Mulligan," but not his replacement, Colonel Tucker.[3] Mulligan's administration was the least distinguished of any commander for this length of time. No one blamed him. Improvements were not possible during the harsh winter and late spring. It was a dirty job that he did not want, and he only had it because he was in the wrong place at the wrong time. Mulligan received no help from the army, and Hoffman only made a cursory inspection the first week of March. Some friendly visits by Cook County and the city of Chicago resulted in a whitewash but no assistance.

Colonel Mulligan was happy to leave Camp Douglas. Now he could get back to the war. The Irish Brigade marched up Michigan Boulevard to the train depot, and a band played "The Girl I Left Behind Me." The regiment fought many battles in the East but returned without its leader. The war ended for Colonel Mulligan on July 24, 1864, while he was leading his tiny regiment against the center of a 30,000-man Confederate army in Virginia.[4] He received his general's star posthumously. The colonel would not have had it any other way.

Few statistics are available for the time he was in charge of Camp Douglas, because the *Official Records* did not compile data before July 1862. Close to five hundred prisoners had already lost their lives, and 77 had escaped by July 1 according to Camp Douglas records.[5] Mulligan simply turned the camp over to Col. Daniel Cameron when he left. They did not consult Hoffman about it. Only five days later, on June 19, 1862, Cameron gave Col. Joseph H. Tucker the keys and departed for the front. Tucker was an innocent bystander who, at this time, happened to be at camp recruiting a new regiment.

Cameron advised Tucker that about eight thousand prisoners were present, but he was unable to provide any information about his duties.[6] The casual manner in which command was changed for the third time made no sense. Tucker was only a militia officer, and this was the largest prison camp in the North. Federal officers ran many of the departments at Camp Douglas, such as the quartermaster. General Meigs's angry outburst that "state authorities have no right to give orders to an officer of the United States" came home to roost for Tucker. This proved to be the longest summer of his life.

Security was not much better than when the prisoners had arrived in February, and Tucker felt that he had to take immediate steps. His most decisive act resulted in the most criticism. He brought in Chicago police for a massive shakedown on June 23. Tucker was justified in not trusting the garrison to do the job, and subsequent commanders felt the same way. The prisoners thought that using Chicago police violated the rules of war, especially because of their thievery.

William M. Barrow charged that "the yanks came with police from Chicago went around in the prisoners quarters. took watches, money, Guata Percha rings [made from coal] sigars clothes etc. then the Police robbers came through our ranks and searched us, takin pocket knives and money." Many plugs of precious chewing tobacco disappeared. Barrow remarked that after this experience a company of Tennesseans who were thinking of taking the oath "concluded that the Confederacy was the best government."

James T. Mackey described how a renegade prisoner aided the police and stole a daguerreotype. Because of this incident, he was thrown out of the Federal unit he had joined. "A fate deserved," says Mackey. The *Chicago Evening Journal* published a letter about the search, supposedly from a prisoner. "We have suffered all the insults and indignities that an ignorant and ill-mannered city-rabble could heap upon us," the writer complained.[7]

Corporal Barrow was accurate about the stolen property, but he did not tell the whole story. The police confiscated five pistols, two of them double barreled, "and many bullets."[8] They found 57 bullet molds, 54 boxes of caps for the pistols, and 60 packages of gunpowder, in addition. Friends smuggled the arsenal in, or it came into camp through the express office. The prisoners were almost ready to shoot their way out. Police also turned in 189 clasp knives, 15 sheath knives, 26 butcher knives, and 2 compasses. Prisoners needed the knives to prepare food, and these were returned to them.

Many prisoners found that they did not need weapons to escape. A message to the army on June 24, 1862, from Columbia, Tennessee, told of prisoners from Camp Douglas arriving there. "The sutler in the camp knowingly sells them clothing to disguise themselves," the report claimed.[9] Hoffman came to Chicago on June 27 to investigate and found that Tucker already had two detectives posing as prisoners. Hoffman ordered "the inquiries to continue." Tucker's spies did not deceive anyone. The sutler story sounds logical, but the army was looking in the wrong place.

They found a letter that revealed a more sinister character behind the escapes. In it, a prisoner asked his father for $20 in gold. "If you can get it," pleaded the absent son, "if you can send me that amount it will enable me to get home all persons that has money her is making thear escape." Money had to be sent to "frederic Hutson [Frederick Hudson] one of the Express Company in Chicago who would fetch it to camp," he advised. He warned his dad that "if the money is sent to Camp Douglas the commander pais us in tickets."[10] Hoffman never reported what he did to Frederick Hudson, but he quickly disappeared from the Chicago Street Directory.

Tucker rightfully believed that the express office and the mail punched gaping holes in security. Censorship was severe under his administration, as a result, almost paranoid. When William M. Barrow wrote home that "I am going to join the army again," the

Dr. Brockholst McVickar. (Image courtesy of the Newberry Library.)

censor inserted the word "not" and by that changed the letter's entire meaning.[11]

Nevertheless, censorship could not protect Tucker against corruption. In one bribery scheme a soldier obtained Federal uniforms for two Confederates, but a suspicious guard stopped them before they reached the fence. A party of Kentuckians gave a guard $165 to distribute to certain prisoners plus $10 for himself. This was 13 months' pay. No one saw the guard again.[12]

Washington issued an order on June 27, 1862, that would likely have resulted in more escapes. Secretary of War Edwin Stanton blocked commanding officers from granting amnesty. Prisoners could still take the oath of allegiance, but that act did not free them. More than three hundred prisoners immediately remembered that they were British subjects and managed to get word to the British Consul in Chicago who demanded the right to enter Camp Douglas and investigate these claims. "I object!" Hoffman wired Stanton. The British lion did not frighten his boss. "This Department recognizes no right in the British consul to visit prisoners of war taken in arms with rebels against this Government!" he fired back on June 28.[13] No one could accuse Stanton of diplomatic double-talk.

The constant demands for better security and care of the prisoners overwhelmed Colonel Tucker. His business experience had done nothing to prepare him for the ongoing crisis at a major prison camp. Doctor Brockholst McVickar, post surgeon, warned him on June 30, 1862, that "the surface of the ground is becoming saturated with the filth and slop from the privies, kitchens and quarters and must produce serious results to health as soon as the hot weather sets in."[14]

Doctors overcrowded the hospital with 326 patients, and many more were suffering in barracks. McVickar estimated that he needed at least "five surgeons and four assistants to perform the medical duty at the camp in a proper manner." Colonel Tucker had pressed the Chicago doctor into service on June 23. This was an excellent choice, although the prominent physician did not have to be there. Tucker probably chose a civilian over an army surgeon because he identified more with the business and professional community in Chicago.

Coincidentally, Henry W. Bellows of the U. S. Sanitary Commission sent a negative report on the camp to Colonel Hoffman. "Sir: The amount of standing water, of unpoliced grounds, of foul sinks, of unventilated and crowded barracks, of general disorder, of soil reeking with miasmatic accretions, of rotten bones and the emptying of camp-kettles is enough to drive a sanitarian to despair," Bellows moaned. "I hope that no thought will be entertained of mending matters. The absolute abandonment of the spot seems the only judicious course. I do not believe that any amount of drainage would purge that soil loaded with accumulated filth or those barracks fetid with two stories of vermin and animal exhalations. Nothing but fire can cleanse them."[15]

Bellows's remark about cleansing the camp with fire was prophetic. Later that year they burned it—not the prisoners, but Federal troops. However, conditions at Camp Douglas were usual for a Civil War prison. The surgeon general of the Confederate army also warned of pestilence resulting from crowded and unsanitary conditions in the Richmond prison.[16]

Hoffman returned to Chicago because directions on how to run the camp had vanished. He gave instructions to organize the prisoners into companies or divisions and to show on a daily morning report the number present and those who were sick, discharged, escaped, or dead. Hoffman also lectured Tucker on his obsession, the prison fund, "which will be created by withholding such part of the rations as may not be necessary, the surplus to be purchased by the commissary." The only visitors allowed were near relations ("loyal people") of sick prisoners.

Sutlers remained under Tucker's control, and "you will see that he furnishes proper articles and at reasonable rates," Hoffman commanded. Stopping escapes would be easier than keeping the sutlers honest. Regarding mail, "Prisoners will not be permitted to write letters of more than one page of common letter paper, the matter to be strictly of a private nature or the letter must be destroyed." In other words, prisoners had better keep quiet about what was happening at camp. Hoffman and Tucker discussed the need to purchase horses and wagons and a portable saw for cutting wood. Repair of fences and barracks, a bake house, and a running water sewer system were priorities.[17] Prisoners had been in camp four months, and space for latrines and garbage pits was running out.

Colonel Hoffman returned to his headquarters in Detroit on July 1 and drew a dismal picture of Camp Douglas for General Meigs. Guards and prisoners alike suffered from the mud. They reused sinks until overflowing. One guard regiment lived in tents outside the stockade. The camp sat on low, swampy ground that defied draining. Hoffman argued for laying sewers connected to the lake "to float out the filth of all kinds." The sinks should be connected with the sewers "so that during the summer the camp and neighborhood would be relieved from the stench which now pollutes the air," he advised.[18]

Hoffman was happy to strike back at Colonel Mulligan. "There has been the greatest carelessness and willful neglect in the management of the affairs of the camp, and everything was left by Colonel Mulligan in a shameful state of confusion," he stated. "Vital information about the prisoners is lacking." He protested that relieving Mulligan was against his orders and that Colonel Cameron "knew nothing of the affairs of the prisoners."[19] He estimated the cost of building new barracks and repairing the old ones at between five and eight thousand dollars. Installing a system of sewers and drainage could cost about as much.

Hoffman had Bellows's report, and he liked the idea of abandoning Camp Douglas but concluded it was too late. "The hot weather of summer is just upon us and if something is not done speedily there must be much sickness in the camp and neighborhood if not a pestilence," he told Meigs. Incredibly, the University of Chicago, the leading educational institution in the Northwest, was in harm's way just across the road.

Colonel Hoffman's report to General Meigs brought a blunt response on July 5, 1862. "I cannot approve the expenditure involved in the improvements suggested in your letter. Ten thousand men should certainly be able to keep this camp clean, and the United States has other uses for its money than to build a water works to save them the labor necessary to their health," he growled.[20] He also cited the abuse of Union prisoners as additional grounds for rejection.

His refusal to spend money caused Hoffman to set new standards for sanitation, security, record keeping, and roll calls, including a monthly report to his office. Most important, he now furnished detailed forms to enroll prisoners of war in the field, and they had to be accurate.

This proved difficult, as prisoners often gave false information. Accurate prisoner rolls were not a priority after a battle. Officers frequently spelled names by sound and did not always understand what was said. Finally, not many officers had the patience to record each prisoner's regiment and company. Rolls in the National Archives sometimes show 25 different regiments listed on a single page.

Hoffman's new instructions made the surgeon in charge of the hospital answerable to the commanding officer of the camp. His office had to approve all clothing requisitions issued by a prison commander to the army quartermaster. He decreed with his usual stinginess that "from the 30th of April to the 1st of October neither drawers nor socks will be allowed except to the sick."[21]

His highest priority was still the prison fund, to make prisoners pay for their own expense. It would be collected "by withholding from their rations all that can be spared without inconvenience to them," he repeated. A voucher for purchases at the sutler had to be kept with the prisoners' accounts. Family and friends could contribute articles for their welfare, and visitors were allowed only for the critically ill.

Letters were limited to one page on common letter paper, and only the War Department or Colonel Hoffman could order a prisoner released. Two prisoners in the 46th Tennessee, upon hearing of this order, asked to see Tucker on July 8 about going home, "as we are tired of this business."[22] No doubt, Tucker felt the same way.

Hoffman, however, reversed himself about improvements in the face of General Meigs's displeasure. He was glad to be relieved of the responsibility of deciding that Camp Douglas could not have the large expenditures, he told Meigs on July 10. "The condition of the camp excited the apprehensions of the officers and of the neighbors, and I felt bound to submit the plans which had been projected for the improvements, though I was doubtful of the necessity of it to the extent suggested," he backpedaled.[23] Prisoners may have agreed with him. Lack of sanitation was not an issue with them. They were familiar with primitive sinks and understood the difficulty of waste disposal in a confined area.

Nevertheless, open sinks were costing many lives. The *Official Records* listed 589 prisoners sick in July 1862, going down to 558 in August. This was not an improvement, since 117 had died. Many suffered diseases of the lungs and bowels, according to Dr. McVickar. He wrote Tucker on July 15 that barracks held between two and three hundred of the sick, attended by only four assistant surgeons. Hoffman, therefore, allowed Tucker to employ four private physicians, "and four assistants at not over $50 per month," with leave to request a fifth physician.

McVickar was concerned about the steady increase in scurvy, "which will eventually if not controlled give a fatal character to all forms of disease whatever their original character." Lack of vitamin C causes scurvy and produces internal bleeding, sallow skin, bleeding and ulcerated gums, and fetid breath. A postwar medical study agreed with McVickar that scurvy increases mortality from other diseases.[24]

Hoffman could easily have controlled it. An abundant and cheap supply of vegetables lay just outside the gates of Camp Douglas. Who was responsible for this state of affairs became the subject of post-war bitterness. Colonel Hoffman was mostly to blame because he had the authority to remedy the situation. Colonel Tucker could have ignored Hoffman and purchased the vegetable foods. What could Hoffman have done to him? Tucker was primarily a civilian, with a pleasant income from the Board of Trade. A want of compassion had sprung up somewhere along the way.

Tucker had to contend with security problems, an unhealthy camp, and decaying barracks. Moreover, dictatorial orders from Hoffman on running the prison frayed his nerves as he found more problems. "There is scarcely a record left at camp and it will be difficult to ascertain what prisoners have been at the camp or what has become of them," he advised Hoffman. He could not furnish the names or the number of those prisoners who had escaped, were sick, or had died. He also lacked information about who had been released before June 19, 1862.

Tucker began reconstructing records from the memory of guards who made roll calls. He pressured Confederate sergeants to help verify the new rolls and requested their personal records regarding deaths, escapes, and discharges. Clerks transcribed this work onto new official forms and in the camp ledger. "Thus two persons are writing, and one calling off constantly," he proudly told Hoffman.[25]

Statistics about this period remain doubtful. It is not certain whether Mulligan took the missing records with him or never kept them. Tucker found and later exchanged 21 prisoners previously listed as dead, much to their relief. Yet, the lack of records was not much different from other Northern prisons. At Camp Butler, near Springfield, Illinois, Capt. Henry W. Freedley, Hoffman's assistant, also relied on prisoners to verify the rolls.[26]

Tucker counted 7,807 prisoners on hand. Deaths numbered about 650 through July 5, with 260 prisoners in the hospital, and many patients in barracks. Besides these problems, Tucker informed Hoffman on July 9 about a shortage in the prisoners' personal funds.[27] This is where Mulligan proved vulnerable. Tucker discovered the problem after receiving only $2,628.88 from Colonel Cameron who was not held responsible due to the short time he was in command.

The deficit was $1,450.79, after deducting "worthless bills," and the amounts drawn by the prisoners. For Tucker, the banker, it was a nightmare. "In order to gain time and not compromise the colonel," he advised Hoffman, he limited prisoner withdrawals to five dollars, and credited them with only one-half the balances shown in their accounts. Tucker considered them creditors of Mulligan and the Federal government under accepted banking practices. He accordingly asked whether "they will have claims against the United States or Colonel Mulligan."[28] Banks had to remain trustworthy despite the war, in Tucker's view.

Tucker also wished to release prisoners who were dying, and those who proved "that they were forced into the rebel service." Hoffman disregarded the amnesty request but did ask the army if it could refund the missing money. The army made no response. James T. Mackey attempted to withdraw $4.70 from his account. However, his name was omitted from a posted list of balances. "So I will have to lose my money," Mackey reflected, "unless Col. Tucker takes the ledger instead of the list of balances."[29] Tucker had, in effect, placed the prisoners' fund in bankruptcy and was wiping out creditors.

Tucker then appointed a special clerk to manage the prisoners' private funds, "who handled nearly a million dollars of their money over the next four years with an accurate accounting," Reverend Tuttle boasted. This was false, for imbalances in the fund continued.

Hoffman informed Tucker on July 9 that the quartermaster planned no improvements to the camp. He softened Meigs's harsh language into, "The Quartermaster General does not approve of the system of sewage and introduction of water pipes." Barrack repairs were also out. Tucker was to fill the old latrines and dig new ones with "shed houses over them," using prison labor.[30]

Meanwhile, Colonel Hoffman challenged General Meigs to provide better shelter. "Some prisoners are living in old leaky stables which should be rebuilt, and the south fence could be moved further in which is now no obstacle to the escape of the prisoners," Hoffman complained. Old lumber and prison labor could be used to cut expenses, he suggested.

Meigs gave a grudging nod. "Whilst the expensive, not to say extravagant, arrangements for sewage, water supply, &c, could not be authorized," Meigs snapped, "the department will approve the reasonable repair of the sheds to make them waterproof." He grumbled that quarters at Camp Douglas were better than those of Union prisoners in the South. This was true, as the South did not build barracks or even huts for prisoners and seldom furnished tools or lumber.[31]

Hoffman was concerned about the Bellows report because he had allowed this busybody to inspect the camp. "I do not agree with him as to its fearful condition, nor do I think that it is past being put in a wholesome condition," Hoffman explained. "When he asked for my permission to visit the camp in his official capacity I granted it, with the request that he should make no report on its condition, as I should do that myself." Bellows accused Hoffman of a coverup, and Hoffman dared Bellows to release his report.[32]

Bellows did not do so, because this act would have damaged his relations with people in high places. The Sanitary Commission was a private organization that required the cooperation of the administration. Hoffman realized this fact, and the report remained secret. The seasoned soldier had become a skilled politician.

Colonel Tucker continued to insist on the need for a sewer system. "I regard it of vital importance to the health of the camp and safety of the prisoners of war," he warned Hoffman on July 11. Water was insufficient because the only hydrants were in the northeast corner of the camp. This situation created a security problem, "and the water is setting back under the walls of Mrs. Bradley's house adjoining camp," he revealed. Incredibly, mail delivery between Chicago and Detroit only took one day, and Hoffman sent a faultfinding response on July 12.[33]

The sewer system was a dead issue, and Hoffman was angry about the Bradley property. He gave the lady his word that her house would suffer no further injury. Hoffman felt sure that Tucker had obtained the horse carts and other equipment and "that the work of putting the camp in a wholesome state of police was by this time well in progress if not already completed." In other words, he expected Tucker to correct six months of neglect in less than thirty days.

However, a general exchange of prisoners appeared imminent. He ordered Tucker to cancel the saw and "to prevent such a waste of water as has been tolerated." Extending the water lines away from the Bradley property was important, but Hoffman allowed for no additional hydrants.

Meanwhile, deaths increased dramatically to 146 in July, 21 more than Mulligan's worst month of March 1862, but Camp Douglas was not closed for several reasons. The government had to economize. Soldiers had not received any pay for months. Even the president of the Illinois Central Railroad complained to Congress that the army had appropriated the line between Chicago and Cairo without compensation. Hoffman had to stop prisoners from baking bread because of fuel costs. The North raised money by selling draft deferments the following year.[34]

Other reasons for the cutbacks included the enormous expense of maintaining the prisoners as they had been, at two thousand dollars per day. Rations cost more than a thousand dollars for prisoners and guards, and fuel was four hundred dollars. Civilian payrolls and maintenance costs made up the balance. Besides, Washington's attitude was hardening due to horror stories about Southern prisons. "The Confederacy would be bankrupted by the proper feeding and care of Union prisoners," explained its commissary general of supplies.[35] This was not true, since the Confederacy had the money to carry on the war for three more years.

Camp Douglas did not receive much in the way of resources either. A furious round of inspections and correspondence took place after Colonel Mulligan left. Authorities now had some idea of what the prison required for better medical care, sanitation, clothing, and diet. Still, nothing was done.

Efforts were directed at security, instead, and the army declared a state of martial law around Camp Douglas on July 12, 1862. Colonel Tucker's brother, Hiram A. Tucker, who sat out the war on the Chicago Board of Trade, called the colonel derisively "The Jailer."[36] No doubt Hiram was referring to an incident that reached the White House.

CHAPTER 6

The Conspiracy of 1862

Martial law declared—Five women and a child discovered—An agreement to exchange prisoners—Former mayor jailed in escape plot—Mismanagement continues—A prisoner cheers for Jeff Davis—Prisoners exchanged.

Camp Douglas was the only Federal prison affected by the declaration of martial law. It began when guards arrested a Chicago alderman for talking to prisoners through the fence. The alderman brought the matter before a Chicago court, according to Stanton, "and the military authority was sustained." Tucker had to post the martial law decree outside camp and publish it in local papers. Wooden stakes 50 feet apart marked the boundaries, and Tucker posted two hundred notices.[1]

Chicago papers published the decree on July 12, 1862, warning the public that "any person violating military authority within said line will be subject to punishment by short confinement or trial by court-martial at the discretion of the commanding officer."[2] This announcement did not surprise anybody. The military had been trampling on the Constitution since the war began.

Hoffman wrote Tucker to impose martial law "for a space of 100 feet outside and around the chain of sentinels." This order allowed him to extend his jurisdiction as far as he liked by throwing out his picket lines. The decree soon ran as far as State Street, six blocks to the west, and included the University of Chicago across the road. Prison officials planned to keep civilians away from all sides of the camp except Cottage Grove.

One newspaper gleefully warned readers not to misbehave on the State Street cars, and charged Tucker with petty acts, such as banning peddlers. It predicted, "In the likely event of a mass escape the country would be devastated by pillage, incendiarism, rapine, and all the risks which stare us in the face." Tucker was unduly sensitive to such criticism and complained to Colonel Hoffman, who soothed him and advised him to blame the restrictions on Colonel Mulligan.[3] As compensation, he gave Tucker authority to ban "disloyal" newspapers from camp.

Simultaneously, Tucker became entangled in political clout. The Honorable Schuyler Colfax of Indiana, a member of Congress, obtained a release for a prisoner named William P. Jones, Third Mississippi Infantry. Colfax was Speaker of the House from 1863 to 1869 and a future vice president of the United States. He was close to President Lincoln, and Stanton granted the personal favor, "which will open his prison doors," Colfax boasted.[4] Colfax was doing it for a friend, to whom he wrote, "P.S.—As the temper of our people is not in favor of releasing rebels and as I would not have done it but to oblige you make no reference to it in the paper."

However, Private Jones asked Tucker if the parole allowed him to cross Union lines into Mississippi. It did not, so Tucker kept him a prisoner. This action petrified Hoffman. "The Secretary of War's orders give you no discretion in the matter!" he roared.[5] Hoffman wanted Jones booted out of camp at the point of a bayonet, if necessary. The old war horse liked his job, if Tucker did not. Tucker was angry. His plea to release dying prisoners had gone unanswered and those who deserted the Confederate army at Camp Douglas were left to rot. The privileged, however, walked out the gate.

President Lincoln interceded in 11 cases at Camp Douglas, ten of them at the request of influential Kentuckians and other friends. Governor Yates did it once. Influence peddling became a regular business for one Kentucky law firm with ties to the president. The law partners charged a hundred dollars for each case and were successful 20 times in releasing prisoners at Camp Douglas. They even had the audacity to send business cards there.

This situation so offended Capt. E.R.P. Shurly, the adjutant, or administrative assistant in modern terms, that he complained directly to Hoffman. "I presume that accounts for the release of so many prisoners of war who have never made application to take the oath of allegiance," Shurly accused.[6] Hoffman said nothing.

Lawyers were often not necessary, as Kentucky loyalists took advantage of Lincoln's misguided policy to keep that state in the Union. The chaplain of the Fifth Kentucky Infantry requested Lincoln to release his "wayward son" at Camp Douglas, and it was done. A Kentucky woman called "one of the most active Union ladies in Fayette

County" had no trouble in getting her son out of Camp Douglas. She even omitted any pretense that "vicious companions had led him away" or that "he was forced into rebel service."

Brutus Junius Clay, a pro-Union Kentucky legislator, really worked miracles. His "thumbs up" caused Lincoln to pardon a soldier in the Second Kentucky Cavalry who was about to be executed as a spy, and the man was set free on Lincoln's order.[7]

While most prisoners wanted out of Camp Douglas, some were trying just as hard to stay in. An astonishing discovery on July 16, 1862, stunned even the hard-nosed Hoffman. Tucker discovered five young women and a child among the prisoners who had arrived on May 28, 1862, from Camp Randall at Madison, Wisconsin. The stowaways had somehow overcome problems of food, bathing, sleeping arrangements, and hygienic needs for themselves and the child for seven weeks. The latrines were only shallow pits, "many of them merely surrounded by a few poles and brush, insufficient to afford privacy."[8] Possibly, the prisoners had set up a more private location and provided security for their guests.

Most likely the women had disguised themselves as men, but this did not explain the ability of the child to escape detection. Prisoners may have bribed guards who were lax anyway. Even the Chicago police did not find the outsiders during the search of June 23. Tucker did his best to put the group in a good light and explain their motives when he reported them to Hoffman's headquarters.[9] They were respectable ladies, he said, whom he described as:

1. Rebecca Parish, about 28 years of age, from Sumter County, Georgia. She was at Island No. 10 where her husband and two children died in April. "Since then she lived under the protection of her brother, a Confederate soldier."

2. Harriet Redd, about 24 years of age, from Pike County, Alabama. "She was taken prisoner with her husband at Island No. 10 while an invalid."

3. Araminta Palmer, a widow, about 22 years of age, from Great Bend, Meigs County, Ohio. She was a cook in the Confederate hospital at Island No. 10 when taken prisoner on April 8. "Araminta is sickly and her parents were good Union people."

4. Amelia Davis, about 33 years of age, from Vermont. The Confederate army employed her and her husband as stewardess

and cook on board a steamer at Island No. 10, "and both sent prisoners to Camp Douglas together with a little boy eight years of age."

5. Bridget Higgins, from Galway, Ireland. She followed her husband from Island No. 10. She had no relatives in this country and "was in delicate health."

Officers at Camp Randall knew about the women and offered to free them, but they preferred to remain with friends and family. The officers did not report them as a matter of kindness. Some might call it chivalry. Getting inside Camp Douglas was not difficult. Guards probably only counted prisoners as they walked by.

Colonel Hoffman decided that the women could remain as nurses or laundresses but not as prisoners. They had to stay within the camp if employed. Those who could not or did not wish to work could live outside at government expense or receive free transportation to the limits of the Union lines. He did not mention the child, so the women assumed that he would stay with his mother. Such generous terms reflected a warmer side of the iron soldier. Little information is available about the outcome. Only Mrs. Redd and Mrs. Davis and her child remained in camp on September 10, 1862.[10] The others may have left with earlier prisoner exchanges.

Camp Douglas was a safe haven for them, although Tucker still was concerned about lack of discipline. Officers were leaving camp without passes, and they continued to deliver packages to prisoners. Tucker again prohibited this practice and all unnecessary conversation with prisoners. He nagged about troops shopping at the wrong sutler and ordered the Articles of War read to them every Sunday.[11] No one could accuse him of courting popularity.

Hoffman was just as dubious about the garrison. He wrote Tucker on July 20, 1862, to pull in the south fence line and to rebuild and strengthen it. His plan called for sentinel walks 50 to 75 feet apart atop the fence. The supports had to be on the outside "so that the sentinel may have a good view of all inside the fence near his post." Camp Douglas would resemble a prison for the first time.

Hoffman ordered Tucker to use old lumber lying about the camp, "Let it cost as little as possible," he said. He did not specify the height and casually reported to Washington on July 21 that 103 prisoners had escaped since February 20. Hoffman did tighten matters a bit by requiring Tucker to assign officers to call the roll. A major or officer of higher rank had to supervise the operation and make a morning report.[12]

However, improvements came to a halt with the Dix-Hill Cartel of July 22, 1862, providing for a general exchange of prisoners. General Meigs postponed the new stockade, a sewer system, more water hydrants, and better medical care and housing. The army quickly exchanged Colonel Hoffman as a paroled prisoner, and he returned to full military status. Ironically, the Cartel prohibited paroled prisoners from doing military duties, but Hoffman was paroled before the Cartel.[13]

Both governments consented to negotiations between Gen. John A. Dix for the North and Gen. D. H. Hill for the South. The Cartel was a lawyer's document with complicated formulas for exchanging men of unequal rank. It required good will to succeed; therefore, it was bound to fail. Parole of prisoners within ten days of capture was one clause that both sides violated immediately. Another critical provision was that both sides release prisoners then in custody at once. This did not happen either. The North held 20,500 prisoners. Camp Douglas, holding 7,800, was the largest prison.[14] The Cartel failed to mention either government by name, as though the war were raging on another planet.

Besides the Cartel, some new postal agreements moved the "Flag of Truce" to City Point, Virginia.[15] Prisoners could now send mail to other prisons. One man wrote from Camp Douglas to his former commanding officer, a prisoner at Johnson's Island, reporting that the shortages of "vegetable food have rendered our camp somewhat unhealthy." Officials usually checked mail more closely than that for derogatory or political matter. As a result, prisoners sometimes received empty envelopes.

A serious escape erupted on July 23, 1862, despite news of the Cartel. Prisoners rushed the fence with three scaling ladders constructed crudely of boards and cleats. Off-duty sentinels camped in tents adjoining the stockade awoke to the sound of gunfire. A young recruit in the 67th Illinois Infantry, a 90-day outfit, recalled, "We went off in the darkness at a double quick and soon arrived at the point of disturbance just in the nick of time to prevent a general escape. Some sympathizers had arranged with the prisoners by some means that at a certain signal a rush on the guard line should be made." A few men in the 67th Illinois Infantry panicked and fled at the sound of the guns, but the vast majority did their job. Officials at Camp

Douglas did not release the 67th when its 90 days expired, and it stood guard duty five more months.[16]

The *Tribune* reported that "parties were seen skulking about in the Cottage Grove Woods before the attack" and claimed that an officer fired his pistol at one of them. Some readers called for a home guard to reinforce security at camp.

The alarm terrified Mrs. Joseph Frederick Ward, a young woman in Chicago. She was at home with friends "when a troop of cavalry turned off State Street, came to position in front of our house, and were there put through the manual of the saber, sharp and quick, to be addressed in very strong language by their commander, after which they turned about and went jingling down State Street."[17]

The women were unconcerned until the doorbell rang and a man shouted that "armed prisoners were out." They numbly changed from summer dresses to walking suits. "We gathered up a few things in hand-bags, turned out the lights and sat in the dark, stunned and stupid with fear, and waited," Mrs. Ward remembered. "Suddenly there was a volley of musketry—another—a third—then cannon—then all was still."

Colonel Tucker reported that a "treacherous guard" in the 67th Illinois Infantry had left his gun and equipment and fled with 21 prisoners. No one was hurt. Tucker pointed out that Camp Douglas, by its structure and form, was unsuitable for a prison. The guard detail was weak, with only 1 captain, 7 lieutenants, 13 sergeants, 24 corporals, and 382 privates. Tucker also sent out patrols ranging as far as three miles. He had no more than 450 men to guard the prisoners. The 67th and 69th Illinois Infantry on guard duty were regiments in name only.

The number of escapees came to 25, but 20 were recaptured within two weeks. It was fortunate for civilians that prisoners meant them no harm. Tucker had an astonishing solution to prevent escapes. "I have no hesitation in saying that in my opinion martial law should be declared over the city of Chicago and the command vested in the commanding officer of this camp."[18] That was one way to become the mayor of Chicago. Washington did not respond.

One prisoner dismissed the affair as "a highly exaggerated account of a rebellion in Camp." He was right according to Milo A. McClelland, an officer in the 69th Illinois Infantry. He blamed the uproar on hysterical guards and laughed at the report that escapees used ladders but confirmed that prisoners fled through a hole dug by the "traitor." Guards fired cannons to sound the alarm, but these were not loaded, he revealed.

It all started, according to McClelland, when officers confined some prisoners in White Oak dungeon for getting drunk on whiskey supplied by a guard, "and their friends swore that the federals would surrender that night honorably or dishonorably." Some young recruits heard about the threat and nervously fired 10 to 15 wild shots in the confusion, McClelland believed.[19]

A "lad" named Charles Ellis, 20th Mississippi Infantry, returned on his own from the July 23 escape. He was not the last to do so. However, prisoners saw nothing wrong in escaping. Two sergeants in the 42nd Tennessee Infantry petitioned Tucker to release recaptured Confederates from the dungeon because "they did not commit any assault upon the sentinels."[20] Tucker, however, "went by the book."

He drew his picket lines tighter around the prison barracks, leaving stables on the south side of White Oak Square unguarded. Sentinels caught some prisoners hiding there, hoping to flee. One prisoner had the mayor of Rockford, Illinois, write Tucker. "John Hayes would not voluntarily of his free choice join the enemies of his country, because his oldest son had been in the Union army for the past year," the mayor swore.[21] Tucker interviewed the man and recommended that the War Department release him, but this event was not likely unless the mayor had some clout in Washington.

Tucker was in a quandary when many more prisoners asked to take the oath, believing that this meant going home. Some made the usual claim that they were "forced into the rebel service." Others were tired of the rebellion and wanted to return to their loyalty and to their homes, Tucker wrote. Stanton ruled that prisoners could take the oath to avoid exchange.[22] This drove another nail into the Cartel.

Meanwhile, prisoners' ragged condition continued because of poor communication by Tucker. He made an emergency requisition after the army clothing promised in February failed to arrive. "Many of the prisoners are destitute and without a change, while others have portions of citizen's dress which they had received before I assumed command," he mentioned.[23] Tucker wished to replace civilian clothing with captured Confederate uniforms so that people could easily recognize prisoners in case of escape.

He had to cope with the prison break and then deal with Hoffman the next day about escapes and the prisoners' health and welfare.

Tucker surprised Hoffman with a set of plans drawn by an engineering firm for a sewer and water system to carry off surface water and human waste.[24] It rivaled, or perhaps surpassed, anything in Chicago. The sewer would be 3,250 feet long, made of oak, and have three-inch water lines connected to privies and hydrants. The firm's engineers designed three 500-gallon water tanks to help flush waste through the system and planned to provide ten privies. This was only one of many miscalculations. They could not foresee that 18,000 more prisoners would arrive, but how they could specify only three-inch pipes defies understanding. The estimated cost was $8,257.18, using prison labor.

Hoffman took the plans with him but was concerned about more than the sanitary system. He had heard pnothing from Colonel Mulligan concerning his accounting. He probably persuaded Stanton to order Mulligan's arrest at New Creek, Virginia, on July 28, 1862, "and be called to account for the charges made against him in the enclosed letter from Col. J. H. Tucker."[25] Only malice and spite can explain the pursuit of a fighting officer for such a petty matter.

Prisoners to whom money may have been owed were leaving anyway. On July 31, Hoffman ordered Tucker to prepare up-to-date prison rolls, giving him only four days to do so. This was a monumental task, considering the eight thousand prisoners on hand, but the stingy Hoffman did provide for additional clerks. He was to release chaplains immediately. Yet, the prospect of exchange did not slow Hoffman's constant charges of mismanagement. On August 4, he demanded to know why prison officials had not credited $20 to one prisoner's account, according to a letter from his irate father.[26] Mulligan's "shortage" should have become more understandable to Hoffman.

The Mulligan affair was far removed from what mattered. In that momentous summer of 1862, Gen. George B. McClellan led the Union army to defeat near Richmond, and Gen. Robert E. Lee began his disastrous invasion of Maryland. The Confederacy had yet to furnish clothing to Union prisoners, and at Camp Douglas 283 Confederates died and 1,147 became ill during June and July. Scurvy returned, and Colonel Hoffman again blasted Tucker for mismanaging the camp.[27]

"The presence of scurvy among men where there is an abundance of vegetables and antiscorbutics is a novel state of things to me, and I fear grows out of a want of attention somewhere," Hoffman ranted.

Medical Inspector Christopher C. Keeney reported in September 1862 that he "was inclined to believe" there was a shortage of vegetables at camp, but did not verify this fact.[28]

Tucker probably wished that he were back at the Board of Trade, because it was Hoffman who omitted the order to buy vegetables.[29] Another report from Dr. McVickar that the camp was in poor sanitary condition again irritated Hoffman, and he accused Tucker of neglect. "They must air the bedding out at least once a week, with free use of lime everywhere to neutralize all impurities. There can be no excuse for noncompliance with this order," Hoffman warned.

Colonel Tucker was probably a poor administrator, and he had less excuse than Mulligan who had commanded during a terrible winter and spring. For example, Tucker received reports that two buildings holding prisoners were collapsing, one of which was a stable housing three hundred men. Water came through the roof, soaking bedding and blankets. Yet, nothing was done.[30]

Why did Hoffman not simply remove Tucker? Oddly, he never had the authority to appoint or dismiss prison commanders, although he asked Stanton for this power on September 19, 1863. "I beg leave to respectfully suggest that it would facilitate the management of the affairs of prisoners of war . . . if the commanders of stations . . . could be placed under the immediate control of the Commissary General of Prisoners," he pointed out. Hoffman also wanted command of all surgeons serving in prison hospitals. He never received these powers.[31]

Another cause for Tucker's staying on was Governor Yates. Hoffman was aware of his influence and told the governor that his assistant would confer with Yates before inspecting Camp Butler near Springfield, "and any suggestions you may please to make will be carefully carried out."[32] The steely veteran was finding that shot and shell was one matter, politics another.

Imagine Hoffman's embarrassment on August 2, 1862, when he accompanied Yates on an inspection of Camp Douglas, and one prisoner shouted, "Hurrah for Jeff Davis!"[33] The mischief maker was Pvt. Joseph M. Rainey, Company C, 48th Tennessee, the same company as James T. Mackey. Guards hauled Rainey to the dungeon, although Yates wanted to forget the incident.

Tucker, meanwhile, made an astonishing discovery upon questioning recaptured prisoners. The money to bribe guards came from

Company C, 48th Tennessee Infantry at Camp Douglas. Circled at top is James Taswell Mackey, the writer. Below is Joe Rainey, who cheered for Jeff Davis. (Image courtesy of the *Confederate Veteran.*)

Dr. Levi D. Boone, a wealthy and influential Chicagoan. Colonel Tucker promptly jailed Boone at Camp Douglas.

Jailing of civilians by the military was common in the North and the South. Yet, it was odd that Tucker did not request permission beforehand. He uneasily notified Secretary of War Stanton and Colonel Hoffman on August 4, 1862, that he had "arrested a prominent citizen named L. D. Boone." Boone was a Chicago physician and businessman who served as mayor from 1855 to 1857. He was related to the Daniel Boone clan of Kentucky, where he lived before coming to Illinois.[34]

"It is ascertained beyond any doubt that considerable sums of money have been given to prisoners contrary to the regulations of the camp," Tucker charged. Boone had access to the camp under Colonel Mulligan while bringing supplies to the prisoners. This practice continued long after Hoffman prohibited Mulligan from admitting visitors. Tucker was wrong in at least one respect. Nothing about Camp Douglas could be "ascertained beyond any doubt," and the Boone case proved no exception.

Tucker also arrested a former prisoner named W. H. Warren whom he had paroled as a chaplain. Warren admitted giving money to the guards but refused to say where he got it. Another prisoner named E. H. Greene claimed that he received $50 from Dr. Boone. The accused doctor admitted giving Green $20 but claimed that a third person gave him the additional $30 without his authority. Finally, he came up with the excuse that he was three hundred miles away at the time.[35]

Hoffman approved of Tucker's decisive action on August 6. "It is plain that all persons who interfere in any way to endanger the safety of the prisoners under your charge, or to disturb the good order of the camp render themselves amenable to arrest and punishment," Hoffman said sternly. As usual, however, he retreated under political pressure.

Boone was a trustee of the influential University of Chicago, separated from the camp by only a country lane. The mayor of Chicago and several aldermen usually sat on the board of trustees, and their sons were students there. A fellow trustee was Hiram. A. Tucker, Colonel Tucker's brother, who in one instance acted as Lincoln's personal banker. This was not all. Lincoln knew Dr. Boone and argued law cases in Chicago when Boone was mayor. Both had served in the Black Hawk War. Another bizarre twist was that Dr. McVickar had

Dr. Levi D. Boone. (Image courtesy of the Chicago Historical Society.)

shared medical offices with Dr. Boone, and when Boone was elected mayor, McVickar became city physician.[36]

Dr. Boone, no doubt, did supply money to prisoners, both his own and funds received from families. Prisoners from the Deep South, especially, were penniless. However, many believed Dr. Boone to be innocent of any escape plot. This was probably true. Yet, he could have deposited money to their account at camp. On the other hand, Boone knew about the bank shortages. Regardless, giving cash to the prisoners was a serious breach of security. Tucker lost 45 prisoners in July 1862, so his anger was justified.

Tucker felt more confident with Dr. Boone in custody and turned to defending his administration. Hoffman's office gave him a late start in providing vegetables, Tucker fired back, and Dr. McVickar meant in his reports that the camp required a water drainage system, and not that Tucker was doing a poor job. Dr. McVickar confirmed these claims.

Unlike Mulligan, the doctor was dedicated to a job he did not want and made heavy demands for work details to clean, disinfect, and whitewash the camp.[37] Colonel Hoffman must have respected McVickar, because he again approached General Meigs about the sanitation problem. Prisoners would work on the proposed sewer system, he told him, "and I believe that they have not at any time refused to work even in cases of doubtful propriety, such as putting up fences that we may hold them with greater security."[38]

Meigs probably did not understand how difficult the prison was to manage with the commandant being responsible for both administration and security, as well as the Post of Chicago. Infantry and artillery regiments were in training, and the stockade was too small. Tent cities sprang up outside and caused more sanitation problems. The many escapes required much of Tucker's attention, adding to the stress of clothing prisoners and improving living conditions. Meanwhile, Hoffman pressed the matter of Mulligan's accounts, and the War Department filed court-martial charges against him on August 12, 1862.[39]

Truly, the War Department had more important matters than chasing a front-line combat officer for a debt, especially one that Mulligan angrily denied to the adjutant general of the army. "My character, sir, has never been sullied," Mulligan countered, "and I am impatient of the undeserved reproach of this arrest—impatient to vindicate to you and your department that I am an honest man and an obedient officer. I therefore respectfully demand an immediate trial or that the War Office upon the accounting shall vindicate me as publicly as it has wronged me."[40]

More pressing matters than Mulligan's shortage should have concerned Hoffman at this time. He complained that Tucker had not given him clothing estimates for the prisoners and was sharply critical of him for not returning requisition papers.[41] "What have you done to supply this clothing; or are the prisoners still suffering for want of clothing?" Hoffman demanded. He finally bypassed Tucker on August 13 and ordered three thousand each of pants, hats, coats, and shirts. However, this shipment met only half the prisoners' needs. Hoffman canceled another order in August because exchange appeared imminent.

Hoffman blamed some of Tucker's failures on Capt. John Christopher, commissary of subsistence. He complained to Washington that the captain had disregarded Tucker in submitting reports to Hoffman's office. Christopher "was unwilling to recognize the authority of Colonel Tucker," Hoffman charged.[42] Perhaps this situation resulted from Tucker's being only a state militia officer and not a war hero. Christopher had shielded Mulligan from Hoffman's interference. It must have irked him, a regular army officer, to see someone who was only one step above a civilian running the most powerful army camp in the Northwest.

The shortage of clothing put the prisoners on edge while everyone waited for exchange. The delay was costly, with 117 prisoners dying in August 1862. More than one-third were from Fort Donelson. Camp Douglas even took the life of one of Tucker's sons who served with him, the *Tribune* reported.

> **FUNERAL OF CAPTAIN TUCKER**
>
> The funeral obsequies of Captain Lansing B. Tucker, son of Col. J. H. Tucker, were observed yesterday afternoon, at two o'clock, in the grove of the University grounds at Cottage Grove. A large number of his friends from the city were in attendance to pay a last tribute of respect to the young officer who has lost his valuable life in consequence of the exposures incident to the camp.[43]

TABLE II

FORT DONELSON PRISONERS WHO DIED[44]

1862	
February	3
March	125
April	96
May	68
June	69
July	78
August	42
September	37

TOTAL: 518 + one killed in barracks

Money left by deceased prisoners was swelling the hospital fund, while the prospects of exchange faded. Wreckage from the Cartel was smashing prisoners' hopes. Union army officers in the field refused to parole prisoners, as required, and the South charged that three summary executions had occurred in Tennessee.[45]

Colonel Tucker's main concern was time to settle prisoner accounts and the observation of proper banking procedures. Suddenly, on August 28, 1862, he was directed to begin transferring prisoners for exchange "as soon as practical." They were to leave in parties of one thousand, by regiment, via Cairo, Illinois, to Vicksburg, Mississippi.[46] Stanton excluded prisoners classified as guerrillas, but this did not appear to affect Camp Douglas.

Tucker detailed the 67th and 69th Illinois Infantry Regiments as guards to prevent prisoners from escaping and to protect them from outsiders. Rations were issued to take them only as far as Cairo where personal money on deposit at Camp Douglas was due with proper balance sheets. Financial responsibility had to be respected even during war's disruption and bitterness.

Prisoners could decline exchange and take the oath of allegiance to the "United States," Stanton ordered. This violated the Cartel. The oath required that those who took it remain north of the Ohio River. Those without funds or employment usually violated the oath. Regardless, 918 prisoners took it. Add 228 more recruited by Mulligan and Cameron, and the Confederate army suffered a 13 percent desertion rate at Camp Douglas.[47] The reasons vary.

Prisoners from the Western armies of the Confederacy suffered more hardship and deprivation than those in the East and felt little obligation to return to duty. Many from Kentucky and Tennessee once had strong ties to the North and did not mind switching sides. Foreign nationals among the prisoners had no personal interest in the war and decided to step out. Conscripts who never intended to fight took this opportunity to desert.[48]

Finally, men who harbored a romanticism about the South found that war is not an adventure for those who stand face to face with it. The price for defending "Southern Rights" was too high. Captain William H. Harder, 23rd Tennessee Infantry, confirmed ruefully that many of his men who were "eager at the beginning of the affair, after seeing the tusk of the elephant, cease to love war and resolve to do anything but die for the South."[49]

Colonel Tucker held Dr. Levi Boone throughout this turbulent time. Finally, Secretary of War Stanton heard from an exasperated President Lincoln on September 1, 1862.

> I personally know Dr. Levi D. Boone, of Chicago, Illinois, who is not in close confinement, but on limits, on parole, under bonds, and oath of allegiance. From my knowledge of him, and the open, and rather marked part he has taken for the war, I think he should be at least, enlarged generally, on the same terms. If the Sec. of War concurs, let it be done.
>
> Yours truly,
> A. LINCOLN.[50]

Stanton passed the responsibility to Colonel Hoffman, who reported that "there seems no reason to doubt Dr. Boone's loyalty."[51] The aging veteran had learned his Washington politics. Imprisonment for 37 days did not affect Dr. Boone's standing at the University of Chicago, and the board appointed him to a new committee.[52]

Colonel Hoffman never arrived to help Tucker, but the businessman did very well without him. The first ones to take the oath were out the gate on September 1, 1862. The first group bound for Cairo was on the road the next day. Tucker shipped out all prisoners by September 27, except those in the hospital. Seventy-one of them died.[53]

Black prisoners captured at Fort Donelson exercised different options. Two slaves enlisted in the Union army, and two of the soldiers took unconditional releases. They were not entirely safe in Chicago. President Lincoln's Federal marshals were zealous in rounding up blacks under the Federal Fugitive Slave Act. Chicago police could arrest them under the Illinois "Black Code" of 1853 that prohibited the migration of blacks into the state.[54]

Two of the black prisoners chose to return South. The army exchanged Pvt. Isaac Wood, probably for a white Union soldier, as the South was not holding black prisoners at this time. He may have astonished the Federal exchange officer at Cairo, Illinois. Richmond would not have allowed his exchange, had it known of it. The Confederacy was concerned about slaves without masters, and especially free blacks, serving as combat soldiers, since this undermined the basic assumption about slavery.[55]

Black prisoners were a troubling presence at Camp Douglas throughout the war, challenging the army to examine its own prejudices about the black race. In this it failed. The policy for now was to let them choose their own destiny. Samuel Hill, a slave, returned to the Confederate army with his owner, Sgt. J. S. Crawford of the Seventh Texas Infantry. Not everyone wanted freedom. G. Blackwood was a victim of bad record-keeping, and his fate is unknown.

Blacks were not the only minorities at camp. "Tom," an Indian, was a private in the Fourth Texas Infantry. He was captured at Fort Gibson in the "Cherokee Nation." He could have been exchanged in Texas, without the long journey to Camp Douglas.

Another 163 Confederates captured at Corinth, Mississippi, suffered the same ordeal. Railroads and steamships carried them 935 miles to Camp Douglas although exchanges were going on at Vicksburg, only 228 miles away. Colonel Tucker turned this bone-weary bunch around after 11 days on the road and sent them to Vicksburg, traveling 1,253 miles this time. It was an army SNAFU at its best.[56]

The Illinois Central Railroad brought freight cars almost daily to the station two hundred yards east of the camp gate on Cottage Grove. An eyewitness wrote, "It was a spectacle long to be remembered to see these multitudes of men in gray and butternut garb, ragged and threadbare, trooping to the long lines of freight cars drawn up on the lake front, from which point they started on their journey in hilarious spirits."[57]

Tattered they were, as little clothing had come from home since July. Families feared that prisoners could be gone when the packages arrived. They amounted to only 650 shirts, 250 pairs of pants, 150 pairs of shoes, 23 blankets, 201 drawers, 42 vests, 88 hats, and 301 pairs of socks. The army made things worse by reclaiming many blue uniforms and taking some prisoners' own clothing for good measure.[58]

The road back turned lethal when a train derailed 120 miles north of Cairo, Illinois, at Centralia. The impact killed one prisoner and injured ten. Workers cleared the wreckage in four hours and brought up a new locomotive. Otherwise, the operation went much smoother than seven months earlier on the way to Camp Douglas.[59]

Reports differ regarding how 7,192 prisoners traveled down the Mississippi River. Eight or nine Federal transports may have waited for them at Cairo on September 8, with one or two gunboats serving as escort. Private Spot F. Terrell of the 49th Tennessee Infantry estimated that six hundred prisoners were crammed aboard each boat, but some vessels must have held more.[60]

The boats flew a large white flag and only traveled during the day, anchoring in mid-river at night. Sympathizers treated prisoners warmly during refueling at Memphis on September 10. "Multitudes of wimmin crouded around and hallowed for Jeff Davis and the South," Private Terrell reminisced. "Tha give meny Gifts of tobaco apples and peaches candy and all sorts of grappess. The boys gave them rings in return whitch was very acceptable to the Tenn girls." However, several men died on the boats, and Vicksburg was unprepared to receive prisoners. Clinton, Mississippi, a college town 34 miles east, became a rendezvous point.[61]

The road back for prisoners of war was not an easy one. Everything in Clinton was either scarce or too expensive. Watermelons cost a dollar each, and shoes sold for $15 to $20 a pair. Sweet potatoes went for three dollars a bushel. The mess was pickled pork, flour and meal, much worse than rations at Camp Douglas. Everyone between 18 and 40 was conscripted for two years or longer without furloughs.[62] The former prisoners quickly commenced drilling and had again to face the confident Federal armies in the West.

Corporal William Micajah Barrow, who devoured much food and many novels at Camp Douglas, left on September 6. "I hope better luck will be my part next time," he wrote in his last letter. He died of dysentery 15 months later while serving in the army near Resaca, Georgia.

James Taswell Mackey embarked on September 7. "The day dawned beautiful and bright," he recorded, "and found many glad-hearted rebels making preparations to leave a place associated with the most melancholy events of their lives." Upon his return the Confederacy promoted him to lieutenant, but he died of smallpox on January 6, 1865, while a prisoner of war at Fort Delaware. A poetic voice was stilled without a farewell.

Sergeant Charles E. Taylor's last Camp Douglas diary entry was Monday, June 16, 1862. He reported "very heavy thunderstorms tonight." He was only 17 years old. Taylor fought on for two years and died of wounds received at Franklin, Tennessee, on November 30, 1864. Taylor is among the 565 unknowns in the Confederate cemetery there.[63]

Camp Douglas claimed the life of Pvt. C. W. Dozier, Company I, 40th Tennessee Infantry, as the prisoners departed. How could he have known when he left home to follow the Confederacy that one day he would merit an obituary in a powerful Yankee newspaper?

> **THE LAST REBEL GONE**
>
> The last rebel remaining in the Camp died yesterday. He stated in his last moments that he had now three sons in the rebel army, besides four who had been killed in the rebel service. He was an inveterate traitor and maintained his treason boldly to the last minute. He declared that he was dying of grief because he had been so unsuccessful in his attempts to root out the Yankees. The surgeon insists, however, that he died of diarrhea, which is probably the case, accelerated perhaps by his profound melancholy.[64]

Dozier was not "the last rebel gone," however. Private William H. Kilpatrick, who fatally struck Thomas M. Golden, was serving time for manslaughter and would not be leaving for at least a year.[65] Kilpatrick symbolized the common soldier of the Civil War, caught up in forces that he did not understand. He did what he had to according to the code of Maury County, Tennessee, but a Chicago jury could not grasp it.

Tucker had nothing to celebrate as the camp began winding down. His poor performance from June to September 1862 may have resulted from paying too much attention to his own business, rather than the camp's. A Chicago banker remembered him being "in and out" of the bank all the time "and more or less after he went out to take the position of commandant at Camp Douglas."[66]

The administrations of Colonel Mulligan and Colonel Tucker reflected their different goals and personalities. The leader of the Irish Brigade was anxious to get back to the war, while Tucker's interests were local. Mulligan did not care to make a permanent contribution to the camp, but Tucker obtained plans for a water and sewer system that one day revolutionized it. Mulligan made his own rules to keep the prisoners in line. Tucker went by the book. Mulligan's popularity shielded him from personal attacks. Tucker had to suffer them. Mulligan boldly rejected Hoffman's formula for selling rations to build up a prison fund. Tucker achieved the same result by giving it lip service.[67]

Hoffman was frustrated and angry when he issued his final report on the camp in November 1862. He mostly blamed Captain Christopher who had the authority as commissary of subsistence to cut rations and "prevent the consequent great waste of provisions and loss to the Government!" Hoffman estimated that the prison fund lost $10,000 to $15,000 under Mulligan and Tucker.[68]

TABLE III

PRISON MORTALITY IN 1862

February 23 to September 29	
Disease	977
Prisoners killed by guards	2
Prisoners killed by another	1
TOTAL DEATHS	980

The *Tribune* counted 976 deaths by disease beginning March 1, 1862, omitting three men who died immediately on arrival in February 1862 and perhaps not listing Private Golden.[69] This did not agree with Tucker's reconstructed records which counted 781 dead through August 1, 1862. Tucker added 22 more by August 10 and 36 additional mortalities on August 26. Another 71 deaths occurred in the next 30 days, for a total of 910, and Dozier was 911.[70] The *Tribune*'s estimate of 976 deaths may have been more accurate because it kept a continuing count. Prisoners died at a rate of about 11.225 percent to 12.2250 percent, or one out of eight. Deaths among Union troops were not negligible at 240.

The *Official Records* accepted Tucker's figure of 7,192 prisoners exchanged.[71] However, the *Tribune* reported 8,962 at camp on June 9, 1862, a difference of 1,770 men. About 290 had since died, leaving 1,480 men unaccounted according to the *Tribune*'s figures. Of these, 584 were released, mostly by taking the oath, and three went to other depots.[72] This still leaves 893 missing. One explanation is that the *Tribune* based the number of prisoners on Mulligan's records, not Tucker's. Tucker, for example, brought current, as best he could, the total number of dead, escaped, and released prisoners beginning in February 1862. Perhaps, more were released upon taking the oath than records show. Failure to record many deaths is another likely answer.

The second phase of Camp Douglas was now over. First, it had served as a base for recruiting, equipping, and training recruits. Next, it also became a prison camp. The *Tribune* remarked that the camp was lively "in spite of the absence of the secesh." It described barracks as "being left in a most filthy condition" and under repair. "It is no wonder they died so rapidly," said the paper candidly of the prisoners. "It is only a wonder that the whole eight thousand of the filthy hogs did not go home in pine boxes instead of on their feet." Medical Inspector Keeney agreed, finding barracks to be dark, dingy, and poorly ventilated.[73]

Colonel Tucker shipped out the last of the prisoners who could travel on September 29, 1862. However, peace and quiet did not settle over Camp Douglas. It was about to enter a third phase as a camp for Union prisoners of war paroled by the South under the Cartel. They were more raucous, insubordinate, and destructive than the Confederates had ever been. A rigid officer named Gen. Daniel Tyler commanded this lot, and a clash was inevitable.

General Daniel Tyler. (Image courtesy of the USAMHI.)

CHAPTER 7

The Iron Rule of General Daniel Tyler

Union Disaster at Harpers Ferry—Paroled troops arrive—General Daniel Tyler takes over from Colonel Tucker—Tyler battles mutinous troops—Parolees set fire to the camp—Colonel Daniel Cameron replaces Tyler—Prisoners exchanged.

Camp Douglas moved along easily through the beginning of Autumn 1862. Eight regiments of infantry and three companies of artillery were training and caught up in the Civil War.[1] Dress parades every afternoon, good food, and pride in new skills made it worthwhile. The quality of instruction and training caused the army to allot funds for repairing the camp. It was too late, as usual. Events eight hundred miles to the southeast wrecked Tucker's plans. The North suffered one of its worst debacles of the war on September 15, 1862, when almost an entire army corps surrendered at Harpers Ferry, Virginia.[2]

The troops wanted to fight and felt betrayed by their officers. Shame and rage at surrendering their arms to the Rebels hung over them like a cloud of putrid fertilizer. Yet this was probably the only option after the mess created by army command. It was Halleck, kicked upstairs as general in chief of the army, who ordered Col. Dixon S. Miles to occupy Harpers Ferry. The Confederates under Stonewall Jackson seized the surrounding heights and trapped the Union army below. They were the well-known fish in a barrel. The French made the same mistake at Dien Bien Phu 92 years later and lost Indochina. Harpers Ferry was not as disastrous, although many in Chicago would have disagreed.

About eight thousand men paroled under the Cartel begin arriving at Camp Douglas on September 28, 1862. Only a thousand of them belonged to Illinois. Secretary of War Stanton placed Brig. Gen. Daniel Tyler in charge of organizing and moving them to parole camps. However, Camp Douglas had eight thousand troops in training, leaving little room in the stockade. Two regiments of the newcomers camped outside in tents, and the others used stables west of the stockade as barracks.[3] This created another camp which they named Camp Tyler, after their commander. It extended two blocks west to an area called the Fair Grounds.

General Tyler at age 63 belonged to another century. His father had fought at Bunker Hill. Tyler was born in Connecticut in 1799 and graduated from West Point. Denied promotion because of his rigid honesty in dealing with government contractors, he resigned his commission in 1834.[4] Tyler reentered the army as a brigadier general at the outset of the Civil War but was discharged after he incurred blame for the Union defeat at First Bull Run. When his superiors realized that no one man could be responsible, Tyler was recommissioned in 1862. This rigid throwback to a time when men fought with lances appeared ideally suited for the assignment at Camp Douglas.

Tyler immediately complained to Washington that the railroads used freight cars without water or toilets to transport the men. Yet they charged the passenger rate of two cents per mile instead of one cent for freight, at a cost of $632.80 to move eight thousand troops. "I am bound to say," Tyler snorted, "that the price paid for the service is the most outrageous I have ever known!"[5]

His parolees consisted of the 60th Ohio, 32nd Ohio, Colonel Cameron's 65th Illinois, 39th New York, 111th New York, 115th New York, 125th New York, 126th New York, and the Ninth Vermont. Artillery units were the First Independent Indiana Battery, 15th Indiana Battery, 19th Ohio Battery, Fifth New York Battery, and Phillips' Chicago Battery.[6]

Colonel Tucker clashed with mutinous parolees on September 30, when the Ninth Vermont groaned loudly and refused to obey his order to go on guard duty.

Tucker called out the 93rd Illinois Infantry, a regiment in training, and prepared to enforce the law with bayonets. The parolees then gave in. However, General Tyler relieved Tucker of command as the senior officer.[7] Tucker remained to organize and train volunteers, and Dr. McVickar continued as post surgeon. Tyler's failure to replace him with an army surgeon was unusual. Regardless, for the first time, Camp Douglas was under an officer assigned by the War Department, not Governor Yates.

Private Thomas Jefferson Moses of the 93rd Illinois found the barracks shocking. "Oh how dirty and filthy they were," moaned the young man from a small farming community. "Here we got our first introduction to the gray back and plenty of them. We got what the boys called lousy for good. It was a fearful place to put us in." His worries ended in a few weeks when parolees cleansed the barracks with fire. Most of the 93rd Regiment then camped in tents outside, creating a clean new bivouac they promptly named Camp Putnam in honor of their colonel. Sadly, he was killed two years later at the Battle of Missionary Ridge, and the 93rd Illinois was decimated to the point of extinction.[8]

A lieutenant straggling into camp from Harpers Ferry also found the place fearful, with his regiment quartered in "horse sheds" at Camp Tyler. "The floors of the apartment were laid in mud and the roofing perforated so as not to exclude the refreshing rain," he quipped.[9] Since the parolees were used to the hills of Virginia, "large quantities of garbage, rotting hay, etc. was thrown in heaps before the sheds," the officer added.

New York troops divided the stables into stalls 10 to 15 feet square with eight men to a stall.[10] Private Nicholas De Graff of the 115th New York Infantry conceded that "they do not look very inviting, but all hands set to work forthwith to make them as comfortable as possible." The stalls lacked bunks, which even the Confederates had enjoyed, but officials provided piles of clean hay to sleep on. Captain Edward Hastings Ripley, of the Ninth Vermont, preferred the stables because the barracks "are filled with vermin, even if you can keep them as clean as you can," he complained.[11] Horses had used the stables for a few days during a recent fair. One drawback was the lack of windows. Light filtered in through cracks in the roof and walls.

Unfortunately for General Tyler, the *Chicago Tribune* published the Dix-Hill Cartel, under which paroled troops were not to do military duties. "If we comply with this paragraph it appears to me it leaves little else for us to do with the men but feed and clothe them and let them do as they please," Tyler warned the army. Parolees took that to mean that they did not have to drill, but General Tyler thought otherwise. He banned furloughs and passes and required the men to train, stand guard duty, police the camp, and suffer many inspections. His problems increased when officers sided with the enlisted men,[12] causing a state of insurrection far exceeding the Rebel prison break of July 23. Parolees set fire to barracks and fences at Camps

Private Thomas J. Moses. (Image courtesy of Tom Gaard).

Tyler and Douglas and attempted frequent escapes. "And during that whole period the citizens of Chicago slept insecurely," said one who lived through it. "They felt that a volcano existed at the camp which might at any time break forth and overwhelm the city." Camp Douglas suffered $7,652.70 in damages, and Camp Tyler lost $7,937.84 worth of buildings and fences.[13]

The dream of the Sanitary Commission to cleanse the camp with fire had come true. "The immense destruction of animal life in the form of lice," delighted Medical Inspector Keeney. "And had less of the filthy and rickety quarters been spared still greater salutary effects would have been the result," he asserted.[14]

Rioters also tore down new fences and destroyed the guardhouse to everyone's satisfaction. Tyler placed 125 men from the Ninth Vermont on guard duty with useless weapons, and the mutinous troops drove them away with rocks. Several in the guard detail were badly hurt, and one suffered a broken leg. Private De Graff confirmed that enough barracks burned to hold four regiments. "Our boys are very unruly, and do not want to drill or do anything else," De Graff apologized. He was unwilling to be negative and described the rations as excellent on October 18. "Fresh beef nearly every day. Plenty of coffee, and excellent bread and butter." The *Tribune* disagreed and reported that the "beef is musty and sometimes completely spoiled."[15]

Tyler finally brought in regular army troops on October 23 to quell the parolees. He ruled them with an iron hand and probably would have done the same with prisoners of war had any been there. Guards shot two men as they scaled the fence. Nevertheless, many escaped into the city, which Capt. Benjamin W. Thompson of the 111th New York Infantry described as "one vast beer saloon." He and fellow officers hunted their men every night "out of the saloons—and worse places." Chicago seemed a rat-infested rickety place to the New Yorker. General Tyler then enlisted the aid of the Chicago police in rounding up AWOLS, and the army promised to back up the police with troops.[16]

Small wonder that parolees wanted to escape Camp Douglas. Thirty-five of them died between October 8 and November 7, 1862, mainly of diphtheria, typhoid, and pneumonia. The sick were short of clothing and lying in filthy bunks. Refuse and trash lay everywhere, and pools of stagnant water made the place a swamp.[17] Troops and prisoners had worn the place out. It needed substantial repairs and rebuilding to become a proud military camp again.

Yet the army continued to harass Colonel Mulligan. General Halleck issued a terse order on October 27, 1862, for Mulligan to report to Washington and settle his accounts. Mulligan was already there, according to his diary.[18] He said little about a meeting with Colonel Hoffman on October 28. He lacked the insight to grasp why Colonel Hoffman was out to get him and blamed Colonel Tucker. "Colonel Tucker has done his best, poor fellow, to the extent of his limited ability to straighten out his accounts—a very weak Joseph Tucker is our Colonel," Mulligan's diary reads. So, the entire affair was Tucker's fault, Mulligan believed.

Mulligan paid Hoffman $1,384.21 in settlement of the prisoners' accounts at Camp Douglas, a substantial sum. It was not likely that Hoffman gloated, but civilians had to learn to respect professional soldiers, he felt. The matter ended there, as well it should have. Union prisoners in the South lost many thousands of dollars in their accounts when Confederates shifted them around to avoid approaching Federal armies. A Confederate officer in charge of these funds stole three thousand dollars after the fall of Richmond.[19]

Dwight L. Moody, the evangelist, returned to Camp Douglas at the beginning of November 1862 to preach and help ease the plight of the parolees.[20] Private Charles Wesley Belknap of the 125th New York credited him with "working for the poor soldiers nearly all the time in providing for the wants of their families." Moody also distributed a little book entitled *The Great Redeemer*. A Chicago relief effort was started to aid the parolees as though they were prisoners of war.

Some officers relaxed by going to the theater in Chicago. Captain Ripley watched John Wilkes Booth play Hamlet on December 10, 1862. "It was a happy evening. I never enjoyed anything half so well. I never heard the Elder Booth, but the Younger is certainly something," he marveled.

Meanwhile, the Chicago Sanitary Commission reported that the camp's overflowing latrines caused a terrific stench and made nearby barracks intolerable. General Tyler was determined to whip his troops into a fighting machine without spoiling them with clean latrines. Colonel Hoffman was more concerned about economy, even where Union soldiers were concerned, and ordered part of the parolees' rations sold beginning November 11, 1862. Tyler refused, explaining that the parolees were training "and in a healthy state of discipline," and that he did not wish to interfere with any of the government allowances. Tyler next went to war with the powerful sutler's lobby and prohibited sales on credit. He then crushed another ancient tradition by denying sutlers the right to collect debts out of a soldier's pay at Camp Douglas.[21] Tyler's actions were remarkable, considering the bitter feelings his men held toward him.

Tyler's powerful sense of what was wrong with the world proved his undoing again. The army replaced him around November 20, 1862, with the excuse that drilling and training parolees violated the Cartel.[22] Why the army did not cite his mismanagement of the camp is puzzling; Col. Daniel Cameron, himself a parolee, took command, again, by direction of the War Department. This decision also violated the Cartel, so the army probably got rid of Tyler to appease Colonel Hoffman, the parolees, sutlers, and contractors. Captain George H. Park of Cameron's 65th Illinois Infantry replaced Dr. McVickar. No civilian would ever again be post surgeon at Camp Douglas.

Colonel Cameron was descended from the Camerons who fought the British at Culloden in 1746. He emigrated to America in 1851 at age 23. He was an unlikely champion for the Union, being a Democrat, a friend of Senator Douglas, and founder of the *Chicago Times*, a pro-Confederate paper. However, Cameron had sold his interest in 1861.[23] This time the colonel was in command of Camp Douglas 23 days. Halleck requested that he be relieved because "he does not think it proper that an officer on parole should command at Camp Douglas, Chicago, Ill."[24]

Nevertheless, Cameron now had some ideas about running the camp and recommended to Governor Yates that a permanent commander be appointed.[25] He did not realize that the War Department now controlled the camp. Of course, Yates was happy to surrender further responsibility there.

Neither Tyler nor Cameron could come to grips with what was causing so many men to die. The difference in mortality between the prisoners and the parolees is significant. Confederates had suffered a death rate of from 11 percent to 12 percent in 1862, while the parolees died at a 2.5 percent rate. Of course the prisoners were in camp for six months, and many parolees left after eight weeks. Yet, the Federals faced the same diseases, inadequate medical care, and primitive conditions as the prisoners. However, they were in much better shape and, more important, warmly dressed. This appears to have counted heavily. Captain Ripley blamed typhoid fever for most

Colonel Daniel Cameron. (Image courtesy of the USAMHI.)

of the deaths among Vermonters, probably caused by contaminated water and food and exposed sewage.

While Confederate prisoners had departed Camp Douglas in high spirits, the parolees were in a sullen mood when they left. The 39th and 125th New York Infantry traded gunfire aboard the train leaving Chicago for the front on November 22, 1862, and a sergeant in the 39th New York was seriously wounded.[26] Responsibility for the fires at Camps Douglas and Tyler may have caused bad blood between the units. Parolees could imagine not drawing a single day's pay until they had compensated Uncle Sam. Another reason may be that "there was plenty of liquor aboard," according to Private Belknap. The Confederates had been seriously lacking in that department.

The War Department exchanged all parolees, except Cameron's 65th Illinois Infantry, Phillip's Battery, and the Ninth Vermont, by November 30, 1862. It held Cameron and his regiment at Camp Douglas until April 19, 1863. Both Cameron and Illinois adjutant general Fuller protested bitterly, without success.[27] Cameron's long stay is suspicious, since his veteran 65th Illinois was needed at the front, and normally Illinois packed tremendous clout at the White House. Perhaps Cameron's standing as a national Democrat kept him there, and his strong support of Senator Douglas did not endear him to the Republican administration.

Captain Ripley of the Ninth Vermont had no doubt that favoritism decided which regiments were exchanged first. The governor of Vermont felt called upon to travel to Washington himself to see about the matter. In retaliation, the War Department authorized the army to recruit the Ninth Vermont away from its volunteer officers. Loss of 100 to 150 of his best men enraged Captain Ripley.[28] Only farsighted advice stopped him from resigning his commission, and he ended the war a general.

The year 1862 was the busiest for Camp Douglas. Besides 8,962 prisoners, the number of parolees rose to 8,226. Approximately 42,000 men had occupied the camp since it opened in September 1861.[29] About 17,000 were Confederate prisoners and Union parolees, and 25,000 were troops in training. Tents not only reached six blocks west to State Street, but three miles south to Hyde Park, and one mile north toward downtown. Camp Douglas had become a major military base.

TABLE IV

FATAL DISEASES AT CAMP DOUGLAS IN 1862

Typhoid Fever: Causal bacteria are related to food poisoning and dysentery and are spread by exposed sewage and contaminated milk and drinking water. (Contagious)

Diphtheria: Infection of the tonsils and back of the throat caused by many varieties of organisms, particularly streptococci which grow freely in milk. (Highly contagious)

Smallpox: Caused by a virus. (Highly contagious)

Cholera: Caused by a bacillus (a micro organism) communicated in contaminated drinking water and by flies which contaminate food with infected human feces. (Contagious)

Consumption: Tuberculosis which may infect the lungs or any other organ; caused by a bacillus and has been known since 400 B.C. (Highly contagious)

Dysentery: Caused by a bacillus spread by flies, by direct contact, or pollution of water by feces from infected patients. (Highly contagious)

Measles: Acute infectious disease known since the tenth century. It spreads rapidly by infected droplets from the nose and throat coughed and sneezed into the air and can cut down large populations.

Pneumonia: Acute inflammation of the lungs which attacks persons with lowered bronchial defenses and less resistance to infections. Caused by a multitude of organisms or a virus following influenza.[30]

CHAPTER 8

Biological Warfare

Tucker resigns—General Jacob Ammen takes charge—Unexpected flood of sickly prisoners—Smallpox prevalent—Doctors call Douglas an extermination camp—Infected prisoners exchanged—Ammen denies wrongdoing—No more room for latrines.

The Union war machine picked up steam in 1863, and Camp Douglas became a prison again in January. More destitute and hard-luck prisoners arrived due to Grant's movements in the West. They should not have been there, since the Cartel provided for immediate parole. The agreement was short lived, and both countries shared the blame. Indifference by politicians caused prisoners to die on both sides.

Confederate president Jefferson Davis warned that the Confederacy would not treat black soldiers as prisoners of war. This gave the North an excuse to end exchanges, no matter what the cost to men in Southern prisons. It was ironic that the entry of blacks into the Union army stranded thousands of Confederates in prison camps.[1]

Colonel Tucker saw that his time had passed at Camp Douglas. The army was in control now and did not need a state militia officer. He resigned his commission on January 1, 1863, and returned to the Chicago Board of Trade.

One may picture him as stiff-necked and humorless, without the charisma to lead men. This was not so. Tucker once led a hand-to-hand assault against rioting and looting Union troops at Camp Douglas and successfully put them down. He ended with his uniform torn and his face scratched and bruised. Private Benjamin J. Smith, who was at his side, described him with a good deal of respect and mentioned that he was a "classy dresser."[2] Tucker once fearlessly branded a sutler as a "malicious liar" for claiming that Colonel Mulligan had collected taxes twice. In the end, it was Tucker who faced down the battle-hardened Ninth Vermont when it refused to go on guard duty at Camp Douglas.

General Jacob Ammen. (Image courtesy of the USAMHI).

The next commander was a far different product from Tucker or Mulligan. The army ordered Gen. Jacob Ammen to Camp Douglas on January 6, 1863. Ammen was a West Pointer, as was General Tyler. Although born in Virginia in 1808, he grew up in Ohio. He was an instructor at West Point and taught mathematics in civilian life. Officers credited his actions at the Battle of Shiloh with helping to reverse the impending Union defeat.[3] Next, he commanded a division against Confederate general Braxton Bragg in Kentucky.

General Ammen had commanded Camp Dennison, in Ohio, and was the first commander at Camp Douglas with administrative experience. The Department of the Army in Ohio, which included Chicago, thought that he was suitable because of his rank and background. He insisted on discipline, as General Tyler had done, banned liquor, and put a stop to speculation in Confederate currency.[4]

About 1,500 Confederates taken at Murfreesboro, Tennessee, in the Battle of Stone's River struggled against sub-zero blasts as they came through the gate on January 26. They resembled the Fort Donelson prisoners, except that most were not as able bodied, ranging in age from 15 to 68, and many more were conscripts. They also lacked warm clothing as did the prisoners of 1862.

A reporter observed them wearing pieces of carpeting and hearth rugs in place of overcoats. They even had "coffee sacks and grain bags, with holes cut in the ends and sides for the head and arms, linen sheets, bed quilts, bed blankets, horse blankets, etc., etc.," he wrote. "Their hats and caps were every conceivable shape and style—and quite a number were bareheaded, while others covered their heads and bodies with the same quilt or carpet."[5]

The remaining Harpers Ferry parolees felt their hearts sink when they saw the wreckage cast upon the gates of Camp Douglas. This doomed them to remain as guards. Winter had already buried the camp under snow and ice, and frigid winds made guard duty agonizing. "Better to fight and die in Virginia," they thought. The Ninth Vermont's colonel and other officers resigned their commissions and left. Enlisted men did not enjoy this privilege. The 65th and 104th Illinois Infantry, the Ninth Vermont, and Phillips' Battery made up the garrison. This force of 1,737 enlisted men was the largest so far.

The Stone's River captives had barely settled into camp when the Union army captured five thousand more Confederates on January 11, 1863, at Arkansas Post. Also known as Fort Hindman, it guarded the Mississippi River in southeast Arkansas. A Union army colonel refused to parole the prisoners under the Cartel. "It would seem to me criminal to send the prisoners to Vicksburg," he decided. "To send them there would be to re-enforce a place with several thousand prisoners at the moment we are trying to reduce it."[6]

His decision would cost almost eight hundred lives at Camp Douglas alone. Oddly, a mere colonel assumed that he could ignore the Cartel, and the army agreed. These prisoners had fought off Union attacks in cold rain, standing in ice water to their waists, similar to the Fort Donelson experience. Then the War Department repeated the confusion of 1862 about what to do with them. They sat on an island near St. Louis 13 days later in freezing weather without shelter.

General Samuel R. Curtis, commanding the Department of Missouri, was deeply concerned. He wired Hoffman frantically on January 23, 1863, that he had six thousand prisoners on the island, with more on the boats. "Shall I have sheds built on the island? Will you take charge of them? It is not in my power to make them safe and comfortable," he pleaded.[7]

Hoffman told him to ship four thousand prisoners to Camp Douglas, but it appears that about 1,500 were released upon taking the oath of allegiance. The others paid dearly for their loyalty. In an eerie replay of Fort Donelson "they crowded them upon transports without protection from the weather and without proper facilities for cooking their rations, with only the clothes on their backs."[8] Nearly 1,300 prisoners finally rolled into Chicago on January 27, 1863.

About two hundred Southern sympathizers attempted to free them when their train stopped for transfer to the Illinois Central. They passed whiskey through the windows, and some rowdies tried the doors. Like the Conspiracy of 1864 it was all talk. The farce ended with the police making two arrests, while the 34th Iowa guard regiment fixed bayonets to well-worn rifles.

The Iowans were a tough bunch who had fought in Gen. William T. Sherman's Chickasaw Bluffs campaign in Mississippi at the end of December 1862, sometimes called First Vicksburg. They only had one week's rest before assaulting Arkansas Post.[9] They killed one prisoner earlier, and it was fortunate for the crowd that police intervened. Even so, the Iowans managed to bayonet two rioters before their officers controlled them.

These prisoners were mostly from Texas and Arkansas, described as "poor white trash in the main, poorly clothed and overjoyed at the sight of a fire."[10] Upwards of a thousand of them were receiving medicine at camp, according to the *Chicago Tribune.*

Captain Ripley disagreed with the newspaper's opinion. "The Texans here are the finest Southern troops I have run across," he wrote home.[11] Vermonters and Texans knew each other from Harpers Ferry. Now they were prisoners together at Camp Douglas. In another repeat of 1862, Ripley discovered that many prisoners had weapons, and he planned to search them again. "If you want an Arkansas bowie knife," he told his father, "I'll set aside a peck or more for you."

Ammen received little warning about the new arrivals, but 40 carpenters had been working on barracks since January 24, and "had all in good order." Captain Charles Goodman, in the quartermaster's department, spent $15,000 trying to repair the fire damage of 1862, and was repairing 36 stoves at a cost of $89.00. His superiors dropped a batch of 1,500 more prisoners into the middle of his work on January 30, 1863. Reporters described them remorselessly as "being more poorly clad, dirtier, and more cadaverous than any that have been in camp before."[12] They saw young boys of 14, Cherokee Indians, Mexicans, and more black prisoners in this last group. "There are a large number of sick among them, and there seemed a continuous cough from one end of the procession to the other," a reporter claimed. Camp Douglas was again a dumping ground for the deprived, the sick, and the destitute. It now had 3,884 willing and unwilling guests who "were literally broken down in health and spirits."

Captain James A. Potter, assistant quartermaster, warned Colonel Hoffman that the camp was fit for healthy prisoners only. Potter had been there from the beginning and represented the most experienced and knowledgeable officer on hand. Nevertheless, Hoffman disregarded him. The result was an urgent message from Ammen on February 2, 1863, repeating the familiar story, that prisoners were too sick and poorly clothed for the near arctic winter.[13]

The *Tribune* interviewed prisoners the next day about charges in the *Chicago Times,* an opposition newspaper, that three prisoners froze to death. "No!" the men responded. "They were sick when they came," which was faint praise.

Prisoners slept with one or perhaps two other men on a bunk of pine boards, without bedding, mattress, or blankets, unless one had his own. A bunkmate may have been ill with a cold or a more deadly virus. Hay was plentiful, and an 18-hour supply of coal lay on the floor.

Nevertheless, barrack floors were only 18 inches above the icy ground, so that the men required two blazing stoves for warmth. They also stuffed rags and clothing around windows and doors in a fruitless attempt to hold back the Chicago winter. Like prisoners before them, they could not conceive how anyone could live in such a climate.

A lone water hydrant remained frozen, drinking water scarce, and cleanliness impossible. Dirty clothing, haversacks, and equipment hung from the rafters. It was more like a shelter for the homeless than a barrack. Yet mail traffic was heavy despite the dismal conditions. Many prisoners had blank business forms looted from various towns, and the post office was kept busy.[14]

Mortality was soon out of control, as 387 died in February 1863 according to the *Official Records.* Captain Ripley reported as early as February 4 that "mortality among them is undiminished. At this rate we shall have our responsibility all underground before the last of Spring," he said sympathetically. "Their blood is so thin, and they have so little vitality, that their blood seems to stop flowing and curdles when exposed as they suddenly have been, half naked, to this piercing cold." Ripley was critical of eight Confederate surgeons who refused to help and noticed how brutalized the prisoners had become. "If one happens to die, another will roll him outside no matter what the weather and take what he can from the poor wretch."[15]

Other Vermonters also drew a grim picture of life at Camp Douglas as the third year of the Civil War began. One soldier believed that the Union troops were equally prisoners with the "Johnnies," because all were in White Oak Square. "The mercury often fell to 20 degrees below zero," he remembered. "The sight of four sallow men, clad in butternut, bearing the corpse of a comrade to the dead house was an almost hourly spectacle. They looked as though they were clothed in sack cloth and ashes, doing penance for their sins."[16] However, he claimed that the prisoners "were as well fed and comfortably quartered as their guards," and blamed the mortality on being "poorly clad, uncleanly, and sickly."

Six prisoners escaped in February. They had little chance of surviving. Ammen did not bother searching for them. One soldier in the 104th Illinois Infantry was defensive about the terrible toll among prisoners and wrote that "they were provided with as warm and comfortable quarters as our own."[17] This may have been true, as prisoners and guards lived side by side in White Oak Square. However, he lost credibility by claiming that "they were fed the same rations [as their guards], had the best medical attention when sick," and received clothing and blankets.

They could not have received the same rations because Capt. Henry W. Freedley, Hoffman's assistant, reported that $1,115.34 accrued to the prison fund by cutting prisoners' rations in February. Ammen was the first to turn so large a profit and in such a short period. Freedley gave no percentage of the reduction.

The opposition *Chicago Times* guessed it was one-third of their ration. It appears to have been about 7.5 percent. Hoffman told Ammen that accumulating a large fund was not necessary, but "to relieve the Government as far as possible of the expense of their keeping." Prisoners were well satisfied with the food before, especially the coffee.[18]

Prisoners were not starving, but reducing rations during the winter, when they lacked adequate clothing and medical care, showed a want of compassion somewhere. William F. Tucker, a hotel owner in Chicago, was supplying rations. He was no relation of Colonel Tucker, but his son was married to the daughter of Gen. John W. Logan of Illinois, credited with keeping southern Illinois in the Union.[19] This may be why Tucker had the contract.

General Ammen faced another, but more humorous, crisis when a woman by the name of Mrs. Finley opened a contraband food stand. She began operating from a shack on Jane Bradley's property abutting the northeast corner of the fence where the hydrant was. located.[20] The determined woman cut a hole in the fence large enough for a service window and dealt food and beverages to all comers inside. Naturally, she paid no business tax to the prison fund. When officers boarded up the window, she reopened it. This happened 12 times before they finally locked her out. She would return.

Ammen submitted an estimate of prisoners' needs to Hoffman on February 11, commenting that "they suffer severely with the cold." He turned the chapel into a hospital, as Colonel Mulligan had done. Stanton did not interfere this time. Ammen called in Chicago police on February 15 for a shakedown, as Colonel Tucker had done. They confiscated some gold and Federal greenbacks and a cache of handsaws, hatchets, and small axes in the barracks.[21] Headquarters later admitted sheepishly that the tools were there to cut firewood.

Officials suddenly restarted amnesty on February 18, 1863, and commanding officers could release enlisted men who took the oath of allegiance. This could be a great lifesaver if the government was serious and prisoners willing. "A careful examination will be made in each case," Hoffman warned, "to learn the sincerity of the applicant." The penalty for violating the oath was death, and violators could be drafted into the Union army. This was risky, since ex-prisoners would face summary execution by the Confederate army if captured in Yankee uniforms. They were safe, as it turned out. Hoffman sternly informed the colonel of the 16th Illinois Cavalry that Stanton "forbids the enlistment into our ranks of prisoners of war who have been released upon taking the oath of allegiance."[22]

Ammen personally asked each applicant the famous four questions drafted by President Lincoln:

"First. Do you desire to be sent South as a prisoner of war for exchange?

"Second. Do you desire to take the oath of allegiance and parole, and enlist in the Army or Navy of the United States, and if so in which?

"Third. Do you desire to take the oath and parole and be sent North to work on public works under penalty of death if found in the South before the end of the war?

"Fourth. Do you desire to take the oath of allegiance and go to your home within the lines of the U. S. Army, under like penalty if found South beyond those lines during the war?"

Ammen examined prisoners' reasons for being in the army and their attitudes about the war. He reported that those from Texas and Mississippi "are very hostile and do not wish any terms except to fight it out." Ammen released only 51 prisoners in February, with about 100 still in line.[23] Only another dozen were successful. The skyrocketing mortality made the denial of amnesty almost equivalent to a death sentence.

It is likely that those who applied for the oath required protection because Hoffman ordered them placed in separate barracks.[24] He also issued orders to prison commanders, "In all cases where you have to employ prisoners as laborers, whether allowed compensation or not, give these prisoners the detail, if they desire it." Commanders were to severely punish those who threatened these men, but Hoffman did not say how.

General Ammen believed that his main job was security, and he locked down the camp as never before. Even officers needed a special pass to get out, and visitors ceased to exist. Charitable gifts had to be left at the gate. Persons who claimed to be Ammen's friends received no favors. A measure of the man was a statement that his only friends at camp carried guns. This policy resulted in the lowest escape rate ever, only 14 during the three months he was in charge. Captain Freedley, Hoffman's assistant, described the garrison "as vigilant and attentive to their duties." He praised Ammen, saying, "They are well instructed and the discipline is more rigid than in any camp I have yet visited."[25]

Ammen was also a strong administrator. Freedley reported to Hoffman that "he has confined himself strictly to your instructions and they are rigidly enforced. Books and records are properly kept."

Freedley inspected the camp on March 11, 1863, and saw nothing wrong. "I find the condition of the prisoners at Camp Douglas much improved," he reported. "The barracks have all been repaired. The fence which was partly torn down by the paroled men has been reconstructed. The barracks are not crowded and are comfortably heated. Each one is provided with a comfortable bunk, and the prisoners are in every way as comfortably provided for as our own troops."[26]

His report sounded too good to be true, and it was. No doubt conditions had improved by this time, but prisoners were always crowded two and three to a bunk, often without bedding. Barracks were far from repaired, and how could they be in sub-zero weather? Moreover, Freedley never mentioned the chronic problem of supplying warm clothing and blankets.

He was confident about health care under Dr. George H. Park as post surgeon. "I found the hospitals generally neat and clean and are well supplied with cots and bedding," he told Hoffman. "The sick prisoners are well cared for. The medical supplies were sufficient."[27]

To the contrary, civilian doctors who inspected Camp Douglas on February 18, 1862, called it an extermination camp. In a complaint filed with the secretary of war, they drew an unrelenting picture of "wretched inmates; without change of clothing, covered with vermin, they lie in cots without mattresses or with mattresses furnished by private charity, without sheets or bedding of any kind except blankets often in rags, in wards reeking with filth and foul air." The hospital was so inadequate that 130 prisoners died in barracks, with 150 more waiting for beds. "Thus it will be seen that 260 out of the 3,800 prisoners had died in twenty-one days, a rate of mortality which if continued would secure their

The University of Chicago across from Camp Douglas and (below) the smallpox hospital next to it. (Images courtesy of the Chicago Public Library.) *The smallpox hospital (circled).*

total extermination in about 320 days," the doctors warned.[28]

They also alerted Stanton about a newspaper article reporting that a hundred more prisoners were dead at the end of March. Their complaints remained secret, like Bellows's report. It is difficult to believe that Freedley and the civilian doctors were talking about the same camp. Perhaps their disagreement resulted from opposing perspectives. The doctors probably compared the camp with civilian hospitals, while Freedley believed that the sick were doing fine measured against other prisons. Another possibility is that Freedley only told his boss what he wanted to hear and saved himself much stress by a coverup.

Residents near the camp were not as complacent as Freedley. They complained to the Chicago Board of Health about the camp's smallpox hospital established next to the University of Chicago. General Ammen responded on March 2, 1863, by appointing Dr. Park and the surgeon of the Ninth Vermont to "examine into the condition of the pest house, and report to these headquarters if in its present location the safety of those in the University and Public Schools is endangered."[29]

Apparently they made no report, and the Board of Health appointed three civilian physicians, including Dr. McVickar, to investigate.[30] They found smallpox patients well cared for but recommended building a new smallpox hospital farther west. The camp had to establish a smallpox cemetery, with graves six feet deep, and to start vaccinating. Security was important to prevent infected prisoners from escaping. "With these precautions, we feel that our citizens may yield all alarm," the physicians concluded.

Chicago's fears continued. At least two smallpox patients escaped each month. More than a year later the epidemic was still raging and claimed 32 prisoners in the week of November 22, 1864.[31]

University of Chicago trustees believed that Camp Douglas was the main reason for declining enrollment and passed a resolution on March 26, 1863, "that the Hon. Thomas Hoyne [Mayor of Chicago] be requested to draw a petition to Government on the subject of the removal of Camp Douglas."[32] It did not have much chance of success.

Freedley agreed that smallpox was prevalent. "The mortality of the prisoners is quite large," he conceded, "but this is to be attributed to their wretchedly broken down condition. Their general health has greatly improved since their arrival at the camp." Besides the 387 dead in February, he reported 262 prisoners in the hospital. Many sick men were in barracks, and 125 smallpox cases needed beds.[33]

Freedley gave high marks to Dr. Park and the four civilian surgeons but permitted four alleged surgeons among the prisoners to work as doctors. He only had their word that they qualified. "No roll accompanied them by which to verify their statements," Freedley admitted. Hoffman granted permission to use them, provided Freedley verified their credentials first.[34] This was not done, and the consequences proved damaging.

Prisoners drew salt meat almost exclusively with their rations, and Freedley recommended fresh beef five days a week because it was both healthier and cheaper. John Sullivan, a food contractor, had advised Colonel Mulligan that "cured meats, such as bacon, &c." made up eight-tenths of the prison meat ration.[35] These meats must have been loaded with salt and fat. Freedley wanted prisoners to again bake bread. Hoffman allowed them to make cornbread, but fuel costs closed the bakery again.

Prisoners required warm clothing and blankets more than cornbread, but the army furnished little, and only in extreme cases. It appears that Meigs and Hoffman were carrying out the old Johnson's Island plan of requiring prisoners to furnish their own clothing. Large contributions of underwear and outer clothing came from friends and family but were insufficient for 3,540 men.[36]

Ammen heeded recommendations to bury smallpox victims in a cemetery "near Camp Douglas," according to prison rolls. It abutted the west side of the smallpox hospital opposite the camp's south fence. The first recorded interments appeared on August 22, 1863, but they must have started the previous spring, when smallpox became a concern. On March 28, 1863, Maj. Gen. Ambrose Burnside, who commanded the Northern Department, asked Halleck about closing the camp.[37] Halleck responded that only Stanton could order it closed, which meant that it would stay open.

Everyone now considered the site to be a mistake. The environment had crumbled under the unprecedented war-time use, and the former prairie was a swamp one day and a dust bowl the next, or a frozen ice field, depending upon the season.

Mortality was out of control by March 31, 1863. Critics claimed that seven hundred prisoners had died. If true, the toll in two months was only 277 short of the 1862 record, which took eight months to reach 977. The *Official Records* denied it, listing 464 dead for the period January to May 1863. Obviously, this figure was too low, as 387 died in February alone. Suspiciously, the *Official Records* carried no Camp Douglas returns for March 1863.

The *Tribune* believed that the toll could be "upwards of 700," which was incredibly accurate. Camp Douglas hospital records in the National Archives show that 748 prisoners died between January 28 and April 27, 1863. Someone drew a heavy blue line in the hospital register after February 28, and apparently officials stopped reporting deaths at this point.[38] This fact was not known until the registers were opened in 1997.

It was probably the worst coverup in the camp's history, far exceeding the future Camp Douglas beef scandal suppressed by President Lincoln or the later burial swindle regarding the Confederate dead. Concealing three hundred deaths could not have been accomplished without the knowledge of the post surgeon, Dr. Park, and probably General Ammen. Dr. McVickar would have been firing off a furious letter. What did Captain Freedley know, and when did he know it? Preventing the Confederate government from learning of the death toll was most likely the motivating factor. Officials were concerned about the fate of Union prisoners in the South.

Prisoners of war did not die so rapidly until a Confederate prison named Andersonville opened in Georgia on February 27, 1864. Exchange was the only hope for prisoners everywhere, as it had been in 1862. Military needs pressured the Confederacy unilaterally to restart the Cartel. On March 31, 1863, the Federal exchange agent, Lt. Col. William H. Ludlow, sent an urgent wire to Colonel Hoffman. "The Confederates are making heavy delivery of prisoners, and it would be very desirable to get our paroled men declared exchanged as soon as possible. When will the Arkansas Post and Murfreesborough prisoners arrive?"[39]

Vicksburg was no longer an exchange center because of the fighting there. Camp Douglas prisoners went to City Point, Virginia, east of Richmond. The route ran through Pittsburgh, Baltimore, and Washington to Fort Monroe. One group of six hundred prisoners left Camp Douglas on March 31, 1863, only two months after arriving.[40] This was the shortest stay by any group of prisoners. General Ammen assigned ninety men from the Ninth Vermont Infantry as guards.

Ripley, newly promoted to major, commanded this detachment. Thirty Vermonters had to be left behind in the hospital, "and over sixty poor fellows under ground, who found the mud and surface water here more fatal than any exposure in Virginia," he wrote home. Uncle Sam shipped his former nephews back in good passenger cars, with seats that converted to sleepers at night.

Major Ripley was an insufferable snob but showed some concern for the prisoners. He enforced the peace with bayonets when boisterous brakemen kept them awake at night. On the other hand, he considered the trip ruined by "lousy high scented Secesh, for our efforts directed to teaching them sanitation and arousing in them any ambition to cleaning themselves up, were a dismal failure." He did not consider that prisoners were continuously short of water due to frozen hydrants.

Ripley clashed with the wife of a Rebel officer at one train station when she attempted to talk to prisoners and give them money. He threatened to transport her to Baltimore as a prisoner, but "politely" escorted her to her carriage. A more potent danger was the pro-Confederate population of Baltimore. One hundred men of the 151st New York Infantry and 40 police reinforced him there on April 4, 1863, as he marched the prisoners through town. Ripley noticed that "many a handsome Secesh Girl quietly placed the corner of an embroidered handkerchief to her face, to figuratively brush away the tear that stood in her dark blue eye."

However, the road back for prisoners of war proved most difficult, as usual, and Ripley soon struggled with one army SNAFU after another. Not one particle of food or water had been placed aboard the steamer ready to take the prisoners to Fort Monroe. Ripley had to walk around for hours and cut the red tape to obtain five days' rations for them.

Next, Colonel Ludlow had the glad news that Ripley's Rebels were "neither paroled nor exchanged," and that Ripley had to write up almost six hundred paroles. He did so by the next day, April 5, but then became entangled in Confederate red tape. The Rebel authorities did not allow the prisoners to land at City Point on the morning of April 7 because they had no transportation. They expected Ripley to feed them while they remained aboard the steamer.[41]

Ripley refused because he saw no reason for the Confederate government to shirk responsibility for its own men. As usual, the common soldier was caught in the middle, and the road back lay strewn with boulders. A train finally arrived later that afternoon to take the hungry men to Richmond, but it is not likely that any rations were aboard.

Ammen reported to Hoffman on April 6 that 2,534 prisoners left camp on April 3. About 350 patients remained, and Ammen was not hopeful that all would recover. He mentioned difficulties and troubles but did not elaborate.[42]

So far it appeared that Ammen had done a good job. However, a storm was about to break. Alarm spread through Baltimore when doctors discovered smallpox cases from Camp Douglas around April 7. Ten prisoners and one guard were found to be infected and were removed to a hospital. Hoffman learned of the situation from the medical director there and hastened to wire the news to Stanton's office on April 8 before Stanton heard it from someone else.[43]

Hoffman blamed the alleged Confederate doctors. "Examination of the sick was entrusted to the rebel surgeon who was attending on the prisoners and he suffered nine slight cases to be brought with the well men," he explained. A "slight" case died in Baltimore on April 8. Hoffman did not reveal that many squads of Camp Douglas prisoners passed through Baltimore without the knowledge of medical inspectors.[44] Hoffman's carefully orchestrated Civil War career was in danger.

Secretary of War Stanton, who wielded harsh authority, was already enraged about 25 other smallpox cases at Fort Monroe. "I think it is outrageous that the commissary-general of prisoners should allow infected persons to travel through the States and be introduced to our posts," he charged and demanded an immediate report from Hoffman.[45] The old soldier now knew what it felt like to have a boss come down hard.

Hoffman was out to do bodily harm to whoever had damaged his reputation. Harping on the Rebel doctors would be foolish. He wanted to place the blame on Camp Douglas headquarters, but the continuous changes blocked his inquiry. The situation was worse than when Governor Yates had controlled appointments. The army transferred General Ammen to Springfield on April 13, and Colonel Cameron was in command again.

When Hoffman demanded from Cameron the name of the post surgeon when the smallpox cases left Camp Douglas, he was too late. Cameron had departed for the last time on April 19. His regimental surgeon, Captain Park, was the man Hoffman wanted, but he was now safely at the front. Hoffman heard from the new commanding officer, Capt. John Phillips, a parolee from Harpers Ferry serving his seventh month at Camp Douglas. He did not believe that the

Edwin M. Stanton, Secretary of War. (Image courtesy of the USAMHI).

prisoners were examined for smallpox. "I find no record of any order from General Ammen [who was then commanding post] for an examination of prisoners," Phillips advised the frustrated Hoffman.[46]

Colonel Hoffman wired Stanton on April 20 that General Ammen and his principal surgeon had to be held responsible for the shipment of the infected prisoners. General Ammen responded that he did order them examined. Hoffman argued that this was untrue because Ammen allowed the four Rebel surgeons to "take with them all whom they were not forced to reject." He failed to mention that he had given permission for these prisoners to practice medicine at Camp Douglas without credentials.[47] Hoffman was determined to stay on the corporate ladder no matter whose face he kicked in.

The aging warrior ended his telegram with a refreshing show of bravado. "In closing my report I must beg leave to express my deep regret that my untiring efforts to perform the various duties of my office with ability and promptness should meet only with such harsh censure as is contained in your telegram." He fired another shot by pointing out that Camp Douglas should be closed if Stanton took smallpox seriously. Hoffman had brought these troubles on himself by choosing to serve ambitious politicians instead of following his profession.

The surviving Arkansas Post prisoners were quartered near Petersburg, Virginia, by April 24, and a citizen suggested that they work on the defenses.[48] They soon returned to duty without furloughs. The road back home beckoned in their fitful dreams, but it would be many years, if ever, before they saw their loved ones in the Southwest.

No one knew how many smallpox cases General Ammen returned to the Confederate army. This is where the matter rested. It was an early instance of biological warfare, although unintended. A more amusing incident shows how little communication there was between the two countries. Dr. Park saw an emaciated prisoner just released from the hospital eating a pie and warned him: "You ought not to eat those pies, don't you know they are poison to you?" The prisoner took this literally, not knowing it was a Northern expression. A Richmond paper ranted soon after he arrived: "Not satisfied with putting our men to death by suffering and torture, the Yankee demons have taken to poisoning them!"[49] A Union army patrol went looking for the editor after Richmond fell, but he had wisely made himself scarce.

Captain Phillips prepared a final shipment of prisoners to City Point on May 4 and left eight days later. Colonel Hoffman had so little control over appointments that he was ignorant of who managed the prisons and hospitals at any given time.

The prisoners were gone just in time, because the sanitation crisis was beyond solution, as no space remained for latrines or garbage pits. Colonel Hoffman now realized the importance of Camp Douglas as a depot for trainees, prisoners, and parolees. However, it required serious reorganization. He again requested General Meigs to spend the money on a sewer system, reminding him of Tucker's plans submitted in July 1862. Hoffman believed that it was a good project, except during the winter, when pipes would freeze. He estimated that about two thousands dollars could be spent from the prison fund to help pay costs.[50]

Secretary Stanton also believed that the prison system could not continue as in the past. Hoffman submitted suggestions for building a new prison near Lake Michigan, either in Indiana or Illinois. His belief in an early victory was gone, and he planned for a new depot to hold ten thousand prisoners. Nothing came out of these discussions, which meant that Camp Douglas would soldier on as a prison.

Meanwhile, the remaining sick prisoners of early 1863 were dying fast, with 42 answering the long roll in May, and two more dying by July 31.[51] About 18 patients and 32 hospital workers remained from the prisoners of 1863. Colonel Hoffman was now winding up matters at camp. He had to protect property purchased by the prison fund.

TABLE V[52]

CAMP DOUGLAS STATISTICS—JANUARY 28, 1863 THROUGH JULY 1863

Total prisoners received	3,932
Died	792
Released	63
Exchanged	3,003
Escaped	24
Remaining sick plus nurses	50
Main causes of death	Smallpox, fevers, pneumonia

The death toll was a catastrophic 20 percent but still not matching Andersonville that had yet to make its stain on history.[53] Whether medical care under General Ammen met Civil War standards is a matter of controversy. Medicine was not close to discovering the causes or cures for many diseases. The following year a commanding officer charged Camp Douglas doctors with incompetence.

Doctors did substantial surgery, but they knew little about reducing wound infection and postoperative mortality. While smallpox inoculation had been effective in Europe, some Northern prison camps were receiving worthless or dangerous vaccines.[54] Perhaps this is why the virus raged on at Camp Douglas until it closed in 1865.

It was not likely that the food caused so many deaths. However, Captain Freedley found the diet poor. The hospital had sufficient coal. Barracks were not as well supplied and remained in poor condition despite $15,000 in repairs.[55] Primitive sanitation and a shortage of blankets still plagued the camp during severe weather. The failure of the government quickly to furnish warm clothing and blankets was probably the main reason so many lives were lost.

Another explanation for so many deaths is the same as that of 1862, one historian argued. "Arriving just at the edge of winter, they were but indifferently fitted to stand the hardships of the barrack life in what was to them the far north. The fact is that there were too many crammed into the place, and, as a natural consequence, they died off like rotten sheep."[56] Reverend Tuttle thought that nostalgia was another cause.

Concern for prisoners lessened as Northern losses escalated, and the prisons strained resources. Significantly, no Chicago relief committee aided the prisoners this time. Even the respected U.S. Sanitary Commission claimed that "the suffering and privations of prisoners in the South were not due to causes the South could not control, but were rather purposely inflicted by the military and governmental authority of the Confederacy."[57]

A new amnesty policy began in May 1863 that would have done little to help the prisoners. Commanders now required special authority from Washington to release them.[58] No one knew what this "special authority" meant, although a power broker in Washington or Kentucky could do the job if the money was there.

Amnesty was restricted further on August 4, 1863, with tougher requirements. The applicant now had to prove that he had been forced into the Confederate service or have "loyal people" vouch for him. Youths had to show that "they were led away by the influence of vicious companions, his Union friends guaranteeing his future loyal conduct."[59] It was a prescription more likely to aid those with wealth or influence rather than the downtrodden mud slogger.

Hoffman started to work on Stanton at the end of May 1863, reminding him of the Bellows report and the need for improvements. "It is almost impossible to have instructions carried out at Camp Douglas because of the frequent changes of commanders," he complained. "There is no responsibility and before neglects can be traced to anyone he is relieved from duty." He recommended permanent medical personnel for prison camps and permanent commanders with reliable guards assigned to them.[60] The only concession made was the appointment of special medical inspectors for prison camps. Their reports proved most valuable.

Events showed that West Pointers such as General Tyler and General Ammen knew how to enforce discipline and attend to administrative matters. Ammen's blunder regarding the infected prisoners resulted from his reliance on a volunteer officer, Dr. Park. Colonel Hoffman knew better than to trust volunteers.

A warm summer moved in, and the camp was almost empty. Troops departed to fight in major battles of the Civil War. Camp Douglas had drilled and equipped more than 30,000 men by June 1, 1863. Close to 12,000 prisoners had suffered through two winters when temperatures had often fallen below zero. Between 1,400 and 1,700 now lay dead, but officials counted only 615 names on desolate graves far from camp. Between seven hundred and one thousand bodies had disappeared. Somehow, Camp Douglas was exterminating the dead and the living.

Hoffman had no jurisdiction at camp while it held no prisoners or parolees. He could have closed his books had it resumed its role as a training base. However, Camp Douglas would become a prison again with the arrival of Morgan's raiders, the most militant and troublesome prisoners ever to grace White Oak dungeon. Moreover, the powers in Washington had drastically changed the camp's mission in the Civil War, and thereby the history of the war itself.

This battered, ramshackle collection of huts, festering latrines, and sagging fences was now destined to become a permanent prisoner of war camp. No longer will tough drill sergeants introduce raw recruits to the manual of arms at this depot. Veterans of future battles will not boast about having trained at Camp Douglas. Bugles that once called sleepy farm boys and tough slum brats to fall in and be counted will be silent. Never again will troops march up Michigan Avenue to the rollicking strains of "The Girl I Left Behind Me."

Meanwhile, Hoffman pressed Meigs about the sewer project.

CHAPTER 9

Daring Escape From White Oak Dungeon

A sewer system approved—Morgan's raiders arrive—Colonel Charles V. De Land ordered to take command—Shortage of barracks—Inspectors give camp bad marks—White Oak dungeon—Running water toilets begin operating.

Confederate authorities at Andersonville left sanitation to the prisoners. As a result, they had no latrines for six months after it opened. Then it was too late. The surgeon general in Washington estimated that seven thousand prisoners "will pass 2,600 gallons of urine daily, which is highly loaded with nitrogenous material."[1] This report may explain the army's decision to approve the sanitary system Colonel Tucker and Colonel Hoffman had wanted. It was to provide sanitation for the garrison, prison, and hospitals exceeding the standard of living for most citizens.

General Meigs surprised Colonel Hoffman on June 11, 1863, with news that the water and sewer system was to go ahead, but he gave no reasons. Meigs may have thought at the time that the depot would continue as a training base and parole camp for Federal troops. However, the sanitation crisis dictated that the camp be closed. It could not continue operating as a prisoner of war camp without improvements.

Inspectors had denounced it as an extermination camp, and this was not a situation where people could say that they did not know what was happening. Neither were officials inclined to let the prison become a giant cesspool, despite the policy of retaliation. Old latrines were already pushing up to the surface. Finally, financing from the prison fund sweetened the plan.[2] As usual, events overtook the camp and prevented improvements.

On June 27, 1863, Confederate general John Hunt Morgan, with about 2,500 mounted men, pushed rapidly northward through

Colonel Charles V. De Land. (Image courtesy of the New York State Library.)

central Kentucky, via Burkesville, Lebanon, Springfield, and Bardstown, to Brandenburg on the Ohio River. General Morgan was a Colonel Mulligan in gray, only to a greater extent. The raid violated orders and was a frolic of his own.[3]

He cut through southern Indiana at Corydon, Lexington, and Vernon, and then headed east after reaching the suburbs of Cincinnati. His men pillaged, burned, and plundered, but Federal forces crushed them in late July. "Many were drowned in the Ohio River and a few escaped," according to accounts. Most of the men were confined in Northern prisons.[4]

Captain J. S. Putnam, commanding Camp Douglas since May 12, 1863, wired Hoffman on August 13 that "Camp Douglas is in good condition to hold 8,000 prisoners. I have 125 guards." Putnam was another parolee from Harpers Ferry. Captain James A. Potter, the quartermaster, was thunderstruck by Putnam's naiveté and warned Hoffman that even six thousand prisoners were too many. "Please have a commandant sent," he begged, "also a good officer."[5] Presumably he meant that one person should have both qualities. Hoffman had no authority to grant his request, and the next commanding officer happened to be in the wrong place at the wrong time.

Among the units chasing Morgan was the First Michigan Sharpshooters under Col. Charles V. De Land, aged 35. He entered the war as a captain in the Ninth Michigan Infantry in 1861 and saw some hard soldiering. Captured at Murfreesboro, Tennessee, he was the only Camp Douglas commandant to have been in a Southern prison. Perhaps this explains his harsh treatment of prisoners at Camp Douglas. One company of his Sharpshooters consisted of 76 American Indians, Chippewas and Ottawas. De Land was a thin, balding man who had been a journalist and farmer before the war.[6]

After returning from Morgan's Raid, the First Michigan Sharpshooters was assigned to guard duty at Camp Douglas. Colonel De Land innocently became the senior ranking officer and by that misfortune received an order from General Ammen to take command of the camp on August 18, 1863.[7] Colonel Hoffman was not consulted. De Land's combat experience would be mere children's play compared with events during the next seven months.

Private Curtis R. Burke, Company B, 14th Kentucky Cavalry, was one of Morgan's most devoted followers. He arrived at Camp Douglas on August 18, 1863, and saw two streetcars and several carriages of sightseers waiting.[8] The camp appeared large to him, with a high

Morgan's raiders at Camp Douglas. Probably taken by D. F. Brandon. Note their menacing look and ragged condition. A youngster is in the upper right. (Image courtesy of the Chicago Historical Society.)

fence around it. He counted a post office, a barber shop, a picture gallery, two sutler stores, a commissary house, and a chapel. The prisoners were marched to White Oak Square, now empty of garrison troops. He described the barracks as long one-story buildings, four of them forming a square.

"The barracks were divided into little rooms with from two to ten bunks in each," Burke recorded in his diary, "and doors and windows to match, also one long room with a row of bunks on each side of the room, mostly three bunks deep or high, and making room for about eighty men." Separate rooms for commissioned and noncommissioned officers completed the quarters. Outside, in the rear of each barrack, was a kitchen, mess room, and latrine.[9]

Burke's father, Edward Burke, sergeant-major of the 14th Kentucky, was also a prisoner, and Curtis called him "Pa." Burke and his father were not Southerners. Curtis was born in Ohio in 1842, and his parents moved to Kentucky when he was nine. His father became involved in Kentucky politics as a Democrat while he worked in the marble business. Both considered the North a foreign enemy of their beloved South, which neither had seen.

Rations were slow in coming, and eating and cooking utensils were scarce. An Indian guard almost shot Burke and his friend, Henry White, as they searched empty barracks for tableware. "You want to go back there now quick," the guard threatened, "or I'll blow your damned heads off!" "You want to" was the Indians' favorite phrase, and the prisoners soon copied it.

Only one water hydrant supplied the entire camp. It was not working when 558 thirsty prisoners arrived on August 20, causing them to use a contaminated well. A prisoner wrote home, "I took a notion at the start that I must go to fight for Southern Rights, and I have now got enough of them."[10]

Morgan's raiders were different from the Confederates seen before. The earlier prisoners had been captured while defending strategic positions or in the brilliant stroke at Shiloh. Morgan squandered his men in a reckless escapade. Of course, they did not see it that way and considered themselves an elite group.

"Generally they are far better looking men than any of the secesh prisoners we had here before," a reporter conceded. "Those butternut suits and shapeless slouched hats, would make an ugly man of anybody. All the colors of Joseph's coat were represented in their wearing apparel: the butternut was worn by the careless quiet looking individuals, who had their horse blankets and tin cups strung across their shoulders. But the keen, black eyed out-and-out raiders of the dare devil stripe, had either a suit of black broadcloth, or a portion of our own soldiers' blue uniform."[11]

Despite these romantic notions, Morgan's men made war on civilians. In one incident on their raid near Corydon, Indiana, they killed an elderly man who fought with his bare hands to stop them from burning his home.[12] They suspected him of shooting at them from an upper story and killing a raider. They threatened other suspected "bushwhackers" with summary execution. General Morgan had pointed the way for Sherman's march through Georgia.

Prisoners discovered that religion was plentiful at camp. On August 26, 1863, the sermon was "Choose Ye This Day Whom Ye Shall Serve," apparently aimed at the new visitors. The chaplain of a guard regiment preached to 2,500 prisoners later that day, and much singing poured down on the camp. Some did not rely entirely on Northern preachers and formed their own congregation "to improve the morals of the camp."[13] A large supply of religious tracts was available thanks to the Chicago Bible Society and Reverend Tuttle. Nonetheless, card playing was continuous and disturbing to some.

Morgan's men continued to arrive until August 27, bringing their number to 3,100. De Land had six hundred Sharpshooters and 150 men in the 65th Illinois Infantry to guard them. Prisoners captured at Cumberland Gap, 75 miles north of Knoxville, Tennessee, increased the population to 4,234 by September 26. About three hundred men from the Invalid Corps arrived the next day.[14]

The War department recruited the Invalid Corps from disabled officers and enlisted men. It was often a dumping ground for elderly recruits and mental and social misfits who passed the army's crude medical exam. Some cheats managed to sneak into the corps and avoid combat. Their primary duties were to guard prisoners, act as military police, or do hospital duty.[15]

Prisoners were now stranded at Camp Douglas for the duration of the war. The Cartel was dead, and the administration was skeptical about whether prisoners would honor the oath once released. For example, five of Morgan's men earned jobs in the hospital by applying for the oath, but they promptly dug a tunnel and escaped.[16]

An exploding prison population made Colonel De Land's position precarious from the start. Without warning he inherited a slum that rivaled the worst streets and alleys of Chicago, "its barracks, fences, guard houses all a mere shell of refuse pine boards," De Land complained.[17] While the city's poor may have accepted their lot, Morgan's raiders did not. Ironically, the same Confederates De Land had pursued poured into Camp Douglas before he could loosen his tie. Add to this a cantankerous career-driven boss like Colonel Hoffman, and De Land was on his way to a case of ulcers.

He issued comprehensive orders to his tiny garrison. He expected strict discipline and made it a serious offense to fraternize with prisoners.[18] However, the poor condition of the camp and corrupt guards soon frustrated him. It was his own Sharpshooters who were most prone to bribery. General Ammen had had more than 1,700 healthy men to guard fewer prisoners who were exhausted, sick, and dispirited. Morgan's men did not even feel defeated.

De Land found two unsanitary sutlers named McBride & Van Fleet and C. K. Winner & Son selling without authority and employing prisoners to solicit orders. Mrs. Finley, who had been shut out 12 times, now operated a food stand in White Oak Square. Colonel Cameron had given her permission during his last administration in April 1863. Colonel De Land condemned the stand as unsanitary and evicted Mrs. Finley along with the sutlers. She would be back. So would the sutlers when Hoffman ordered them reinstated. The sutler lobby had powerful friends in Congress. De Land allowed Hall & Treadwell, his own First Michigan sutler, to open for business.[19]

The "extensive repair to barracks" in early 1863 was only a bandage, as it turned out, and De Land used outbuildings and kitchens to house prisoners. Hoffman did not see any emergency until September 23, when he recommended to Washington "that the buildings burned down last winter not yet rebuilt may be put up with as little delay as possible."[20] The new sewer system would make it possible to greatly expand the camp.

Improvements moved ahead, and infantry prisoners were digging a ditch for water pipes by the middle of September 1863. De Land changed cooking arrangements, with messes of six men to cook and draw food. Inspectors sharply criticized this arrangement. De Land mistakenly believed that what worked in the army could do the same at Camp Douglas. Burke's mess fixed a room with shelves and other items. Rations were prepared in the long room, or dormitory, of the barracks.[21]

The army still failed to furnish clothing, but this was not a problem for affluent Kentuckians. They simply sent a list of their needs to friends and family. However, instead of receiving cash from home, all they saw was the empty envelope with an amount noted on it. "Then we had to take the sutler's checks for it and pay whatever the sutler choose to ask for his goods, which made the profit very large," Burke complained. They had been introduced to the Camp Douglas banking system that had almost ruined Colonel Mulligan.

Equally astonishing was the free run of the camp. Nothing prevented prisoners from leaving White Oak Square and going to the hydrants in the northeast corner of Garrison Square. One of three usable hydrants was reserved for troops, causing prisoners to wait hours for water.[22] This was a bone-chilling ordeal as cold winds whipped through the camp.

Despite the lack of utilities and general run-down condition of the camp, Washington accepted no applications to take the oath of allegiance after October 1863. The reason was practical. It needed Confederates to exchange for Union prisoners if the Cartel restarted. This made no difference to Morgan's raiders, who were mostly loyal to the South. They planned to escape, not take the oath. Two men in Burke's mess who attempted it four times were successful on the fifth, aided by civilian clothing and a corrupt guard.[23]

Loss of prisoners caused Colonel Hoffman to open a can of worms. He requested Dr. A. M. Clark, medical inspector of prisons, "to see how far the regulations are carried out." Hoffman received a distress call from Colonel De Land soon afterwards. "The camp being so dilapidated, it cannot house all the prisoners," De Land advised. "I also desire the erection of an additional hospital building and a hospital laundry," he added.[24] He was learning prison administration on the run.

Dr. Clark studied conditions on October 9, 1863, and was shocked to find 6,085 prisoners, but only 978 guards. Of these, no more than 651 men in the First Michigan Sharpshooters and 309 in the Invalid Corps were available for duty. Cameron's veteran 65th Illinois Infantry had departed.[25]

Clark described the water as insufficient, but "quality and effects, good," which showed how little he knew about Chicago water. Otherwise, he described a camp that matched the worst Southern prison. He found open sinks, "twenty feet long, six feet wide, four feet deep" running through the middle of White Oak Square. Regarding sink management, he said, "No management at all, in filthy condition."

Hospital capacity and bedding were almost nonexistent, with only 50 beds for guards and 120 beds in the prison hospital.[26] The chapel was being prepared as a hospital for the third time. Dr. Clark reported that it was "against the protest of certain good ministers of Chicago, who claim that the prisoners' souls should be looked after at the expense of their bodies." He recommended a 600-bed prison hospital. Even that figure was too small, and it barely reached half that goal by war's end.

Believing that the air carried diseases, Dr. Clark moaned, "Ventilation utterly lost sight of." The main killers were typhoid fever and pneumonia. Measles was also on the increase. Fifteen patients were recovering from leg amputations. A lack of "strict discipline" for Rebel nurses concerned him. Incredibly, he did not mention the smallpox hospital.

He predicted that the sewer system would be inadequate because it only ran along two sides of the camp. This assessment proved correct. The three hydrants in Garrison Square continued to leak and create pools of water, but plans called for seven new ones. Prison barracks sat on very uneven ground, permitting stagnant water to collect. While Dr. Clark noted that the quarters and grounds of the Invalid Corps "are models deserving the highest commendation," he condemned the rest of the camp as "simply filthy." This beat-up prison camp must have seemed like a nightmare to him compared with regular army posts that boasted thick lawns and shaded pathways. The barren landscape of Camp Douglas said no to beauty, no to hope, and no to life.

He estimated that the camp could house only 4,500 prisoners, under the best of conditions. Many barracks were a wreck, lacking heat, flooring, and siding, with roofs badly in need of repair. "There is not a door and hardly a window among them," Clark observed. Prisoners were short of bunks and heating stoves, while the guard barracks were too hot.

Clark mentioned that prisoners were not required to work, but many volunteered. His report denounced "the authorities," meaning De Land, and described "discipline in camp—very lax." Authorities paid no attention to the cooking in barracks or to policing the camp, he charged.

He did not explain what he meant about the cooking. True, "Johnny Reb" was a terrible cook at first. Southern newspapers attributed much sickness in the army to improper food preparation.

However, the soldiers soon learned how to prepare staple items and specialties such as pies and baked "possum."[27] The saying, "too many cooks spoil the soup," defined the problem. De Land needed to develop central mess halls, with a few skilled cooks to take charge of rations and feed large groups of men.

While Dr. Clark was specific about food and hygiene, he gave little information about prisoners who died. He did discover that the camp was not properly reporting the number of deaths to Hoffman's office. Prisoners were buried in a place called City Cemetery, he wrote. He did not say where it was or how the dead got there. Who was responsible for the burials and keeping the cemetery records remained a mystery.

Clark reported about 1,200 prisoners without blankets and expressed a negative opinion of their personal hygiene, noting that "some would be cleanly if they could, but most are filthy." He advised Hoffman that De Land withheld army clothing from the prisoners because he worried about escapes. Doctor Clark disagreed with his thinking. "This should be looked to, for many of the prisoners are miserably clad, and already suffer much from the cold."

He criticized White Oak dungeon as "utterly unfit for that purpose." A hatchway in the ceiling of the guard room opened into an underground space measuring only 18 square feet. One small barred window was the only light, and a sink gave off an intolerable stench. He found 24 prisoners confined there because of escape attempts. "The place might do for three or four prisoners," Dr. Clark estimated, "but for the number now confined there it is inhuman. At my visit I remained but a few seconds and was glad to get out, feeling sick and faint." Four prisoners felt the same way and petitioned for their release, promising "not again to attempt escape."[28]

The risk of ending up in the dungeon did not deter others. De Land informed General Ammen on October 13 "of a stroke of bad luck in the loss of twelve prisoners Sunday and Monday nights, and I strongly suspect collusion and bribery." One escapee's father had been in camp for two days with a pass from department headquarters. De Land was fortunate to have lost so few prisoners. Discipline had declined among his Sharpshooters to the extent that he offered the Chicago police a ten-dollar reward on October 5 to arrest soldiers without passes. Nervous guards fired several shots at prisoners on October 14 for trivial offenses. However, a substantial stockade was under construction, and Hoffman promised that he would send no more prisoners and that a thousand would be transferred out of Camp Douglas.[29] Both promises were illusory.

Captain Charles Goodman, promoted to assistant quartermaster, purchased 550 pounds of tobacco to pay prisoners working on the stockade and other projects. The men preferred chewing tobacco to the smoking kind. It cost an inflated $1.50 per pound, and the prison fund paid the bill. Goodman had enough tobacco to put five hundred men to work. They almost completed a new stockade by October 17, 1863. It boasted a parapet, or platform, for the guards to walk on. Burke estimated the height to be 15 or 16 feet. Water lines followed the building projects, and prisoners drew water from new hydrants near their barracks.[30]

However, the construction work provided hiding places, and a most desperate escape occurred on October 18, 1863. Two prisoners entered the unfinished sewer, a wooden box-like duct two feet high by 18 inches wide and filled with water. They emerged outside the camp after 16 hours in this hellish box.[31] However, patrols recaptured them in Chicago, where they had lingered too long. The city was not only a commercial and industrial center, and a hub of religious revival, but also a world-class den of prostitution, vice, saloons, and "gambling hells."

"There were many fissions in the city's social pattern," a historian claimed. "Among them, the Prairie Queen, on State Street, which offered uninhibited dancing, erotic shows of degenerate detail, dogfights, and a monthly prizefight, bare knuckle-style, for the pay of two dollars a fight and, for the winner, a free bed with one of the house whores."[32]

This is not to suggest that every Rebel fled north to State Street instead of south to Dixie. However, when 12 men escaped through massive bribery, one of them got drunk in town and revealed the entire affair. Eleven evaded capture but not without adventures in Chicago. They had the nerve to file police complaints against a taxi driver who overcharged them, which delayed their exit from the city.[33]

Ministers claimed that the city's corruption extended to Camp Douglas. Twenty card tables were in use at the sutler.[34] Burke watched but did not play. The sutler rented the tables and profited more by selling the playing cards. Camp Douglas commanders were weak on religion, which may explain why gambling went on.

Chicago had much to offer other than gambling and vice. Willie

M. Barrow and James T. Mackey, for example, would have enjoyed fine acting at McVicker's theater. John Wilkes Booth continued to play in Shakespeare, and Chicago critics agreed that he was a star. "The simple announcement of his appearance will fill the theater," a critic gushed.[35] Burke and his father may have liked the new game of baseball, played just west of downtown. A special racing day at the Chicago Driving Park would have been pleasant, when track officials banned liquor, and only the "best people could attend." Captured Confederate musicians could have heard visiting orchestras in Chicago playing "Daisy Dean," "Babylon Is Fallen," and "Before the Battle, Mother."

Colonel De Land was also in need of some recreation. Dr. Clark's report exploded on October 24, with Colonel Hoffman quoting the most derogatory parts. "All these deficiencies must be remedied at once," he lectured. This would be at the prisoners' expense, paid for out of the prison fund. Worse, Hoffman imposed new restrictions that made management of the camp more difficult.

Cooking stoves had to be replaced with 40-gallon boilers. Not only would this destroy the quality of prison rations, but cooking stoves had been critical items for survival. The reason for this regulation was not economy, for the boilers did not last long, but retaliation. Prisoners never learned who ordered this policy. It could have come down from Stanton or Meigs. Another possibility is that Hoffman pushed for it to bootlick his superiors and climb the corporate ladder.

More changes included the baking of bread in camp, again, instead of using outside contractors. Hoffman ordered De Land to build two more hospitals with the prison fund but still grumbled. "The hospital affairs must be very badly managed if the hospital fund is not sufficient to purchase all the furniture of all kinds that they require for the hospital," he lamented. Mismanagement was not the cause, but the large number of sick, and an increase in the cost of rations.[36]

Hoffman agreed with Dr. Clark about the army clothing and ordered De Land to cut off the skirts, trimmings, and buttons and have them issued. De Land finally distributed 1,000 blankets, 1,000 jackets, 1,000 pairs of pants, 2,000 woolen shirts, 2,000 pairs of drawers, 2,000 pairs of socks, and 1,000 pairs of shoes.[37] Prisoners did not appreciate wearing the stripped uniforms because it made them feel ugly, and they still had their pride.

Did Colonel De Land have any pride? Hoffman demanded a

report from him within six days on how he had remedied the shortcomings in Clark's report. Why did he take Hoffman's abuse? Camp Douglas was not his responsibility. It was not a world that he made. He could have demanded a transfer for himself and his regiment or have scrapped his commission and gone home. It turned out that De Land was simply not a quitter.

Colonel Hoffman's criticism had some effect, however. De Land purchased cooking utensils, a hundred barrels of lime, 24 whitewashing brushes, and a substantial amount of lumber to repair barracks. Beginning October 25, De Land required that prisoners clean their quarters and police the grounds immediately after roll call.[38]

About 161 escapes plagued De Land, the most of any commandant, and his small garrison was unable to cover train stations and look for prisoners. The War Department further reduced his guard strength by detailing men to escort deserters to other cities. He could no longer enforce the martial law decree of 1862 and told Ammen, "It is known to the prisoners that a large number of persons are constantly outside the prison."[39]

Even the army created problems by issuing passes to relatives and friends of prisoners. De Land refused to admit any of them, including a minister. Headquarters in Cincinnati complained to General Ammen. "De Land has no authority to limit permits to visitors at Camp Douglas," the army charged. Ammen supported De Land and warned him about the minister, a Reverend John Frimble, "who is agitating to get into Camp Douglas to convert souls."[40] Colonel Hoffman agreed with Ammen and ruled that the army was not to issue passes for anyone to enter Camp Douglas.[41]

The weak security force encouraged Morgan's men, who filled White Oak dungeon for insubordination and break-out attempts. The building was in the shape of a cross, with the first-story walls entirely blank. A guard room occupied the second floor, and a ladder lowered prisoners into the dungeon below. "It is the determination of those in command at Camp Douglas, that the secesh there domiciled shall behave themselves; and they have got to do it," said the *Tribune* sternly.[42]

Nonetheless, 26 prisoners made an extraordinary escape from the dungeon on October 26, 1863. They cut a hole through the plank floor, then dug about four feet into a garbage pit adjoining the dungeon, according to De Land's report.[43] They continued through the pit ten feet under ground, past the fences, right under the feet of the guards. The army never learned how they did it. "I cannot see how anybody is to blame for it," De Land told Hoffman, as he tried to cool him down. "It was one of those desperate things that desperate men will sometimes do, and was done with great cunning, rapidity, and secrecy, as well as success."

De Land refused to accept blame. "For six weeks I had less than 600 effective men as garrison," he pointed out. "During all the time we have been building, fencing, laying sewers, water pipes. Prisoners have slid out of the holes in the dark, have passed out as workmen, and in a variety of ways have eluded the vigilance of the guards. Several have been killed and others wounded, and yet some escapes could not be prevented. But thank God, the crisis is past!" He made the point that the garrison and prisoners lived side by side in White Oak Square, which gave more opportunity for bribery and corruption. "I have instituted some extremely severe punishments to restrain the men," De Land claimed but gave no specifics.

He added that the sewers were finished, the water pipes laid, and the fences nearly completed. "Three or four days more will make Camp Douglas so safe and secure that not even money can work a man out. The only danger then will be in tunneling and that will not be tried often." This was a disastrous prediction.

De Land was ill throughout this stressful time but made a vigorous defense of his administration on November 3.[44] The situation was similar to the time when Colonel Tucker had to explain Dr. McVickar's reports of a crisis at camp. De Land argued that poor conditions in the hospital came from terrible overcrowding. "How could it be otherwise with so many sick thrown upon our hands?" Food preparation was difficult for lack of utensils. However, he had improved garbage collection. Workers were building two new hospitals and a laundry, and the new sewer system would begin to operate in three days, on November 6, 1863.

It included sinks constructed over the sewers. Forty funnels from each sink connected to a soil box. Each funnel fit one man, and a movable hydrant would flush the soil boxes into the sewers each day.[45] Engineers designed three 500-gallon water tanks to wash the filth through the sewers and into Lake Michigan. No one considered that Chicago's water intake crib was only five miles away and close to the shore. The city laid a large water main under Cottage Grove to serve the new system. However, three-inch pipes inside the camp proved a serious defect.

The prison camp at Elmira, New York, had similar sanitation problems after it opened about July 1, 1864. Lack of a water supply defeated a plan to build water closets like the ones at Camp Douglas.[46] Prisoners dug pits at the edge of a pond, which quickly became a cesspool. Colonel Hoffman allowed the Elmira commander only $120 to connect its sewers to a river a half-mile away. In desperation the commandant did the job at a cost of two thousand dollars.

De Land was blunt about the cooking boilers. "We have tried the Farmer boilers and they are a failure," he warned Hoffman, suggesting that the prison kitchens use brick and iron cooking stoves similar to the garrison's. The iron top was fitted with openings to accept all types of cooking utensils. The stoves measured three feet wide and 12 feet long, with 16 holes to burn four-foot wood.[47]

De Land believed the stoves were cheaper to operate and cooked much better than the boilers. He was right but did not consider the paranoia gripping Colonel Hoffman and the War Department. The stoves were too good and did not conform to the new policy of retaliation. De Land surprised Hoffman with a bit of news about the bread. It was now beyond his control, as all rations at Camp Douglas had come under the jurisdiction of an officer in Springfield named Capt. Ninian W. Edwards who managed subsistence for Illinois military depots by order of the army's commissary department in Washington.[48] Edwards may have been closer to President Lincoln than any other man and owed him his commission.

Ninian Wirt Edwards, born in 1809 in Kentucky, was a lawyer by training and a merchant and politician by profession. He sponsored the first public school law in Illinois as a member of legislature in 1855. Proud and aloof, he was married to the elder sister of the future wife of Abraham Lincoln, with whom he had long been associated in politics. It was in Edwards's home in Springfield that Lincoln met Mary Todd. It was there that they were married after Edwards encouraged the turbulent engagement.[49]

Edwards contracted with vendors to supply meat and other rations to military camps. His contractors delivered rations directly to the prisoners at Camp Douglas, bypassing the camp commissary. One contractor furnished equipment for the prisoners to use to make "Johnnie cakes." Curtis R. Burke commented about the poor quality of these rations. "We draw fresh beef every other day, but it is not a number one article being mostly neck, flank, bones and shanks," he recorded in his prison journal.[50]

Ninian W. Edwards. (Image courtesy of the Illinois State Historical Society.)

De Land had to know about the low-quality meat, because the garrison was receiving no better, but he did nothing. Perhaps Edwards's political clout intimidated him. De Land concentrated on construction and spent $20,000 improving the camp, employing a hundred prisoners daily. They were paid in clothing and tobacco. "This cost the government nothing," De Land boasted, "as they purchased the tobacco with prison funds and much of the clothing came from Kentucky." He assured Colonel Hoffman that Camp Douglas would be a model military prison by the end of November 1863. "If I fail, the fault shall not be mine," he said smugly.[51]

Nevertheless, Dr. Ira Brown of the 65th Illinois Infantry reported that the number of square feet per prisoner in the barracks was far below army standards. Such overcrowding made it impossible to keep them sanitary. Tar paper was missing from roofs, and many barracks were boarded up for lack of windows. Some of those in use had no bunks for the men to sleep on.[52]

Understandably, prisoners were reluctant to come to Camp Douglas, and one of De Land's officers carelessly "lost" 11 prisoners whom he was transferring there from Louisville, Kentucky. Hoffman chewed De Land out as though he were a private. "It is your duty to see that those under you perform properly their duties assigned to them!" Hoffman raged. "It is not sufficient that you give these orders, but you must see that they are obeyed!"[53] De Land did not respond. Perhaps he was beginning to enjoy his position.

Pressure mounted for De Land to plug the security leaks, but conditions were against it. Disabled soldiers of the Invalid Corps limited the garrison's efficiency, and his guards had made bribery a way of life. Quartering both guards and prisoners in White Oak Square created a climate for corruption. Preventing escapes was almost impossible, given the arrangement of the camp. These problems ushered in a new era of brutality.

It started with the killing of a black prisoner. "The first prisoner they shot after we were put in was a small fourteen year-old negro boy," one prisoner wrote. "I saw him the next day in the dead-house, and the rats had eaten off his ears."[54]

CHAPTER 10

Cruelty Under Colonel De Land

A serious shooting—Attempted coup against De Land—Prisoners tortured—The great tunnel escape—Camp Douglas beef scandal plagues the Lincoln administration—De Land relieved of command—General William W. Orme takes charge—Prisoners testify about conditions.

Maintaining accurate prison records was a priority for Hoffman, but not essential in De Land's view. He felt that controlling the prisoners was most important. Hoffman notified De Land on November 2, 1863, that his rolls were short a hundred men. In another incident De Land found eight Confederate officers and did not know where four of them came from. This discrepancy resulted from carelessly counting prisoners as they came through the gate, instead of forming them into ranks.[1]

De Land's get-tough policy started with a serious shooting on November 3, 1863. An escape tunnel had been found under the Eighth Kentucky Cavalry barrack. De Land lined up the regiment and told guards to shoot "if any sat down," according to T. D. Henry. A guard fired when a sick man fell, Henry claimed. "One man was killed dead, two others were wounded, one of them losing an arm, as it was afterwards cut off."[2]

Curtis R. Burke investigated and found that "there was at least a dozen different reasons given for the shooting." He was not able to learn the truth about the affair. "Some fifteen or twenty finally stept out and acknowledged being the principal diggers and were sent to the dungeon," he concluded.

Another serious matter occupied De Land three days later when a case of smallpox was found in the Invalid Corps. He issued a thundering order to vaccinate "every officer, soldier, and camp follower!"[3] Presumably, he meant employees and contractors. This was the only mention that doctors also vaccinated civilians at Camp Douglas.

The camp employed about 20 civilian workers, with pay scales set by Colonel Hoffman. Doctors received $100 per month, the controller of funds, $50 per month, clerks and mechanics earned 40¢ per day; copiers, who duplicated every document sent or received, eked out a mere 25¢ daily.[4] Their work fills about 20 volumes in the National Archives. Hoffman exploded when he learned that soldiers doing personal services for officers received an extra 40¢ a day. "An orderly is a choice job," he muttered, and reduced the pay to 25¢.

Colonel Hoffman finally heard from Washington on November 7, 1863, regarding his proposal to build many more barracks. Stanton's rejection reflected a hardened attitude: "The Secretary of War is not disposed at this time, in view of the treatment our prisoners of war are receiving at the hands of the enemy, to erect fine establishments for their prisoners in our hands."[5]

One woman caused excitement the same day when De Land jailed Sarah C. Goodwin at camp, "charged with plotting and conspiring to obtain the release of five prisoners of war." De Land arrested another young woman on the same charge a few weeks later, but she was saved from confinement in Camp Douglas and resided in an officer's home while being investigated. The *Tribune* reported, "She belongs to a family of high respectability in Kentucky, and her brother is one of Morgan's men." Other women, perhaps less respectable, gathered near camp, not to aid in escapes, but "to indulge in the grossest licentiousness with soldiers," according to the paper.[6]

Regardless, preachers were more concerned with propaganda than sin. On November 8, Chaplain S. Day of the Eighth Illinois Infantry held a special service for the prisoners. His message was clear, according to a reporter. "Chaplain Day spoke to them from the words of the Prodigal. I will arise and go to my father,—giving a brief resume of the parable—the departure from home of the prodigal—the sad consequences it involved—and the return and reception of the erring son. Chaplain Day assured his audience as hearty a welcome from their heavenly Father as the prodigal received—on his return home, —provided they came to God, through Christ, with the sincerity and patience which this sinning son manifested."[7]

One of De Land's officers cared little about patience. Colonel Benjamin J. Sweet, commander of the Eighth Regiment of the Invalid Corps, suddenly challenged Colonel De Land's authority on November 9, 1863. Sweet was ambitious and viewed Camp Douglas as a high visibility post. He complained to Colonel Hoffman that he should be in command because his commission from Wisconsin predated De Land's from Michigan.

De Land responded that the government had recognized his commission first. "I do not wish to remain in command unless clearly entitled to it," he assured Hoffman. "I neither court nor shrink from responsibility, but it will be a pleasure to yield the command to any officer you may direct."[8]

This was not the first time that Colonel Sweet had tried to undermine his commanding officer. He had made derogatory remarks about his colonel in the Sixth Wisconsin Infantry in 1861, which resulted in a request that Sweet go home and raise his own regiment.[9] He had been kicked out of what was to become the famous "Iron Brigade," one of the highest visibility outfits in the Union army.

A serious fire in Garrison Square on November 11, 1863, probably worked in De Land's favor and against Sweet. Some fences burned down, and there was nothing to prevent prisoners from leaving adjacent White Oak Square and escaping. De Land sent a company of his trusty Indians to force the prisoners into barracks, ordering that they shoot if necessary.[10] The Indians swiftly sealed the area, and not one prisoner was lost. Sweet's Invalid regiment could not have acted as quickly.

Burke estimated that the fire destroyed three hundred feet of barracks, fences, and the sutler's shop. "The fire was accidental and caught from a stove pipe," he reported in his journal. Burke was fast becoming a fine investigative reporter and keen observer of prison life. Colonel Sweet added that "much more damage was prevented by the arrival of a city fire engine called 'The Little Giant,' and another one that raced up belonging to the Illinois Central Railroad."

De Land felt thankful when General Halleck suddenly ordered him away from Camp Douglas. Halleck directed him and his regiment to immediately "join General Grant's army," leaving only three hundred guards to watch six thousand prisoners. Captain Potter urgently wired Hoffman "to stop it." Hoffman frantically got Stanton to intercede, but De Land said nothing. The battlefields of Virginia looked inviting compared with Camp Douglas. He had discovered, besides his other problems, that the garrison was "selling slops and swills to unauthorized persons."[11]

The canceled order to ship out nevertheless caused De Land to think about the lack of discipline among his men, and he ordered daily drill. They even had to drill in barracks in case of bad weather, an impossible task in such confined quarters. He went so far as to decree that "profane swearing or obscene language will be suppressed by company commanders."[12] This was no more possible than finding an honest sutler.

Colonel Hoffman finally settled the De Land-Sweet dispute with a curt order for De Land to remain in charge. It was surprising that Hoffman sided with him in the power struggle. Perhaps De Land's optimistic reports influenced him. The old grouch seemed to have regained his composure and told the beleaguered commandant that he was "pleased" to learn about his reforms.

However, Hoffman continued to insist on using boilers for cooking. "A Farmer's boiler, which cost $25 to $35, will cook for 120 men, with a very small supply of wood," Hoffman argued, "and there can be no plan so cheap, and if they have failed at Camp Douglas it is because those who used them did not want to succeed."[13]

Hoffman warned De Land that the prison fund was low because previous commanders had not followed his orders. "Now I must insist that my instructions shall be strictly carried out." De Land had to reduce rations according to Hoffman's formula. He would not gamble his career on the uncertain quality of volunteer officers and intended to exercise personal control at Camp Douglas.

He began by ignoring Ninian Edwards and ordering De Land to contract for bread with a Chicago baker. He had to cut the weight two ounces per loaf to save money. Edwards was to know nothing about it. He also wanted the bakery ovens repaired so that the prison could eventually produce its own bread. De Land was directed to hire a baker for $75 to $100 a month. "And he can soon have a savings of from $200 to $300 per month," Hoffman promised. "I depend on you, colonel, to put my plans into successful operation," he concluded.[14]

De Land was happy to see Hoffman as little as possible. Therefore, he was unnerved upon learning that the ogre was coming to investigate the fire of November 11. De Land did the unthinkable and bribed many prisoners with liquor to clean up the camp. The grounds must have resembled West Point when Hoffman arrived on November 15, because he made no derogatory remarks. He agreed with Burke's conclusion that the fire was an accident, "but there probably was some carelessness with it," he had to add.[15]

With customary stinginess, he suggested to Secretary of War Stanton that he only compensate enlisted men for the loss of clothing in the fire and that should be limited to one issue. Hoffman had never served in the ranks and only identified with top brass.

He had secret talks with Colonel Sweet in a downtown hotel about replacing De Land. Sweet was confident that he could do the job with about a thousand men of the Invalid Corps. Hoffman was skeptical, especially after the recent fire. He believed that Invalid regiments were inefficient. The meeting did not lead anywhere because Hoffman did not see how Sweet could change matters.

Still, De Land was overwhelmed, and a new commander may have been worth trying. Prisoners occupied former cook houses in White Oak Square because of the barracks shortage, and they continuously crowded the hospital. Yet, no prospect of exchange was in the air. Hoffman again thought about sending a thousand men to his new prison at Rock Island, Illinois. That did not happen, any more than completion of a new prison hospital. However, the sewer system was working, and Hoffman found the camp clear of trash and garbage. He did not seem concerned that De Land only had 859 enlisted men to guard "between 6,000 and 7,000" prisoners.

De Land needed reinforcements after being ordered again to retaliate for the reported ill treatment of Union prisoners in the South. Tension in White Oak Square must have increased considerably. Now, only families could send clothing, "nothing from friends and sympathizers," a fact impossible to verify and showing the paranoia setting in. "If a prisoner has a suit he can wear, nothing more can be given to him," Hoffman's order read.[16] Prisoners were allowed only two dollars of personal money in the bank, but the amount later was raised to ten dollars. More than likely, these restrictions were Stanton's idea, and they came as a Chicago winter was setting in.

Yet some prisoners found cash hidden in packages from home. They bought a barrel of flour for $20, eight dollars above the market price in Chicago. However, the sutler accidentally delivered a barrel of sugar, instead, and "vinegar pies," a Southern delicacy, soon flooded the camp. Burke's mess joined with another on November 16 to buy a cooking stove and utensils in Chicago for $12 and were "well satisfied."[17]

General Ammen, commanding the district from Springfield, was not "well satisfied" with De Land's roll call and reorganized it. The supervising sergeant was to list prisoners by squad on a morning report. A

Rebel sergeant in charge of the squad also filled out a morning report, and the two lists were checked against each other.[18] Guards soon discovered five Confederate officers among the prisoners. Their aim was to plan and lead escapes and generally cause trouble.

De Land suffered through another inspection around November 18, this time by Brig. Gen. William W. Orme, who reported directly to Stanton and who had been selected to succeed De Land as commandant. Orme felt that the food ration was good, "being three-quarters of a pound of bacon [1 pound of fresh beef three times a week], good, well-baked wheat bread, hominy, coffee, tea, sugar, vinegar, candles, soap, salt, pepper, potatoes, and molasses all of good quality." For every one hundred men prison officials issued daily 10 pounds of hominy, 10 pounds of coffee, 1 1/4 pounds of tea, 15 pounds of sugar, and 4 quarts of vinegar.

Each prisoner received 1 1/4 pounds of candles, 4 pounds of soap, 3 3/4 pounds of salt, 1/4 pound of pepper, and 30 pounds of potatoes. One quart of molasses went with every 100 rations. Beans and rice were added to the hospital ration, but no tea. The cost of the hospital ration was $18.42 per hundred and $14.08 for the prison. The commissary issued rations between 11:00 A.M. and 4:00 P.M. Orme proved how difficult it was for an outsider to know what was going on. For example, he failed to learn about the rotten beef ration.[19] He soon would.

Orme did show that De Land had not resolved the lack of any system for cooking. "The result is a great waste of food and fuel, the latter of which especially is a serious item of expense at the camp," he reported. Colonel Hoffman must have chewed his nails when Stanton handed him the report. Orme warned that the garrison was dangerously small at 876 men and needed a "chain of sentries" outside the fence. Sixty-one prisoners had gotten out in the three-month period ending November 18, 1863. The clean condition of the camp and a good situation in the prison hospital were in De Land's favor.

With only a small garrison behind him, De Land decided that he had to take extreme measures to prevent escapes. He promptly hanged three men by their thumbs for allegedly threatening an informer. They endured the punishment for over half an hour in silence and then began groaning and crying out.

"It made me almost sick to hear them," Burke wrote. "Several times the Yankee officers asked them if they were ready to tell what they knew, and they answered that they knew nothing to tell. A

Yankee surgeon examined them to see how much they could stand. There were some citizens there and they tried to get Col. DeLand to take the men down. The men were taken down after having been tied up so that they had to partly tip toe for an hour. One of the boys fainted, and another threw up all over himself. Their names were James Allen, John Sweeney, and Wm. Wason [*sic*]."

John Sweeney of the 14th Kentucky Cavalry died on May 19, 1864. William T. Wasson of the Second Kentucky Cavalry died on May 3, 1864. Most soldiers considered hanging men by their wrists or thumbs to be inhuman. Sometimes comrades released the victims and risked the same punishment.[20]

De Land lectured the prisoners about threatening informers and hanged two more by the thumbs. "They were let down when this traitor Stovall said that he forgive them," Burke said. Another prisoner also swore that De Land's punishments were severe and that he knew of him hanging men by their thumbs to extract information.[21] Stovall did not return to the regiment.

De Land cracked down more by requiring stoves to be out at Taps and threatened his own men with a court-martial if they were absent without a pass. He frequently turned prisoners out of barracks while searching for tunnels, and the hired prisoners took over Burke's quarters on November 24. "We call them the chain gang," Burke sneered.

These changes were chaotic, as De Land did not arrange for new quarters. Burke and his mess had to crowd in with a different regiment, but carried their cooking stove with them, which was some satisfaction. The food situation was also poor. Prisoners complained to Capt. Levant C. Rhines of the Sharpshooters about short rations, and he ordered the commissary to increase them.[22] This meant less money for the prison fund, but Rhines could do it because of a close relationship with De Land.

An important source of food was eliminated when the army shut down the sutlers on December 1, 1863, as additional retaliation. A sutler's establishment was a well-stocked general store selling most items except liquor, "including cider, butter, eggs, milk, canned fruits, boots, and underclothing." The liquor ban was hard on Kentuckians, who persuaded a woman selling milk from a tin can to fill it with "something more in keeping with the needs of a grown-up individual." Burke noted that the sutler closed down on December 12, 1863.[23] This meant that postage stamps, envelopes, and paper were no longer readily available. However, prisoners could make these purchases from the camp commissary.

De Land now took time to strike back at Colonel Sweet. He pretended to hear about alleged complaints that Sweet was shorting his men on rations and demanded a written report. The inference was that Sweet was profiting, but this appears to have been unwarranted.[24]

De Land soon forgot Colonel Sweet as another disastrous escape threatened his administration. His prediction that he had put a stop to tunneling was on a par with the *Tribune* editorial that no prisoners would come to Chicago. A new and massive escape resulted from setting barracks on the ground.

De Land had the "disagreeable duty to report a serious break of the Morgan prisoners in this camp, on December 3, 1863."[25] About a hundred prisoners in White Oak Square succeeded in leaving through a tunnel. De Land was fortunate. The entire prison could have strolled away had they not become reckless.

"They dug a small, round hole just under the frozen crust of the ground, the dirt being secreted under the floors of the barracks and cook-houses," De Land attempted to explain. "During the day this hole was covered with a board, over which was kept about six inches of dirt. This same barrack was searched every week, but the device was too perfect, and the officers failed to detect it."

Dark and foggy weather shrouded the camp on the night of the breakout, so guards were on patrol outside the stockade. Nevertheless, prisoners poured through the tunnel from 8:00 P.M. to 9:30 P.M., when discovered. "If there had been less hurry among them many more could have escaped," De Land conceded. The fence had no lights, and the square was very dark. "This is the eighth attempt which tunneling under the fences has made to escape from here, only two of which have been successful," the dispirited officer muttered.

The shaken commandant was unable to give a clear picture of where and how the tunnel began. Stanton assigned General Orme to investigate. "They began the tunnel under a bunk, and ran it the length of the building," Orme found. "At this point, they started a tunnel running at right angles with the barrack [the barrack being nearly parallel with the high fence enclosing the camp] the distance from the barrack to the fence being about forty feet." Orme did not say how far under the fence the tunnel ran, but legend had it at ten feet.[26] The need to hide the dirt and replace flooring was the tricky part of this operation. Orme placed no blame on De Land.

It was a miracle that any prisoners were left with so few guards available. The army had detached some to distant Boston at the end of September 1863, and Company I of the Sharpshooters was on duty at Detroit. De Land reported that the guard regiments "are broken down from measles and lung disease."[27] Only 250 men and ten officers were available for duty through December. Why did prisoners simply not walk out the front gate? The main reason was that Hoffman had armed the guards with six-shot revolvers on November 27, 1863. He believed that these were the best cards held by the garrison.

De Land, aided by police and troops in Chicago, sent patrols south and west of the city for 20 miles in search of the escaped prisoners. About 50 were quickly recaptured due mainly to the telegraph. Half had already obtained civilian clothing. Communications behind Union lines were well organized, with railroad stations connected to telegraph lines. The army recaptured all but 20 escapees who had got out since August 1863.[28]

De Land conceived a drastic remedy to counter the tunneling. "In view of this I have ordered all the floors removed from the barracks and cook-houses and the spaces filled with dirt even with the top of the joist," he reported to Hoffman. "This will undoubtedly increase the sickness and mortality, but it will save much trouble and add security." De Land understated the case. Uprooting the barracks in this manner brought Camp Douglas down to the level of Andersonville, where men lived on the ground without shelter. It was a complete reversal of the policy to make the camp more habitable and made a mockery of the modern water and sewer system.

An angry garrison tore down partitions in the barracks, making them one large dormitory. "They also tore up the floors except under the bunks," Burke laughed, "and we enjoyed ourselves by jumping around on the sleepers." They enjoyed themselves less when they began living in the frozen mud. The escape so unnerved guards that one fired at a prisoner who was hard at work repairing a roof.[29]

De Land also confiscated warm coats sent from home. This may have been done to prevent escapes, but was more likely retaliation. Burke angrily denounced the replacement coats as "some thin cottonade pepper and salt jackets, and some thin black rediculous looking tight spade tall Yankee coats! Some photographs were even taken of our men!"[30]

Sergeant Oscar A. Cliett. (Image courtesy of Robert L. Marchman III.)

Oscar A. Cliett, a sergeant-major in the 55th Georgia Infantry, believed that De Land "was one of the most bitter enemies of the South that I met during my war life."[31] Cliett suffered retaliation when he reported to De Land that his men rejected an offer to join the navy, "as we couldn't swim." Mulligan would have laughed. Tucker might have frowned. General Daniel Tyler might have lectured him on military courtesy. Ammen would not have responded. De Land ordered Cliett chained in the dungeon for 21 days on bread and water.

However, the outlook for prisoners brightened considerably when President Lincoln proclaimed a general amnesty on December 8, 1863. It called for releasing all prisoners below the rank of general. Nevertheless, prison officials closed the barber shop and newsstand on December 17 as punishment for the escape. They even banned sales of stamps, envelopes, and writing paper. The army had never denied prisoners such luxuries before, especially their precious newspapers.

It was likely that the loss of prisoners and De Land's administrative failures caused the next change in command. The War Department ordered Brig. Gen. William W. Orme to take over the Northern District of Illinois at Chicago, including Camp Douglas, on December 16, 1863. Orme relieved De Land as commander on December 23, 1863.[32] About four hundred reinforcements arrived the next day, representing six companies of the 15th regiment of the Invalid Corps under Col. James C. Strong, a most colorful and determined officer.

De Land was not totally disgraced, as he remained in charge of the garrison. This veteran officer felt hurt by the demotion, despite his previous assurance to Hoffman that he was willing to step down as commandant. He was so upset that he continued to sign himself as "Commanding Camp Douglas" on prison correspondence. An irate Hoffman ordered General Orme to put a stop to it.[33] Nevertheless, De Land's new position represented an historic step in prison administration at Camp Douglas. Command had been decentralized to the extent that General Orme did not have to supervise the day-to-day running of the prison.

Orme was a favorite of President Lincoln because he and Leonard Swett, one of Lincoln's intimate friends, were partners in a Springfield law firm. Lincoln regarded Orme as a most promising lawyer. Born in Maryland in 1832, Orme moved to Illinois and was admitted to the bar at age 21. He became colonel of the 94th Illinois

General William Ward Orme. (Image courtesy of the USAMHI.)

Infantry at Bloomington, Illinois, in 1861 and was in combat until June 11, 1863. Orme became ill with tuberculosis after the campaign at Vicksburg and could not continue in active service. This led to his post as prison inspector and his appointment to Camp Douglas.[34] His experience with the prison system was promising. He already perceived the need for changes in security at Camp Douglas. Orme's plans would revolutionize the camp and change its appearance considerably. As usual, however, events intervened to put such ideas on hold.

Taking command was as troublesome for Orme as it had been for previous commanders. Back in 1862, the camp had been tossed into Col. Arno Voss's lap as he was leaving for the front. Colonel Cameron once handed Tucker the keys while he was there recruiting. The army twice gave Cameron the command as he was fighting to get out the gate with his regiment. De Land was hit with a deluge of prisoners before he could sit down. Now, General Orme had to investigate food contractors instead of settling into his new job.

Strangely, this scandal surfaced after a complaint by a Canadian, named Montrose A. Pallen, about "great suffering in Northern prisons." Secretary of War Stanton ordinarily would have fired off a blistering denial. Instead, he ordered Colonel Hoffman to investigate. Stanton was probably seeking the good will of the Canadian government because Confederate agents had set up bases there for operations against the North. Hoffman issued an order on December 19 for General Orme to report on Camp Douglas.[35]

Orme mainly "found abuses" regarding the quality of the beef and other supplies. He submitted written questions to the Confederate sergeant-majors on December 24, 1863, to gather more information. They covered medical care, bunks, clothing, blankets, and the quantity and quality of the rations. Orme assumed that the sergeants were truthful men, which was justified. One prisoner even wrote a separate report to Orme to make sure that he did not misunderstand his sergeant-major. The sergeants of 24 squads drawing rations responded to the questionnaires. Among them was Burke's father, Edward.[36]

The meat ration: The main problem, according to 14 of those reporting, was the short weight and poor quality of the beef. Some answers included carefully worded understatements: "It is proper to say that there may be an honest difference in the scales. By our scales the bread holds out." "The beef does not weigh out with other rations, according to our scales." "I presume all are gentlemen connected with the department." "I rely on the gentleman in charge to do justice to the prisoners."

Medical care: All but two of the 24 squads reported prompt medical attention. One sergeant gave a fair rating, saying that his men would have "benefited by a more prompt admission into the hospital in several instances."[37] Another said dryly, "Not having had any sick cannot tell." The pharmacy promptly filled prescriptions, according to the sergeants, who praised four Confederate surgeons. Post surgeon Dr. Arvin F. Whelan of the Sharpshooters received a grudging nod. Respondents did not mention the smallpox hospital.

Blankets and bunks: The camp had issued seven thousand blankets for 5,822 men, which was not sufficient for winter. One sergeant reported that some of his men were without blankets. Two sergeants complained that many of the blankets were "much worn" or "light and ragged." Another added that the four hundred blankets in his squad were "all sent by friends."

The bunk situation was unfair. Smaller squads of about a hundred prisoners were doing fine, though they slept three to a bunk. The larger squads, comprising almost an entire regiment, were in desperate need. Two sergeants reported that their men had no regular quarters, because of the bunk shortage, and could not be found for roll call. They were vagabonds, drifting from barrack to barrack trying to find a place to sleep, homeless persons in modern terms. One sergeant snarled, "There are bunks for all who stay in the workmen's quarters!"[38]

Clothing: These responses were dismal. Only the smallest squads of less than a hundred men had received sufficient clothing. Eight sergeants refused to answer the question, in protest. Most of the larger squads of more than two hundred men had received only one-third of their clothing needs, and this was of poor quality: "The cottanade jackets, substitute for coats, are very uncomfortable for the season; many men are suffering for clothes," one sergeant stated bitterly. Many said that most of the clothing, about two thousand suits, came from home. One squad of 233 men had received only 22 shirts, 35 pairs of socks, 5 pairs of pants, 42 pairs of shoes, and 3 coats, at camp.[39]

Quantity of rations: The disbelief was evident in one response about whether rations were issued regularly: "I am informed by the commissary that we do."[40] Another sergeant dodged the question by saying that the rations were drawn regularly, "but very irregular." Two non-coms hedged with the response that rations were drawn regularly "generally" or with "a few exceptions." Twenty sergeants agreed, however, that rations were issued regularly. None of them claimed that the rations were inadequate.

It seemed that the sergeants were not as open in their responses as one might expect. Perhaps they feared retaliation. More likely, they found it impossible to accept this gesture of good will. The war had opened too deep a chasm, and the Camp Douglas experience had made it impossible to bridge. No one would shake hands there when the war ended.

Captain Rhines confirmed the responses. "I most fully believe the prisoners have been shamefully treated by the contractor for fresh beef," he assured Orme, who sent the reports to Colonel Hoffman in Washington. He concluded that contractors had habitually cheated the prisoners and ordered General Orme to investigate further. Hoffman wanted to know to what extent the rations were inferior or short in quantity and who benefited. Ironically, Hoffman had cut rations by one quart of molasses and two ounces of bread the day before Christmas.[41]

General Benjamin Butler followed a different policy at his prison and personally questioned Confederate sergeants drawing rations at Point Lookout, Maryland, on December 24, 1863.[42] Prisoners had been there only four months and were living 16 to a tent with few stoves. Six sergeants drew rations for 1,500 men each, about double the number of men the sergeants at Camp Douglas had to cover.

Unlike Camp Douglas, those in charge of rations had no scales and did not even know what the official allowance was for each man. However, they told Butler that they "had complete trust" in their Yankee commissary sergeant and felt comfortable with the situation. "We have got very fine beef," one responded, but he could only describe it as "from four and a half to five and a half quarters." The beef ration was insufficient, but prisoners received turnips, beans, and carrots by the barrel, and thus scurvy was absent. General Butler, also known as "Beast Butler," was not the type of man that Hoffman would have dared short on vegetables.

The lack of blankets and clothing at Point Lookout was the same as Camp Douglas. A sergeant from General Lee's army had drawn only one pair of pants and one shirt since August 9, 1863. Butler also wanted to know about brutality by the guards, a question not raised by General Orme. Prisoners reported no abuse, except having to build barracks and work on the grounds. This was no longer a problem since many now volunteered for these tasks.

Butler asked prisoners to compare their standard of living at the prison to what they had received in the army. A sergeant in the Seventh Texas felt that the Western armies of the Confederacy had less to eat. One from the Army of Northern Virginia told Butler, "We lived better in our army than we do here." The main complaint was lack of clothing.

Back at Camp Douglas, Orme finally had time to convene a post council of regimental officers to audit the prison fund and to add clerks to organize camp records. Hoffman was pleased. He believed that Orme would "bring about all the necessary reforms so much needed and produce a state of discipline and police which will be highly satisfactory."[43] Hoffman did not know that Orme was dying.

Orme was satisfied that coal stoves heated all prison barracks, and that "they [prisoners] are well cared for in the hospital and receive every medical attention." He retained Captain Rhines as commissary of prisoners. Rhines used clothing rather than tobacco to pay for prison labor. Much of this came through friends or family of other prisoners and was confiscated from those not considered "needy."[44] Since September 23, the needy received confiscated clothing in the form of 953 jackets, 796 trousers, 1,955 drawers, 2,033 shirts, 2,106 pairs of stockings, 1,280 blankets, and 1,114 pairs of shoes. These far exceeded what the army was furnishing.

However, Rhines found it necessary to deliver 1,280 more blankets by December 26, 1863, but the pure wool wore out quickly under hard usage. Each bunk now received 12 to 14 pounds of prairie hay monthly. Stoves used 1,412 cart loads of wood or 350 cords. Prisoners also consumed 294 cart loads of coal, amounting to 196 tons, each month. Captain Rhines did not consider the coal supply sufficient in extremely cold weather.[45]

The shortages of food, clothing, and blankets had caused a class structure to spring up. At the bottom rung was the infantry who had to work for additional clothing and food. Above them was the leisure class of Kentuckians who were able to buy what they needed from the sutler and even from Chicago merchants. This was in addition to the many packages they received from home. Burke and his father were members of the leisure class, thanks to Mrs. Burke's family.

They enjoyed regular shipments from Ohio, including cash for their bank accounts.

One group of prisoners asked Rhines to settle a ration dispute near the end of December 1863. About 80 men in Byrnes's Battery complained that their sergeant-major was only obtaining two days' rations for every three days. This was hardly his fault, but they petitioned Rhines "for the privilege of withdrawing from Byrnes' Battery, and to elect our own Sergeant-Major."[46] Not content with seceding from the Union, they now wished to secede from their own regiment. Rhines wisely stayed out of the dispute.

Meanwhile, President Lincoln's amnesty proclamation of December 8, 1863, was causing some Confederate officers to waver. One of Morgan's steadfast raiders wrote home from Camp Douglas: "I am sorry for our regiment. I do not know what we will do if all the commissioned officers take the oath. I believe it will play out entirely."[47]

Better news came for one last detachment of the Ninth Vermont Infantry, forgotten and abandoned at Camp Douglas since June 12, 1863. They received marching orders for the front on December 22, and like released prisoners they whooped and hollered their way to the train station.[48] They could still win some victories.

Burke was preparing a Christmas dinner as the year began to close. He did not dream that he would give another at Camp Douglas. He and his friend, Henry White, were flush with orders on the army commissary because the sutler was still closed. On December 25 they purchased "10 candles, one box of pepper sauce, two lbs. of coffee, 7 lbs. sugar, 1 paper of black pepper, 1 paper of allspice, 1 lb. butter, and 1 lb. lard," at a total cost of $2.45. The old saying, "money talks," held true at Camp Douglas, and the commissary was well stocked for those who could afford it. The prisoners did not expect gifts, but Burke's father gave him a pair of buckskin cavalry gloves, a pair of socks, a fancy shawl pin, and a 50-cent sutler ticket. It was pleasant to have generous Yankee in-laws.

Burke's dinner was late because other messes were also cooking. Hoffman had not been successful thus far in eliminating all of the cooking stoves. Prisoners had resisted no other policy at Camp Douglas so fiercely, not even the smallpox vaccinations.

Burke's menu was biscuits, tea, beans and bacon, buttered baker's bread, toasted molasses, boiled onions laid in water, cheese, peach pie, apple pie, onion pie, plain doughnuts and sweet doughnuts. This holiday mood even affected a guard officer, who asked humorously while inspecting barracks if any "goffer business is going on."[49]

Guests had filled and refilled cups, mugs, and glasses with "something more in keeping with the needs of a grown-up individual," and Henry White offered the "Toast of Morgan's Men."

"Unclaimed by the land that bore us,
Lost in the land we find,
The brave have gone before us,
Cowards are left behind,
Then stand to your glasses, steady,
Here's a health to those we prize.
Here's a toast to the dead already,
And here's to the next that dies."[50]

General Orme, meanwhile, was trying desperately to get a grip on administrative problems beyond the beef scandal during this holiday season. On December 29 he wrote to Colonel Hoffman that he found no regulations or directives on how to run the camp. It was a repeat of the situation encountered by Colonel Tucker after the departure of Colonel Mulligan. Orme also learned that De Land had paid two detectives a hundred dollars per month out of the prison fund and requested instructions.[51] De Land was the first commandant to put detectives on the payroll, while Colonel Tucker had used them only for special assignments.

Orme increased security on December 29, with the officer of the day to "personally inspect the quarters of the prisoners of war and satisfy himself that nothing is going on to endanger the safekeeping of the prisoners." Officers had to report how often they visited guard posts during a tour of duty.[52]

The new hospital was still under construction, and Henry White took some lumber to make a new storage bin for their extra food. The year 1863 was noteworthy for the water pipes and the sewer system that began operating on November 6. However, the task of replacing the pipes with larger ones had to be faced. Morgan's men set an escape record in 1863, and the mortality rate continued inexorably high. About 1,010 more prisoners had died since July 1862, and approximately 6,144 Confederates had arrived since August 18, 1863.

Disappointing news came on December 31. President Lincoln had changed his mind about a general amnesty for prisoners of war and now said that it did not extend to them. At least that is what the army claimed. "A general jail clearing, as you express it, could not certainly have been contemplated by the President in issuing his proclamation," the judge-advocate-general proclaimed in answering a question from a prison commander, "and such a result would, I think, be in every way to be deplored."[53] The army had overruled the president, and Camp Douglas would soldier on to the end of the war and beyond as a prison camp.

General Orme unexpectedly exonerated Ninian Edwards and his contractors in the beef scandal as the year ended, blaming the subcontractors. Orme believed that the beef ration had been short for some time. However, he reasoned that the contractors were not responsible, as their subcontractors furnished the beef. This was an odd position for a lawyer to take, and no judge would have agreed. "I am further induced to this belief by the character and standing of some of the contractors, whom I personally know," Orme added shamelessly.[54]

Meanwhile, Orme instructed Capt. Ninian Edwards to withhold payment to the beef subcontractors. Finally, he informed Hoffman that various contractors and businesses at camp employed prisoners, asking, "Has this practice met with your sanction?" Camp Douglas enjoyed a free market economy amid the unprecedented war-time prosperity, and sutlers had sped away in their ruthless pursuit of free enterprise. However, unlike sutlers at the front, they drove home to family and fireside when they closed up shop, perhaps humming a few bars of "The Girl I Left Behind Me."

CHAPTER 11

Unfit for Use

More charges of prisoners freezing to death—Black prisoners released—Rats killed and eaten—A new Prisoner's Square takes shape—Health deteriorates—A coverup in the beef scandal—Colonel De Land ordered to be court-martialed.

A blizzard started the new year in Chicago style. Temperatures fell to 18 degrees below zero on January 1, 1864, and 25 below at night. A heavy snowfall added to the crisis.[1] Surgeons hospitalized six or seven guards, and Burke was cut off from Pa's barrack. "I put a pot of dried peaches to cooking on the stove to bake a big peach roll for dinner," Burke recorded. "The night was very cold, but the guards kept the coal stoves red hot all night, which kept the barracks warm, and we slept well."

M. J. Bradley, who described Camp Douglas as "that hellish den of iniquity," claimed that the garrison had warm gloves but refused to help prisoners haul wood to their barracks. "Many men were frost bitten and many perished," Bradley charged. He was wrong. None perished, although R. T. Bean said he would have died coming back from the wood pile had guards not taken him into their barracks. Bradley was probably referring to some prisoners who escaped and were found frozen to death nearby.[2]

Dr. C. S. Brunson, an able Confederate surgeon, reported a childhood friend "frozen to death" in barracks during the winter of 1863-64. Brunson headed a Confederate medical corps of ten doctors established by Colonel De Land. Private T. M. Page, captured at Chickamauga on September 19, 1863, claimed that the Federal surgeons challenged Brunson's diagnosis but backed down when Brunson requested an autopsy. However, this incident may have resulted in more coal for the barracks.

General Orme requisitioned 50 more coal stoves and 350 joints of stove pipe on January 4, sufficient to make 25 barracks comfortable. Private Page had an interior view of events as secretary to the

Confederate surgeons. Dr. Brunson had awarded this coveted position to him for predicting wrongly that Page would die when first examined at Camp Douglas.[3] No one could accuse Brunson of having a good bedside manner.

Page alleged that guards stripped him of blankets before his arrival on October 4, 1863, and that prisoners whom they treated similarly were freezing to death in their bunks. His account, written in 1900, is questionable at times. For example, he wrote that about 539 prisoners died in October 1863, which seems unfounded, based on other information. True, blankets were scarce then, but Captain Rhines had issued 1,280 by December 1863.[4]

The *Tribune* described how, during the sub-zero emergency, "supply trains make their regular trips, despite the weather, and immense wagon loads of beef, bread, wood and coal can be seen several times each day wending their way to Camp Douglas." Prisoners did not mention this rescue effort.

Coal yards gouged the poor in Chicago from $1.50 to $2.00 more per ton than in 1863. Wood, also, was up $2.00 per cord. Mortality in the city for the year 1863 provided another explanation for why so many prisoners died "like rotten sheep." Scarlet fever raged through the city killing 475 people; smallpox accounted for 215 victims; cholera, typhoid, typhus, dysentery, and diphtheria also came in for their share, like scavengers flocking to a kill.[5]

General Orme was working on New Year's day and wrote Hoffman about black prisoners from Morgan's raid. "These negroes have been at Camp Douglas for some time and I submit this statement to you for such instructions as you may deem advisable," Orme reported. Hoffman responded that their release depended upon whether they were slaves or soldiers. Orme should release them if they were slaves. "If soldiers they are not to be exchanged against their will."[6]

TABLE VI

BLACK PRISONERS FROM MORGAN'S RAID[7]

Isaac Cox, negro. Co. L, 2nd Kentucky Cavalry. Captured 7-26-'63 at Talinnville, Ohio. Remarks: Released by order of Secretary of War, February, 1864.

Alex Bogan, negro. Co. I, Wood's Tennessee Cavalry. Captured 7-26-'63 at Talinnville, Ohio. Remarks: Unaccounted for.

Henry Marshall, negro. Co. B, 14th Kentucky Cavalry Captured 7-26-'63 at Talinnville, Ohio. Remarks: Unaccounted for.

Marshall Henry, negro. Captured 7-14-'63 near Cincinnati, Ohio. Remarks: Released by order of the Secretary of War, February, 1864.[8]

Robert Marshall, negro. Servant of Dr. Marshall. Captured 7-15-'63 at Logan, Ohio. Remarks: Released by order of the Secretary of War.

Berry Black, negro. Co. D, 15th Tennessee Cavalry Captured 7-20-'63 at Cheshire, Ohio. Remarks: Died November 5, 1863.

John A. Rogan, negro. Captured 7-14-'63 near Cincinnati, Ohio. Remarks: Released by order of the Secretary of War.

Reading Buffer, negro. Co. G, 15th Tennessee Cavalry Captured 7-20-'63 at Cheshire, Ohio. Remarks: Unaccounted for.

General Morgan had ignored orders from Richmond to report the presence of blacks in his army. As a result, many were captured on free soil in Confederate uniforms. The army held black prisoners at Camp Douglas despite President Lincoln's Emancipation Proclamation of January 1, 1863, which declared that slaves captured with Rebel forces would be "forever free." A War Department order on April 24, 1863, reinforced this command, declaring that slaves captured from belligerents were "entitled to the rights and privileges of free men." It seems that these men were not considered slaves.[9]

General Orme concluded his investigation into the surviving black prisoners and advised Stanton to release them. He ruled that Robert Marshall, Isaac H. Cox, and John A. Rogan were slaves, despite evidence to the contrary. He decided that Marshall Henry was a "free negro, not listed as a soldier and not having been in the Rebel army." Orme's findings resulted more from compassion than attention to facts. Marshall Henry was a free man from a border state, captured with Confederate raiders near Cincinnati, Ohio. He hardly qualified as a tourist. Rogan was on the prison rolls as an infantry private, not a servant.[10]

Private Berry Black was buried with his white comrades at Oak Woods Cemetery in Chicago. Orme made no inquiry into the fate of three missing black prisoners. Neither did anyone else. One Union general protested the exchange or release of black prisoners and wanted them put to work. Hoffman, however, stood by his original orders to General Orme.

Orme next turned his attention to new prison regulations and drafted many restrictions. Burke counted them off: "1st that we must only write every thirteen days and then only one letter of two pages of note paper each. The whole number of prisoners in camp was divided into thirteen squads each having a certain day to write. 2d. That we can not visit the other squares unless we get a pass from the officer of the day. 3d. That we must be in our barracks by five o'clock p.m. and put all lights and fires out at the beating of the drum at eight o'clock p.m. and no one allowed out side of the barracks till day, except to go to the sink."[11] He observed that while General Orme signed the restrictions, Colonel De Land along with his officers "still remains in office."

Orme's guard schedule was different from Colonel Tucker's. Reveille and roll call started at sunrise, breakfast was at 7:30, and sick call came an hour later; changing of the guard in Garrison Square was at 9:30 A.M.; drill and another roll call came at 3:00 P.M. Guards made two more roll calls by 9:00 P.M., and lights out for the garrison was at 9:30. An officer supervised the garrison roll call, and company commanders made daily inspections of garrison quarters and mess halls.[12]

Morgan's men were busy writers, which caused the mail restrictions. This clamp-down did not deter one smitten prisoner. "Fortunately I found a man of a Mississippi regiment whose name was the same as mine except for the middle initial," he recalled in later life. "He allowed me to use his name in writing to my rebel girl in Kentucky." His letters proved effective, and the couple were married after the war. Prisoners with money might "persuade" the Yankee barracks sergeant to "take out five letters per day until the regular writing day."[13]

Oscar Cliett recorded that guards operated an underground mail service to rival the Chicago post office. "Gen. Morgan's command was made up principally of the wealthiest people of Kentucky," he believed.[14] Kentuckians sent cash to these guards for the benefit of loved ones, according to Cliett. This was likely, since a similar pipeline ran through the Adams Express office in 1862 when Frederick Hudson appeared.

The commandant at the Elmira, New York, prison camp discovered a similar underground, running hundreds of letters around the censor. He arrested "one commissioned officer, one acting assistant surgeon, and two enlisted men."[15] Detectives and spies were not able to make a dent in this lucrative business at Camp Douglas, probably because they joined it.

Newspaper carriers also found White Oak Square a free enterprise zone, but they fell under trade restrictions. "Newsboys are prohibited from going to rebel quarters on any pretext, and from selling anything to the prisoners of war," Orme decreed.[16] This order hurt the guards who shared in the profits. Licensed vendors, paying a business tax at camp and Federal income taxes in Washington, had probably complained to Orme about the duty-free market.

Newsboys were better off out of the way. Colonel De Land ordered guards to shout only one challenge to a prisoner seen near the fence or outside his barrack at night. The guard was then to fire if the prisoner did not obey. Prisoners going to the latrines had to leave their clothing in barracks, no matter how bitter the weather.

Orme made the mistake of issuing winter clothing without Hoffman's permission, and the crabby old soldier read about it in the *Chicago Tribune*. He lectured Orme on January 5, 1864, that "great coats have not been authorized by the Secretary of War, and I have approved no regulations calling for such articles."[17] Hoffman reprimanded Orme for trying to save lives during the worst Chicago winter of the war. Orme probably considered the Vicksburg campaign a mere stroll in the park compared to running Camp Douglas and dealing with Hoffman. How did Orme obtain Union army overcoats for the prisoners without going through Hoffman's office? They probably came down some "good ole boy" pipeline, or perhaps Orme called in some chips.

Orme did not answer Hoffman because he was busy creating a system of ground patrols on January 8. This was the most significant new security measure ever undertaken. Patrols had "to break up congregations of prisoners in or outside of their barracks" and consisted of two divisions of 15 enlisted men each and one officer and one corporal.

Armed patrols and prisoners would be in close contact for the first time. Patrols also had to watch the guards and report "derelictions of duty." In addition, they had authority to arrest soldiers "who were straggling among or holding conversations with the prisoners." Patrol officers had to inspect the prison quarters twice a day to search for escape tunnels.[18]

Some prisoners killed and ate rats, despite the patrols, when workers demolished a kitchen on January 10. The North denied these reports. Burke says that he saw it. "Two of the men gathered them up to clean them and to eat them. I understand that rat eating is very extensively carried on in the other squares, but my curiosity has never made me taste any rats yet." A man named Stoton reported that rat meat was "as tender as a chicken." Stoton survived the rats and Camp Douglas. Some anonymous characters reminiscing 37 years later said that prisoners raised the kitchen floor to catch "big gray rats" which they made into rat pie.[19]

Daniel F. Brandon, the camp photographer, was dining quite well, however, until charged with violating security. Orme had issued an order on January 16, 1864, banning prisoners from all commissaries, offices, and shops, unless they worked for the quartermaster, were assigned to the prison hospital, or had a pass. Even Confederate sergeant-majors no longer left the square to draw rations, and guards now carted food to the barracks.

Orme banished Brandon from camp after two prisoners were found at his photo studio in Garrison Square. Brandon denied that he had employed prisoners and swore that he "has nothing to do with prisoners, except those who come into my gallery for pictures. And may I say, General," Brandon added, "that I hate a rebel and his cause as bad as the Devil ever hated Holy Water."[20]

Orme relented, perhaps impressed by such deep religious feeling. However, Brandon's "hatred" did not prevent him from doing business with any Rebel who could pay his fees plus the two cents tax. Brandon had opened a studio on Cottage Grove opposite the camp in 1861 and operated a second one in Garrison Square by 1862. He had come to Chicago from Pennsylvania before the war and was married with two small children.[21]

In addition to the new patrols Orme planned radically to change the shape of Camp Douglas. His investigation of the mass escape on December 3, 1863, had convinced him that a totally new prison was necessary. He decided to move prisoners from White Oak Square, on the southeastern side of camp, to the western part. "I have the honor further to state that a prisoner of war, once beyond the camp lines, finds in this city so many active friends and sympathizers as to render his recapture almost impossible," he told Hoffman.

His plans called for all prisoners to be in one place for the first time, enclosed by a 12- or a 14-foot stockade with a guard walk. He scheduled completion of the new square for March 15, 1864. Ground patrols would walk a beat 24 hours a day and have an office inside the gate. Orme also planned separate barracks for them. Hoffman was shaken by such extravagance. He limited these new facilities to bare wooden walls, without plaster or ceiling, and ordered that the work had to be done free by prisoners who wished to take the oath.[22]

Hoffman now had General Orme's letter blaming the ration scandal on the subcontractors. He rejected Orme's attempt to shift responsibility. "The parties contracting with the government are responsible that its terms are faithfully complied with," Hoffman ruled.[23] Orme had to know this fact. Hoffman wavered on whether prisoners could work for vendors but finally decided against it. They could perform all duties related to themselves, only, such as hospital work, Hoffman said. However, they could not attend their own sick, probably to guard against escapes. This rule was quickly disregarded in the smallpox hospital where nurses were too scarce for such restrictions. Orme's report on the rations would go to Stanton when completed.

Dr. Edward D. Kittoe, of the surgeon-general's office, arrived on January 18, 1864, for another inspection. Colonel De Land conducted him about the camp. General Orme felt the pressure now. Damp winds from off of Lake Michigan immediately soured Kittoe on the location. Noxious odors from nearby meat-packing companies added to his dismay. He found the garrison well off compared to the prisoners. Guards were living in new barracks raised off the ground, their rations were good, "and their persons are clean, also their privies," Dr. Kittoe noted.[24]

The prisoners' story was different. They were deep in mud and filth due to the lack of flooring. Crowded barracks were swarming with vermin in White Oak. Three of the 100-foot buildings held 440 men, almost three times normal capacity. De Land told Kittoe that "he finds it impossible to make these men observe the ordinary rules of decent cleanliness of persons or quarters." Quarters occupied by Morgan's men already living in the new Prisoner's Square "were preeminently filthy," the doctor wrote.

Cooking was deficient, and garbage littered the streets again. Kittoe graded the prison rations as "good and ample" but stated that the cooking arrangements were bad, so that food was improperly prepared with much waste. He did not explain his objections to the cooking, but they probably related to the many small messes instead of central cooking.

Kittoe discovered that workers had not sealed the old sinks

properly and that waste was seeping up through the ground. Camp Douglas sat atop an environmental disaster. About 5,616 prisoners were present, with 1,595 guards available for duty from three guard regiments. The First Michigan had 812 men, the Eighth Regiment of the Invalid Corps under Colonel Sweet, 447 men, and Colonel Strong's 15th Invalid Regiment totaled 409. Four companies of the 11th Regiment of the Invalid Corps were due to arrive momentarily, but he did not know how many.

He gave high marks to the hospital and medical care for prisoners, but doctors had filled the 234 beds, while 250 patients remained in barracks. A new hospital was still under construction. Serious illness among the prisoners was an appalling 36 percent, with 57 deaths in December 1863, according to Kittoe. The garrison had 29 percent very ill and six deaths. Mumps, measles, pneumonia, and sinus infections racked the camp. Guards stationed on the fence suffered a higher rate of respiratory disease because they were "exposed to the full sweep of the cold and damp winds," Kittoe believed. Camp Douglas was not an ideal place to be either a guard or a prisoner.

Kittoe concluded that the camp was unfit for use. Unrelenting cold added its own misery to the barren landscape, so that any feeling of warmth in a prisoner's life became a distant memory. Prisoners going to the sinks on winter nights had to leave clothing in barracks no matter how bitter the weather. A cold and miserable guard fired at a prisoner one January night, missed, and the bullet may have fatally wounded another. The perceptive Burke feared "that a great many prisoners will take the oath before exchange comes again."[25]

He was not one to admit that Morgan's raiders had a breaking point, but when that time came it hit close to home. Courage does not wear out quickly at age 21, and Burke still had a lot of it in his bank account. Older prisoners had been making withdrawals without putting anything back, and their grit was wearing as thin as their clothing.

General Orme's great move from White Oak Square to the new Prisoner's Square began on January 20, 1864. Burke had to vacate his barracks on January 27. Much labor was required to move the 300-foot long structures on rollers, and plans were made to cut them down to just 90 feet. At first the non-paid prisoners helped, but a dispute with the Yankees soon broke out, and they quit. Many barracks were still en route as night fell. Guards retaliated by preventing prisoners from sleeping in them, and they had to use makeshift shelters in White Oak Square. The mud, the cold, and the many rats upset by the move made this a memorable night.

However, work had to stop without substantial help from the prisoners. In all fairness, why should they work to build a more secure prison? Orme was forced to bring in an outside contractor with horses on January 29. A time was coming, however, when prisoners would either work or risk punishment or death. Orme's move took about two months, and some prisoners remained in White Oak Square until April.

The new square could hold about 12,000 when completed. It ran two city blocks from north to south and two blocks from east to west, covering about 40 acres. It occupied land between present Vernon Avenue on the east and Martin Luther King Drive on the west. The north end is now East 31st Street, and it extended to 33rd Street on the south. Andersonville confined 35,000 Union prisoners on a field of 30 acres in August 1864.[26] Only a third of them had any kind of ragged shelter.

The difficult move to Prisoner's Square was not Orme's only problem. Corruption reduced the already understaffed medical department on January 28, 1864, when Orme arrested Dr. William D. Lee, a Chicago contract surgeon, as co-conspirator in a bribery scheme. "I have so much to contend with," Orme wrote to Colonel Hoffman, "in the way of attempts at bribery (and successful attempts too) of persons on duty at my camp that nothing short of severe punishment will stop it."

Dr. Lee was found out when police arrested a drunk near the Prairie Queen. A search revealed that he was a Confederate officer sent to organize escapes from Camp Douglas. Letters described plans and implicated Dr. Lee. They revealed one of the most promising escape plots ever hatched at camp. The doctor allegedly confessed but claimed that he had acted for humanitarian reasons. This may explain why escaping from the hospital was easier than any other area of the camp. Lee then had the gall to request that Orme send his salary to his "destitute" family in Chicago.[27]

Lee's arrest left only three Chicago doctors, the post surgeon, and about four Confederate surgeons to treat almost six thousand prisoners. Inspector Clark returned on February 1, 1864, and confirmed their lack of cleanliness.[28] With the sewer and water system working, Dr. Clark believed that "a little care would suffice to keep sweet and clean." Clothing was also dirty, and of poor quality, mostly

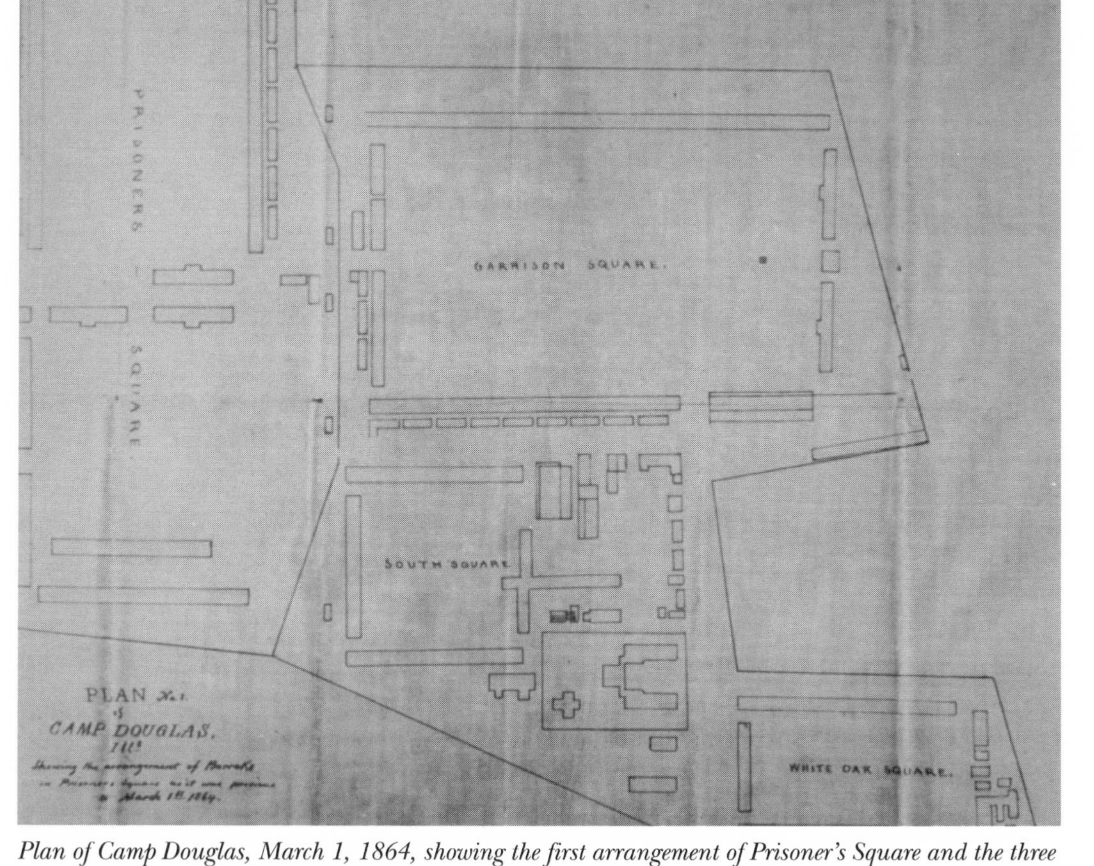

Plan of Camp Douglas, March 1, 1864, showing the first arrangement of Prisoner's Square and the three other squares. South Square contained all hospitals except the smallpox facility. (Image courtesy of the National Archives.)

donated and condemned army items. What did Clark expect? The men had been living atop the dirt since De Land stripped their barracks of flooring, and they had no means of thawing frozen hydrants.

Clark continued to be critical of Orme's administration. "Police of camp—very much neglected," he snapped. "Discipline in camp—very lax." The running water sinks delighted Clark, but "they are not well managed," probably meaning that they were dirty. Cooking was better, "mostly done in well-furnished cook houses."

De Land ignored inspection reports and concentrated on security. He tightened control of the guardhouse on February 2, 1864, by requiring a morning report on the number of prisoners held.[29] Similar to Colonel Tucker, he ordered army regulations and the Articles of War read at guard mounts and reliefs.

Dr. Clark could not understand why prison officials did not raise barracks off the ground to prevent tunneling. They followed his simple suggestion, resulting in healthier living conditions. Burke's new quarters arrived in Prisoner's Square on February 4, 1864. Two days later he helped place short legs under the building and laid the floor. They no longer had to live in the dirt, thanks to Dr. Clark. Pa moved in with his son, and the transfer of barracks from White Oak continued.[30] They set them around the sides of Prisoner's Square, close to the fences. These were old garrison barracks, as officials had never built new ones for prisoners. Kitchens also backed up to the fence, allowing prisoners to continue tunneling.

Clark glowed over the prison hospital. Patients were neat and clean, and so were the buildings and grounds. Kitchens, diet, and utensils rated very good. He gave no credit to Dr. Whelan, post surgeon from De Land's regiment. However, many patients lacked beds. Even the chapel contained 66 patients. A new prison hospital was under construction, designed to hold only 189 patients in four wards. Those responsible may just as well not have bothered. Hospital laundry was done under contract, but the new facility would have its own.

Dr. Clark was unduly optimistic about controlling smallpox. Burke and many others avoided vaccination because the infections were almost worse than the disease, but "considerable uneasiness" about the rise in smallpox cases made the camp nervous. Finally, the prisoners were rounded up at gun point and marched out for vaccinations on February 14.[31] It happened to be Valentine's Day, and Burke mourned the loss of romance in his young life. "I see nothing here to remind me of such old times," he reflected sadly.

Burke had more to contend with when he found Pa reading aloud to the barracks his letter from a young lady. Burke did not appreciate the "joke," as Pa called it, which shows that parents can be difficult sometimes. Apparently, a "pen-pal" network was active in the South, because Burke was writing to three young women "at their request."

General Orme was trying to build a criminal case against the subcontractors, and this situation so intrigued Colonel Hoffman that he did not mention the negative inspection reports. Orme had submitted his findings to Colonel Hoffman on February 8, detailing how four contractors had been supplying the camp since April 1863 under the name E. S. Fowler. All four continued doing business under another name when the contracts were renewed on November 10, 1863.[32] These agreements allowed them to bypass the camp commissary and issue provisions directly to the troops and prisoners.

The beef ration was exactly as reported, the poorer parts of the animal, and those in short weight. Beef was up to 40 percent below contract requirements "and has inured to the benefit of the subcontractors," Orme reported. He placed no blame on Capt. Ninian W. Edwards, who had been demoted for an earlier incident at Springfield, Illinois.

This happened long before the beef scandal at Camp Douglas. In a significant letter about the Springfield problems, dated June 22, 1863, his superior, Gen. Joseph P. Taylor, wrote to Edwards that he had just seen the president about him.

"The President does not doubt you in any manner or shape but is embarrassed by circumstances should you remain at Springfield," Taylor advised. "Therefore I have or will today direct Colonel Kilburn to locate you in Chicago, which will be very agreeable to the President, and under the circumstances, I hope will be agreeable to you. The President would very much regret should you resign and I also would much regret to lose you from the Commissary Department."[33]

Something was rotten in Springfield. Otherwise, why should Lincoln be "embarrassed by circumstances" and banish Edwards to Chicago? And why did Edwards offer to resign his commission? Possibly, he was a silent partner in the government contracts. His critics charged that Edwards "was making $15,000 from his office."[34]

The contractors were all from Springfield, where Edwards had long-time business connections. He owned a store there under the name N. W. Edwards & Co, and Lincoln had an account with him before the war.

Enemies raised questions about his honesty when Edwards paid large sums to his creditors. He claimed that he could "retire $13,000 of his indebtedness" through frugality.[35] The president was skeptical, but the coverup by the administration succeeded.

Edwards's presence in Chicago during the Camp Douglas violations added to his earlier problems. He had tried to protect himself by asking Colonel De Land, then in command of Camp Douglas, to give his opinion of the rations. De Land had responded on December 9, 1863, that he was "perfectly satisfied" with Edwards. "How any fault can be found is beyond my knowledge, unless it is because you are too strict & cautious to shield the government & its troops from pecuniary loss & from all cause for dissatisfaction."[36] De Land would regret this letter.

Edwards also asked Orville Hickman Browning, a former Illinois senator in Washington, to intercede for him. Browning, a lawyer and politician, filled Senator Douglas's seat from July 4, 1861, to January 30, 1863, and was Lincoln's floor manager in the Senate. Some believed that "the president's office and the president's secrets opened to Browning when they opened to no other." Browning was an unscrupulous influence peddler who simply prepared an order for Lincoln's signature to get what he wanted.[37]

For example, he recorded in his diary on Monday, December 14, 1863, that he went to Willard's Hotel to meet a Dr. Brown, and "went with him to the President to try and get Henry Warfield, a lad of 18 years old, a rebel prisoner at Camp Douglas, and a brother in law of Dr. Brown committed to the custody of the Dr." Lincoln saw to it that the necessary paper work went through Hoffman's office. Browning's fees must have been substantial.[38]

He again "went to the Presidents, and got an order for the release of Ludwell Y. Browning, a rebel prisoner at Camp Douglas." He was also working to free prisoners of war at Camp Chase in Ohio and Camp Morton in Indiana.[39] Browning's power was so well understood that he often went to Colonel Hoffman directly.

Browning wrote a revealing letter to Ninian Edwards on December 30, 1863, about the Camp Douglas beef investigation: "Your several letters have been received," he assured Edwards. "I have had repeated conversations with the President in regard to you, in all of which he has expressed himself most kindly, and as having unshaken confidence in your integrity and capacity."

Browning also met with General Taylor twice, "who informed me that the whole thing was finally disposed of—that the last contract taken by Mr. Baker & others [E. S. Fowler, R. E. Goodell, E. L. Baker, and John McGinnis, Jr.] would be rescinded—the contract relet and you continued in command at Chicago under the supervision of Col. Small, and to report to him, and that nothing further would be done. This I presume, will be entirely satisfactory. The Genl expressed himself in the kindest terms respecting you. You have had a hard time of it, but I trust now you will be let alone, and permitted to discharge your duties in peace. I suggest that you do not talk about this matter. It is not necessary that the public shall know that either you or the contractors have been subjected to annoyances."[40]

The Camp Douglas scandal was not as dangerous to Lincoln as the Springfield matter, since this time it merely looked like negligence. However, Washington terminated the E. S. Fowler contract, and Edwards was placed under supervision in Chicago.

The army finally stripped him of control over subsistence around January 27, 1864, despite Lincoln's belief in his "integrity and capacity." This time the president did not intervene. The army now purchased rations through competitive bidding. About two dozen Chicago suppliers submitted bids of more than $100,000 to supply subsistence to the army and prison camps. "Chicago beef and Chicago pork have an excellent reputation among soldiers," the *Tribune* boasted, "and Government has come to appreciate this fact, and to govern itself accordingly." The problem persisted, however. The army charged a new contractor named A. P. & D. Kelly with furnishing inferior beef to the garrison and prisoners at Camp Douglas and ordered Capt. E. R. P. Shurly to investigate.[41]

Orme found that the loss in defective beef amounted to $1,416.89. Federal troops had received the same low-quality meat. Three different size loaves caused confusion about the bread ration. Orme lamely concluded that no intentional shortage had occurred and claimed that the bread was of good quality. He soon changed his mind and ordered an investigation into the inferior quality of the bread supplied by O. Kendall & Sons.[42]

Kendall operated the bakery in Garrison Square with prison labor. Sergeant Cliett described how "sixteen prisoners baked twelve thousand loaves of bread per day." He wrote his memoirs 34 years after the war, but was referring to the time of Orme's investigation.[43] Bakery workers took large quantities of bread to sell in Prisoner's Square, according to Cliett, hiding up to 160 loaves per day under their clothing.

Burke confirmed that prisoners sold the bread for 25¢ to 50¢ in Federal money or sutler's checks, more than five times the price in Chicago. One of Morgan's men wrote at this time, "My Dear Dad: Please send at once $100 or a coffin." The censor sent it back endorsed, "Do you think we are all damn fools up here?" Guards soon caught the prison bakers, according to Cliett, when the bakers overloaded their clothing one day. Then, rumors about the ration scandals finally surfaced. The *Tribune* claimed defensively that "the rations daily distributed are the same as those given to our soldiers, notwithstanding the reports to the contrary."[44]

Orme decided that pork and bacon were not deficient and that contractors had watered down beans with peas, but at no profit to them. Rice and hominy were good, and it was no surprise that ground coffee at ten cents per pound was terrible. Green coffee was good, except that no one knew about it. The prisoners were not great tea drinkers, so not much was drawn. However, contractors had cheated them on soap, pepper, and molasses. Vinegar, candles, salt, and potatoes were not deficient.

Orme discovered that contractors paid far below contact price when repurchasing prison rations, thus reaping additional profits. Orme saw no violation here, since the camp did not require contractors to buy back any rations. Orme considered only the legal, not the ethical aspects. He ignored the fact that additional profit to the contractors represented less money for the prison fund and an additional burden on the taxpayers. Surprisingly, hospital rations were in full compliance with contracts.[45]

Captain Arvin Whelan, post surgeon, reported to Orme that the ration in the prison hospital was the same as that for the post hospital, consisting of "bacon, beans, fresh beef, soft bread, potatoes, rice, tea, coffee, sugar, &c." The hospital fund purchased butter, eggs, vegetables of all kinds, chicken, oysters, fresh fish, and several varieties of fruit. Smallpox patients, though, did not see much of it.[46] While the prison hospital drew underwear, shirts, socks, and bed linen, none of this reached the "pest house." Most likely, inspectors considered these patients dead men.

Hoffman omitted Ninian Edwards's responsibility for the ration shortages and beef fraud when he set the matter before Secretary of War Stanton in February 1864. Hoffman recommended that the contractors make good on all deficiencies, including the beef. He placed blame not on Edwards but on Colonel De Land and recommended that he be court-martialed for "failure to see that his command received the rations which they were entitled to under the contract."[47]

Hoffman had again surrendered to political pressure and personal ambition after telling General Orme that the contractors had to be held responsible. Edwards was Mrs. Lincoln's brother-in-law and the president's lifelong friend. No one now expected Lincoln to lose the next election or be assassinated. Stanton's eyes were fixed on a Supreme Court nomination, and Hoffman saw a general's star in his future. Both dreams came true. De Land had fallen into their hands with his heaven-sent letter absolving Edwards of any wrongdoing.

Colonel De Land was the third commandant whose reputation was "sullied" at Camp Douglas. However, the contractors thought it unfair to be fined $1,416.89, so they hired Orville Hickman Browning to get the debt canceled. Browning went to Colonel Hoffman's Washington office to see him about the matter on February 13, 1864, but did not find him in. He returned on February 19 and missed him again. Browning's chance of success was excellent, however, as he was urging Lincoln to name Hoffman's boss as chief justice of the Supreme Court.[48]

CHAPTER 12

The Fall and Rise of a Commandant

The agony of Charles V. De Land—General Orme loses command of garrison—Prisoners forced to work—New stockade and ground patrols—Modern prison hospital opens—General Orme resigns—Command assigned to Colonel Benjamin J. Sweet.

Orme finally had time to consider another pressing matter. The indomitable Mrs. Finley was back. The Post Council of Administration appointed her sutler to the prisoners, and her prices were quite high. It is likely that she had a powerful political sponsor. Not satisfied, she stole business from Benjamin Nightingale, the garrison's sutler. Major Lewis C. Skinner complained to Orme on February 25, 1864, that he could not tax Nightingale while Finley "is trespassing upon his rights." Orme closed her store for good on February 22, Washington's birthday.[1]

Prisoners honored Washington's memory, but the Yanks did not seem to care about him, Burke noted with surprise. Meanwhile, major improvements in Prisoner's Square continued rapidly. On February 27, workers laid new floors in all the barracks, which were raised five feet on thick timber legs.[2] Regardless, they were still old barracks from White Oak Square.

Another serious blaze in Garrison Square on February 29 showed the need for fire equipment to protect Prisoner's Square. It destroyed a sutler's store and two hundred yards of barracks and kitchens. The Chicago Fire Department probably had a fire station nearby, because "two steam fire engines and two hand engines were soon on hand," Burke reported.[3]

De Land did not have a chance to remedy the fire hazards because he finally left Camp Douglas. He was the longest serving garrison commander by the end of February 1864 but could not remain after Hoffman's charges in the meat scandal.

His previous experience had not equipped the former journalist and farmer to handle the Camp Douglas assignment. He was not a jailer, after all, and the job required expertise. However, he did much better in supervising improvements. He took command under desolate conditions, when the camp was not prepared to receive prisoners, but completion of the sewer and water system and repair of barracks went rapidly. De Land built the first real stockade, and he cleared out unauthorized and unsanitary sutlers. However, he made the barracks unfit for use by removing the floors. Persistent escapes frustrated his management efforts and led to serious cruelty and retaliation on his part.

On the other hand, he tried to release youngsters and told General Ammen in 1863 that anxious parents in the South were willing to post bonds for them. The prison held about 50 youths, ranging from ages 14 to 17. The plight of 16-year-old James Simmonds particularly moved De Land. "The boy is a slender youth, enticed into the Confederate army as a substitute for his uncle, who has since swindled him and his mother," he wrote Hoffman.[4] Nothing was ever done about these teenagers.

Hoffman's plan to court-martial De Land came to nothing. The army did not put him on trial for the same reason it did not prosecute Colonel Mulligan. Fighting officers were a priority for the showdown in Virginia. De Land and his regiment, numbering 785 men, minus about 20 deserters, left for the front on March 11, 1864. They fought in the Wilderness campaign and at Spotsylvania Court House in May, and De Land suffered two wounds.[5] Captain Levant Rhines, who had supported the prisoners in the beef scandal, assumed command of the Sharpshooters.

Rhines, now a major, was killed at Petersburg, Virginia, on June 17, 1864.[6] De Land returned to duty on July 15 only partially recovered. He suffered a third wound at the Battle of the Crater on July 30. De Land again returned to the fighting not fully healed and went down with his fourth wound on September 30, 1864. This time he was left to die on the field but fell into the hands of the Confederates and survived. The former commandant who had hanged prisoners by the thumbs was in enemy hands. However, the Southerners did not retaliate, probably because of his wounds, and they exchanged him in February 1865. His war was over, with a promotion to brigadier general. He joined Colonel Mulligan as a Camp Douglas commander who had won his star on the battlefield. He would not be the last.

Meanwhile General Orme became despondent and thought of resigning his post and returning to the war. His good friend, Federal Supreme Court justice David Davis, was aware of Orme's poor health and wrote on February 19, 1864, trying to dissuade him.[7] Regardless, Orme was being eased out of command.

The War Department bypassed him in appointing Col. James C. Strong, commanding the 15th regiment of the Invalid Corps, to replace De Land. Orme notified Colonel Hoffman that "on the 1st of March a new set of officers were placed in charge of the prisoners." Strong had only 526 men in Sweet's Eighth Invalid Regiment and 450 of his own, although four companies of the 11th Invalid Regiment were scheduled to arrive soon.[8] About one-third were too sick or disabled to go on duty, so the garrison had barely 650 men to contain almost six thousand prisoners. This situation substantially weakened Orme's security.

Colonel Strong was a native of New York state and served in New York regiments until devastated by wounds in 1862. His injuries were featured in *The Medical and Surgical History of the War of the Rebellion.* Many people mistook him for General Grant.[9] Strong preferred to live in Chicago despite Hoffman's orders to take up residence at Camp Douglas. However, he displayed a relentless determination to make the prison efficient.

This terribly wounded man did not hesitate to make enemies and complained to the army about the poor condition of his weapons. He claimed that few pieces in his command were in firing condition and ended by demanding that Capt. Franklin A. Perdue in Cincinnati "be severely punished for sending me worthless trash!"[10] No Camp Douglas officer had ever sent such a letter.

Strong prepared new prison rolls without regard to the old records. He showed that 84 prisoners were unaccounted for. Orme reported that "the discrepancy is not as large as I anticipated." Hoffman had his own ideas about that issue. Orme remained in command of the district and the post, but Colonel Strong was the boss over the garrison, not a happy situation. Surprisingly, Ninian W. Edwards appeared at the gates of Camp Douglas. He had again been demoted, this time to food commissary and treasurer of the prison fund.[11] President Lincoln did not intervene.

Colonel Strong kept up his pressure, and prisoners received new orders from his officers, according to Burke.

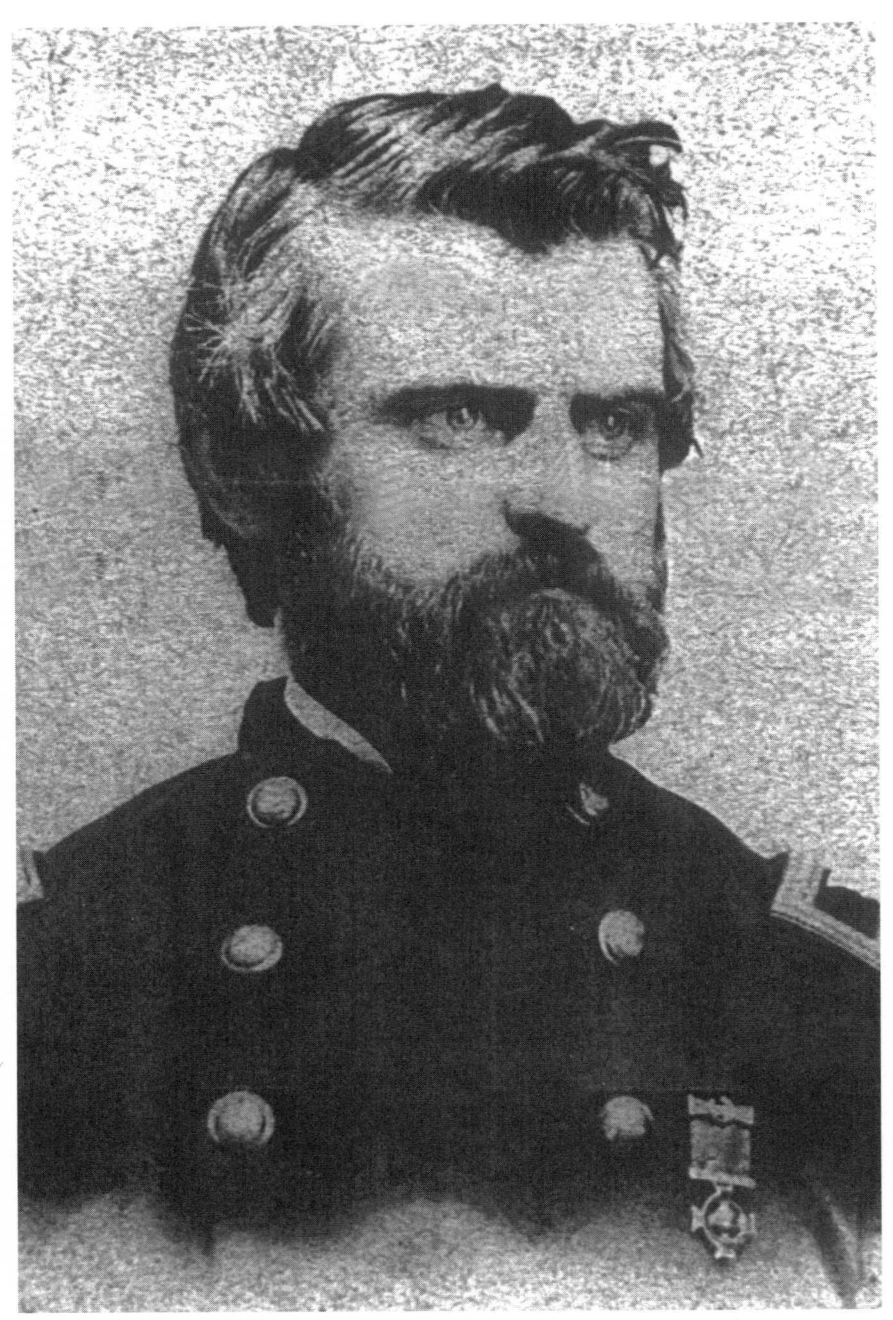

Colonel James C. Strong. (Image courtesy of the USAMHI.)

1. To rise at sound of bugle at sunrise.
2. Roll call one hour later.
3. Dismissal and breakfast.
4. Work detail from 8 a.m. to noon.
5. Dinner at 12:30.
6. Work detail at from 1 p.m. to 5 o'clock.
7. Supper at 5:30.
8. Lights out at 7 o'clock.[12]

Strong was the first garrison commander to exploit forced labor, and he searched the barracks ruthlessly to conscript prisoners for work details. "Our Yankee sergeant brought six spades, one rake and two wheelbarrows and called for a detail of nine men to dig a ditch in front of the barracks," Burke said resentfully.[13] Sergeants called men out in alphabetical order when no one responded voluntarily. The first detail worked until 1 P.M., and then another detail was conscripted until 5 P.M. It was not exactly a slave labor camp. Burke and John Curd dug 150 feet of ditch under the close eye of the sergeant. Both men were exhausted, sore, and angry after such abuse.

This was far different from the days when prisoners were free to quit helping move barracks to Prisoner's Square. However, some prisoners wanted to work when the improvements benefitted them. Medical Inspector Clark reported as early as October 9, 1863, "Duties in camp—none required of the prisoners; many volunteer to work."[14]

Many prisoners probably felt that the war was over for them, and that they had to stay busy to avoid the demoralizing effect of prison life. Burke's mess stole a barrel of coal from infantry prisoners on February 16, not thinking or caring about what this theft meant. They were supposed to be on the same side. The small garrison was unable to enforce the law and protect prisoners from each other. About 166 men, amounting to 10 percent of the guard force, were ill on March 1, 1864. This emergency caused Colonel Strong to bar civilian workers from leaving camp "until all Prison workers had returned to their squares."[15] He was referring to Prisoner's Square and White Oak Square, where some prisoners remained.

Stanton eased conditions because of the weak security. Prisoners could make purchases from a small room, not a sutler store, during the day, but only authorized items such as: tobacco, cigars, pipes, snuff, steel pens, paper, envelopes, lead pencils, pen knives, postage stamps, buttons, tape, thread, sewing cotton, pins and needles, handkerchiefs, suspenders, socks and underclothes, caps, shoes, towels, looking glasses, brushes, combs, clothes brooms, pocket knives, and scissors.

Groceries consisted of crushed sugar, syrup, family soap, butter, lard, smoked beef tongues, bologna sausage, cornmeal, nutmeg, pepper, mustard, table salt, crackers, cheese, pickles, sauces, meats and fish in cans, vegetables, dried fruits, lemons, nuts, apples, matches, and yeast powders. Table furniture items available were crockery, glassware, and tinware.[16]

Stanton had, in effect, put sutlers back in business, and they stayed open from sunrise to sunset. The vegetables necessary to prevent scurvy were most important. Many prisoners sold their rations to obtain articles from the store. Burke's mess was not concerned when it ran short. "We buy from the infantry prisoners at the rates of ten cents per pound for sugar and from five to seven cents per pound for fat meat," said Burke with a trace of guilt. "The infantry from the extreme south need a little cash to buy things they cannot draw so they save up part of their rations and sell them," he rationalized.[17]

Stanton lifted the ban on packages from friends on March 11, although "excess clothing" was forbidden. He issued an unprecedented order on March 17, 1864, to form a board of inquiry when a prisoner was shot. "Rigid discipline must be preserved," he ordained, "but great care must be observed that no wanton excesses or cruelties are committed under the plea of enforcing orders."[18] Officials at Camp Douglas did not take him seriously.

The following day, March 18, 1864, was one of great satisfaction to the Invalid Corps as they were renamed the Veteran Reserve Corps. Everyone promptly labeled them the "VRC."

Conditions continued to improve with a curious contraption for washing clothes. It was a boiler with six feet of pipe attached to it, and "looked like locomotives on a small scale at a distance," Burke thought.[19] Each barracks had two, fired by wood or coal.

However, conditions for the guards were not that good. Colonel Strong found his 15th VRC quartered in old barracks without floors in White Oak Square. He complained to General Orme that they were damp, poorly ventilated, and with terrible odors from decayed animal and vegetable matter. His men were living atop a garbage dump while he resided comfortably in Chicago.[20]

Regardless, he was in camp every day, busy changing the cooking and roll call procedures. Each prison mess now had three permanent cooks. The Rebel sergeant-majors had to account for missing men at roll call, and prisoners could not leave ranks until the morning rolls were completed. They stood in line for more than three hours once because one man was missing.[21]

Some Confederate sergeants petitioned Major Skinner to change the rules so that this did not happen in bad weather. Skinner never answered grievances. Perhaps his crippling wound at age 25 made him ill mannered and bad tempered. However, keeping the prisoners in ranks was Orme's idea.

An ingenious escape plot almost succeeded in March 1864, because Orme's new Prisoner's Square could not yet hold all of the prisoners. Some who still lived in White Oak started a tunnel through the large brick and iron stove in their kitchen. They built a cunning trap door to protect the hole while the stove was in use. An officer uncovered it one day, much to the "astonishment of the rebs." The prisoners suspected treachery, but they were wrong. Reverend Tuttle wrote that Capt. Wells Sponable discovered the hole after spotting a prisoner running to the kitchen at one o'clock in the morning.[22]

Orme reported on March 22, 1864, that the fence separating the new square from the rest of the camp was complete. Camp Douglas began to look like a maximum security prison, but it was not, and would never be one without locked cell blocks. The patrol had grown to 1 captain, 1 lieutenant, 10 sergeants, 20 corporals, and 38 privates. Orme barred prisoners from leaving the square without permission, but giving orders at Camp Douglas was much easier than having them obeyed. He was greatly disturbed to find that prisoners strolled out of both squares to go to the pharmacy and the "Picture Gallery."[23]

This laxness contributed to 32 escapes between January 1 and the end of March 1864 when 5,462 Confederates were present. Strong had only 550 men available for guard duty during this period. Orme's defective design of Prisoner's Square encouraged prisoners to tunnel out. He realized this fact and had the buildings moved toward the center of the square. They were arranged on parallel streets, sitting on five-foot posts with double flooring, and were 90 feet in length. This was only the first of many redesigns. Hoffman also delivered tents with the consequent rumor that prisoners lived in them. That never happened.[24]

Colonel Strong was angered when his superiors sent two more

guard companies away on detached duty. He complained to VRC headquarters in Louisville, Kentucky, about "the demoralizing effect of scattering a regiment." Therefore, he requested that the commandant send him his 18-piece band for guard duty. "Bands are liable to entirely forget their obligations as soldiers," Strong warned. He knew how to whip pampered musicians into shape. Louisville did not respond, and the band played on.[25]

This loss of manpower made Orme more serious about resigning and returning to the war. He now viewed the Vicksburg campaign of 1863 with nostalgia. Justice Davis sent a frantic letter on March 29 warning, "You must not go into the field anywhere! If you desire to remain in the army, remain in Chicago!" The jurist also informed his friend that he had seen Stanton to insure that he approved Luman Burr, Orme's choice to be the new sutler.[26] Such personal influence by a Supreme Court justice would cause an uproar today. Burr and his wife were old friends of the Orme family.

Burr's prices were "very high" when he issued his first checks. He needed to recover losses suffered when prisoners looted the store before he opened. Headquarters no longer issued sutler's checks, which were now his responsibility. He printed them "on thin paper, steel engraved, and thus harder to counterfeit," the men observed.[27]

Along with Burr's new store, a new 225-bed prison hospital was finally completed around April 10, 1864, between White Oak Square and Prisoner's Square. It cost the prison fund $10,000, an exorbitant price.[28] Its exact nature is difficult to learn because of varying descriptions.

Inspectors first described it as a two-story building with two wings, each containing four wards and 180 beds.[29] It had a mess room, kitchen, and adjoining two-story laundry. A furnace heated the water for laundry, bathing, and boiling clothes. Each ward contained a running water toilet connected to the main sewer, and the entire place was whitewashed. "State of Art" would be too mild a term to describe it. Regardless, the cost of the hospital was at least double what it should have been. Economy was not the watchword, and Chicago contractors took full advantage.

Colonel Hoffman almost had a stroke when he learned of the laundry and the flush toilets. First, the three-hundred-dollar price tag for each for the two laundry boilers was outrageous. "The sixty gallon farmer's boilers cost I think about thirty-five dollars each," he groaned. Worse, the toilets at six hundred dollars each were far too costly. Hoffman wanted them "arranged as they are in the city with removable boxes to be emptied by the prisoners." He conceded that the resulting disagreeable odor would require lime.[30] It was too late, unless he wanted to rip out the plumbing.

Hoffman's reference to the city related to a general hospital the army had recently built three miles northwest of Camp Douglas, near downtown. It treated sick and wounded Union soldiers from all sections of the army and included an eye clinic. Apparently, this hospital had the old-fashioned dry toilets.

However, the new prison hospital was too small, probably because of a lack of space. It was squeezed into the area between Garrison Square, White Oak, and the new Prisoner's Square. Five hundred more beds would be needed as the prison population doubled. Two old buildings were added, amounting to only 70 more beds. A converted cavalry stable outside camp and just west of the university still served as the smallpox hospital.

Camp commanders had a continuous problem in finding a site for the "pest house," because no one wanted it in his back yard. Orme instructed Capt. Charles Goodman on March 28, 1864, to move it from the west side of the university to a site called "Adele Grove, one-half mile south of Camp Douglas." This placed it on the south side of the university, facing Cottage Grove. Adele was Senator Douglas's widow, so the hospital undoubtedly remained on the Douglas estate rent free. While the new location may have made Camp Douglas breathe easily, it did nothing to help the university. It contained two wards and began operating by April 15, 1864. Burke estimated it to be four hundred yards south of camp. An inspector reported that it was only two hundred yards away. Burke, as usual, was more accurate.[31]

While medical facilities for prisoners were growing, so was the oppression. Colonel Strong gave more authority to the patrols in Prisoner's Square, and a sergeant, two corporals, and five privates controlled each barrack. One of them, named "Old Red," was reputed to be vindictive and dangerous.[32] They now guarded the prisoners at roll call, prepared work details, and saw to it that guards delivered fuel and rations to the barracks—besides patrolling the square at night.

Prisoner's Square changed dramatically when Orme attached many bright oil-burning reflector lamps to the fence. They were "so close together and the light so brilliant that it would be almost

A prisoner wearing his time piece at Camp Douglas. (Image courtesy of the Illinois State Historical Society.)

impossible to get to the fence without being discovered by the guards on the parapet," Burke reported. Workers soon installed bright reflector lamps at the end of each street. The "deadline" was a low railing about 18 inches high and 10 feet from the fence. Guards patrolled this area, besides their posts on the platform.

Discipline of prisoners grew more rigid under Colonel Strong. On April 10, 1864, the patrols made some prisoners stand on barrels for purchasing whiskey from a guard. Another punishment was to make violators wear a box or barrel with a placard attached: "For disobeying orders," "For washing in barracks," "Lousy," "For meddling with other people's business," "For going to the other square."[33] No reports of hanging prisoners by the thumbs have been found for this time, but punishment almost as severe was on the way.

A new dungeon of heavy timbers arose inside the gate to Prisoner's Square. It measured about eight feet square and seven feet high, with a door in front and two diamond-shaped windows or air holes on two sides. Previously, White Oak was the only dungeon. Prisoners called it the "Four of Diamonds." Guards named it the "Monitor." Three men spent a night there for climbing on a roof to watch horse racing.[34]

Ball and chain also saw extensive use. A cannon ball, weighing 32 pounds or more, with four or five feet of chain, was attached to a lock going around the ankle. Prisoners carried this contraption by leather straps and called it their "time piece." Camp officials punished several prisoners this way after they applied to take the oath and changed their minds. Even sick prisoners wore the time piece. One prisoner with the unlucky name, John Shackelford, returned from the smallpox hospital still in ball and chain. "On his way in, the 64 lb rolled out of the old ambulance nearly jerking his leg off before the ambulance could be stopped," Burke said in amazement. "At night he suffered a great deal with his leg."[35]

Inspectors paid no attention to such cruelty, but on April 16, 1864, a mere lieutenant colonel from the inspector general's office "sullied" General Orme's reputation for other reasons. "General Orme gives very little attention to his command at Camp Douglas," said Inspector John F. Marsh.[36] Orme apparently did not like Colonel Strong. "There is a want of courtesy on the part of the commanding officer toward the commander of the garrison," Marsh noted. Lax control of the sutlers shocked him. This was Orme's fault, and believable, with his friend Burr as sutler to the prisoners. The camp also had one for the Eighth, 11th, and 15th VRC. Only the 15th's had a price list. "Sales restricted to articles authorized by law," Marsh naively reported.

He noticed that a private contractor came around to collect garbage and grease from the kitchens and paid prisoners with tobacco to carry it to his wagon. Barracks were in poor condition, again, with floors ripped up, bunks filthy, bedding not aired, and grounds wet and in poor police. "Colonel Strong and Major Skinner would be valuable officers serving under an efficient commander," Marsh said insultingly.

Reverend Tuttle believed that he could keep a lid on the camp by distributing religious newspapers to the 5,435 prisoners. Not all were appreciative. "Some of the reading we respect, but most of it, the abolition articles we read with the utmost contempt," Burke sneered.[37]

General Grant weighed in on April 17, 1864, with bad news for all prison camps, North and South. He canceled negotiations for exchange of prisoners unless they included black Union soldiers in Confederate hands. This was Stanton's policy, not Grant's, and probably came down from President Lincoln. Prisoners at Camp Douglas read about it in the papers but were "still more confident of the success of our cause," as April came to a close. However, about 1,500 of the six thousand prisoners applied to take the oath of allegiance, which they called "swallowing the dog." Some prisoners threatened defectors, and Hoffman ordered severe punishment for any prisoner "who threatens or insults them in any way for expressing a desire to return to their allegiance."[38]

The dying General Orme made a fateful move when Grant canceled exchange talks. Without authority, he fired Colonel Strong on April 27, 1864, and replaced him with Colonel Benjamin J. Sweet. Only two days later, someone, possibly Inspector Marsh, told Orme to correct the problems at camp, and he abruptly resigned on April 29, 1864. Camp Douglas had now sullied the reputations of five commanders, Mulligan, Tyler, Ammen, De Land, and Orme.[39]

The War Department assigned the powerful district and post to Colonel Sweet on May 2, 1864, without comment. Sweet was the only one who ever sought the job. Did two days make a difference in killing one career and launching another? Probably not. The War Department knew that the valiant Strong was too crippled and in too much pain to bear the responsibilities of the Post of Chicago and Camp Douglas. Colonel Strong was deeply disappointed, but the job probably would have gone to Sweet without Orme. The War Department heard nothing from Colonel Hoffman regarding Sweet and, as usual, he had no say in the matter.

Orme's main contributions to Camp Douglas was Prisoner's Square and the system of ground patrols. Some may argue that causing the release of black prisoners was the benchmark of his administration. Exoneration of the contractors in the beef scandal and disregarding Ninian Edwards's responsibility were ethical failures. His postwar career in law and politics lay in Illinois, and he acted accordingly. General Daniel Tyler would have acted differently.

Colonel Sweet was in an ideal position compared with past commanders. He had been at camp for seven months and had gone to school on the problems faced by De Land, Orme, and Strong. Unlike De Land, he did not get hit with a flood of prisoners before he could bite off the end of his cigar. Neither did he have to spend his energy on a ration scandal. He knew what needed to be done and had experienced officers in place to carry out his plans. The former Wisconsin lawmaker saw his opportunity and made the most of it. Meanwhile, a once bright star was going out. General Orme had but two years and three months to live.

Colonel Benjamin J. Sweet. (Image courtesy of the USAMHI.)

CHAPTER 13

The Beat of a Different Drummer

Colonel Sweet reduces rations—Fatal stabbing—Prisoner's Square rearranged—Weapons used by the garrison—Garbage eaten—The wooden mule—Sutler's prices—Prisoners eat a dog—Problems with religion.

Benjamin J. Sweet was born in New York state in 1832, but his parents moved to Wisconsin around 1848. Sweet was a lawyer and member of the Wisconsin senate when the war started. He volunteered early, although he had a wife and four children. Right off the bat, he tried to undermine his commanding officer in the Sixth Wisconsin Infantry, and that attempt landed him back home. There he recruited the 21st Wisconsin Infantry and was assigned to the Army of the Ohio. Colonel Sweet suffered a wound in the right arm when his regiment saw action for the first time at the Battle of Perryville, Kentucky, on October 8, 1862.

His 21st Wisconsin poured "a withering fire" into the ranks of a much larger Rebel force, according to official reports. It appeared that Sweet played an important role in starting the Confederacy down the road to defeat long before Gettysburg. However, some now have doubts about his wound and the behavior of his regiment. For example, Sweet told the unlikely story that two of his men, neither one a doctor, dressed his shattered elbow and tended a wound in his chest.[1]

Disbelievers today also question the "crippled" right arm, but he qualified for the Invalid Corps and became colonel of the Eighth Regiment. The army assigned him to Camp Douglas around September 26, 1863.[2]

Sweet moved his headquarters downtown after taking command of the post from General Orme, but he wisely left Colonel Strong in charge of the garrison. He strained relations with Hoffman by refusing to live at camp. This was puzzling in view of his ambitions. The reason must have been his young daughter, Ada, who was with him. She had just passed her 12th birthday.[3]

"About this time Colonel DeLand is ordered to the front," T. D. Henry remembered. "He was succeeded by Colonel B. J. Sweet as commandant, Colonel Skinner as commissary of prisoners, and a fiend named Captain Webb [Wells] Sponable as inspector of prisoners. From this time forward the darkest leaf in the legends of all tyranny could not possibly contain a greater number of punishments."[4] Skinner was responsible for rations, while Sponable managed the patrols.

Sponable's patrol force had increased, with 2 lieutenants, 10 sergeants, 20 corporals, and 38 privates.[5] These interior police did not have to account for their actions and continued to regulate rations, cooking arrangements, and work details. A squad of one corporal and four privates patrolled Prisoner's Square around the clock.

The patrols benefitted prisoners by enforcing the law. It was the captor's duty to insist on discipline and protect the men from each other. Lawless bands of Union soldiers called "The Raiders" roamed the stockade at Andersonville, and robbers invaded the hospital tents. It became so bad that an inmate remarked, "Our own men are worse to each other than the rebels are to us."[6]

Officers arrested one guard at Camp Douglas for robbing a prisoner and sent a Confederate to the new dungeon "for selling several suits of clothes that were sent to other persons in his care." Patrols protected sutler's checks against thieves and impostors.[7] The patrol badly beat a prisoner named Joseph McCarney for stabbing two brothers in a fight on May 12, 1864. He ended up in ball and chains in the new dungeon, Burke reported. One brother, who later died, took the blame and asked authorities to release McCarney. Nevertheless, he remained in the dungeon.

Guards received similar treatment. Captain Shurly ordered a man in Company D, Eighth VRC, confined to White Oak dungeon "on bread and water" for ten days with ball and chains.[8] The offender was drunk two days in a row and was "an habitual shirk, at most," Shurly charged.

Nonetheless, Sweet gave the garrison a good deal of power. He intended to become independent of Hoffman and eliminated hominy and candles from the ration.[9] Prisoners used candles for tunneling out, he believed. However, they needed candles during the long gloomy winters. Reading and social activities became impossible without any light after the short winter days; nor did Sweet consider that the sick in barracks needed care at night.

However, Hoffman finally had a commandant who seemed to think similarly as himself. Major Skinner wished to eliminate tea, and Ninian Edwards urged Sweet to take away rice and vinegar, as well. Worse, the commissary substituted meal for flour and fed prisoners pickled pork instead of beef three times in the last ten days of April.[10]

Union prisoners at Andersonville received "one pound of beef, or one-third pound of bacon, one and one-fourth pounds of meal, with an occasional issue of beans, rice, molasses, and vinegar." How long it had to last or the number of men it fed is unknown. Of course, they also lacked cooking utensils and shelter in that bleak Georgia location. The toll was 1,026 dead in the ten weeks after it opened on February 27, 1864.[11]

Colonel Sweet was less interested in providing comfort than expanding on the experience of General Orme. He placed the increasing number of barracks along parallel streets in Prisoner's Square. This was done with forced labor, and guards constantly searched barracks for men. Obtaining water for thirsty workers was difficult due to the three-inch pipes.[12]

Meanwhile a court-martial had been sitting to decide the unusual case of Dr. Lee, who had allegedly aided prisoners to escape. Why had he traded in his bright blue uniform and a guaranteed hundred dollars per month to cast his lot with the prisoners? Was it out of pity, as he claimed? These questions went unanswered, and his court-martial concluded on May 9, 1864, with a finding of guilty. The board sentenced him to the prisoner of war camp at Fort Delaware. Mulligan had only drummed Lt. Patrick Higgins out of the army for operating an escape ring in 1862.[13]

Sweet wanted to insure that prisoners had no ready cash to bribe doctors or guards and continued the daily search for contraband. The men usually succeeded in hiding their money, however. Guards searched Pa, once, although out of respect for his rank he did not have to take off his boots, where his money was hidden.

Prisoners were less worried about searches than rumors that the sutler was closing. They were warned on May 19, 1864, to spend their checks. Burke was unconcerned because he knew that the sutler store would reopen. "Some of Colonel Sweet's friends are expected to succeed the present sutler, Mr. Luman Burr," he predicted. Two weeks later Sweet ousted Burr and substituted Benjamin Nightingale. One prisoner claimed that Nightingale was Sweet's brother-in-law.[14]

He was probably correct, since prisoners knew everything that was happening. Gossip and loose talk ran through a pipeline from the front office to Prisoner's Square.

Sweet also established a new system of banking for the prisoners' money without Hoffman's permission. The clerk who kept prisoners' accounts went to Prisoner's Square each day with his account books, order forms, and a checkbook. He filled out the form upon request and issued a check to the prisoner according to his order. Sweet intended to benefit the sutler by giving prisoners easier access to their funds.[15] Hoffman saw the danger of bribing guards with these checks and canceled the system.

Sweet took an unprecedented step in trying to verify the number of prisoners. He counted them all at once in a giant roll call on May 24. The men were dressed in their best clothing because they expected searches while they were out, and "excess clothing" was confiscated. Lines of prisoners filled the square in proud military formation. For a moment the 5,277 men were soldiers again. They could have added five regiments to the Confederate army. Sweet had created a situation where they could attack the fence with overwhelming power, but they lacked leadership. Sweet required reinforcements badly, and the army gave him only one company of the Seventh VRC on May 30.[16]

Burke described the ration at this time, designed for eight men and to last ten days: "Meal 24 cups, pickle-pork 22 lbs, hominy 4 qts, fresh beef 18 lbs, light bread 24 loaves, parched coffee 4 pts, molasses 3 pts, sugar 5 qts, potatoes 1 peck. No soap, flour, candles, pepper, peas, beans, or vinegar was issued this time. Our beef and bread is not all issued at once, but we draw them in three different drawings during the ten days, so that we get them tolerable fresh."

Fresh beef amounted to only two and one-fourth ounces per man. The potato ration was about four ounces per day for the ten days, not enough to prevent scurvy. The meal and bread came to only one-third of a cup of meal and one-third of a loaf of bread daily. The loss of peas, beans, and flour made charges of starvation understandable. Men had to go hungry if a mess ran out of food, unless they had money to buy provisions at the sutler or from other prisoners.

Besides food and sanitation problems, the top soil became so eroded that the garrison was wearing "green goggles" against blowing sand and dust. Prisoners almost had to close their eyes to move about. Similar to Willie Barrow, Burke declared this part of the country unfit to live in. He also was concerned about the Confederate dollar. Gold stood at $1.9125 per ounce, and Southern currency was rapidly becoming worthless. On May 27, Sweet ordered Captain Goodman to improve Prisoner's Square with two more sinks for the sewer system and more than six thousand feet of pine board to repair barracks.[17]

Sweet completed another rearrangement of Prisoner's Square on June 1, with streets 50 feet wide and four barracks on a street. This arrangement moved them away from the fence and prevented tunneling. Thirty-two barracks sat on blocks, and prisoners whitewashed them inside and out. They measured 90 feet long, including a 20-foot add-on kitchen, and could house 165 men with two to a bunk.[18]

Prisoners realized that the new arrangement made tunneling difficult, and they attacked the fence on the night of June 1, 1864. The assault was well coordinated, with some prisoners smashing the lamps, and others rocking the fence so that guards on the platform had difficulty firing. Another group went at the boards with axes. Only one guard rifle discharged, but patrols on the ground ended the assault with revolvers. Miraculously, no injuries occurred. Colonel Sweet complained to Hoffman that the rifles had been condemned months before, and the prisoners knew it.[19]

A February 1864 report showed that the rifles were "an old and probably condemned lot of arms, unserviceable and positively dangerous to the men using them." Only one company of the Eighth VRC had new Springfield rifles. The guards had five hundred revolvers besides rifles, but these were also from a condemned lot. Prison security did not have high priority in Washington. Bullets did find their mark from time to time, however. One escapee disguised in a shawl was found dead from revolver shots.[20]

Despite the unrest in Prisoner's Square, officials soon added Nightingale's sutler store, an express office, D. F. Brandon's photo studio, and a pharmacy. Sweet was proud of the improvements and argued for the erection of 39 more barracks, "which would give a capacity to hold 11,880 prisoners, or would accommodate, by placing a few more men in each barrack, in round numbers, 12,000 men," he told Hoffman.

"A few more men" meant overcrowding, but Washington accepted Sweet's estimate, and the camp expanded just as he said. The cost, including kitchens, amounted to $19,600. Colonel Sweet

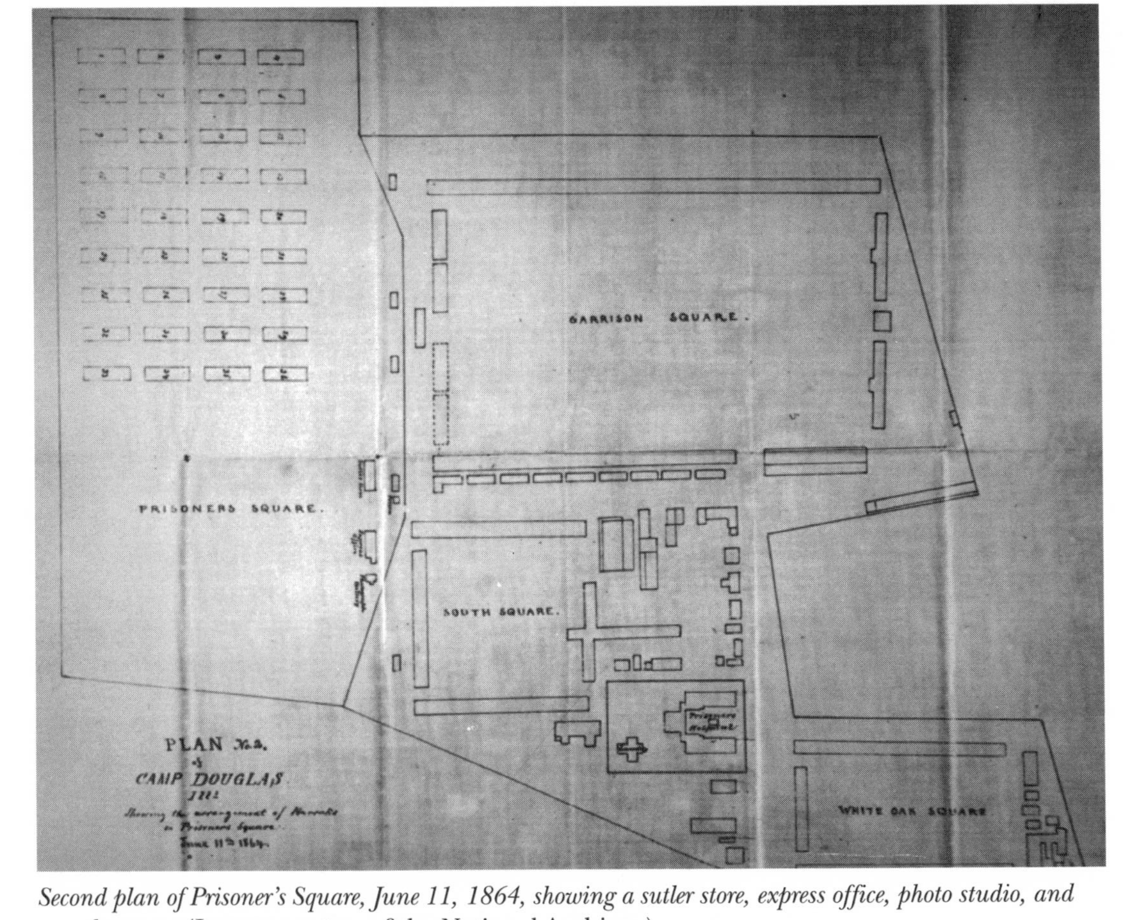

Second plan of Prisoner's Square, June 11, 1864, showing a sutler store, express office, photo studio, and new dungeon. (Image courtesy of the National Archives.)

knew that his boss would not agree to use the prison fund, and he gave Hoffman a subtle warning. Authority for expanding the square could be found in a War Department letter of April 29, 1864, he wrote.[21] Precisely as Hoffman would not risk his career on volunteer officers, Sweet refused to let Hoffman stand in the way of his own future.

Sweet must have understood Hoffman well, because he promptly ordered prisoners housed in old tents. Sweet coyly replied that he had only new tents but that his men could renovate old barracks in Garrison Square and move them into Prisoner's Square, "should you desire it." He set four more barracks in place by June 11, totaling nine rows of four, and the area could hold seven more rows. Contractors submitted bids for new barracks at five hundred dollars each plus a hundred dollars for an add-on kitchen. Unaware that Sweet had set up more barracks, Hoffman ordered "worn" tents for two thousand prisoners.[22] Sweet wrote Captain Goodman to furnish two hundred tents "for use of prisoners at Camp Douglas," but no one ever lived in them. Mulligan had simply disobeyed Hoffman's orders. Sweet maneuvered around them with the swiftness and cunning of an escaping prisoner.

The War Department again reduced rations as the new square began filling. It restricted tea, sugar, and coffee to the sick and wounded and eliminated molasses. The gain went to the prison fund. It did this at General Halleck's suggestion, "to reduce the ration to that issued by the rebel Government to their own troops."[23] Oddly, Halleck could not let go of Camp Douglas, even from his position in Washington as general in chief of the army. Perhaps it was nostalgia. He saw no need for prisoners at Camp Douglas to eat better than the Confederate army. This was a matter of retaliation, not economy. General Taylor, who conspired with President Lincoln to hide the Edwards affair, agreed with Halleck.

Each prisoner was left with the following:

Meat

Pork or bacon in lieu of fresh beef . . . . 10 ounces.
Fresh beef . . . . 14 ounces.

Bread

Flour or soft bread . . . . 16 ounces.
Hard bread in lieu of flour or soft bread . . . . 14 ounces.
Corn meal in lieu of flour or bread. . . . . 16 ounces.

Vegetables

Beans or peas per 100 rations	12 1/2 lbs.
or rice or hominy per 100 rations	8 ounces.
Soap per 100 rations	4 ounces.
Potatoes per 100 rations	15 ounces.

For sick and wounded, only:

Sugar per 100 rations	12 ounces.
Coffee per 100 rations	5 lbs. ground.
or	7 lbs. green.
Tea per 100 rations	1 lb.

Even with reduced rations, Colonel Strong required that each barrack furnish a work detail of six men for the day, "two to bring water and cut wood for the kitchen, two to keep the barrack and street in front well swept, two to carry out the waste water."

Families could send food packages, including clothing and tobacco. The guard took a handful of cigars when Burke received a box at the express office. Inspectors usually snatched something for themselves. Otherwise, everything was there: a gray jacket and vest, socks, soap, crackers, marbles, and two novels for Curtis. Pa received a hat, socks, soap, thread, a pair of shoes, and part of a box of cigars. The package reached camp from Kentucky in only three days.

Burke saw John T. Shanks from his regiment working in the express office when he picked up his package. Shanks may have been a spy for Colonel Sweet. He was Sweet's agent in the Camp Douglas Conspiracy of 1864. Something was wrong about the man, because the prisoners already had his number. An incident intrigued them in which a prisoner named William Calameze struck Shanks. Neither one revealed the cause of the quarrel, which fueled more curiosity and suspicion. It was possible that Shanks forged Calameze's name for a sutler's check while working at headquarters.[24]

Most of the square was out of food, after reductions in rations by Sweet and the War Department. "It will be three or four days til we draw again," Burke guessed. By June 17 the men were living on scraps, and later they were supplied only two meals a day. "I saw one poor fellow who had lost his mind for fear of starving to death, and his cries for bread were pitiful in the extreme," R. T. Bean claimed.[25]

Guards punished anyone caught taking bones from the garbage by fastening the bone between his teeth, across his mouth, and then tying it like a gag. "And then the poor fellow was made to fall down and crawl around on his hands and knees like a dog, a laughing stock for Federal soldiers, spies, and camp followers," Bean recalled bitterly. "There is more inventive meanness in the Yankee composition, than any other nation upon God's green earth could conceive of during thousands of years!"[26]

Did the prisoners eat a dog? A small terrier owned by Lt. Joel A. Fife was often seen in Prisoner's Square. "This dog is a great favorite and pet of the prisoners," according to the story, "but one day the cooks in one of the barracks entice the dog into their kitchen, kill and dress it nicely, and cook it; then invite quite a number of other prisoners to dine with them, as they had a rare dish for dinner—they ate the dog and drank the soup."[27]

Fife posted a reward notice for the dog's return and someone wrote under it, "For lack of bread the dog is dead, For want of meat the dog was eat."

Private J. M. Berry added, "We also ate all the rats we could catch. No doubt many died after the war from disease contracted on account of these things. I have written the foregoing in no spirit of ill will, but simply to state facts. It will not be long until we shall all pass under review in a better world than this. I am now sixty-three years old and am crippled and helpless."[28]

Eating the dog may have been for revenge more than hunger. Lieutenant Fife commanded patrols who made life miserable and interviewed men who wished to take the oath. Sweet soon discovered the gourmets and stopped their rations. They scattered among the rest of the prisoners who fed them. The poet was never found.

Despite the hunger, Sweet was anxious for prisoners to look presentable to inspectors. On June 12, 1864, he issued shoes, dark blue pants, gray jackets or coats, high crowned gray hats, cotton drawers, woolen shorts, and a few socks. Burke argued that he had a right to the clothing and was scornful of those who worked for it. He and Pa received packages regularly from relatives in Ohio, and he had never been threadbare or hungry at Camp Douglas.

Sweet made sure that Prisoner's Square did not fall into disrepair, and heavy drafting of prisoners to dig ditches, level off the ground, grade streets, and repair barracks continued. Colonel De Land had never seemed able to address these problems. Burke did his best to dodge work details, and he loafed on the job at every opportunity. For him the war continued, and any cooperation with the enemy was dishonorable.

The identical appearance of barracks became a source of hilarity as the prisoners often entered the wrong one, and they soon numbered them with black paint. However, the men turned on each other more often as hope of exchange faded. Arguments and fights were common by the summer of 1864. Something as trifling as a rusty plate set off a battle.[29] Others intervened quickly, because no one wanted a repeat of the McCarney stabbing.

Continuing barrack changes caused tension over bunks. The men raced to new quarters because leaking roofs made top bunks the worst. Cold floors affected the bottom bunk, leaving the second tier as their choice. They discussed putting a stop to this "devil take the hindmost" mentality by drawing new bunks by lot. Nothing came of it.

One prisoner named Jerry Murphy refused to sleep with anyone, and the other men tolerated him, although this meant less bunk space for others. One night he came back from the sink and found someone in what he thought was his bunk. His roar of anger awakened everyone, only Jerry had wandered into the wrong barrack. The laughter could almost be heard in Chicago, as he retreated very apologetically. Miraculously, he was not shot.[30]

These conditions contrasted sharply with life just outside the camp. Burke was working on a roof detail one day and noticed a crowd at the racetrack nearby. It was the Chicago Driving Park, four blocks west of Prisoner's Square. "By war's end the Chicago Driving Park was the place to be seen in new duds, with new loves, new fortunes, followed by the busy pickpockets," a cynic observed. "Gay parasols revolved in dainty gloved hands, as bodies in whalebone corsets went by dragging the trains of whores and society wives."[31]

Some Union army veterans would not mind using artillery to end the laughter there. "The people walking about as if there was no war going on, and here I have been wasting part of the prime of life in this miserable place a prisoner, and not knowing how much longer I will be forced to remain," Burke reflected. "I could not help envying them their liberty, yet I try to be contented."

Mulligan's problem with religion returned to baffle Colonel Sweet. He consulted Colonel Hoffman when the Catholic bishop of Chicago requested permission to hold services for prisoners. Hoffman advised Sweet that Catholic clergy had the same limited rights as other clergymen to see the sick in the hospital or preach on Sunday. However, Colonel Sweet barred nuns because he did not feel that Hoffman included them. The mayor of Chicago prevailed upon him to allow the sisters to distribute food on the hospital wards, and they restored peace. Sweet sent his Camp Douglas band to serenade them occasionally because Ada was a pupil at their academy. They reciprocated with huge cakes for the Eighth VRC.[32]

A Catholic priest from nearby St. James Church visited Camp Douglas regularly and baptized more than 250 Confederates. Many names appear in the church's records today, such as: "Bartholomew Server, Rebel Prisoner, Age 22 years, 54th Va.; George F. Reynolds, Rebel Prisoner, Age 44, 3rd Miss.; John L. Chadwick, Rebel Prisoner, Age 19 years, 39th Ala."

Of those baptized, 77 soon died. This is the only Camp Douglas document that shows the prisoners' ages. They ranged from 17 to 50. One was a captain in Forrest's Mississippi Scouts who died at age 38, one week before the war ended. The ladies of Grace Church in Chicago formed the Camp Douglas Aid Society to help the sick. Out of their experience, they established St. Luke's Hospital in 1864, now part of the giant Rush-Presbyterian-St. Luke's Medical Center.[33]

The presence of nuns and other female nurses was most welcome to prisoners. Depression deepened with short rations, mostly bread and water twice a day, the third week of June 1864. The sutler sold butter at the astronomical price of "65 cents per lb. and other things in proportion," Burke complained. Forced labor made Burke stiff and sore. Every day was nearly the same to him. "Time like a sweeping billow, rolls steadily on, and nothing as yet intervenes to break the dull monotony of our prison life," he moaned.[34]

Something did intervene, when Hoffman ordered Brandon's photo studio and the privately owned express company evicted from Prisoner's Square. The grumbling was considerable, but it seemed to Hoffman that these luxuries conflicted with the policy of retaliation. Sweet allowed the photo studio to go but defied Hoffman on the express office as convenient for his administration. The sutler, like the postal service, remained untouchable. Brandon continued to enter the square and photograph prisoners anyway. Careful poses concealed their troubles from families back home. A fearsome animal had been set loose in camp.

"The Yanks have fixed a frame near the gate with a scantling across it edge up, and about four feet from the ground, which they make our men ride whenever the men do anything that does not please them," Burke reported in his journal on June 28. "It is called The mule. Men have sat on it till they fainted and fell off. It is like riding a sharp top fence." Prisoners used their hands to brace themselves and avoid damage. Regardless, no one walked away from the mule with dignity.

Adding weights made it more painful. "Sometimes the Yanks would laugh and say, I will give you a pair of spurs," which was a bucket of sand tied to each foot. Other prisoners confirmed that men rode the mule in the worst winter weather. It grew to 15 feet tall by 1865 and required a ladder to mount. Guards in White Oak Square came to know it also, only they called it the "horse." Major John Piper of the First Michigan Sharpshooters sentenced a guard named David Parkhurst to ride it two hours out of every six, day and night, for one week during the sub-zero weather.[35] Records did not state his offense, and Piper was killed in action in 1864.

Medical inspectors never mentioned the mule but worried very much that cooking was "deficient." Sweet experimented with new mess arrangements at the end of June 1864. He assigned cooks to prepare rations for an entire barracks. Cooked food was then drawn in messes of ten. This break with tradition was an early step toward central mess halls. Ironically, troops in the field continued to prepare their meals individually.

Rations were again sufficient by July 5 for two full meals without breakfast. Men ate cornbread, pork, sour hash, and beef. They had to scour cooking utensils, clear the trash, and get rid of everything not in use.[36] Colonel Strong was aiming for a thinner, meaner camp. Colonel Sweet was still living in Chicago, however.

Hoffman reported him to Secretary of War Stanton who wrote Sweet to move to Camp Douglas "in order that your personal attention may be given to the affairs at that camp." Sweet responded that he was near the telegraph, provost marshal, and quartermaster in the city. The real reason was probably his daughter, Ada. He never explained why she was not living in Wisconsin with his wife and his other three children. Regardless, Stanton's order was conclusive, and Sweet moved back to camp with Ada on July 15. It appears that he did begin stricter enforcement of sanitation.[37]

This was necessary, except the cruelty. "The Yanks make us keep the camp very clean, and are always on the alert to catch any prisoners that may break any of the rules and regulations," Burke said. T. D. Henry wrote that "if the least sign of water or spit was seen on the floor the order was, Come, go to the mule or point for grub, which was to stand with the legs perfectly straight, reach over, and touch the ground with the fingers. If the legs were bent in the least, a guard was present with a paddle which he well knew how to use."[38]

M. J. Bradley described how "another mode of punishment, was to make a man stoop forward, keeping his legs stiff, and touching his hands to the ground, remain in that position with the blood rushing to his head, and every vein in his body swelling until the protruding eyeballs became bloodshot, and almost bursting from their sockets with pain."

Prisoners got some relief from the oppression on July 4, 1864. Garrison Square was festive with speeches, fireworks, and bands playing, while the mood in Prisoner's Square was somber. Prisoners heard partying at a beer garden outside and racing at the Chicago Driving Park. The Confederates responded by singing their own version of the former National Anthem:

> "Oh say can you see, by the dawn's early light
> What so proudly we hailed at the twilight's last gleaming,
> Whose cross bars and 'leven stars thro' the perilous fight,
> O'er the breastworks we watched were so gallantly streaming,
> And the rockets' red glare, the bombs bursting in air,
> Gave proof thro' the night that our flag was still there.
> Oh say, doth that cross spangled banner yet wave
> O'er the land of the free and the home of the slave."[39]

Like Humpty Dumpty in the old nursery rhyme, putting the country back together again would not be easy. This feeling of separation and alienation was not a passing thought but lived into the next century. The rupture deepened at Camp Douglas in the months to come. Many prisoners were about to begin a second year of imprisonment, and even the most irrational rumor could not whip up the hint of a general exchange.

Meanwhile, hunger, cruelty, boredom, and disease were fast killing the smiles and the laughter. These were not the same men who had once vowed to make the Southern dream come true. Camp Douglas was stamping out their hopes that all would be well in the end. Regardless, Colonel Sweet had to struggle to keep them prisoners with his limited resources.

Colonel Strong was in a philosophic mood on that July 4, 1864. The Federals had driven the Army of Northern Virginia across the Rappahannock River for the last time on November 23, 1863. Since then, it had been all misery for the Union army as it pressed from the

Wilderness to Cold Harbor, or Coal Harbor, as the South called it. Grant had closed his campaign with another brutal, dismal loss to Lee's defending army. The winding roads cut by the bluecoats through the Wilderness and the pines of Spotsylvania Court House were paved with their own bodies.

None of this was lost on the valiant Colonel Strong. The war was over long ago for him and the Veteran Reserve Corps. So, he enlivened the holiday by comparing the stimulation of battle with the dullness of guard duty, where "the soldier walks his lonely beat merely from a sense of duty and the earnest duty to perform it." He thanked everyone for the good condition of the camp and the small number of escapes. Colonel Sweet was on leave.

One reason for fewer escapes may have been the lack of contact between Morgan's men and the infantry prisoners they called "web feet." Burke and his friends considered them inferiors. The raiders heard singing in the infantry barracks every Sunday. "I suppose they have been preaching," Burke reflected sadly. "I have never visited them to see. We have not had a sermon or even a hymn since we moved into this barrack." Morgan's men were paying a price for their false pride.

CHAPTER 14

What a Child Saw at Camp Douglas

A guard is killed—Loyalty to old regiments—Women restricted—Smallpox rages—More prisoners crowd the camp—Artillery zeros in—Prisoners denied vegetables—Some famous escapes—Weekly inspections ordered.

Guards usually did not pay for even serious offenses, until one was killed on July 17, 1864. Colonel Mulligan had allowed one officer to completely escape punishment for engineering escapes. Five of Colonel De Land's First Michigan Sharpshooters had let out 12 prisoners, and the bribe money had bought rounds of drinks in every brothel downtown. No report of punishment can be found.

How one guard came to pay the ultimate penalty on July 17, 1864, was carefully concealed. Colonel Sweet issued a vague statement that Pvt. James Kennedy, Company A, Eighth VRC, arrested for "disobedience of orders," was shot in Chicago by Pvt. John Stonebreaker of the same company and regiment while Kennedy was attempting to escape. Both men were on patrol duty in the city. A military commission found, "Private John Stonebreaker is deserving of praise for the prompt manner in which he carried out his orders."[1]

Sweet never revealed the whole story. Possibly, Kennedy refused to go on duty because patrolling Chicago was much more dangerous than guarding prisoners at Camp Douglas. Deserters from both armies and the worst criminals infested every rat hole along Wells Street. They did not hesitate to shoot it out with patrols that came looking for them, and one of the Eighth VRC was killed on Christmas night 1864 in Fitzsimmons' Saloon. These establishments made the Prairie Queen look like a Sunday school.

Kennedy's offense was probably less than others who came to Sweet's attention. He soon had to deal with a corporal in the 15th VRC who not only allowed a deserter to escape but was caught picking the pockets of a brother soldier on the streetcar.[2]

Life was quiet in Prisoner's Square by comparison, and Burke wrote all day to catch up on his journal and not lose scattered notes. He was upset, however, when he received news on July 23 that his mother had returned to Medina, Ohio, "in the neighborhood of her relations and purchased a little home for the present only, as Pa says he cannot live north and will not. And I say the same!" Nonetheless, he and Pa never turned down packages and money from Ohio relatives, some of whom had served three years in the Union army.

Colonel Strong, meanwhile, had been doing an excellent job of managing the prison from Chicago. No doubt, the colonel found it easier to nurse his terrible wounds in a comfortable hotel downtown. However, he received a sharp letter on July 27, 1864, ordering him to live at camp. W. A. Nichols, assistant adjutant general of the army, reminded him that Colonel Sweet was required to do the same. One reason Strong should be there was the turmoil that resulted when Major Skinner tried to consolidate new prisoners with other regiments.

Prisoners fiercely resented these arrangements, as most men wished to maintain their old units. It was the only refuge they had amid their degrading circumstances. For example, they continued to elect noncommissioned officers at Camp Douglas, but strangers could try to elect one of their own as sergeant-major. Pa barely won re-election after 38 outsiders were added to the 14th Kentucky and voted against him.[3] Loyalty to the old regiments continued during that steamy July in Chicago, even after the defeat at Gettysburg and the fall of Vicksburg. It did not appear that the prisoners understood or wished to face these enormous events.

Sweet allowed them to go under the barracks during the intense heat, and they enjoyed debating issues of the day on the cool sandy prairie. They were well informed, thanks to the *Chicago Tribune,* the *Post,* and the *Journal.* The sutler sold these papers for 10¢ each, more than triple the price in Chicago, which included home delivery. The banned *Chicago Times* sometimes came over the fence tied to a rock or was smuggled in.[4] Prisoners suspected a Confederate victory when newspapers were stopped. This did no good, as they bought contraband papers from guards and the sutler.

A *Tribune* dispatch from Washington excited the prisoners near the end of July 1864. Two disgraced officers of the First Michigan Sharpshooters had arrived there. One was named De Land and may have been related to Colonel De Land. Both men had been convicted of cowardice and were to be stripped of buttons and shoulder straps and sent to the "Dry Tortugas," the prisoners read with satisfaction. "Such is the fate of men who assisted in tieing up prisoners by their thumbs to extract secrets, or supposed secrets last fall in this camp. We all say Amen," Burke wrote happily.[5]

Hoffman was also pleased when Camp Douglas received its best inspection report ever on July 25, 1864. Medical Inspector Charles T. Alexander wrote that "seeing the camp and hospital, you would be pleased at the general condition and management." He gave no credit to Sweet or Strong, but to Major Skinner and Captain Sponable. He told how Skinner confiscated money the prisoners earned by selling boots. Skinner and Sponable had a vendetta against boots, and allowed none to reach the prisoners.[6] It had to be a question of morale. If a man's boots were taken away, he did not feel as tall. Stanton and Hoffman overcrowded barracks, however, with 170 men each.

Alexander noted that the prison fund was $19,691.50, and contractors owed more to it. Sweet had sold many rations to earn this amount, although the fund had also received income from business taxes. The hospital fund had only $503.85. Alexander recommended six-inch water pipes to make the hydrants and sewers more efficient. He said little about the smallpox hospital. It did not appear that inspectors gave it much attention, which is understandable. Alexander only mentioned that it was still a stable "converted into a comfortable ward." No patient confined there would have agreed.

He described the new prison hospital, completed in April, as "a good two story building adjoining a two-story laundry," and confirmed that it cost ten thousand dollars. It stood in a separate enclosure between White Oak Square and Prisoner's Square, which the officials called "Hospital Square." He reported that doctors had stopped smallpox vaccinations for some time because of unhealthy ulcers that developed, but they were resumed on July 21, 1864. Five men from Burke's regiment alone had died of the disease since April. Alexander believed that the doctors were efficient, but he said nothing about scurvy.

The present system at the sutler was to give him an order to draw on the prisoner's account, with the sutler issuing the corresponding number of checks. Dr. Alexander did not mention gouging, but Nightingale's greed was monumental. For example, Burke received a new gray uniform jacket, but an inspector had removed the

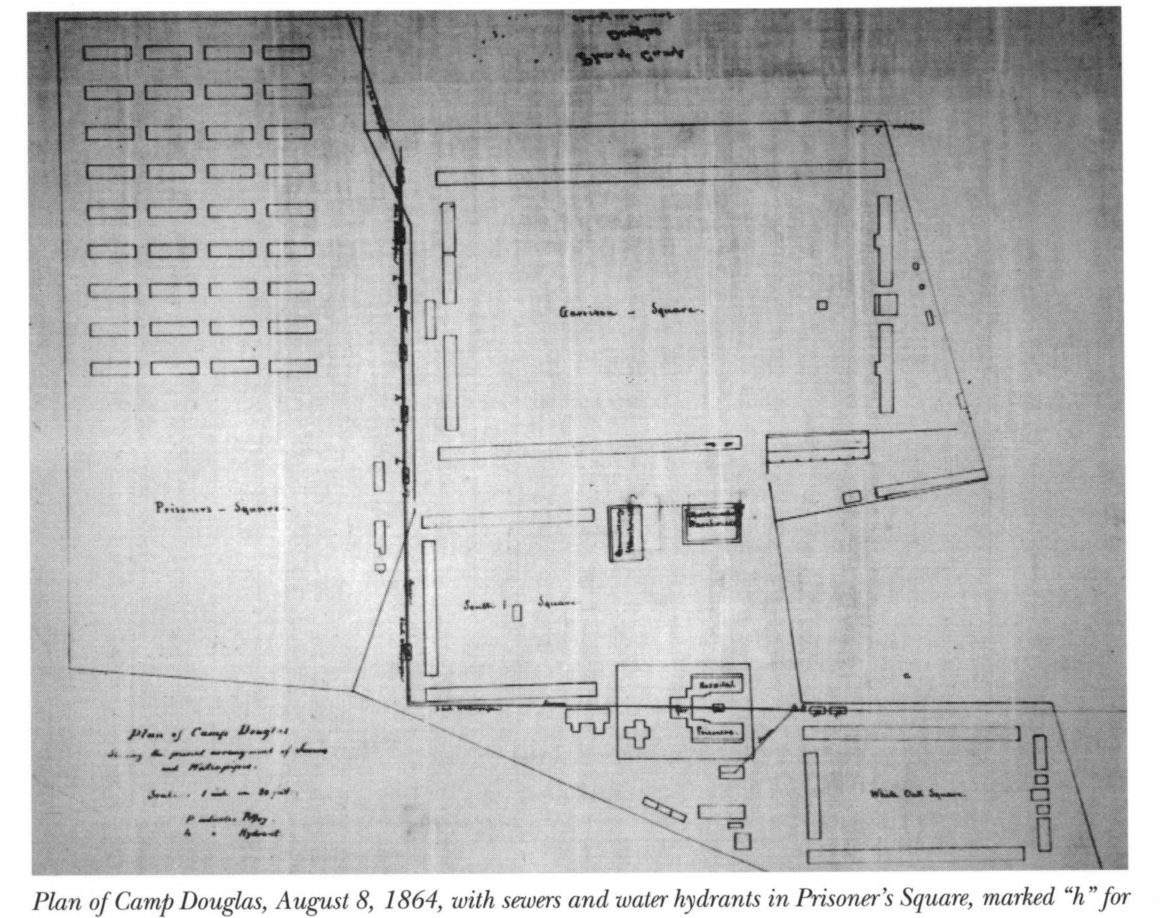

Plan of Camp Douglas, August 8, 1864, with sewers and water hydrants in Prisoner's Square, marked "h" for hydrant and "p" for privy. (Image courtesy of the National Archives.)

Confederate buttons. The fanatical Burke had the option of either purchasing Union army buttons or having none. He ordered Union buttons, and "two skeins of yellow sewing silk and a quarter of a yard of bright yellow cloth" for trim. Nightingale charged him four dollars for the order, a 300 percent profit.[7]

Something of a romantic nature must have occurred, because Colonel Sweet suddenly issued an order on July 29, 1864, concerning women. He allowed none at Camp Douglas "except members of officers' families or family servants, or laundresses, not to exceed one for every twenty-five men."[8] Apparently he felt that this was a safe margin. It was a waste of paper, as authorities discovered an officer with two ladies in his room a few months later.

Prisoners were concerned about a woman who they learned had arrived from Georgia with two children, not knowing that her husband was dead. She was destitute and stranded in Chicago. The men raised $116.35 for her, about four hundred dollars today. She was very grateful and took the list of donors home. Their compassion was striking, and so was the Federal money in their possession. One joker went to Captain Sponable and said that he wished to surrender his money as required. It was a half-dollar I.O.U. issued by the city of Sparta, Tennessee.[9] He suffered a few bruises and a shower of curses, and made himself scarce.

It was amazing that anyone could play the comic, since vaccinations were not slowing the flood of smallpox cases. Colonel Sweet informed Hoffman on August 5, 1864, that the smallpox hospital was hazardous to both the camp and the University of Chicago.[10] "The Hospital is now too near the camp for safety," Sweet feared. "It has broken up two terms of school of the University and materially injures the property of the estate of the Hon. Stephen A. Douglas."

Smallpox worsened as more weakened prisoners shuffled in, with eyes sunk in blackened faces, clothes worn through, shoes, if any, in shreds. Their guards, also straight from the battlefield, did not look much better, and it was difficult to tell who was guarding whom.

Sherman's Atlanta campaign and another raid by General Morgan sent almost 2,500 prisoners to Camp Douglas in July and August 1864. The old hands questioned them closely. Surprisingly, the Confederate army had plenty of food, "and coffee every few days, with whiskey in bad weather." The new arrivals caused a good deal of tension and upheaval, because the old hands refused to give up their quarters and had to be forced out by the garrison. Burke complained about having "to move from our nice little room into the long room of another barracks to make room for the newcomers."

Some oldtimers, including Burke, were ungracious toward the newcomers because they felt that "a good many of them did not try as hard as they might have tried to keep from being captured." Morgan's raiders believed that they were in a hopeless situation when they surrendered, and now they passed judgment on what other men did under fire. About this time an escaping prisoner attempted to surrender and was shot, regardless. Sweet held no inquiry as Stanton had ordered. The case against the guard was probably too flagrant.[11]

A substantial increase in prisoners caused Colonel Sweet to again request reinforcements. Units of the Eighth and 15th VRC were in other cities. He had to further reduce the garrison when more went on patrol in Chicago. They had authority now to arrest enlisted men without passes. The good old days when Chicago was a wide-open town for AWOLS and deserters had ended. Business at the Prairie Queen suffered considerably, no doubt, and the patrols probably accounted for many recaptured prisoners. Sweet ordered $50 worth of streetcar tickets for them to ride downtown.[12]

Reinforcements began rolling into camp on August 13, 1864. They were poor quality, amounting to about 802 inexperienced men in the 196th Pennsylvania Infantry. It was only an untrained hundred-day outfit determined "to do their part," and the prisoners would soon test them.

The pampered civilians were shocked to find themselves crowded three to a bunk. Worse, they learned of a hundred smallpox cases in camp and suffered vaccination.[13] They had never seen a battlefield but came to know the reality of war Camp Douglas style. The killing was just as real. They soon realized that shooting a man was a far cry from going to the office. The 24th Ohio Independent Battery of 145 men signed in on August 29. They quickly pointed six cannons at Prisoner's Square. It seemed that these guns were the best cards Sweet held. Surprisingly, Hoffman did not think so.

Regardless, the arrival of artillery crowned an incredible 12 months. The prisoners of 1862, the parolees, and the Arkansas Post captives would not know how to find their way at this camp. Prisoner's Square, new hospitals, a high stockade with a sentinel walk, and sewers and water closets were only a few of the changes.

Burke, who had lived through it all, took time to count his

blessings as a second year of imprisonment began. "1st. My general good health with generally enough to eat, and 2d. The privilege of corresponding with friends and receiving provisions, clothing, etc."[14]

His remark about "generally enough to eat" clashed with reports, including his own, about short rations and hunger. However, Yankee food packages and Yankee money had kept his stomach full. Ten dollars had just arrived from his uncle, William H. Burke of Canton, Ohio, almost a month's pay for a garrison soldier. However, the flow of money and packages was soon shut off. Even the privileged did not escape the new crackdown.

Reprisal against the prisoners had intensified because the South was allegedly refusing to allow clothing and other articles to reach Union prisoners. A circular from Colonel Hoffman dated August 10, 1864, ordered Confederate prisoners treated in the same fashion. Only the sick could receive packages from outside.[15]

"Prisoners will be allowed to receive clothing or other articles from relatives and friends residing beyond the lines, when forwarded by flag of truce, so long as the prisoners of war held at Richmond and other southern prisons are permitted to receive the same articles in the same manner from relatives and friends in the loyal states," Hoffman ranted. "No articles above referred to will be delivered to prisoners of war at this post after Aug. 25th, 1864."

Hoffman's pompous tirade probably confused many prisoners, but it meant that authorities had cut off Burke and Pa from generous relatives in Ohio, and their survival was at risk. They would remember the period August 1863 to August 1864 with longing, compared with what was coming. Sutlers could sell "writing materials, postage stamps, tobacco, cigars, pipes, matches, combs, soap, tooth brushes, hair brushes, clothes brushes, scissors, thread, and needles, handkerchiefs, towels, and pocket looking glasses."

The War Department banned vegetables and other foods essential to avoid scurvy. Wealthy prisoners were now down on the ground like everyone else. Stanton had silenced money at Camp Douglas. Hoffman replaced the system of Sutler's checks for about the fifth time. Prisoners filled out an order for the purchase, and the sutler cashed it at the post cashier.[16] This prevented the men from using checks to bribe guards and explains why few bribery cases arose under Sweet.

Those who relied on the sutler complained the loudest. "He has nothing to eat except sugar at 70 cents per pound," Burke griped.

"We are getting boiled beef and sour light bread six days out of ten, and boiled pickle pork and sour light bread the other four and coarse hominy for dinner extra." He was not used to such a mean diet.

New prisoners felt hunger pangs more than the old hands and hovered around the barracks begging for refuse meat and bread. "They have not worn the wire edge off their appetites yet," Burke observed. The hired prisoners were eating well, however, and had their own mess hall with six long tables and benches. "They get coffee, sugar, etc. regular," Burke raged. Prisoners hated the paid workers "nearly as bad as Yankees for humbling themselves to the Yanks."[17]

This hatred led to more attacks on the fence. Prisoners believed, with justification, that the boards were paper thin. Hoffman had ordered Tucker to repair the fence with old lumber about the camp. "Let it cost as little as possible," he said. De Land rebuilt it entirely of oak boards, not logs. The *Tribune* described it as 14 feet high, supported by 16-foot posts, with a three-foot guard walk near the top. Burke believed that it was 15 to 16 feet high.[18] Carpenters had placed several sentinel boxes on the platform by mid-December 1864.

The high stockade made it easier for guards to find targets, and a commission of Camp Douglas officers investigated the wounding of two prisoners around August 13, 1864. They concluded that firing at prisoners without warning was legal and commended the guards. A new rash of shootings broke out during more suicidal escape attempts. Sweet reported five prisoners shot in one week in August, one of whom died. A group of six working on a detail in Garrison Square tried to flee over the fence in plain sight. Only one made it. The best time to escape was on the way to camp. Twenty prisoners disappeared while coming from Alton, Illinois, on August 14, 1864.[19]

Some escapes achieved the status of Greek mythology and were passed down through the years. One prisoner who had obtained civilian clothing went to the gate and told the guard that he would hang every "mother's son of the rascally secesh." The guard demanded a pass. When the pretended visitor said he had none, the guard kicked him out the gate instead of arresting him. In one apparently true legend, a contractor gave his pass to an "expert penman" among the prisoners. Soon he was signing Colonel Tucker's name better than the colonel did, and several prisoners escaped this way.[20]

Another famous escape occurred when Nightingale's prison clerk convinced him that a barrel contained sugar he could sell in Chicago. The clerk had himself sealed in the barrel and carted out of camp. He scared the wits out of the driver when he suddenly popped up on the way to town. He also stole "two or three hundred dollars from old Nightingale," Burke heard. Officers arrested the other clerks, and the place was closed. Another prisoner pulled a copycat stunt by shutting himself in an empty vinegar barrel that was placed on a trash pile outside Prisoner's Square. Ada Sweet remembered hearing about this incident "and being glad for the poor fellow."[21]

She personally wished a prisoner bon voyage while living in Garrison Square. "The man slipped away from the other prisoners, and hid in our basement," she later recalled. "At night when I came home from school I saw him hiding there behind a barrel. I just kept quiet and didn't say a word. About an hour later his absence was discovered. The alarm was given and a search was made, but it was too late. The man had run the guard and escaped. It was one of those things a child will do."[22] Ada was wrong. It was one of those things she would do. She could not play the informer, even though her father was the commanding officer.

Colonel Sweet unexpectedly requested permission to move back to Chicago, probably because Camp Douglas was not the best place for Ada. An officer remembered her as a "little girl" running in and out of headquarters. She had no one to play with, as other officers did not want their children at Camp Douglas. Hoffman turned down Sweet's request to live in Chicago, writing, "I feared that in your absence from the camp it would necessarily fall into other and less reliable hands, and for this reason I asked for the change."[23] Hoffman's conciliatory tone showed a close relationship between the men. Sweet had plenty of options regarding Ada. He could resign his post, or send Ada to his family in Wisconsin, or board her with a family in Chicago. He chose to keep her at Camp Douglas, where childhood diseases killed adults.

While the camp remained in Sweet's "reliable hands," Burke described depressing conditions in barracks. August 6, 1864: "There were two candles burning all night, and several of the men sat up with the sick flux [diarrhea] patients. The barrack assumes the appearance of a hospital. Permission to have a light is often given in cases of extreme illness. I did not sleep much." August 7, 1864: "Everybody walks light and speaks in whispers on account of the sick.

Ada C. Sweet at age 29. (Image courtesy of the Chicago Historical Society.)

About 11 o'clock John Duckworth of Co. D died, and about 3 o'clock Jessie T. Hunter of Co. D died.[24] Both died in their bunks of the flux. They were good soldiers and gentlemen. Duckworth is from Bath Co. Ky. and Hunter is from Wilkerson Co. Miss. They received all the attention that could be given them under the circumstances. Medicines of the right kind could not be procured."

Prisoners washed and laid out the bodies, and an ambulance came with rough coffins. This was the last loving care the dead received. Private T. M. Page, secretary to the Confederate surgeons, accused the post surgeon of rejecting a request by the Confederate doctors to have medicines sent at no expense. Page's accusation seems true, for he named Dr. J. C. Whitehill, surgeon of the 11th Illinois Infantry, in charge of the general hospital at the time. "Respectfully disapproved," Whitehill said, "as all medicine is strictly contraband of war, excepting only such as is supplied by and through these headquarters."

Whitehill was spouting nonsense, as prison authorities had freely accepted medicines from relief committees in 1862. Whitehill wrote a memo in 1903 claiming that the contract surgeons at Camp Douglas were incompetent and that there was a 95 percent mortality rate among the smallpox patients.[25] This report may have been accurate, but he did not help matters.

Desperate conditions did not deter Hoffman from issuing another order on August 13, 1864, to remove the cooking stoves. Prisoners presented a petition against the order signed by 41 men representing 44 barracks and even including the Yankee doctors. This was the entire prison. The surgeons argued that many sick prisoners remained in barracks due to lack of hospital space and that only a stove could cook something for them. Washington denied the petition.[26]

Prisoners offered to purchase their own stoves, but Hoffman rejected the idea because fuel was too costly. They could not bake cornbread without stoves. The Irish among them called it "Yaller Hammers," and white bread was "gun wadding," which they preferred. Otherwise, 60-gallon farmer's kettles boiled the rations to shreds. T. D. Henry commented, "There was no more nutritious matter in it than an old dish cloth, for dinner one pint of bean soup and five ounces of bread, this was our living!"[27]

Chicago raised no relief committee this time, but Southern friends were much concerned about reports of scurvy almost within sight of downtown. Burke reported, "A good deal of flour, cabbage, potatoes and pickles were sent to the prisoners through the kindness of Mrs. Norrus [Mary Morris] of Chicago."[28] Mary Morris, of Kentucky, was the wife of a prominent Chicago attorney, also a Kentuckian. Her sister was married to a Confederate general. Authorities had named their brother, Dr. Luke Blackburn, as the principal villain in the "Yellow Fever Plot" against the North, and Mary ended up as a defendant in the Camp Douglas Conspiracy trials of 1865.

However, conflicting signals from Washington confused the prisoners. The policy of retaliation, on the one hand, was a ruthless waste of lives. Yet, the government seemed determined on making Camp Douglas a modern prison. A large crowd gathered in Prisoner's Square on August 27, 1864, to see the first fire hydrant tested. It threw water 50 feet, and a guard amused himself by wetting prisoners.[29] Firemen no longer had to worry about running out of water.

Neither did retaliation extend to medical treatment. Sergeant Oscar Cliett admitted, "The yankees gave every attention to the sick that was necessary. They provided good beds for them and plenty of wholesome diet and good medical attention."[30] The irony was that only the hospitals supplied a vegetable diet.

This conflict between retaliation and providing reasonable care took another bizarre turn on August 15, 1864, when the War Department issued an unprecedented order. Sweet had to appoint a special inspector, "an active and reliable officer, whose duty it will be to inspect the camp in every part daily and to give all necessary orders for policing,"[31] the order read. He had to submit a written report to Sweet every Sunday. Sweet was to add his comments and pass the report to Hoffman. Surprisingly, the order's broad sweep covered hospitals, sutlers, Prisoner's Square, and even the garrison.

Sweet tried to outmaneuver his superiors by appointing not an "active officer" but a disabled Eighth VRC lieutenant who had reason to get even with the prisoners. However, Lt. Morris Briggs took pride in his new title of "Special Inspector." Appointees sometimes live up to the job, rather than the boss's expectations. Colonel Tucker had his Dr. McVickar, De Land had his Dr. Clark, and now Colonel Sweet found himself under siege.

Briggs was a former enlisted man, as were most VRC officers, and this may be why he identified with the common soldier. He was crippled at the Battle of Perryville by a gunshot wound through the left shoulder joint. This caused a permanent stiffening and loss of use in his arm. The army assigned him to Sweet's Eighth VRC after he commanded a company of convalescents pursuing General Morgan in 1863.

His first report on August 28, 1864, found the prisoners and the grounds to be very clean, but noted that the three-inch water pipes did not supply enough water for the 7,500 prisoners. Sweet soon received permission "to substitute a 6-inch water pipe for the 3-inch one" and to install as many hydrants as required in all the squares.[32] Such requests by previous inspectors had come to nothing.

Colonel Sweet did a good job of keeping the camp and the men clean but could not solve the major problems of health, clothing, and housing. Of course, neither could prior commanders. Nothing was done to repair roofs and windows and provide more clothing and blankets. Hospital space was hopelessly inadequate and remained so to the end of the war. Long hair, however, came under attack. John Curd was appointed as barber. "For every ten men he operated on he was to be excused from work detail one day," Burke laughed.

The men did not give up hope of receiving help from their own government. Atlanta was about to fall, but many, especially Morgan's men, did not believe that the war was yet lost or that escape was impossible. They knew that Sweet did not have a rock-solid garrison behind him. Governor Yates felt it necessary to come and give the 196th Pennsylvania a pep talk on August 28. Even Gen. William S. Rosecrans, the loser at Chickamauga, spoke to them about the importance of their job.[33]

Another inspector from the Northern Department of the army reported an explosive situation on August 31, 1864. "There appears to be more than usual discontented feeling among the prisoners of war and a disposition, especially on the part of the Kentucky prisoners to escape," the inspector observed.

He joined many others in condemning the farmer's boilers. "It would be a matter of economy to place cooking stoves in the kitchen used by the prisoners, or even common camp kettles would be preferable." He did not realize that the boilers were there in retaliation. In addition, he noted that the pharmacy did not promptly fill prescriptions for medicine; "the consequences, more sickness and more death."[34]

Company H, 196th Pennsylvania Infantry outside Camp Douglas 1864. (Image courtesy of the Chicago Historical Society.)

CHAPTER 15

The Puny Boys of Summer

Nervous Pennsylvania troops guard prisoners—Desperate attempts to escape—Water shortage—Prisoners enlist to fight Indians—The Pennsylvanians whipped into shape—Inside the smallpox hospital—Prisoners launch a major offensive—5,000 more prisoners approach camp.

The 196th Pennsylvania did not inspire much respect or fear among the prisoners. "I notice a good many puny-pale-gosling looking boys on guard on the parapet," Burke sneered. "I understand that they are one hundred day men."[1] The Northeastern states had agreed to supply fully equipped men for one hundred days to release veterans for combat. The University of Chicago furnished many hundred-day men, but none served at Camp Douglas. Students had done relief work there, and they knew the prisoners.

Morgan's men soon challenged the "puny boys" and charged the fence on the night of September 7. They broke a plank, and between 11 and 17 escaped. Burke counted only two bullet holes. "Bad shots for fifty yards," he judged. At least three guards in the 196th Pennsylvania failed to fire.

Frightened Pennsylvanians made more noise than the escapees. Some prisoners thought for a moment that drunken guards were attacking them. They fired five or six pistol shots between the barracks, and one guard on the parapet would not stop yelling, "Corporal of the guard" at the top of his voice. He continued to bellow even after the attack ceased and all else was quiet.

Not all the Pennsylvanians were young men, however. Edwin Greble thought that he was older than President Lincoln when introduced to him at the White House in March 1864. Lincoln denied it and held Greble's hand in sympathy after learning that Greble had also lost a young son.

Nevertheless, Greble and his comrades displayed arrogance not seen before. They called Prisoner's Square the "Bull Pen," and

Etching of Prisoner's Square, around September 1864. Note guards patrolling between the deadline and the fence at the end of the street and the number 13 on barrack at right. (Image courtesy of the Illinois State Historical Society.)

viewed prisoners as mere targets.[2] Conversation between garrison and prisoners was nonstop when they were in White Oak. Now, only the patrols were in direct contact.

This distancing was evident when patrols recaptured three prisoners in nearby haystacks after officers probed them with swords. "One of the Rebs yelled," Greble says without emotion. "An officer struck another with his sword, called Fat Jack." Greble showed no sympathy when prisoners received the "glad" news at roll call on September 8 that they could no longer walk between the barracks and the deadline. The penalty was shooting. They had to stay on the streets as punishment for escapes. Curiously, the North and South agreed to release all prisoners from close confinement. This agreement emptied the dungeons at Camp Douglas and freed Joseph McCarney, who had killed a prisoner named Scroggin.[3]

The inspector from the Northern Department returned in September and saw an increased water supply, barracks under repair, and the prisoners being forced to practice good hygiene. He was more concerned about the danger of a mass escape. "There is an apparent restlessness that augers mischief among them if they are not well watched," he warned. He believed that the garrison was too weak for safety, "especially at this time, when everything tends to show that the prisoners of war expect succor from some quarter."[4] This perceptive officer also noticed another weakness; the garrison was housed too far from Prisoner's Square. No one had thought of this before. Only the patrol force had barracks near the entrance to the square.

The pressure on Sweet was considerable, with inspectors from the Department of the Army and his own Lieutenant Briggs roaming about the camp. Briggs denounced the War Department, Sweet, and Hoffman in his next report, but did not say that he foresaw a mass escape. Instead, he complained that the new prison hospital was too small, leaving two hundred sick in barracks, 12 of whom had died in the past week. In addition, the barracks were dilapidated, many prisoners lacked blankets, and the farmer's boilers, Hoffman's cherished idea, were a disaster.[5] Briggs confirmed that "the supply of medicine was insufficient for the actual wants of the prisoners." He could forget promotion.

On September 9, 1864, Union army general Benjamin F. Butler proposed an exchange of sick and wounded officers and men to ease prison conditions. It applied only to those who would not be fit for duty for 60 days. His idea may have come from the story about a delegation of Andersonville prisoners traveling to Washington to see President Lincoln.[6]

The South had reportedly released them to carry a petition detailing the horrors of Andersonville and begging Lincoln to negotiate their release. While the petition charged the South with barbarities, it also pleaded the Confederate case to restart the Cartel. They were not too concerned about black prisoners. "It is true that they are again made slaves," the whites conceded, "but their slavery is freedom and happiness compared with the cruel existence imposed upon our gallant men."

News of Confederate general John H. Morgan's death reached Camp Douglas amid stories about the Andersonville prisoners, but his men did not believe it any more than they did the Andersonville reports. The general had made another disastrous raid into Kentucky early in June 1864, one year after the suicidal expedition through Indiana and Ohio. Again, Union forces destroyed or captured most of his command. He was preparing to launch another campaign when he was killed on September 4, 1864, at Greenville, Tennessee.

Federal cavalry attacking through darkness and heavy rain caught the general with his pants off. The Yankees had finally learned how to mount a night operation. Morgan was unarmed and "desperately pleading for his life" when a laughing trooper deliberately shot him. One of Morgan's grief-stricken officers reported that "the bullet struck the gallant raider square in his left breast, ranging downward, passing through his heart, and exiting from the back of his left shoulder blade." Troopers flung the corpse into a rain-filled ditch and stripped it for souvenirs.[7] All the glory and adventure of war had fled this dismal scene.

Some people benefitted from the war, however, when about this time Colonel Sweet allowed John J. Nelson of Chicago to build and operate an "eating saloon" in Garrison Square. He could serve food and oysters to officers, only, with no "loungers permitted." On the other hand, Sweet had cut the prisoners' potato ration only a week earlier, "whenever a less amount of potatoes can be issued to the prisoners without material detriment to their health."[8] Any reduction had to be harmful. The potato ration had grown to about nine ounces per prisoner for five days but was still not sufficient to fight scurvy.

Colonel Sweet uncovered an astounding reason for the loss of six prisoners on September 7. He found that guards were removing percussion caps from their rifles when changing shifts. This was minor compared with the discovery that the Eighth and 15th VRC were not loading weapons at all.[9]

The guard would go on duty with empty guns to avoid cleaning them. A Civil War musket became fouled whether or not it was fired, because gunpowder had to be poured down the barrel to load it. The prisoners were probably aware of this laxness, just as they knew everything else happening in camp. Of course, officers had failed properly to inspect the weapons. They had believed in the past that the guns had not fired because they were defective.

Danger of a general escape loomed when high winds ripped the camp on September 9. The guard platforms suffered substantial damage, but the stockade held. Winds also tore up the new prison hospital, and two prisoners escaped.[10] The War Department made an unusual offer to the prisoners by inviting them to join a regiment of U. S. Cavalry to fight Indians. Burke saw a large crowd around the recruiting office all day on September 14, 1864, but did not know how many enlisted. This was one way to solve a shortage of seven hundred suits of clothing, 1,500 blankets, and a severe lack of hospital space. Burke wrote on September 15 that "we deeply mourn the loss of John H. Morgan."

Edwin Greble of the 196th Pennsylvania was in Chicago that day observing the construction of a new water system. Engineers extended a tunnel two miles out into the lake, "in order to get good water," Greble remarked. The improvement came too late for Camp Douglas.

Workers installed ventilators and chimneys on barracks around September 17. The square was kept very clean. "The prisoners were obliged to carry all slops and dirty water to the sinks," reported Briggs. However, he wrote a depressing report of barracks without windows, roofs leaking, and the need for new floors. Some prisoners lacked blankets, and many needed clothing. Another harsh winter threatened, because Greble reported heavy frost during the night of September 18, and guards had already drawn their overcoats after a snowfall. Barrack 41 was now a convalescent ward holding 80 men.[11] It also needed repairs and was not warm enough for patients. Worse, they were in harm's way from wild-shooting guards on the nearby fence.

Colonel Sweet's wife and three other children arrived in the fall of 1864 for a winter visit. They lived in officer's quarters at the east end of the parade ground, far from Prisoner's Square near the Cottage Grove gate.[12] The children were soon heard singing the bugle calls. For sick call: "Are you all dead yet? [very slow]. Are you all dead yet? [slower]. [Voice] Come get your quinine. Come get your quinine! Come!"

The children's presence did not seem to worry Sweet when he discovered plans for a concerted effort to escape on September 19. Prisoners were depending on draft riots in Chicago to help them. Sweet intended "to let them make the effort and punish them in the act, and made dispositions accordingly."[13] Nothing happened. The plotters probably guessed that Sweet knew their plans, and no draft riots occurred. Thousands of the Rebels had been there for over a year, and Sweet observed "that the prisoners are restive and inventive to an uncommon degree of late."

Private Greble confirmed that "troops were alerted for a prison break." All weapons were loaded, and the two VRC regiments took up positions outside the stockade. Greble heard reports that "700 rebels in Morgan's command have taken an oath either to regain their freedom or die in the attempt," and that the prisoners had killed an informer. He was skeptical, and rightfully so.

Greble had more pleasant moments when he attended the play, *Our American Cousin* in Chicago. The city now had an eerie preview of the Lincoln assassination, with John Wilkes Booth and the play Lincoln was watching at Ford's Theatre both appearing in town. Some of the men enjoyed other diversions. "Captain had two women in his room," Greble wrote with disapproval on September 20. Presumably, they were neither relatives nor laundresses.[14]

Sweet did not punish the romantic captain, but prisoners felt the lash quite often. Even an elderly Confederate surgeon suffered severely for a minor violation. A new rule prohibited walking between the sutler store and the express office. Dr. Pettus, who should have been at home, was sick in the hospital when the edict came down, and he did not know about it. Nonetheless, he was forced to ride the mule on September 24, 1864. After this brutal and degrading incident, the doctor's health began slipping, and he failed to diagnose a smallpox case the following week.[15]

Colonel Sweet made a rare appearance in Prisoner's Square on September 26, but it was not a success. Prisoners chanted "More bread! More Bread!" so violently that he had to retreat. Almost immediately, a patrol fired two shots at a prisoner for starting toward the sinks before dismissal from roll call, but fortunately missed without killing anyone. Lieutenant Fife placed more restrictions on letters requesting packages from home for express delivery. Two Rebel clerks in the express office read the letters, and a Yankee corporal told them what to strike out. Prisoners cursed the hired hands for "everything good or bad," including a two-hour roll call.[16]

As September closed, Sweet occupied himself with having a prisoner executed. Private James P. K. Thornhill, Company C, Fourth Alabama Cavalry, was the only Confederate to enter Camp Douglas under sentence of death. Sweet hurriedly wired Hoffman on September 27, "There is danger that the prisoner will not arrive at Huntsville, Alabama in time for the execution."[17] He was worried that "if the day passed without a new time being set, that the prisoner goes unpunished." Sweet needed to curry favor with Hoffman to pay his detectives from the prison fund. This appeal did not work with Hoffman, who yielded only under political pressure.

Private James P. K. Thornhill, along with William Thornhill, and a third man named Jefferson Sisk, had gone on a rampage against Union loyalists near Huntsville, Alabama, on May 11, 1864. They had taken six to ten horses from four plantations and had targeted an alleged Union militia man named Patillo for execution. James Thornhill, an illiterate, was the leader of the group, and Sisk shot Patillo at his order. Miraculously, Patillo survived to testify against Thornhill before a Union army court on June 8, 1864. Judges rejected a plea for Thornhill's life "because he was only a beardless boy."[18]

The "beardless boy" would have gone to his death by firing squad at Huntsville except that he had been shipped to Nashville, Tennessee, by mistake, then to Chattanooga in error, and finally to Camp Douglas. Hoffman quickly ordered Thornhill returned to Huntsville in response to Sweet's telegram. He should have arrived there by the 29th in plenty of time to be shot, but was somehow lost at Louisville, Kentucky, along with his guards.

The provost marshal there telegraphed a frantic Major Skinner in Chicago that the prisoner had not been delivered. The condemned man somehow surfaced at Huntsville on October 7, but the military refused to execute him because his death warrant had expired.[19] It was never renewed because Gen. Oliver O. Howard,

Confederate officers in front of sutler store in Prisoner's Square, around September 30, 1864. Note the fire and water hydrants in foreground. One prisoner standing on right appears to be a civilian. (Image courtesy of the Chicago Historical Society.)

Enlisted men in Prisoner's Square, taken at the same time. (Image courtesy of the Chicago Historical Society.)

who had to sign it, had fought the Battle of Atlanta and then marched on to the sea with Sherman. Thornhill had singlehandedly exhausted every shred of luck allotted to the Confederate army.

Sweet did not have time to marvel at such bungling, because prisoners struck the fence in a surprise attack on September 27, just as the army inspector had predicted.[20] This operation was unusual because 13 men who spearheaded the assault come from nine different regiments, consisting of infantry, artillery, and cavalry units. Normally, they would have betrayed or accidentally revealed plans of this size. The raid had possibly been organized by some Confederate officers who should not have been kept at Camp Douglas anyway.

About 30 prisoners charged out at 10:00 P.M. and made for the northwest corner of the square where the Olivet Baptist Church now stands at East 31st Street and King Drive.[21] The leader threw a blanket over the light and took a bullet in the face. His squad pressed on, however, and battered away furiously with axes and hammers. Meanwhile, the garrison drummer brought out security forces with a long steady roll. The attempt ended quickly as patrols come up and fired into the corner with revolvers. They may have wounded another prisoner, and the others retreated into the darkness. Sweet reported that the leader would die, but he survived.

Sympathizers supplied help outside, with two rockets going off as signals, followed by several shots fired at pickets. The "puny boys" in the 196th Pennsylvania did much better this time. "Our men in Co. C fired at them," Greble wrote with satisfaction. Even more satisfying, their rifles worked, while many of those in the VRC did not. Officers of both VRC regiments complimented the 196th on the speed with which it answered the alarm. Hoffman's belief that Sweet's detectives were incompetent was confirmed.

Twelve prisoners ended up in irons. This was almost a successful escape and proved that Camp Douglas could not be a maximum security prison without locked cell blocks. "In some of the barracks nearly all the men were ready to escape," Greble observed.

The assault did have some effect, because the following day, September 28, notices were nailed to the barracks announcing an easing of restrictions.[22] Destitute prisoners could now receive from home one suit of gray or dark material of inferior quality and one change of underwear. Bedticks and overcoats could be sent from home without limitation. However, the coats could not be taken in case of a

Etching of interior of prison barrack, with a view of the triple-tiered bunks. (Image courtesy of the Chicago Historical Society.)

prisoner exchange. As a result, some of the men swore that they would not request them.

Because of the expected stream of packages, all requests for express delivery had to be approved by Lieutenant Fife. Colonel Sweet returned to the square for another inspection on September 29, and prisoners again shouted "more bread!" The ration was continuously short. This time Sweet retaliated by marching out one barrack of prisoners for punishment. They had to mark time in place until exhausted. Sweet also ordered six more sets of ball and chain "for punishing prisoners of war."[23] Two days later he issued an extraordinary bulletin in Prisoner's Square revealing that he knew about an escape committee called the "Supreme Council of Seven."

"The Colonel Commanding has information, which leads to the conclusion that there is an organization among the prisoners of war at Camp Douglas, having for its object a combined attack, to overpower the guard and effect an escape," the notice read. Sweet was straightforward, conceding that a prisoner had the right to escape and that he "would be actuated by the same motive if he were a prisoner." He warned that should there be a mass attack on the guards, "the necessary means to repel it and restore order will endanger the lives of all in the prison square, the innocent as well as the guilty."[24]

Apparently, Sweet intended to use the artillery. Why did he not say so? He may have wanted the prisoners to try it. He was also conciliatory, promising "to make the prisoners barracks comfortable, and to clothe and protect them from cold and disease." However, he ordered another guardhouse built in Prisoner's Square.

Prisoners had organized the Supreme Council of Seven after the deadly winter of 1863-64. Many felt that their chances of survival at Camp Douglas were less than on the battlefield. Six or seven of Morgan's men formed the committee to plan a mass escape in the early spring of 1864, according to B. R. Froman. The Supreme Council members were Clayton Anderson, Harmon Barlow, Otway B. Norvell, A. W. Cockrell, Winder Monroe, John H. Waller, a member of Burke's Company B, 14th Kentucky, and E. M. Headelston. They realized the difficulty of secrecy because of spies, traitors, and the indiscreet among the prisoners. Therefore, the recommendation and the unanimous consent of the Council were necessary before anyone was approached. The candidate was then sounded out and made to take an oath if he agreed to join.[25] R. T. Bean was one of those selected.

"The oath was administered to me by Mr. Waller, who, I thought was a Texan," Bean recalled. "We went under my barracks, and with my hand grasping a Bible, I repeated after him the most terrible, blood-curdling oath ever concocted by the brain of man. Every word seemed branded upon my mind with letters of fire, and for weeks afterward I hardly knew who or what I was."[26]

However, Bean later called the escape plans "wild and reckless in the extreme." Prisoners were too weak to walk back to the South, and there was little chance of stealing a train to travel that distance. Regardless, the Supreme Council was going ahead with its plans. Through bribery, it was able to obtain a report on guard strength and the location of weapons and munitions.

According to former prisoner Thomas S. Longwood, the Council recruited about two thousand prisoners. Longwood settled in Chicago after the war and succeeded in business. He became president of the Confederate Veterans of Chicago and lobbied Congress for the erection of the Confederate monument in Oak Woods Cemetery. R. T. Bean believed the number recruited was closer to 1,500.[27] "Many times the solemn ritual was interrupted by the guard, or a careless or too inquisitive prisoner," Bean recalled.

The Council did not recruit Burke, probably due to his poor health. They planned to flee west after smashing through the fence and free prisoners at Rock Island, Illinois, 120 miles away. Their idea was to combine the two groups and attack Sherman's army in Georgia. Imagining the weakened prisoners taking on Sherman's powerful army of well-equipped and hardened veterans is impossible.

The problem was too many uncoordinated escape committees. The attempted breakouts in 1864 seemed by different groups, and the Supreme Council had no control over events. It was so cautious that it became paralyzed.

Sweet was now busy with matters other than escape plots. He received orders from Colonel Hoffman on October 1 regarding General Butler's plan to exchange sick and disabled prisoners. Surgeons were to determine who qualified. Sweet would ship these men to Cairo, Illinois, unless they chose not to go. From there the Federal government agreed to transport them by boat to exchange points farther south. Camp Douglas had to supply three days' cooked rations, but officials stripped invalids of all "U.S." property, including blankets. Meanwhile, guards purchased items for the prisoners and were paid for their services by "keeping the change."[28]

Medical inspections began on October 2. Burke, barely able to stand, and racked with chills and fever, was rejected. His stance about the war was well known. Fourteen of his friends, including John Curd, who was not very sick, made the list. However, all remained in camp.[29] The plan had cooled off. The War Department released only 60 disabled by the end of 1864, and 162 more were set free in January 1865, mostly for taking the oath, not because of illness or wounds.

If any prisoner should have left his bones in Chicago, it was Burke. However, two infections and a case of smallpox did not stop him from living into the next century. He suffered a tooth extraction in 1863 with unsterile instruments and without anesthetics or antibiotics. A week later he caught a severe cold, which was often fatal. Now he had chills, and doctors treated a hacking cough with a stick of licorice. In the meantime he had to remain in his quarters for lack of hospital beds. October was a cold month during the war years, and Briggs's report of October 2, 1864, mentioned that barracks still needed repairs to floors, windows, and roofs. Some lacked stoves in the already chilly weather.[30]

Burke was hospitalized with smallpox on October 5, 1864. A red ambulance carried him through the camp's south gate and drove about four hundred yards southeast to the smallpox hospital. The old cavalry stable still rested at Adele Grove, on the south side of the university. The site had no water hydrants or sewers, and privies remained the old-fashioned pits. Water came from wells which had been polluted by latrines. About eight men died in the pest house each day. The hard-pressed Dr. F. A. Emmons, a contract surgeon from Chicago, was in charge.[31]

Attendants gave each new patient a canvas cot with a mattress and two blankets, probably covered with the scabs of those who had gone before. The hospital issued no clothing, and patients slept in what they wore. Only one stove fought to keep out the cold and dampness penetrating the cracks and holes in the walls. An oil lamp hung from the ceiling, and the roof let in the cold fresh air. Nevertheless, the stench from the sick was powerful despite the scrubbed floors.

Patients were discouraged against drinking water or washing, as "this was bad for smallpox." Three meals a day were the same: sliced bread, coffee, milk, sugar, crackers, and roast potatoes. About 13 male nurses, including three prisoners, ran the wards. The Yankee nurses were kind if patients gave them no trouble. Two of the Rebel nurses stole money and tobacco from the sick and escaped.[32]

Several men would likely die during the night, and nurses tramped up and back with coffins. Patients did not die comfortably and filled the ward with raving, ranting, cursing, and praying. One man spoke most eloquently against a death sentence from an imagined judge and assured his family and sweetheart of his innocence.[33]

New patients cowered under putrid blankets, but the fowl air underneath was worth the price of shutting out scenes worse than the battlefield and more horrifying than anything the sick could have imagined in their sunny Southland. When they finally saw the morning light come filtering in, it was more welcome than any infantry regiment sent to rescue them. A brave woman approached within a few feet of the hospital to sell milk at 10¢ a quart and buttermilk for 10¢ per gallon. Patients would have preferred something "more in keeping with the needs of a grown up individual." However, they were desperate, even for milk, as water was practically forbidden and their medicine was dark bitter stuff called "number one."

Lucky patients felt the bumps on their faces begin to dry. They could now go to the sink by themselves but only in shorts and shoes. The privy was a roofless shed set over a slit trench. Winter had come on early, and the patients shivered with sickness and grew dizzy from the stench. One wandered away into the darkness and cold and could not be found.

T. M. Page accurately stated that doctors discharged patients who were still infectious and exposed them to a freezing journey back to camp. Lieutenant Briggs confirmed the serious shortage of hospital beds and prisoners dying in barracks.

Nurses moved a recovering patient to the convalescent ward after two weeks. Doctor Emmons usually ordered such patients discharged about 15 days after admission, ready or not, although some still had running sores. The many patients and the lack of facilities left Emmons no choice. He gave no medical examination before discharge, and departure started with a bath, two men to a tub. The water was heated, but patients bathed in a cold, dilapidated open shed and became thoroughly chilled. The hospital staff burned their old clothing and issued each patient a new blue suit, thin shoes without socks, a pair of unlined pants without shorts, a good gray shirt, and a mutilated frock coat. These were inadequate in the cold weather, even for a healthy person.

Ironically, Union soldiers sent to the pest house fared no better. More than 50 percent of them died, according to Camp Douglas hospital records in the National Archives. Danger to the civilian population was significant when 18 patients escaped on October 11, 1864.[34] Meanwhile, doctors vaccinated the entire garrison again.

Those who returned from the hospital barely recognized Prisoner's Square after the many improvements and new barracks that had sprung up in only a few weeks. Comrades welcomed them as heroes for returning from the pest house alive, though just barely so. Burke was ill for the next two months and, being infectious, may have sent some of his comrades to answer the long roll.

Officials vaccinated the 196th Pennsylvania again, and Greble mentioned that four of his comrades had died. Burke complained about "soreness and slight pain on the left side of my neck under my jaw between the ear and apple of the throat. It increased so by night that I could hardly eat a couple of biscuits and cup of tea that Pa brought me." He had infected tonsils, probably diphtheria from drinking milk. Civil War medicine could only treat infections locally, so the Confederate surgeon gave Henry White a prescription of nitrate of silver to burn the ulcers. The treatment was excruciating.

Burke was still suffering with his throat the first week in November 1864, burning the ulcers and gargling with potash. The cure hurt more than the illness. Patients applied poultices of lye, bread, onions, and vinegar several times a day. Meanwhile, another of Burke's comrades died. Burke was unable to answer roll call for nine weeks. Survivors reported more than two hundred cases at the smallpox hospital, many of the sick were lying on the floor and suffering from frostbite. "To the helpless agony of this situation smallpox added its own horror," Page mourned.[35]

Briggs's reports had alerted the army to these conditions, and Colonel Hoffman approved a plan to move the smallpox hospital again to a place called Dull Grove, so that the university could reopen. That is where his concern lay, and not with the prisoners. He required that the ground be rent free and that the new building be paid for by the prison fund. Officials planned two wards like the existing one, with windows for ventilation. Hoffman vetoed the idea of raising the building three feet from the ground, as "this would be too expensive."

Dull Grove cannot be found on maps of the area. Page claimed, "The victim was removed to an isolated hospital miles away out on a sandy waste, a removal which was a fatal journey to many men when the phenomenally cold winter of 1863-64 came on." He overstated the case. Medical inspector Dr. Richard H. Coolidge placed it "one mile from the camp," and so did Burke.[36] It was probably southward on the lakefront. It had begun operating by the end of December 1864. While the new location benefitted the university, it offered no new or better treatment for its patients.

Barracks at camp did improve steadily, according to Briggs, but many needed windows and stoves. Prisoners were clean and comfortably supplied with clothing and blankets. "The kitchens are scrupulously clean and the messes are prepared as well as could be expected with the cooking utensils allowed them," Briggs added sarcastically.[37]

The army promoted Hoffman to brigadier general on October 7, 1864, jumping him two grades from lieutenant colonel. Doubtless, his Washington office saw some celebrating. Camp Douglas was less festive with 7,402 prisoners on hand. Briggs reported that Prisoner's Square was still shabby but that new barracks and repair of the old ones should help. The prisoners were not only clean but "very neat in appearance."[38] Briggs was about the only one who could be trusted to tell the truth about them.

Camp Douglas was becoming more livable, but that situation would change when the population almost doubled in the next two months. The weak spot, as usual, was inadequate hospital space. Briggs warned that "50 men in barracks have acute diseases."

Between June 1 and October 1, 1864, about 304 prisoners died, with 1,354 being sick. Another thousand patients were in barracks, which increased the mortality.[39] This situation alarmed Colonel Sweet after he had done so much to improve the camp and heighten his reputation. "In my opinion," he wrote Hoffman, "this increase springs from three causes," which he proceeded to lay out.

First: Prisoners had been confined for a long time, which caused depression and disease, "although they have the range of the prison square, which is kept in excellent sanitary condition."

Second: Dr. A. M. Sigmund, a volunteer officer who became post surgeon on June 22, 1864, was not competent to direct so large a medical department. Sweet charged "a lack of efficiency" at the prison hospital and in Prisoner's Square. He gave no specifics, and none of the medical inspectors agreed with him on this point. Doctor Alexander gave Sigmund good grades in his July report.

Third: Hoffman was responsible for the mortality because he stopped the sutler from selling vegetables on August 10, 1864. "This want has been distinctly visible as a cause of disease," Sweet charged.[40] The commissary issued potatoes from time to time "upon a surgeon's certificate," but not in sufficient quantities to stop scurvy. Sweet was the first prison commander to charge Hoffman with misconduct. This charge was long overdue, and Sweet planned to carry it to higher authority.

He recommended that competent medical officers be sent for and that the sutler be allowed to sell vegetables and other antiscorbutic to the prisoners. However, many of them were destitute, and Sweet did not suggest that the government should furnish vegetables. His plan favored only wealthy prisoners who could pay sutler prices. Worse, he had enough money in the prison fund to buy all the vegetables needed.

Sweet then bypassed Hoffman, going over his head, and complained to the adjutant general of the army on October 11 that mortality at camp was up 35 percent since June.[41] Thirty-four prisoners died that month, 49 in July, 98 in August, and the September toll was 123. No other Camp Douglas commander had dared to complain to higher authority. This was the third time that Sweet had tried to undermine a superior. He would not mind having Hoffman's job. No doubt Hoffman planned revenge, as he had done against Mulligan. Eventually, Sweet would find himself at Hoffman's mercy, and it would not be a pretty picture.

Meanwhile, the prisoners were desperate for help against scurvy. T. M. Page described how Mary Morris donated seed to grow vegetables, and prisoners raised a crop between the fence and the deadline. However, officers and guards ate the harvest, according to him. His reference to Mary Morris makes the incident probable. Burke described a vegetable garden belonging to the garrison that was 20 feet wide. "A small squad of prisoners are often pressed to work in the Yankee garden," he complained in his journal.[42]

Why Colonel Sweet did not use the substantial prison fund of almost $20,000 to purchase vegetables is a mystery. It ranks as the blackest mark against any commandant, at Camp Douglas or elsewhere. Colonel Mulligan and Colonel Tucker would very likely have spent the money. General Tyler and General Ammen, for sure, would not have tolerated scurvy with such a large fund on hand. De Land may not have cared. General Orme showed compassion in more than one instance and would have purchased vegetables.

Sweet was probably hoarding money for the Democratic convention, when he planned to enlarge his network of detectives and spies. The Democrats were suspected of plotting an attack on Chicago and Camp Douglas, according to Sweet's detectives. Prisoners showed great interest in the convention scheduled for August 29, 1864, in Chicago.[43] They believed that the election of a Democratic president could end the war on favorable terms for the South.

The convention gave Sweet's detectives an excuse to make heavy demands for money. This caused a dispute with Hoffman, who ordered Sweet personally to reimburse the prison fund $183.02 paid to them. This was payback time for Hoffman, and the whole business began to look like the Mulligan affair. Eleven days later Hoffman disapproved Sweet's request to put a detective on the camp payroll for a hundred dollars per month. Sweet had shown no proof that detectives had prevented a single escape from Camp Douglas. Hoffman said he would approve a lesser amount "if it can be shown that these detectives have rendered any services which have been of any value."[44] He was confident that such proof would never be presented, and he was right.

Detectives were less essential because drill instructors had whipped the "puny boys" of the 196th Pennsylvania into fighting shape. They suffered through the manual of arms, heavy drill twice a day, by battalion and regiment, target practice, cleaning weapons, and brutal inspections. This was the training that Camp Douglas had once been known for, and Major Skinner praised Greble for the beautiful condition of his rifle.

Ironically, new recruits only stayed overnight on their way to training camps elsewhere. Greble saw 130 of them outside barracks on October 2. "Six of them were Negroes!" he said with amazement. Mainline Philadelphians had little contact with the black race. Later, Greble saw 250 draftees in White Oak Square, and they were gone the same day.

General Joseph Hooker reviewed the garrison on October 15 and named the 196th "the finest Hundred days regiment he ever saw," stating that if the regiment reenlisted "he would like to have it under his command."[45] None of them did so, but Sweet must have been proud.

Sweet's other project was Prisoner's Square, and Briggs noted that major repairs and erection of new barracks were continuing as late as October 16. "The barracks are generally well policed; the floors are sanded every morning and dry rubbed," he reported to Hoffman. "The kitchens are in the best of order; their dishes, cooking utensils, and tables are scoured daily. Most of the prisoners wash their underclothing once a week," he continued. Water was somewhat limited, but blankets and clothing were sufficient for present use.[46]

Colonel Hoffman finally answered Colonel Sweet's inquiry about filling Prisoner's Square with barracks. The approach of almost five thousand more prisoners made additional housing essential. The number of barracks had to be increased or they would be terribly overcrowded. Hoffman wanted the work done cheaply, as much under five hundred dollars per barrack as possible. He believed that the barracks had been raised too high from the ground and there was no reason lathing could not cover the seams in the floors, using clay plaster as an insulator.

Hoffman promised to lay the medical needs of the camp before the surgeon general, but he refused to relax his ban on the sale of vegetables. He suggested using the prison fund to purchase "a reasonable quantity" or raising the money by selling part of the meat ration. Colonel Sweet told him bluntly that he would not cut the meat ration because winter was coming on.[47] This response surprised Hoffman because Sweet had cut rations and candles on his own. However, Sweet knew that he could only reduce rations so far, with opposition newspapers watching the camp. Regardless, Hoffman had given permission to use the prison fund to buy vegetables, and Sweet refused to spend the money.

Briggs right now was concerned about the lack of stoves and fuel for the prisoners. A wash house with six large boilers was nearly complete, and workers were busy laying six-inch water pipes throughout the camp. Prisoners suffered while the hydrants were shut off. They sank barrels in the ground to trap moisture, but with little success.[48] Briggs continued sharply to criticize the farmer's boilers in his October 23 report, which angered Hoffman. Briggs never inspected the sutler, who also came under his jurisdiction.

Nightingale charged the highest prices for shoddy goods. Inferior coffee was $1 a pound; poor quality black tea, $2.50 per pound; common brown sugar, 60¢ per pound; butter, 80¢; small apples, 5¢ each. Three large apples for 10¢ was a normal price. Nine envelopes and nine sheets of note paper sold for 30¢, double the normal cost. Prisoners labeled Nightingale "a high priced singer."[49]

Meanwhile, scurvy reached a malignant stage and brought an

View of Camp Douglas, September 1864, looking southwest, with Prisoner's Square at the western end containing 48 barracks in 12 rows, and Garrison Square and White Oak Square in the lower front. (Image courtesy of the Chicago Historical Society.)

eloquent denunciation from R. T. Bean: "Lips were eaten away, jaws became diseased, and teeth fell out. If leprosy is any worse than scurvy, may God have mercy upon the victim! It was shocking, horrible, monstrous, and a disgrace to any people who permitted such conditions to exist."[50]

October 24, 1864, was a bad day for Colonel Sweet, with prisoners pressing home successful escapes. About four Rebels tunneled out from the cellar of the prison hospital next to White Oak Square, all the way under the fence and parapet. Others slipped over the fence by ladder, right past a sleeping VRC guard. Worse, Sweet's detectives failed to warn of a serious attack that came four days later.

Colonel Sweet had left Capt. E. R. P. Shurly in charge during the time while he was on leave. Shurly was only an administrative assistant. It is puzzling that Sweet placed him in command rather than Skinner who had been promoted to lieutenant colonel on August 1. Captain Edward Richard Pitman Shurly was a transplanted Englishman. He had settled in New York and was commissioned a first lieutenant in the 126th New York Infantry early in the war. Shurly had suffered serious wounds at the Battle of Fredericksburg in 1862 and ended up in the Eighth VRC.[51]

A prison informer reported that an evening assault on the western fence of Prisoner's Square had been planned, "to be spearheaded by 100 prisoners with 11,000 to follow." Shurly believed his story because of unusual agitation in the barracks.[52]

Captain Shurly placed the Eighth VRC outside the western fence of Prisoner's Square after dark. Another regiment took up position at the eastern edge of the Chicago Driving Park, four blocks away. Shurly was just in time, as prisoners attacked at eight o'clock in the evening and broke through the fence. The Eighth VRC fired a volley that drove them back. As usual the guns did not cause much harm. Only ten prisoners suffered slight wounds. Eighteen prisoners escaped, according to the report, but were rounded up by troops advancing from the Driving Park.

Shurly had no intention of using the artillery. Hoffman again was skeptical about the cannons, except "overawing the prisoners, and its judicious use must depend on the ability of the commanding officer." Infantry would have to defend the guns, Hoffman believed, making the five hundred revolvers a better choice.[53]

Sweet would have used the big guns. He said earlier that he was anxious to punish the prisoners while in the act of escaping and that he had no confidence in the rifles. Some prisoners got by the VRC despite direct fire. Artillery would have shredded them at such close range, including those in the nearby barracks.

The *Tribune* described how guards rushed in to fire at 25 to 30 prisoners in the square after the break started. They breached the fence, but only four of them escaped before troops arrived on the outside to seal the hole, according to the paper. Guards wounded only one prisoner. John Shackelford, who had been in irons twice, was one of the leaders. He was soon on his way back to the dungeon with the familiar ball and chain. The newspaper warned that "this was a complete surprise and a close call." It concluded that the departure that day of eight hundred men in the 196th Pennsylvania encouraged the attack.[54]

Colonel Sweet retaliated by stripping prisoners of extra blankets and clothing to the extent that two wagons were required to haul the material away. Burke did not doubt that the "Yankees may be determined to reduce us to one suit."[55] It is surprising that prisoners had anything left to take. Officers had stripped the barracks of all extra shoes and clothing the previous week.

The attack of the 28th reflected on the Camp Douglas Conspiracy. This alleged plot to assault the camp occurred less than two weeks later, on November 8, 1864, and supposedly even threatened Chicago. It was unlikely that those in the attempted escape on October 28 were aware of it. The Supreme Council was unable to stop it, even if it had known. The November 8 attack would have had little chance of success if the Council had not been able to take control.

An inspector from the Northern Department disagreed with Hoffman about the artillery. He recommended that two howitzers should be added and that the farmer's boilers were fire hazards because of their worn-out condition. Sweet was after Hoffman again, reminding him about his statement that he could pay detectives out of the prison fund if "results were reported."[56] Sweet claimed that such employment "has given the names of rebel sympathizers, thus indicating where to look if they escape." Accordingly, he presented bills of $78.50 and $186.66.

His detectives had discovered the "workings and the ultimate designs of the Sons of Liberty, a treasonable organization having for its main object the success of the rebellion and the overthrow of the Government of the United States," Sweet blustered, and he warned of an "intended insurrection among the inhabitants of this and other states." Employing detectives for the next three months was essential, he argued.[57]

Colonel Sweet was either a scoundrel or a fool to suggest that dissidents could threaten a government that controlled the most powerful army on earth. Lincoln had sent veteran troops from the Army of the Potomac to crush the murderous New York draft riots in August 1863. Sweet was no fool. Neither was General Hoffman.

Captain Thomas H. Hines, CSA. (Image courtesy of The Filson Club.)

CHAPTER 16

Whether 'Tis Nobler in the Mind

The Conspiracy of 1864—Martial law in Chicago—Civilians rounded up—Fourteen die—Army hysteria—Military justice—Mary Morris takes the blame—The decline and fall of an adventurer—Colonel Sweet made a general.

Conspiracy is peculiar in that it is punishable without any crime having been committed. If one person plans to rob a federally insured bank and steals a getaway car, but decides to go bowling instead, he or she is only guilty of auto theft. However, if two people plan to rob the bank and steal a getaway car, they have committed a Federal crime by conspiring to rob the bank. Conspiracy law is useful in times of national stress to prosecute political dissidents or perceived enemies for alleged plots that do not have much chance of success.

Opposing views about the Camp Douglas Conspiracy of 1864 continue to surface. Some historians believe that the conspiracy existed. Others conclude that it was a hoax concocted by scoundrels and self-seekers.[1] It appears that the truth lies closer to the hoax theory. Many plots to free the prisoners were hatched before 1864. However, none captured the attention of the media, or alarmed the North, as did the Conspiracy of 1864.

Many Northerners found reasons for believing in a plot. Tension existed in the southern part of Illinois called "Egypt." Officials passed resolutions in two of these counties on April 15, 1861, "to effect a division of the state and to attach Egypt to the southern confederacy." Illinois congressman John A. Logan "was understood to have approved the resolutions."[2] He denied it, but his pro-Southern bias and sponsorship of the Illinois "Black Code" of 1855 gave credence to the story. His legislation provided for arresting blacks who migrated to Illinois and selling them if they could not pay the fine.

Bitter clashes developed between draft officials in the southern counties and mobs opposing conscription. Guerrilla bands attacked

Unionists, and five men died on April 28, 1864. The "Clingman" gang caused much damage until it was broken up.[3]

A Union army thrust toward Atlanta supposedly led Confederate president Jefferson Davis to plan an uprising in the North. The plan was to use "Copperheads," such as the Order of American Knights, renamed Sons of Liberty, Knights of the Golden Circle, and the Sons of Illini.

Richmond gave Capt. Thomas Henry Hines an assignment to go to Canada on March 16, 1864, and contact Confederates from General Morgan's old command. Hines supposedly had engineered one prison break and had contacts among pro-Southern groups in the North. He was to find friends in Canada and persuade them to organize and give aid to the South. "He will likewise have in view the possibility, by such means as he can command, of effecting any fair and appropriate enterprises of war against our enemies," the orders stated.[4]

The Confederate government sent a commission to Montreal under Jacob Thompson as director and treasurer to oversee the agents. Two more commissioners arrived in May 1864 under instructions from President Davis "to further the interests of the Confederacy." They reportedly had eight hundred thousand dollars in Federal greenbacks to spend.[5] This amounted to about $5 million in Confederate money. It was unlikely that the Confederacy invested such a huge sum in a project with no plans or strategy.

Hines selected Camp Douglas for mounting an attack because of the large number of Morgan's men held there. He foolishly believed that Chicago contained large Copperhead organizations, perhaps numbering five thousand members. Confederate agents allegedly met in Canada with Clement Vallandigham, a prominent Copperhead. He assured Hines and Commissioner Thompson that he controlled three hundred thousand men, many of them Union army veterans. They were ready at his command for an armed uprising to take over the state governments in Illinois, Indiana, and Ohio. "All that was needed was money," the blowhard said. The Confederates conceded afterward that they were naive to believe him.[6]

Hines and his agents set an attack to take place on the Fourth of July, the day of the Democratic convention in Chicago. Charles Walsh, an alleged leader of the Sons of Liberty, would arm two thousand of his followers. Walsh was a successful Chicago businessman with a wife and ten children, one of them an infant.[7] He did not plan to lead the attack.

Those in charge discussed the possibility of capturing a Federal gunboat on Lake Michigan and turning its guns on the camp. This suggestion never came up again. Perhaps it dawned on the conspirators that the guns would most likely kill many prisoners. The plan included freeing prisoners at other camps simultaneously with the attack on Camp Douglas and seizing all three governments of the northwestern states, Indiana, Illinois, and Ohio.[8]

Yet, plotters did none of the planning for such a large-scale insurrection. They failed to map or assign assault positions. Leaders went unnamed, and an opportune hour for an assault was never set; no discussions took place about weapons and munitions, no provision was made for dead and wounded, and no thought was given to escape routes or rear guard blocking units.

Small wonder that when the Democratic convention was postponed to August 29, the Sons of Liberty decided to do the same with their plans. Hines, convinced that the promised troops were eager to fight, persuaded them to make July 20 the starting date.[9] Again, no plan existed.

The Chicago conspirators soon reneged on the July date and sent word that they were not ready, but gave no reasons. Hines allegedly met with them again in Chicago, and they agreed upon August 16 as the day of action. The con artists soon requested another postponement of the assault, arguing that the Confederate army had to launch attacks into Kentucky and Missouri to divert Federal forces away from Chicago. Hines and Thompson should have realized that they were wasting time and money. Instead, they reset everything for the day of the Democratic convention, August 29, 1864.[10] Hines stipulated no more delays.

A major reversal occurred when Vallandigham withdrew from the plot and returned to Ohio. There went three hundred thousand troops, limiting the uprising to an attack on Camp Douglas. Braggarts in Canada and sympathizers in Chicago boasted of an attack on the prison, not to mention the tales coming from spies and informers.[11] Many men, and perhaps women, on Union and Confederate payrolls, were making a good living out of the whole affair.

This time Captain Hines made himself responsible for planning the assault. He came to Chicago, "and using the Walsh home as a vantage point, drew an accurate map of the camp and its approaches and planned the attack upon it as a textbook military operation," the conspirators wrote seriously. "A night assault was aimed at three of the four sides of the camp; as soon as it started, the prisoners were to attack the guards from the rear."[12] Those involved planned to cut telegraph lines and bribe railroad employees to transport freed prisoners. "The first stop was the prison camp at Rock Island, Illinois," they concluded.

Omitting doubts about the railroad scheme, it is difficult to believe that Hines actually planned to use civilians who had never fought together as a unit. He expected these inexperienced volunteers to mount a successful night operation without training or rehearsal? More unbelievable, he paid no attention to the University of Chicago astronomical observatory towering over the camp. Colonel Sweet had taken notice and had stationed one to two companies of riflemen there.[13] They could unleash a devastating fire on the camp and any attack force while enjoying the protection of the stone tower. Sweet overmatched Captain Hines before the game even started. An attack would be uncertain even for highly trained special forces.

Copperheads rescued Captain Hines and his agents from their own folly when they made no assault on August 29. Their army existed only in the imagination of Charles Walsh or, more accurately, in the imaginations of the Confederates. The many thousands of assault troops came to 25 men.[14]

Originally, the Supreme Council of Seven at Camp Douglas knew nothing about the Hines group. It planned a mass breakout, probably for the spring or summer of 1864, but gave no date.[15] Then it received a coded letter from friends that Capt. Thomas Hines was in Chicago, but otherwise the letter was unclear. Again, no date was given.

The Supreme Council postponed its plans but paid a garrison officer $130 to allow a prisoner to escape. He carried a code to Chicago for communicating by mail. This story has a ring of truth because the bribe money was raised partly "by selling sutler's checks at enormous discounts to the Federal soldiers on duty as patrol guard." Soon, John Waller, who invented the code, received a letter from Mrs. Sarah B. Waller (no relation) on August 4, 1864.[16]

Mrs. Waller requested prisoners "to contribute some curiosities of their own manufacture to be sent to a fair to be held in Liverpool, England for the Confederate prisoners' benefit," according to Burke. It is too much coincidence that this Southern woman, active in prison relief since 1862, sent the request to John Waller. It appears certain that Confederate agents were in contact with the Council by August 4, 1864. Sweet told Hoffman on October 11 that his detectives had discovered "channels of communication" between Chicago and a prisoner of war organization at camp.[17]

B. R. Froman stated, "In this way we were informed that Captain Tom Hines, St. Leger Grenfel, Captain Castleman, and others, with about eighty of our comrades who had not been captured, were in Chicago, had come thither by way of Canada, for the purpose of liberating us, and they expected to be joined and aided by one or two hundred Copperheads, as they were then called, from Southern Illinois."

Froman gave no date for this planned assault, nor did he say that the Council had received more letters. He wisely objected to postponing their own plans, but was overruled. Hines confirmed that "information had been conveyed to prudent prisoners that aid from the outside would come and they were to be watchful for the attack without as a signal for resistance within."[18] Such a signal never came, as the Sons of Liberty failed to produce an assault force.

Hines perceived the Sons of Liberty as "being sincere and not lacking in courage." Now he believed that they had become timid and had overestimated reinforcements sent to Sweet. "It was necessary, therefore, to look beyond Chicago for a field of action," Hines decided. He and fellow agent John Castleman suggested to the Sons of Liberty that they attack the Rock Island, Illinois, prison camp and seize the state capital.[19] Castleman was a Confederate officer who had ridden with Morgan.

No one responded to this suicidal plan, so "the Confederate officers accordingly deemed it wise to leave Chicago," according to Hines, "as the safety secured by the presence of the Convention was removed, and the agents of the Government had been aroused to greater vigilance and activity."[20]

The Camp Douglas Conspiracy was now over, but not if Colonel Sweet could help it. The rest of the tale was his invention. It was improbable that the few civilians intended to attack the camp. It was not their war, not their flag. They had no cause worth dying for. It was the money that mattered, and Hines and Castleman were no match for their cunning.

Colonel Sweet, however, set out to convince his superiors that he was about to crush a dangerous uprising. He had to act without authority and present them with an accomplished fact before they stopped him. They had made no response when Colonel Tucker requested martial law in Chicago, yet when he arrested a prominent citizen, it caused a furor. Colonel Sweet planned to do both. Where Tucker had failed, Sweet succeeded, because Tucker was a businessman, while Sweet was a skilled politician.

At 8:30 P.M. on November 6 Sweet dispatched a hand-delivered message to Gen. John Cook in Springfield, because "he was not entirely sure of the telegraph." The real reason was to have time to act without being questioned. Cook had given Sweet specific orders on November 6 to arrest only two "rebel agents" in Chicago on Monday morning, the seventh, "at 9 o'clock," and seize their papers. That was all.[21] Sweet's messenger could not have reached Springfield by rail until after midnight, and probably did not see General Cook until the morning of the seventh. By that time it was too late to stop the operation.

Sweet must have flabbergasted Cook with his message. He warned that "the City is filling up with suspicious characters . . . and others who were here from Canada . . . plotting to release the prisoners of war at Camp Douglas . . . I have every reason to believe that Colonel Marmaduke of the rebel army is in the city . . . and also Captain Hines . . . also Col G. St. Leger Grenfell . . . My force is only 800 men . . . to guard between 8,000 and 9,000 prisoners. I am certainly not justified in waiting to take risks . . . The head gone we can manage the body. In order to make these arrests perfect, I must also arrest two or three prominent citizens . . . I regret that I am not able to consult with you on my proposed action before acting without letting an opportunity pass which may never again occur . . . "[22]

Nevertheless, Sweet had written letters to the Northern Department of the Army at Cincinnati on November 1 and did not mention these fears. He only protested his heavy work load as military commander of Chicago besides other duties. This office furnished security to hospitals in the area and provided transportation for soldiers in transit. In a second letter, Colonel Sweet recommended that the department appoint Colonel Strong military commander of Chicago.[23] "I am only one man," Sweet complained, "and cannot divide myself without causing inconveniences." The department never asked that he explain why these letters gave no hint of danger.

Even more damning was the 196th Pennsylvania Infantry. Why did

Sweet permit eight hundred trained and healthy troops to depart on October 28 if he anticipated an attack on the camp 11 days later? This left only the disabled Eighth and 15th VRC. The term of service for the 196th did not expire until November 15, and Sweet could have requested Washington to extend it. Washington had done so with the 67th Illinois Infantry in the Dr. Levi Boone emergency of 1862.

Sweet had two reasons for wanting the Pennsylvania regiment gone. His main excuse for the preemptive strike was the tiny garrison. "My force is only 800 men," he told Springfield. Most important, he would have had to give Washington some reason for keeping the 196th. Then, the army would have been certain to send in its own strike force, if it did credit his story. It was no accident that Sweet was in Wisconsin when the Pennsylvanians went home. This allowed him to say, if need be, that he would have stopped the departure if he had been there. It also explains why he left Captain Shurly in charge of the camp, instead of Lieutenant Colonel Skinner. Skinner was so ruthless, decisive, and efficient that he would have prevented the 196th from leaving.

With the 196th out of the way, Sweet unleashed the most able-bodied of his VRC on November 6, 1864. Arrests began that night and continued into the morning of the seventh. Helped by Chicago police and mounted civilian vigilantes, the troops gathered in alleged leaders of the plot and supposed foot soldiers. Martial law had come to Chicago. At 10:30 A.M. on the seventh, Sweet wired to Colonel Hoffman a list of the persons arrested.

"Col. G. St. Leger Grenfell, and J.T. Shanks, an escaped prisoner of war at the Richmond House; Col. Vincent Marmaduke . . . Brig Gen. Charles Walsh, of the Sons of Liberty; Captain Cantrill, of Morgan's command, and Charles Traverse . . . at the house of General Walsh; Judge Buckner S. Morris, treasurer of Sons of Liberty . . . also capturing at the same time in Walsh's house about thirty rods from Camp Douglas arms and ammunition." These were sufficient to arm only 569 men, far short of the two thousand troops Walsh had supposedly promised. No warrant to search the Walsh home was issued by any judge, as was required under the vanished Constitution.

Found on November 7 at Walsh's, according to Sweet: "142 shot guns, double-barreled, loaded; 349 revolvers; 13,412 cartridges; 3 boxes of cones; 265 bullet molds for pistols; 239 cone wrenches for pistols; 8 bags buck shot, No. 4; 2 kegs powder, partly filled; 115 holsters for revolvers; 8 belts for holsters."

Buckner S. Morris. (Image courtesy of the Chicago Historical Society.)

Mary E. Morris. (Image courtesy of The Filson Club.)

Seized on November 11: "47 shot guns, double-barreled; 30 Allen's breech-loading carbines; 1 Enfield rifle."

Sweet did not explain why this stockpile was not found on November 7. Attempts by the defense to inquire about it at the conspiracy trials were overruled by the court. This second arsenal would have been difficult to overlook in the first search, and it may have been planted after Walsh was in custody.

Sweet claimed that he had "complete proof" of Morris's "assisting Shanks to escape and plotting to release the prisoners at this camp." Their plan was to attack on election night, he claimed. His charges against Buckner S. Morris proved false. He was the second former mayor of Chicago to be imprisoned at Camp Douglas.

On November 10, in response to an inquiry about Morris, General Cook repeated Sweet's charges but admitted that he had "no written order for his arrest especially."[24] Cook's evasive answer confirmed that Sweet had no warrant. Buckner Morris was twice a widower with two grown daughters when he married Mary Parrish, a young Kentucky widow, in a May-December match in 1856. She was devoted to the Southern cause and used the Morris home recklessly for Confederate activity.

"In addition," Sweet continued, "the patrols aided by Chicago police arrested on 7 November 106 bushwhackers, guerrillas and rebel soldiers, among them many of the notorious Clingman gang of Fayette and Christian counties of this State with their Captain, Sears, and Lieut. Garland, all of whom are now in custody at Camp Douglas." His claim of 106 men arrested on November 7 was probably true, but more than half of those were subsequently let go according to Camp Douglas records.[25]

One Camp Douglas register in the National Archives lists 18 prisoners from Chicago, but patrols arrested only six in the city on November 7. Sweet seized the others on the 12th through the 16th of November, and Edmund C. Waller was arrested in Cincinnati on December 2. A second list shows 108 suspects, 103 from southern Illinois and five from out of state. Incredibly, authorities arrested only 69 in Chicago, the others were taken into custody in their home counties. Even more astonishing, of the 69, Sweet found only 51 in the city on November 6, 7, and 8, the remainder on November 12. Sweet could barely show that 57 "traitors" were on hand for the attack, and only 25 of these had shown up.

His boast about Sears and Garland was also untrue. Guards had a

George Garland in custody on November 8, but he disappeared from the rolls by December 10, and was probably the wrong man. No one named Sears was ever there. Apologists for Sweet put forward the tangled argument that it is a matter of punctuation. Sweet never claimed that he had captured Sears and Garland, but meant only that they were the captain and lieutenant of the Clingman gang.[26] This is a preposterous reading of his report.

Sweet jailed "bushwhackers, guerrillas, and rebel soldiers" at Trinity Church downtown before moving them to Camp Douglas. The *Tribune* even reported that "military barracks" were set up inside the church.[27] Imprisoning people in a house of worship showed a lack of sensitivity somewhere. Doctor Pratt had to give his permission, because Trinity was too prestigious for Sweet to just walk in and take over. Doctor Pratt had preached the first sermon to Confederate prisoners at Camp Douglas in 1862 and had asked them, "What will you do if you still have doubts about religion?"

On November 7, General Hooker, commanding the Northern Department of the army, not knowing what Sweet had done, wired, "I apprehend no attack on you." He advised Sweet to gather all of the military forces he could find and hold them ready until he had passed the crisis of the election. "The Board of Trade and other loyal citizens will take care of Chicago, if necessary," Hooker said confidently. "This will leave you a handsome battalion to fight with, if required." He was not aware that Sweet had let go of the 196th Pennsylvania. "I have requested General Cook to reenforce you with two companies from Springfield," the general concluded.[28]

Stanton telegraphed his approval of Sweet's actions, and Governor Yates placed the Chicago militia under his orders. General Hooker fell into line and dispatched five hundred more men to Chicago "under fighting officers." The 48th Illinois Infantry rushed in the following day along with "three car-loads of armed troops" from Camp Butler near Springfield. Sweet soon had two thousand troops at his disposal in addition to the garrison and extended a guard line outside Camp Douglas for miles.

Sweet arrested five more alleged members of the Sons of Liberty on November 14. One was Richard T. Semmes, whom Sweet named as the nephew of Confederate admiral Raphael Semmes, another lie. Sweet jailed Dr. E. W. Edwards who had allegedly harbored Confederate agent Vincent Marmaduke. Marmaduke, like Semmes, was another innocent bystander with the wrong name. On November 15,

Sweet's men grabbed a young Englishman from Canada, "who proved to be a messenger" between the conspirators and guerrillas in Kentucky, according to Sweet. Edmund C. Waller was also in custody. He may have been the son of Sarah B. Waller, who sent the coded message to the Supreme Council. Colonel Sweet advised the adjutant general that Waller's family resided in Chicago and that he was being held as a witness at Camp Douglas.[29]

Taking Sweet's figures, the threat to Camp Douglas on November 8 amounted to seven alleged leaders and 106 foot soldiers. Camp Douglas records reduced this number to 57. Add eight or nine more suspects taken on November 14 and 1,5 and the total force was perhaps 66 men. More ludicrous, Sweet could name only 143 "prominent members of the Sons of Liberty" statewide.[30]

Colonel Sweet saw the making of his career in the rumors of a conspiracy. Washington promoted him to brigadier general on December 20, 1864, and his postwar career was assured. He had his star, but the cost in lives was substantial. He ended his reports with the recommendation "that the officers of the rebel army, and as many of the Sons of Liberty and guerrillas above mentioned, as the interests of the Government may require, be tried before a military commission, and punished."[31] The army heeded his advice.

Sweet requested that the military trials be held in Chicago, but Maj. Henry. L. Burnett, in Cincinnati, was an experienced prosecutor, and General Hooker decided that this is where the conspirators would be moved.[32] However, General Sweet would have an active role in Chicago, gathering evidence, interrogating witnesses, and holding defendants in custody until they went to Cincinnati. The Sixth Amendment to the prostrate Constitution had once prohibited removing defendants to a different jurisdiction.

President Lincoln sent no word, but his humorous telegram to Frankfort, Kentucky, on November 10 should have made him skeptical about the conspiracy: "I can scarcely believe that General John B. Huston has been arrested for no other offense than opposition to my re-election; for if that had been deemed sufficient cause of arrest I should have heard of more than one arrest in Kentucky on election day," Lincoln joked. "General Burbridge will discharge him at once," he ordered.[33]

Lincoln distrusted the military, and his instincts were correct. On November 28, 1864, Sweet advised Major Burnett, the prosecutor, on how to entrap two alleged Camp Douglas conspirators already locked up in Cincinnati. "I have no doubt," Sweet wrote, "if they are sent here and confined with a man who will be an important witness in Cincinnati, and fasten guilt upon some of these leading Sons of Liberty."[34] Sweet did not name his jailhouse informant, but it was John T. Shanks, who pretended to be an escaped prisoner and plotter.

It was no surprise that General Hoffman remained silent. He had continuously denied Sweet's requests to pay his detectives, believing they were worthless. Now Sweet's men seemed to have triumphed. By November 12 the hysteria in Chicago was so intense that General Hooker's adjutant requested additional men from Springfield. General Cook reported that soldiers had found more weapons in Walsh's barn. "We have not touched bottom yet!" Cook warned sternly.[35]

Chicago newspapers took sides about the plot depending on their politics. The *Tribune* felt that Chicago had escaped a volcano. "A GENERAL SACK OF THE CITY INTENDED—PLUNDER, RAPINE—FIRE—BLOODSHED IN THE STREETS OF CHICAGO."[36] This came directly from Sweet's reports.

The pro-Confederate *Chicago Times* felt that not the slightest danger existed for an attack upon Camp Douglas. "That such an attack was contemplated by half a dozen rebels is probable, but that they could have relied upon any local assistance in the undertaking is wholly improbable," the editor claimed. This was not an understatement.

Sweet did not arrest Mary Morris, despite the frenzy. He was after her husband because that was where the publicity lay. Buckner Morris was born in Kentucky in 1800 and sat in the state legislature at age 30. However, he destroyed his career by proposing to abolish slavery. He then moved to Chicago where he was elected mayor from 1838 to 1839. Morris later became the first judge in Illinois to allow scientific evidence in a murder trial. He ran a losing campaign for Illinois governor in 1860 as a Breckinridge Democrat, the breakaway Southern faction of the party.[37]

Sweet considered Charles Walsh almost as important as Buckner Morris. Walsh was a major player in Chicago's economic and political scene and had been the Democratic candidate for sheriff of Cook County in 1862. The district included Chicago and Camp Douglas, along with substantial patronage. The weapons and munitions stored on his property were the only evidence that might tie Walsh to a conspiracy.

George St. Leger Grenfell was probably Sweet's trump card in collecting support for his actions. Grenfell was an Englishman with a criminal record, whose show business name suited his wasted life and tall tales. He had been close to Gen. John Hunt Morgan as adjutant and advisor once and had done credible administrative work for Confederate generals Braxton Bragg and Joseph Wheeler. His army career ended when officials filed felony charges against him in Tennessee for stealing horses and a slave. He jumped bail, however, and Gen. J. E. B. Stuart then employed him as inspector general of cavalry in 1863. He resigned at the end of the year under veiled circumstances.[38] Grenfell's life in the American Civil War was as obscure as his past and is only dimly glimpsed, like fish in a muddy pond. He was ideally suited to be a defendant in the conspiracy trials.

Major Henry L. Burnett, the army prosecutor, overruled Sweet's decision not to arrest Mrs. Morris. It turned out that Sweet's strategy had been correct, as Mary's self-incrimination at the trials destroyed the case against her husband. A story, fictitious no doubt, told how Colonel Sweet had ordered Mrs. Morris sent to White Oak dungeon after arresting her on December 19, 1864. Captain Shurly, the adjutant, defied him and housed the Morris couple in his quarters.[39] This would have been typical of Shurly, who considered himself, with some merit, a "Christian gentleman."

Shurly would do nothing for Grenfell, however. Sweet held him in a tiny unheated cell in the guardhouse, under what Grenfell labeled "inhuman conditions." He complained to Sweet that he was a British citizen and inquired anxiously about his dog which had been captured with him.[40] Sweet made no response, and the animal's fate is unknown.

Military justice was swift, if nothing else. The army sent Buckner and Mary Morris, Walsh, Grenfell, Shanks, and other defendants to Cincinnati around January 1, 1865, for trial by a military court. Military trials of civilians during the Civil War usually took place in the territories or war zones.[41] The spectacle of the army trying civilians in Cincinnati, while the state and Federal courts were open, horrified those who were concerned about liberty. Attorneys for the defendants argued without success that the tribunal had no jurisdiction in the matter. The darker shadows of the rebellion were moving across the Northern landscape now, and the "peculiar" Constitution had packed up and left for parts unknown.

Benjamin M. Anderson, a "conspirator" put on trial at Sweet's suggestion, committed suicide in jail, which the military court took as an admission of guilt. Anderson was a deserter from a Kentucky regiment that had been part of Morgan's command. Grenfell testified that Anderson left the army in September of 1862, "since which time I have never heard from him or of him."[42] This was probably one of few truthful statements made during these proceedings.

The star witness against the defendants, next to General Sweet was John T. Shanks, Company D, 14th Kentucky Cavalry. His enemies labeled him a "forger, thief, traitor, spy, liar, and perjurer." Thomas Hines charged that "a blacker-hearted villain never lived!"[43] One would expect Shanks's enemies to exaggerate, but it appears that they did not.

Officials accused Shanks of "forging land warrants" while a clerk in the Texas land office in Austin before the war. He probably gave buyers fake land titles and pocketed their money. He was indicted on five criminal charges and ended up in the penitentiary. He managed his release by enlisting in the 15th Texas Cavalry, but quickly deserted. Shanks then made his way to Tupelo, Mississippi, and became a clerk for the Confederate army. There he made false entries in record books and defrauded army suppliers. Prosecutors filed additional charges against him for stealing a saddle and marrying a Mississippi lady while he still had a wife in Texas.[44]

A court-martial found him guilty on all charges, and he could have been shot. The army delivered him, instead, to civil authorities for trial on the bigamy charges. He promptly escaped and fled eastward to Tennessee or Kentucky. Shanks later joined the so-called 14th Kentucky Cavalry of Morgan's command. This unit was created for the benefit of Col. Richard C. Morgan, General Morgan's brother. Shanks surrendered with Morgan's raiders in June 1863 and landed at Camp Douglas. The ex-convict was ideally suited to be a prisoner of war.

General Sweet's pretense that Shanks was not his agent, and that Buckner Morris had helped him escape from Camp Douglas, was his most devious lie. Sweet revealed the truth in a letter written to Hoffman on March 29, 1865, only recently found in the National Archives. In it, he requested permission to give Shanks one year's pay from the prison fund at a hundred dollars per month. "John T. Shanks had been employed for more than a year as a clerk in the office of the Commissary of prisoners without pay," Sweet wrote, "being a prisoner of war and was a very careful, efficient clerk—In

November last at the time of the rebel raid from Canada he was taken into my confidence, went into the City of Chicago, detected the presence and identified the presence of some of the officers and prisoners engaged in the Conspiracy, and performed faithfully a very important public service for which on my application he was afterward released."[45]

Sweet argued that to pay him "is no more than a fair compensation for the amount of labor he performed." Significantly, the going rate for one of Sweet's detectives was a hundred dollars per month. Records do not show that Hoffman approved the request.[46] Sweet's role in employing Shanks remained buried in army files and later lay undetected in the National Archives. Major Burnett, the army prosecutor, was out to convict innocent men and women and must have guessed that Sweet employed Shanks. Hoffman failed to expose them. To do so may have damaged his career. General Daniel Tyler would have acted differently.

Grenfell wrote the British embassy during his trial that "Shanks invention is most fertile, he sticks at nothing, one tenth part of his assertions if true would be sufficient to hang me." They did, in a way. Incredibly, the army court sustained an objection by Burnett, when defense counsel asked Shanks about his criminal convictions in Texas, but Shanks had the audacity to snap, "I never was!" This opened the door for defense witnesses to testify to the contrary, and Burnett was forced to concede that Shanks had been "imprisoned, tried and convicted at Austin, Texas."[47] The army handed down convictions anyway.

The trials lasted until April 18, 1865, with strange results.

George St. Leger Grenfell: Sentenced to death. Influential people, including General Sweet, interceded for him. Sweet already had Anderson's suicide on the table. This was no longer a comic opera. The court commuted Grenfell's sentence to life in prison at Fort Jefferson in the Dry Tortugas, another death sentence. Grenfell seemed to find himself there and worked with Dr. Samuel Mudd, the convicted Lincoln conspirator, to save lives during the terrible epidemics that ravaged the island. The adventurer showed an astonishing selflessness and strength of character this time.

No evidence existed that Grenfell played any role in the alleged conspiracy other than testimony from slimy characters such as Shanks and others working for Sweet. Even more despicable than Shanks was Winslow Ayer, a quack who pretended to be a doctor, and who was, perhaps, Sweet's most trusted agent. No doubt Grenfell was aware of rumors about the plot. Otherwise, why was he in Chicago on November 7? His story that he just happened to be passing through town after a hunting trip was absurd. Most likely he sought employment in attacking the camp, since Morgan's raiders knew him, and so did Hines. No matter how inept Hines was, he would not have trusted Grenfell with any secrets, and Grenfell received no warning when they fled.

"Colonel" Vincent Marmaduke: He was not even a "Kentucky Colonel," but some luckless civilian who was in the wrong place at the wrong time with the wrong name. Sweet probably associated him with Gen. John Sappington Marmaduke, a former U.S. Army officer from Missouri who fought ferociously for the South. He did not appear to have had a relative with the same family name.[48] Small wonder that the court described Marmaduke's role in the conspiracy as "unknown" and acquitted him.

Richard T. Semmes: Originally from Maryland, he refused to serve in either army. His downfall was the name "Semmes" and belonging to the Democratic club, which was the alleged center of the Copperhead plot.[49] He received three years in prison for being an innocent bystander but was later freed.

Charles Walsh: An army veteran of earlier wars, he supported the war at first and helped to raise Mulligan's Irish Brigade. Lincoln's Emancipation Proclamation embittered him, which may have led him to purchase weapons and munitions for the Confederates. Walsh claimed that he only intended to arm his local Democratic club to protect the polls on election day. His story is no more believable than any other about the conspiracy, although the small number of weapons seems to support him. Regardless, the guns implicated Walsh only. However, Burnett tied him to the other defendants through the testimony of Shanks and three more dubious characters working for Sweet.[50] The court ordered five years imprisonment, and he was also pardoned.

Buckner S. Morris and Mary E. Morris: The military court acquitted the judge. Even Shanks had conceded under cross-examination that he had dealt only with Mary, not her husband. However, the trials bankrupted Morris, and he became dependent upon his daughters who were needy themselves.

Major Burnett charged Mary as a conspirator but did not put her on trial, probably in exchange for her testimony. She took the blame and thus lent credence to the plot. The army court banished her to Kentucky, and the destruction of the Constitution was complete. She and Buckner never lived together again. However, Mary became first lady for her brother, Dr. Luke P. Blackburn, in the governor's mansion in Kentucky after the war.

Doctor Blackburn was the center of an infamous "Yellow Fever Plot." His diabolical plan was to gather "infected clothing" from yellow fever victims for shipment to Northern cities.[51] Fortunately, the "infected clothing" was no more dangerous than the Camp Douglas plot, since only mosquitoes carry the disease.

The trials were discredited in 1866, when the again U.S. Supreme Court resurrected civil liberties by vacating a military death sentence against Lambdin P. Milligan of Indiana, an alleged Copperhead. It ruled that the military could not try a citizen where civil courts were open. This decision should have freed Grenfell, as it did the other defendants, but it did not.[52]

He had incurred Stanton's special wrath for allegedly promising that he would not engage in operations against the North. The sinister Judge Advocate General Joseph Holt conceded that the only direct evidence of Grenfell's complicity in the Camp Douglas conspiracy was Shanks. "His testimony is minute, direct, and full, and completely implicates the accused in one of the most stupendous projects of causeless and profitless crime known to modern times!" Holt ranted.[53] On March 6 or 7, 1868, after three brutal years of imprisonment, Grenfell escaped into the ocean and perished. Another eagle had fallen.

Yet, Grenfell was insignificant compared with Capt. Thomas Hines, who broke things up and let others put them back together again. Hines claimed that he was staying at the Morris home when soldiers arrived on the night of November 6. He "was saved from the patrol," according to his account, "by being placed between two mattresses on a bed while two ladies reposed in apparent sleep upon the upper mattress, with suitable bed clothes." Legend also placed him at Dr. Edwards's home, this time under the mattress of Mrs. Edwards.[54] The South compensated Hines with a seat on the Kentucky Court of Appeals after the war.

Unlike Hines, many others reaped a harvest of pain and death. Eighty-one prisoners arrested in November spent four to five months at Camp Douglas; the last releases were on April 19, 1865. Twelve of them died. This brought the toll to 14 in the conspiracy hoax, counting Anderson and Grenfell. General Sweet put some on trial at Camp Douglas. "A court martial has been sitting for some weeks at camp, trying the leading cases; it has now been adjourned," the *Tribune* disclosed. "The findings are not made public." Secret military trials violated the Articles of War that supposedly were still in effect.

Unfortunately, President Lincoln had suspended the Writ of Habeas Corpus for persons in military custody. This famous Writ, embodied in Article I, Section 9, of the torn-up Constitution, was an order issued by a judge to deliver a person from illegal confinement. No civilian court could now question the "probable cause" for their arrests.[55]

On the other hand, Lincoln now set about to protect two high-ranking plotters from prosecution. The army caught John Castleman, but his sister, Virginia, was married to Judge Samuel M. Breckinridge of St. Louis. The judge was a fellow Kentuckian and on a first-name basis with the president. Lincoln was happy to oblige "Sam" and "Virginia" by interceding for Castleman. Then, just before going to Ford's Theatre, Lincoln ordered the warrant for Jacob Thompson, the former Confederate commissioner, torn up so that he could leave the country.[56] Compare these events with the treatment accorded the ill-fated Grenfell.

Camp Douglas may have seen its largest insurrection had the Supreme Council not postponed its own plans. Otway B. Norvell claimed that any object that may have served as a weapon was hidden away, and the plot was ready by midsummer 1864.[57] The conspirators planned simultaneous attacks for 3 A.M. on the guardhouse to arm themselves, on the parapet, and against the stockade. They aimed to seize the artillery once they had penetrated the fence.

A sudden attack by close to two thousand men against only eight hundred disabled guards had potential. This would have been the first mass attack on the garrison. By November 8, it was too late. Ironically, the "interior conspiracy" had a better theoretical chance of succeeding than the exterior one.

On the other hand, the Council made some serious miscalculations. It believed that the garrison consisted entirely of "perfectly raw troops," and it made the unwarranted assumption that the 24th Ohio Artillery would not immediately fire into Prisoner's Square. Finally, it overlooked the danger of betrayal. Sweet told Fuller about a plot by four to five hundred prisoners working in Garrison Square to seize arms and munitions.[58] The information must have come from a prisoner; otherwise, Sweet would have credited his detectives.

Believing in the Camp Douglas Conspiracy is a matter of faith. Confederate agents wished themselves into believing they had created one, and General Sweet made their dreams come true. It was the nature and the character of men like Grenfell, Hines, Castleman, Shanks, and Sweet that gave life to the hoax.

The excitement barely made a ripple among the prisoners, who were busy darning their socks. They used yarn taken from worn-out socks, a darning needle, and a small stick about the size of a lead pencil. They sewed the damaged sock over the stick, which they then removed. Burke heard that "there were rumors about arms, etc. being found near camp. At night we had unusually strict orders to keep quiet. The Yanks seem afraid of the rebs making a break."[59]

Sweet continued to employ John T. Shanks. On April 6, 1865, he placed the Sixth U. S. Volunteer Infantry Regiment in his charge to march it to Camp Frye, a subpost of Camp Douglas. He insured Shank's continued loyalty and silence by making the felon an officer and a gentleman in the U.S. army on April 21, commanding Company I of the Sixth Regiment. The War Department approved this extraordinary commission at a time when career soldiers and West Pointers were seeking promotion.

It was all ahead of Shanks now, at the age of 34. The road lay westward to Fort Leavenworth and the Indian wars. He was on the winning side again. Like General Sweet, Captain Shanks saw his opportunity in the Civil War and made it pay off. However, 1866 was not a good year for the captain after Indians wounded him in January. Then the army investigated him for not paying his men.[60] Shanks gave the unacceptable excuse that they were "insubordinate." The payroll stuck to his fingers, most likely.

With the Camp Douglas conspiracy fading by the end of November 1864, the forces of nature moved in to fill its place. Soon another dreary winter lay over the camp. Sleet and snow swirled off the lake, while daylight fled the city as though it were a plague. Darkness fell on the hearts of guards and prisoners alike.

CHAPTER 17

The Long Winter of the Confederacy

General Hoffman takes a breather—Pa deserts—General Hood's shattered army arrives—More charges of prisoners freezing to death—The no-talking rule—Description of cruel guards—Food and bedding reports—Prison population reaches 12,082—Chapel destroyed.

The turmoil in Chicago did not stop Special Inspector Briggs from criticizing Morgan's men for lack of cleanliness. Otherwise, the camp was finally in excellent condition, "The guards perform their duty well," he thought, "and the sick have plenty of attendants; the hospital is well supplied with food necessary for the sick," including "plenty of vegetables." Smallpox patients were in bad shape as usual.

Briggs suggested that prisoners be allowed to receive from home "uncooked garden vegetables, such as onions, potatoes, cabbage, turnips, &c." Continuing retaliation scuttled this sensible idea. Families could again ship clothing, bedding, and ticks, "but no articles the sutler sells."[1] Nightingale must truly have been Sweet's brother-in-law.

Hoffman's policy of providing vegetables only to the hospital caused chaos in the medical community. Hospital surgeons refused to discharge patients because of the scurvy in barracks. They could have sent back half the 250 cases taking up beds. Surgeons pulled their hair out as a thousand patients suffered in barracks, of whom four hundred required hospital care.[2]

Scurvy at Elmira was worse. There Hoffman refused to order fresh vegetables even for the hospital, and he rejected needed repairs on barracks. This explains why Elmira had a higher mortality rate than Camp Douglas. Far fewer escapes occurred, but it produced an appalling sick list. "In March 1865 an average of sixteen prisoners died daily," one historian observed. "Out of 12,123 soldiers imprisoned at Elmira, death claimed 2,063, nearly one out of six."[3]

The Elmira prison never lacked a substantial stockade, however.

Officials had to reinforce the one at Camp Douglas with more lumber around November 15, 1864. Burke described the work as "an extra coat of plank." They nailed it "as high as a man can reach" on both sides of the fence. Conscripted prisoners had to carry the planks and were furious with the paid prisoners who did the carpentry "for hiring themselves to the Yanks to nail themselves and us up," Burke raged.

Meanwhile, water was shut off again for repairs. Men gathered snow near the barracks to brew coffee and crossed the deadline to gather more. Patrols fired at them, and one prisoner was shot in the head.[4]

The prison hospital also suffered a water outage, with both hydrants down. Dr. J. C. Whitehill, post surgeon, implored Captain Shurly to furnish carts for hauling water. More bad news from the hospital was that the roof leaked, the laundry required a ventilator, and the contractor had failed to connect wash tubs to the sewers.[5]

Better news for General Sweet was that General Hoffman had lost his Washington office on November 15, 1864, and now supervised only lesser prisons west of the Mississippi River. General H. W. Wessells replaced him as commissary general of prisoners in the East. Wessells was known for the loss of Plymouth, North Carolina, on April 18, 1864, including the capture of his entire garrison.[6] Washington gave no reason for the changes. Hoffman was likely ill or exhausted.

Sweet tried to convince Wessells that releasing prisoners upon taking the oath was a bad idea. Most of them were "unreformed Kentuckians from Morgan's command," according to Sweet, "among whom there is scarcely one who has any love for his country, or can be trusted." Sweet claimed they went home to become guerrillas or went underground in Chicago to aid escapes and "Copperhead plots."[7] Sweet exaggerated, since few of Morgan's men took the oath, and not one paroled prisoner was involved in the alleged conspiracy. He was correct about Morgan's men not having any love for the once United States.

Nightingale reopened the sutler store around November 21, 1864, employing two civilian clerks, "and two half loyal rebel clerks," Burke laughed. The prisoners cheated them because they were unaware of Nightingale's "high prices." However, Nightingale ran wild in Hoffman's absence and worked a deal with prisoners to go into business for themselves. They purchased supplies from him and resold them at high prices for Federal money.[8] The bright side was that they sold onions and potatoes to fight scurvy, but only wealthy prisoners could afford them.

General Sweet still failed to buy vegetables for the prison. He did attempt to force Rebel cooks to take flour owned by prisoners and use it for the general mess, but the cooks refused. Those who owned flour baked their pancakes on the coal stoves, while keeping a sharp lookout for the patrol. Even the efficient express office became a casualty with Hoffman gone, as inspectors stole many articles from packages.[9]

Sweet found that dealing with General Wessells was much easier than approaching Hoffman. He allowed the money without bickering when Sweet requested permission to spend $1,028 on the smallpox hospital for enlarging the building and enclosing it with a board fence.[10]

Camp Douglas now held many civilian prisoners, and Sweet extended the guardhouse in White Oak Square to 90 feet long by 16 feet wide, including six windows and two more doors.[11] More guards arrived with two companies of VRC, one each from the Seventh and the 12th regiments.

The camp took final shape as Prisoner's Square expanded. Sweet placed sixty barracks in 15 rows of four each by the end of November 1864. A vestibule inside the outer door, six feet in length by four feet in width, was one improvement. It conserved heat, but patrols also hid there to spy on prisoners. The quartermaster furnished barracks with spitboxes, and patrols were zealous in trying to prevent the men from staining the floor with tobacco juice.[12]

Burke again complained about favoritism shown some prisoners, but these were not the paid workers who received special treatment. "The Reb free masons (Master Masons and higher) have been rubbing their heads together and have succeeded in getting a barrack to themselves where they will have a lodge," Burke fretted. "It was obtained through the influence of Yankees who are free masons and free masons outside."[13]

Barrack Number 49 was reserved for this group. Privileges there must have been substantial, because Pa, who was a Mason, resigned as sergeant-major of the 14th Kentucky Cavalry to live in Number 49. Another eagle had fallen. Burke could not hide his hurt and disappointment at Pa's desertion. It went beyond that. What kept the prisoners going was not letting down their friends. Pa had done so, but who can point a finger? He was past middle age in a young man's war, and his bank account was short on courage by the end of November 1864.

A. W. Cockrell, one of the Supreme Council of Seven, was in Number 49 and became president of the "Prisoners Masonic Association of Camp Douglas, Ill." The Yankee guard assigned there was a Mason. Burke observed with disapproval that "they all appear to be getting along as well as could be expected under the circumstances!"[14]

Briggs seemed to think that the rest of the prison was getting along very well also. Morgan's men continued to be a problem in not keeping clean. He gave no reason, and they probably just enjoyed breaking the rules. Whatever made the Yankees unhappy delighted them. Briggs was enthusiastic about the bath and wash house in operation by November 20. "A gray back is seldom seen!" he exclaimed. "Prisoners were comfortably clad, with few exceptions." Each barracks had a good stove "with plenty of coal."[15] However, short rations, especially vegetables, caused suffering.

Washington probably warned Sweet to prepare for many more prisoners, because he placed a cannon at the entrance to Prisoner's Square, "in the event of any trouble among the prisoners of war during the time they are formed for roll calls."[16] He gave furloughs to 11 men of the 15th VRC while awaiting survivors of Gen. John B. Hood's army. The Yankees had shattered them in the battles of Franklin, Tennessee, on November 30, 1864, and at Nashville on December 14 and 15. The 49th Tennessee Infantry was one regiment that had higher hopes.

John M. Copley was only 15 years old when he enlisted in Company B, of the 49th Tennessee. He missed Fort Donelson due to illness. Otherwise, this would be his second visit to Camp Douglas. Hood's men were typical of the hard-luck Confederates sent to Chicago. A Union general recalls that "it rained and snowed and hailed and froze, and the roads were almost impassable," as Hood's army made its way toward Franklin.[17] There, on a short November afternoon, they "fought with what seemed madness and despair," suffering severe losses, including the death of many Confederate generals.

Yet, the Tennesseans were in good spirits as the men advanced on Franklin. They almost caught and destroyed the enemy near Spring Hill, some 12 miles to the south. Franklin was a different matter, surrounded by massive breastworks "filled with soldiers wearing the blue uniform, their guns and bayonets shining with a dazzling brightness in the sun." Copley's regiment was gathering beans to make soup when it was ordered to storm the Union lines. This caused "our patriotic enthusiasm and most sanguine hopes to wane," Copley admitted, "and ere the dawn of another day had given place to feelings of bitter despair."[18]

They knew what to expect. The situation was similar to Fredericksburg, two years earlier, when 12,000 Union veterans fell before Confederate guns entrenched on Marye's Heights. Hood also ignored the lessons of Gettysburg, where Union troops decimated 15,000 of Lee's men in front of Cemetery Ridge.

"A profound silence pervades Hood's entire army," as it prepared to attack at Franklin, Copley remembered. The advance was deceptively easy at first as they overran some outer works, but artillery and rifle fire soon shattered Copley's regiment.

He could see "the slaughtering of human life as far as the Columbia and Franklin pike." Copley reached the main line of Federal breastworks to find himself in a shallow ditch under heavy rifle and cannon fire. The living tried to hide behind the dead who almost completely filled the ditch. They wished to surrender, but their colonel refused. Enemy fire killed 16 Confederates as they turned to flee.[19] Federals even shot dead one of their own soldiers trapped out there. Finally, a kindly Federal officer behind the breastworks ordered his men to stop firing, and called out, "Throw down your arms, boys, and come over." About six hundred survivors did so.

Copley discovered that "my left arm, from shoulder to hand, was covered with the blood and brains of some one; my haversack and canteen had been shot away; my clothing well perforated with minnie balls." He reflected mournfully that in losing this battle, "our beautiful Sunny South had received a blow from which it could not recover." He was right. The dikes raised to keep out the world were all down now, and the flood would soon come in and erase the landmarks.

Union soldiers also suffered. Private William Taylor lost a leg through amputation at Franklin. A local doctor named Rainey did it. "Probably was anxious to try his hand on a Yankee soldier," a Camp Douglas surgeon growled.[20] This was untrue, as Taylor's hospital chart showed that gangrene had set in.

"Ragged, dirty, and blood-bespattered," the remnants of Hood's army were herded toward Nashville in weather so severe that even civilians in the city were desperate for firewood. Nevertheless, the victors exhibited prisoners at the capitol, and Copley claimed that Gov. Andrew Johnson came, not to praise them, but to curse them.

They then began the journey to Chicago in unheated boxcars. Many knew Camp Douglas by reputation or experience. The camp lived up to expectations as warmly dressed guards forced them to undress outside the gate where they searched them for valuables and weapons. The captives stood for a long time in ice and snow on that grim December 5, numb and shaking, while guards robbed them, according to Copley. Chicago had now received prisoners from most major battlefields of the Civil War, except Gettysburg and Antietem.

The situation was brighter in some respects than that facing Arkansas Post prisoners and others who had arrived the previous winter. Most barracks were in good repair, according to Briggs, with comfortable bedding and plenty of water. Food, on the other hand, while of "good quality is hardly sufficient" Briggs stated in his December 4 report.[21] He asked Sweet to increase the meat ration and to see that each man had more than one blanket.

The prisoners of 1862-1863 had sufficient food, but Hood's men would go hungry according to Briggs. Add the shortage of blankets, warm clothing, and vegetables, and the result was likely to be more suffering and more death than had occurred earlier. The war was not over for Hood's army as it came through the gates of Camp Douglas. Another struggle for survival was beginning, and the odds of success were no better in Chicago than at Franklin or Nashville.

However, the arrangement of Prisoner's Square impressed Copley. "There are fifteen rows of barracks with four to each row, and number from one to sixty," he noted. "Two hundred men are assigned to each barrack. Each barrack had a kitchen attached to one end. The main door or place of entrance to the barracks was near the center in one side." He described an interior with "bunks from the floor to the roof, in tiers or rows above each other the entire circumference of the barrack, divided by narrow strips of plank."[22]

Carpenters had partitioned off the kitchen and had built a square opening with a sliding panel for issuing rations. Prisoners called it the "Crumb Hole." Copley likened it to a teller's window in a bank.

This kitchen arrangement was no blessing for the garrison, according to Colonel Skinner. Not only was it too small to eat in, but steam escaped into the barracks and dampened weapons, equipment, clothing, and blankets.[23] Colonel Sweet ordered kitchens and mess halls built outside the guard barracks. This was the arrangement when the camp opened in 1861.

Skinner warned Colonel Sweet that guard quarters were too small for 98 men, but almost twice that many prisoners were crowded into the same size barracks. Skinner counted only 1,575 square feet of living space in guard quarters, whereas army regulations required 3,750 for 98 men. Small wonder that communicable diseases ravaged Prisoner's Square.[24]

The men were equally at risk from kitchen fires near to where they slept. Sweet did not have to consult the city when he decided to organize a fire department on December 7, 1864. He simply did it. It had one captain, a lieutenant, five sergeants, ten corporals, and 135 privates, and rivaled the Chicago Fire Department with five fire engines.[25]

Despite the many fires at camp, officials never accused prisoners of arson, although the men had plenty of matches for cooking, smoking, and heating. An unspoken agreement may have existed that burning the camp was not fair play. Federal parolees in 1862 had felt no such restraint.

New six-inch water pipes kept the latrines running smoothly. "A sewer conveyed the filth from the sinks to the outside of the prison walls, the water being conveyed by hydrants into the sewers to wash off the filth from the prison," Copley wrote. "Wash-houses were conveniently located on different parts of the prison grounds. These were supplied with hydrants, which conveyed the water to the inside, and also with tubs, buckets and soap, but minus towels."[26]

Friday of each week was wash day, and officers held inspections at Sunday morning roll call. However, prisoners could wash on any other day they wished. Some went into the laundry business, charging two to five cents per garment. Those who lacked a change of clothing washed shirts in the morning and pants in the afternoon.[27] Burke described the wash house on a typical day.

"We found the house already very much crowded and about three inches of water all over the floor," Burke recorded. "The troughs that the tubs set in were full of tubs, so we sat our tub on the floor and got hot water from one of the eight large two lb. boilers and went to work on our bag of duds. I counted a hundred tubs all in use. After we had given our clothes one rubbing we put them in one of the boilers and boiled them. By this time it was late in the evening. We had washed 29 pieces."[28] Prisoners ended their cleaning routine with baths for themselves.

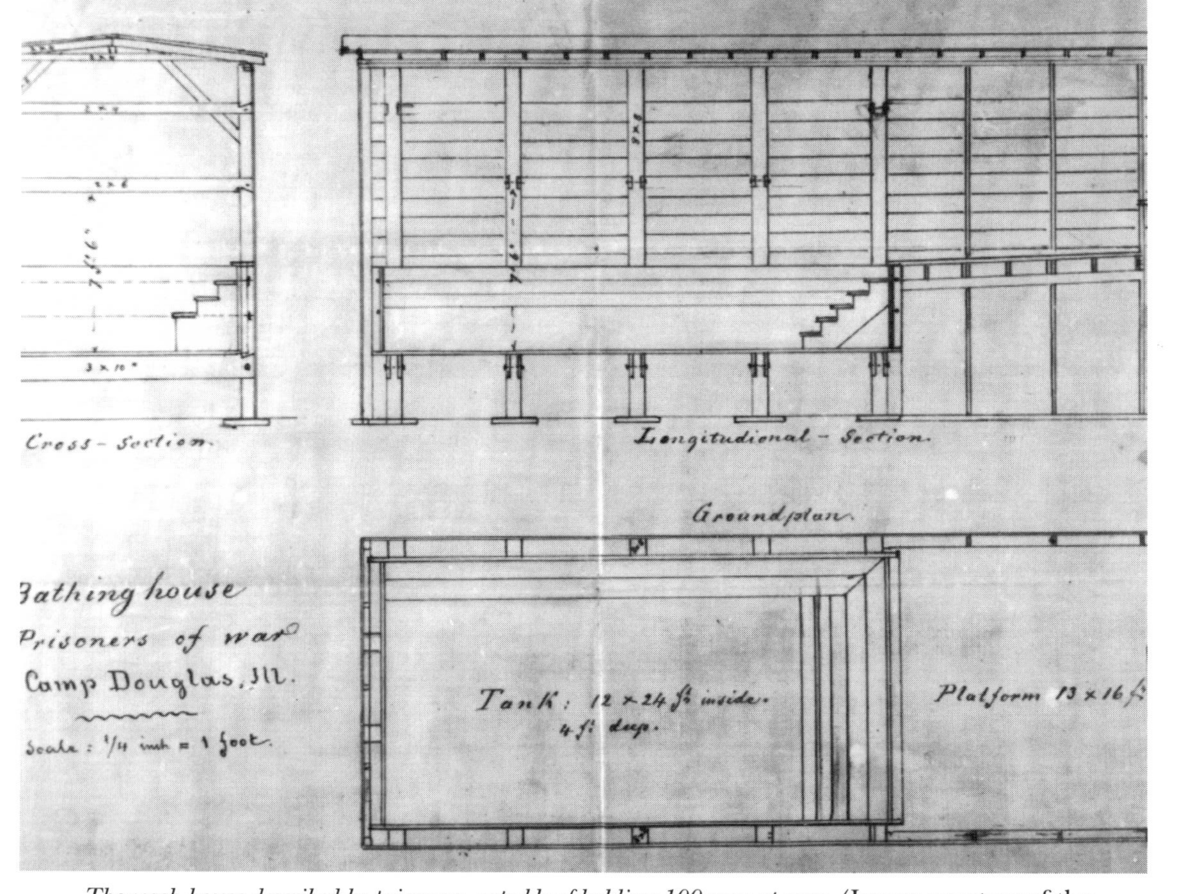

The wash house described by prisoners, capable of holding 100 men at once. (Image courtesy of the National Archives.)

Any man who failed to keep clean found himself on trial before his peers, according to Copley. "The sentence of the court, after the jury found him guilty as charged, would be that he be taken by the sheriff to the wash house, there stripped, and two men thoroughly scrub him with soap and rags, until the skin was red. One dose of this was sufficient; it never had to be repeated upon the same person. He was then compelled to wash his clothing."

The accused had to pay court costs, as well, just as in civilian life. He could settle this debt with thirds of bread or chews of tobacco. The court waived costs if the party could not pay. "All the property a man owned was on record in his own name, and not hid behind his wife," Copley said smugly. "Hence we all knew the exact amount of property owned by each man in the barrack."[29]

The alternative to barrack justice was turning the accused over to the garrison, which was a last resort. Many thefts involved food. In one case, a man admitted stealing flour from a fellow prisoner and agreed to submit his punishment to "a fair trial."[30] A jury of 12 from his and other barracks was sworn, witnesses were called, and a prosecutor and defense counsel argued for an hour each. "A large crowd was collected, but perfect silence was maintained, and things went on in the same manner as a regular court," Burke reported. A. W. Cockrell prosecuted, and John Waller acted as judge. John Curd was sheriff, and William McConally defended the accused.

The jury ordered one side of the defendant's head shaved, and his name, company, and regiment placed on the bulletin board as a thief. John Curd cut the man's hair short on one side. The defendant submitted with dignity and returned home with more than one scar. Kilpatrick had felt called upon to carry out summary punishment when Golden broke into the kitchen in 1862. That was no longer permissible. However, not all prisoners accepted the criminal justice system. One prisoner convicted of stealing and selling a blanket threatened revenge against the "sheriff" who was about to whip him.[31] This caused him to feel the strap much harder.

Both garrison and prisoners had an established routine by the fall of 1864. The bulletin board near the gate in Prisoner's Square carried many advertisements, notices, and news items. Perhaps the most important person in camp was the bugler. He entered Prisoner's Square twice a day, at 6:30 A.M. to wake the men and at 8:00 P.M. to retire them to bunks. Prisoners never saw him, and he was the subject of great curiosity.

Sergeants notified prisoners when money came in, and they could draw a purchase voucher for the sutler. Heavy traffic caused problems in sending mail, and lines formed all day to see the censor. A Yankee sergeant delivered incoming mail at roll call or picked it up at the sutler. A "dead letter" office in the square collected stray mail. The post office continued to be sacred, and no prisoner claimed that his mail was withheld or not sent. Oscar A. Cliett of the 55th Georgia told how a sergeant delivered a letter to him in the dungeon where De Land had him chained on bread and water.[32]

Garrison troops now left camp regularly to patrol the city. They also camped outside the fence as they had done under Colonel Tucker. They built a door in the west side of Prisoner's Square for easy access. Guards on the stockade stood 50 to 100 feet apart and were relieved every two hours. They had to call out regularly on their beat at night so the officer of the guard knew they were awake.[33] Guards carried a Springfield rifle, a bayonet, and a pistol.

The most important routine for the prisoners was eating twice a day. One third of a loaf of bread and a small bit of meat boiled into "a dish rag" in the farmer's boilers was consumed at 8:00 A.M. The army had long ago eliminated coffee, and it cost one dollar per pound at the sutler. Dinner was at 1:00 P.M., consisting of bread and beef water or soup.[34]

Copley found that the men formed "rings and cliques." He associated mostly with three comrades in his company. A major concern was protecting their few valuables from thieving guards, especially "Old Billy Hell." Bread came from outside the prison, and Sunday was a special day because prisoners drew two ounces of bacon. They improvised most of their tableware from tin cans and pieces of wood. The prison fund was intended to provide these items, but General Sweet was hoarding it as though it were his own money.

Next to food, or perhaps even more important, was tobacco. It was as valuable as "thirds of bread," as the prisoners called it, or one-third of a loaf. "Camp Douglas was one place where no living prisoner was ever caught by any other prisoner taking a chew of tobacco," Copley warned. The sutler sold smoking tobacco for 60¢ to $1.50 per pound, and chewing tobacco cost an astronomical $3.00 per pound.[35] Those who could afford it often shared. Oyster cans made good cooking pots and sold for a third of bread or three chews of tobacco.

Perhaps warmth was more important than tobacco as Chicago winters made prison life a fight for survival. Some prisoners claimed that deaths from freezing occurred during the winter of 1864-65. P. H. Prince charged that "often our fellow prisoners were found frozen dead in their bunks in the morning."[36] No one else claimed that this happened "often," and Prince, writing 43 years later, did not say that he ever actually saw it. He was the only survivor out of 39 men from his company sent to Camp Douglas on November 23, 1864. Twenty-three died within two weeks of smallpox and pneumonia, and 15 more perished before the final surrender. Prince blamed the mortality on inadequate food and clothing. Three of his four brothers and 14 uncles and first cousins died in the war on the Confederate side.

Accusations had been made in the winter of 1863-64 about prisoners freezing to death. This came up again the following year when Burke claimed that "a man froze to death in barrack 28 last night [December 8, 1864]." This report carried great weight, although Burke did not live in Number 28. Yet, he took too much pride in his journalism to fabricate stories.

With Lieutenant Briggs on the prowl, Sweet had to take steps. Even Copley admitted that "during extreme cold weather the guards would detail two prisoners to each stove to keep the fires burning all night. This kept the barracks very comfortable and warm."[37] On the other hand, the guard in Burke's quarters threatened to shoot prisoners, "if caught putting coal in the stove after taps." Treatment varied depending upon the barrack guard. During severe cold on December 8, 1864, "a man was allowed at each stove along with a bucket of water," even in Burke's quarters.

Cold temperatures in barracks very likely killed off some sick prisoners who should have been in the hospital. That Chicago winter was devastating. The death toll reached 217 for November 1864, another 323 died in December, 308 in January 1865, and 243 more answered the long roll in February.[38] This loss of 1,091 lives in only four months was the heaviest for any like period in the camp's history. It equaled the deaths at Andersonville from February to May 1864.

The near-arctic weather lent itself to cruelty, as well. "Another [punishment] is to make the men pull down their pants and sit, with nothing under them, on the snow and frozen ground," according to T. D. Henry. "I have known men to be kept sitting until you could see their prints for some days afterward in the snow and ice," he remembered with bitterness. "When they got weary of this, they commenced whipping, making the men lay on a barrel, and using their belts, which had a leaden clasp with sharp edge, the belt would often gather wind so as to turn the clasp edgeways; every lick inflicted thus cut entirely through the skin."[39]

One prisoner swore that when sufferers attempted to sit on their coattails for protection "they were cruelly kicked in the back by the guards and forced to sit longer on the barebones." Guards forced prisoners to stand in the snow for hours without moving, another man claimed, while they checked footprints to see if any had budged. Copley alleged that those who did received 40 to 100 lashes.[40] He exaggerated, but no doubt such beatings did take place.

Some prisoners lost feet, fingers, and ears to the bitter cold. One described "a fellow whose feet had been frozen while in Camp Douglas, necessitating their amputation. He improvised two wooden pegs as substitutes for feet and hobbled around surprisingly well."[41]

A rule prohibited conversation between prisoners after 8:00 P.M. during that winter. Constant talk was a means of survival in a Civil War prison, especially during the long cold darkness in Chicago.[42] Little information exists about when the rule went into effect or by whose order. Burke first mentioned it in July 1864. Preventing escape plots was one purpose, and cruelty another.

Punishment was harsh for talking. "When the men see a Yankee coming, they give the alarm consisting of hist, hist, which can be heard on all sides," according to Burke. Patrols were maniacal in enforcing the rule, but it was a losing game. They threatened everyone with punishment when the patrol heard someone talking. Burke recalled one incident when the guard "ordered all of us to get up but before we got our clothing on two of the guilty men owned up and we were ordered back to bed again, and the guard marched the men off to ride the wooden mule." The men soon began talking again. "We saw the light of a large fire on the west side of camp in Chicago," Burke recalled. "The night was cool and rainy. I did not rest well."[43]

Harsh treatment also extended to relatives. M. J. Bradley's lasting hostility toward the North may have resulted from an incident in December 1864. His wife, stepchild, and the sister of a fellow prisoner arrived at camp, but guards barred them from entering. A kindly clerk intervened, but officers required the women to take the oath of allegiance. The visit was limited to 20 minutes in the presence of guards and officers. "The following memorandum is attached to the oath demanded of my wife:—The above named Mollie J. Bradley, has blue eyes, auburn hair, is 26 years old, and is five feet four inches high."[44]

Prisoners poured in relentlessly, amounting to 7,670 arrivals in 1864, with only about three hundred hospital beds available. Around 1,547 patients filled the barracks. This averaged 25 in each building, and many of them died of dysentery or diarrhea. Burke criticized Confederate doctors, saying, "All of our Doctors deserve censure for their neglect of duty for some time past."[45]

Patrols in the square had absolute authority, which added to the suffering. General Sweet seldom entered. Copley did not object to strict sanitary regulations, but claimed that men were still being hanged by the thumbs. He blamed certain guards for much of the brutality.

Copley named "Red" O'Hara as one of the most cruel. "He was a large man whose oily skin appeared to be infected with vermin." "Little Red" was another. "His eyes were of a steel-gray color, giving to his countenance a cold and hard expression; the mouth large and filled with a set of unsightly and disgusting teeth; it was a perfect harbinger of filth, the stench emitted therefrom when it opened, would permeate the atmosphere for a distance of several feet."

Red O'Hara was Edward O'Hara, Company C, Eighth VRC, "on daily duty with inspector general of prisoners at Camp Douglas, Ill," according to records in the National Archives. He was no bargain for the Union. O'Hara was in the hospital from his date of enlistment in Company C, 23rd Kentucky Infantry, until transferred to the VRC in 1863. His evil temper may have resulted from not getting paid for 13 months due to the transfers. He finally deserted. He was court-martialed and acquitted. The court knew the futility of trying to correct army payroll records.[46]

Copley found Billy McDermott, known as "Old Billy Hell," unforgettable. "Two small squint eyes which resembled those of a hog; his mouth large, but kept somewhat in the background by a pair of large, thick lips; a short neck, which appeared to be swallowed up by the shoulders; the knees were perfect strangers to each other."

Records listed no Billy or William McDermott with any guard regiment; possibly he used a false name in the square. "Prairie Bull," also known as "McCurley," was the most infamous. "His hideous features, coupled with a demoniacal expression, revolted every living thing near him," Copley raged. "He carried the expression of a demon wherever he went."[47]

Prairie Bull was a Southerner of Union persuasion, born John McCurley in Gilmore, Georgia, in 1844. Records describe him as a farmer, with blue eyes, light hair, and fair complexion, five feet six inches tall. He enlisted in the First East Tennessee Cavalry in 1862, developed a hernia in 1863, and ended up in Company C, Eighth VRC. His nickname probably came from working in Prisoner's Square, often called the "Bull Pen." The dreaded guard found himself in the guardhouse on June 14, 1864, for "drunkenness and missing guard duty."[48]

Copley's anger had not cooled after 18 years. "They were the unsightly, hideous, midnight ghouls in human shape, who prowled over the prison square after night to find some frivolous excuse to exercise their assumed authority," Copley ranted. "They were the ghastly and hungry hyenas digging into the prison barracks for little trivial violations of some foolish and insignificant rule of their own manufacture, and of which the prisoners knew nothing until marched out for punishment."[49]

J. W. Cook was also angry years later. "A Texas comrade in the April Veteran asks if any Camp Douglas prisoner remembers Prairie Bull and Billy Hell! My recollections of them are more vivid than pleasant. They were inside guards, but called themselves inspectors."[50]

Prairie Bull held Cook on the mule one frigid night until he was frostbitten and then threatened more punishment. "I backed off entirely out of reach of that dreaded club," Cook said. "Thousands of men will remember Bull, many of whom have answered the long roll, brought on by exposure just to satisfy his spleen."

Bull almost killed P. H. Prince for going out before reveille. Prince hoped to get first chance at the wash house. "I heard the Prairie Bull, whose voice I knew well, swear at me an awful oath, and at the same time he shot at me, the ball passing through the top of the tub that my hand was on," Prince shuddered. "I knew it meant death if I did not get away so I jumped to the door of Barrack 13, and he sent another ball at the door facing me, and then followed me with cursing."[51]

Prince hid in Number 13 and escaped. Prairie Bull, frustrated and enraged, drove two hundred men outside without their clothes. "The snow was from one to two feet deep and the thermometer twenty below zero, and the wind blew as only it can blow off of Lake Michigan," Prince recalled. "Many were marched off to ride the mule."[52] Prince gave no date for this incident, but his responsibility for causing it lends credence to the story.

Copley accused McCurley of shooting a prisoner who was sick and hardly able to walk. Copley often retold legends from the past. J. M. Berry blamed the First Michigan Sharpshooters. "I remember when one of them shot a poor, sick confederate who had gone out of his quarters and was scarcely able to stand alone." Prisoners had to undress before going to the sink at night or pay the fatal consequences. Prairie Bull supposedly killed another prisoner who had accidentally tripped him.[53] No dates for these alleged shootings were given, and none of them were investigated. Prisoners did not say whether they had witnessed what happened or had only heard about these incidents. Therefore, whether Sweet allowed a serial killer to run loose is open to question, but such a possibility exists.

Burke claimed that the most hated guard in the camp was not Prairie Bull but O'Hara. "He is always on the alert, watching for a chance to shoot somebody. I often hear it whispered through the ranks, lookout here comes Old red. He bayoneted several of the men, and we have no particular love for him." Spilling some water on the floor once petrified Burke. He quickly dried it before a guard punished him.[54]

Simultaneously, R. T. Bean formed a warm relationship with a guard almost 50 years of age who had enlisted to stop a mortgage foreclosure on his property. A Federal law protected soldiers and sailors against creditors. The guard's wife refused to make biscuits, which he loved, and at which Bean excelled in making. Soon Bean was furnishing the flour, and the guard was bringing the butter. The guard made a chair for Bean, the only prisoner in the square to have one.[55]

Prisoners believed that O'Hara was jailed in Chicago for five months in 1864, but this is when he deserted. The army gave him back his patrol job after the court-martial acquitted him. However, he was arrested on January 3, 1865, for trading with the prisoners.[56]

"Old Red broke up religious meetings in barracks 13 and 25, and said that if he caught any more singing and praying in the barracks he would put them in irons," Burke fumed. "Some of the men saw Capt. Sponable about it, and he told them that the guard had no orders to break up such meetings, but that he left such things to the guards and if they chose to break them up he would not interfere."[57]

One prisoner accused O'Hara of killing a man in the 64th North Carolina Infantry for laughing when O'Hara slipped and fell on some ice. This may be true, because prisoners from this regiment were present at the time. Ironically, Southern Unionists petitioned Washington to release the 64th as a pro-Union regiment.[58]

Another guard who did not endear himself was "Old Socks," described as tall, rawboned, long-legged, hump-shouldered, and green-looking. He earned his name while punishing two prisoners by answering, "I'll sock ye!" to one man's plea for time to don his socks. The following month Old Socks was beating prisoners because they crowded around the stove on a cold December day. It was this pettiness that angered the men. Guards destroyed precious food and containers for the crime of cooking on the stove, and marched the prisoner out for punishment.[59]

This kind of behavior made prisoners bitter against their fellows who switched sides or took the oath. Defectors required protection to retrieve their belongings and move to "Loyal Row" in White Oak Square. Guards who escorted them had sometimes to draw their pistols because of the outrage.

Politicians finally heeded the suffering prisoners and their families, leading to the most bizarre incident of the Civil War. The enemies agreed to supply their own men in prison camps with clothing, blankets, and provisions. However, the South pleaded poverty. Consequently, the North gave Confederate brigadier general William N. R. Beall, a prisoner of war, a parole of honor to sell Southern cotton in New York City. The profits would go to pay for the South's part of the deal. Beall swore by the code of chivalry "not to reveal to his government what he learned or saw as he traveled in the north on business." Officials posted a notice at Camp Douglas on December 12, 1864, informing prisoners about the arrangement.[60]

The North benefitted financially if the South provided for Confederate prisoners. Sale of the cotton, on the other hand, pumped Federal dollars into the Confederacy at a time when its currency was collapsing. This agreement meant jobs for Southern industrial workers, profits for agriculture, and hard cash for the Confederate war machine. One irony is that Southern factories and farms used slave labor. Another is that while the North blockaded cotton in Southern ports, it now moved freely to New York City by rail.

Prisoners at all camps were directed to establish committees and determine their needs for General Beall. Barracks at Camp Douglas elected delegates who selected a committee of four to receive the supplies. The chairman of this committee was A. W. Cockrell, who appeared to have found his calling at Camp Douglas. The promise of clothing, blankets, and food from General Beall came at an opportune time because rations were several days behind, and another reduction was threatened, according to rumor. No official intention to reduce rations can be found, although Briggs warned that the meat allotment was insufficient and that one blanket per man was not enough.[61]

General Sweet's administration became more severe after the Beall agreement. He did not like it. Guards and patrols on the ground fired at prisoners gathering snow near the deadline after the hydrants froze. They hauled nearly naked bodies of smallpox victims out of barracks "like a dead horse or dog."[62] Copley's bunkmate had smallpox for two weeks before being removed. Miraculously, Copley never contracted any illness and attributed his good health to clean habits and a cold bath at the wash house every morning.

Regardless, the constant cold, repression, hunger, and dreary landscape took their toll. One night a prisoner bolted into the street toward the lights, shouting, "There's Jesus! I see his light!" He tore a lamp from the fence and ran with it shouting, "Glory! Glory! I have got Jesus." A bullet smashed the lamp from his hand, but he was unharmed. The guards caught him at the gate and took him back.

Red O'Hara punished prisoners who grumbled about rations and restricted mail to five or six lines per letter. Postal service remained above the conflict, however. It made no difference when a Camp Douglas prisoner mistakenly directed a letter to Flag of Truce, New Orleans, on December 15, 1864. An efficient Federal post office simply delivered it to the correct Flag of Truce at City Point, Virginia.[63]

The Camp Douglas relief committee working for General Beall issued its report on December 16, stating their needs. It counted "163 1st Sgts, 508 Sgts, 406 Cpls, 32 Citizens, 9,107 Pvts," on hand, "Total: 10,216." However, it did not know that more than three thousand prisoners were coming. The committee stated that it would not share the Confederate bounty with those who were openly deserters, those who took the oath, or those who worked for the garrison. Naturally, Sweet vetoed the report.

"The prisoners will determine what supplies to apply for, precisely as they are instructed, and in the same order make a table and sign the same!" Sweet ordered. "Dissertations on the duty of rebels to remain as such, and matters relating to other than such supplies will not be forwarded," he growled.[64] Out of the "32 Citizens" counted by the committee, about 30 were Sweet's prisoners from the Conspiracy of 1864, and the committee apparently intended to share with them. Any enemy of Sweet was a friend of the prisoners, they felt.

Briggs's report of December 18, 1864, bluntly warned Hoffman that winter weather required more bedding and food. The situation worsened when prisoners arrived on December 23 from the fighting at Nashville, some so frostbitten that they had to be brought from the train by ambulances. About 3,341 of them crowded in by the end of December 1864, raising the prison population to 12,082, its highest point ever. Doctors frantically vaccinated them, and those who wished to renew vaccinations could do so. Guards allowed fires all day in barracks because of the sick. Many more men were dying there than in the hospital. Workers built a coal house 25 feet wide by 50 feet long on the east side of the square to supply fuel more efficiently.[65]

Captain Goodman, assistant quartermaster, staggered under the burden of keeping the camp glued together. Even the guard quarters in Garrison Square were crumbling. One of the 15th VRC barracks needed a new roof, and the Eighth VRC quarters required new floors. The ambulance to carry the sick was worn out, and the post surgeon requisitioned two new ones. Goodman was ordered to dig latrines in the frozen ground for the two barracks serving as hospitals in Prisoner's Square. Authorities gave no thought to sanitary needs when they converted these unsuitable buildings.[66]

Burke gave no thought, right now, to the crowded unhealthy conditions in Prisoner's Square because funds from Ohio were late for his highly anticipated Christmas dinner. New prisoners overflowed his barrack, with three men crowded into a bunk made for two. This caused a good deal of tension. Burke described how "all of the bottom bunks and some of the middle and top bunks had to double up three to the bunk."

New arrivals had a good deal of "new issue" Confederate currency worth one Federal cent. Naturally, they promptly named them the "New Issue," and they chased the blues by singing "The Girl I Left Behind Me." Two more favorites were "Massa's in the Cold Cold Ground," and "Old Uncle Ned."[67] They saw nothing odd in their affection for black music.

General Sweet aggravated the bunk shortage by transferring civilians from the guardhouse to Prisoner's Square. Burke described them as bewildered. They claimed they were "U.S. Citizens" and had done nothing wrong. Sympathy for "U.S." citizens was scarce, however.

Burke obtained his funds and cooked a magnificent meal on Christmas day, with many ingredients purchased illegally at the army sutler.

Burke's *"Bill of Fare," Christmas, 1864.*

Boiled Beef	
Biscuit with short[en]ing.	Molasses.
Tea with sugar.	Chip beef.
Potatoes with butter.	Cheese.
Soft Bread.	Salt, pepper & vinegar

Delicacies.

Prune pie	Tarts
Apple pie	Ginger cake
Onion pie	Spice cake
Potato pie	Apples.
Vinegar pie	

This must have put a dent in his bank account, with flour costing $20 per barrel, and butter 80¢ per pound. Men still cooked on the coal stoves in spite of severe punishments. The one who made the fire in the morning cooked his breakfast first.

Briggs issued his last report on Christmas day, 1864. Barracks held too many sick, as usual, but smallpox was steadily decreasing. Briggs was wrong on that score. He was much concerned about the new men. "The prisoners received during the last week are poorly clad; many of them are nearly barefoot and destitute of blankets," he complained.[68]

Many of his reports were published in the *Official Records of the War of the Rebellion* and were studied long after he disappeared into history. Briggs spoke fearlessly for those who had no voice, no friends, and no power, He undoubtedly caused improvements in food, shelter, and clothing. This was phenomenal, since he had been crippled in battle, and his reputation had been sullied in the mass tunnel escape of December 3, 1863. He was captain of the guard that night, and the great escape fell on his watch and on his record.

A Federal inspection was scheduled for the last day of the year. The sutler removed illegal items from his shelves, and a guard called "Smiler" made the men straighten up their quarters. Smiler had earned the name by his murderous nature. Ticks were folded back on the bunks, and blankets were folded "nicely on top of the ticks." Prisoners took anything hanging up and folded it into the bunks. Utensils "such as tin stew pots, plates, cups, etc. had to be scoured anew and taken to the kitchen." The barrack detail went to work and cleaned thoroughly.

The men said goodbye to 1864, "Long to be remembered by the prisoners now at Camp Douglas," Burke recorded. Many probably remembered the year for its shortage of food, the cruelty of the guards, and the widespread disease. Post-war studies showed that the number of illnesses suffered by the prisoners was about the same as what they had experienced in the army. However, the fatality rate at Camp Douglas was 10 percent higher. Surgeons attributed this increase to depression, monotony, savage winters, inadequate clothing and blankets, and lack of hospital space. The new hospital received high praise in 1864 medical reports, while doctors criticized the presence of scurvy. Major improvements were six-inch water lines and the introduction of wash houses.[69]

About 2,235 prisoners had lost their lives since the prison opened in 1862, according to the *Official Records*. This may be 967 short of the true figure. Persistent inspections resulted in repairs to barracks and better medical care. Regardless, food, bedding, clothing, and hospital space could not keep up with the collapsing Confederacy.

Forty-one prisoners had escaped since Sweet's reorganization of the square in June, a surprising number. Seventeen escapes had occurred in October 1864, so it is likely that more prisoners got out on October 28 than was shown. Some 93 prisoners managed to flee in 1864, another disastrous record but much better than the 161 escapes in 1863.

Officials claimed that Prisoner's Square cost $61,000 in repairs for 1864 and $80,000 more for new buildings, which is questionable. Hoffman complained about paying six hundred dollars per barracks, including a kitchen.[70] The army could have built two prison camps for $141,000, with enough money remaining to supply sewers and water for downtown Chicago. Either the figures were wrong or contractors reaped another windfall. One historian claimed that "the daily expenses of camp, aside from the officers' and soldiers' pay were $8,540." It was two thousand dollars per day in 1862. The prison population was three times as large now, so the 1864 figure may be accurate when inflation is added.

General Sweet tore down the chapel in 1864 because he needed the lumber to repair barracks. Later he learned that the chapel was exempt. This led Reverend Tuttle to campaign for construction of a new one seating six hundred people. Prisoners built it with money from the prison fund, and Sweet reluctantly contributed the value of the lumber he had used.[71]

Sweet experienced some of Colonel Tucker's troubles when "a small number of vicious men" created disciplinary problems on the streetcars and in town. Garrison soldiers broke into the Chicago Driving Park and wrecked it. Investigators discovered few cases of bribery, although one guard sold civilian clothing to three prisoners who used a ladder to get away on Christmas day, 1864. They stayed at the warm and luxurious Sherman House in Chicago, courtesy of Southern friends.

Outside, a bitter Christmas night closed in on Camp Douglas. Many thought about what was happening at home, in the North as well as the South. Everyone realized that the Civil War was the defining moment of their lives, and some suffered the penetrating cold to visit other barracks and exchange gifts. They could not know for sure that this was the last Christmas night of the war, although many suspected it. This, even more than past holidays, was a time for reflection, for thinking about what might have been and what the future promised. Somehow, dogs were running loose inside the stockade. They yelped and barked and scratched on the barrack doors, hoping for a little warmth, a sliver of food, or the feel of a kind hand. No one knew how they got inside, and General Sweet threatened to shoot them.[72] It was a bad omen for the holiday season.

Federal inspectors failed to arrive on New Year's day, 1865, and Burke cooked another magnificent dinner. His casualness is astounding in the midst of so much death and suffering. One explanation is the financial security provided by Yankee relatives in Ohio. He would be 23 years of age in three weeks.

The year opened in Camp Douglas fashion: "At dusk a new prisoner was shot in the mouth for going under his barrack [Number 30] to the sick men's tub," Burke sadly noted. "The detail had failed to set the tub out in the street when the retiring bugle sounded, and the prisoner not knowing that he was liable to be shot for going under the barrack after dark. This is a bad beginning for the first night of a new year."[73]

CHAPTER 18

The Tower

A tower is built to see the prisoners—How the men react—Art, literature, music, and crafts behind the walls of Camp Douglas—Prison newspaper questions the duty of loyalty.

Visitors were welcome distractions in Prisoner's Square. Twelve Indian chiefs stopped in on their way to Washington. They were "tall and portly and dressed out and out in full Indian costume," according to John Copley. General Joseph Hooker visited the square by dashing in on horseback with a fine escort and dashing out again. Prisoners were disappointed at not hearing a speech. Governor Oliver Morton of Indiana and Governor Richard Ogelsby of Illinois came in a fine carriage after the surrender. Morton spoke to the prisoners about having them released and restored to their citizenship. They were deeply moved and would have voted for him to be president.[1]

However, the prisoners did not enjoy the insensitive gapers who climbed to a wooden tower on the east side of Cottage Grove to stare at them. A businessman built it for this purpose. Artists made drawings of the camp from this vantage point.

M. J. Bradley reflected how the prisoners felt about the spectators: "They could look down on and inspect us as objects of curiosity, as they would wild beasts in a menagerie. And I suppose it was well, for some of the visitors who crowded that platform had never in all their lives seen a gentleman, and the sight was one well worth the money."[2]

Summertime was especially irritating, when Chicagoans made it an outing to take the streetcars to Camp Douglas and climb the tower. "Summer gardens opened to serve the public because of these never-failing Sunday crowds," a reporter observed. The trip from downtown took an hour. Businessmen built a similar tower at Elmira, where the entrance fee was 15¢. In Chicago it was 10¢. These towers added their own heartache to the degrading life. They were wooden

The observation tower at Elmira, New York, similar to the one at Camp Douglas. (Image courtesy of Chemung County Historical Society.)

structures, about 25 feet high and 10 feet wide, with a lower and upper deck enclosed by railings.[3]

Some prisoners fought back by making obscene gestures, "which they seemed to enjoy," Oscar Cliett remembered. Even escaped prisoners climbed the tower to view their former home and wave at comrades.[4] One visited too often, and someone betrayed him.

Prisoners may have astonished the rubbernecks with the considerable activity in the camp. Arts, crafts, entertainment, and gambling emerged from the poverty and decay of Prisoner's Square. A Union soldier observing prisoners in 1862 wrote condescendingly, "There are of course among so large a number many intelligent faces to be seen."

Records reveal little information about Joseph M. Dunavan who composed and arranged "Twas A Pleasant Home of Ours Sister." He dreamed of an independent South he could call his own country. This artist and composer belonged to Company D, Second Kentucky Cavalry, in Morgan's command. His enlistment papers give no age, indicating only that he joined on November 1, 1862, at Gallatin, Tennessee.[5]

He arrived at Camp Douglas on August 18, 1863, the same day as Curtis R. Burke. They probably knew each other. Dunavan left camp on March 2, 1865, for exchange, but it was too late. His beloved Confederacy was breaking up and drifting away. Authorities held him at Point Lookout, Maryland, long after the war because he refused to take the oath of allegiance. The army finally gave up and released him on June 24, 1865, at Charleston, West Virginia. Nothing more is known of him.

The prisoners of 1862 were less productive than Dunavan and his comrades. Letters from this period contain some valuable data about prison life, but it does not appear that they were as creative. Reverend Tuttle claimed that "there were many stabbings among those who were continually gambling."[6] One prisoner set up a faro table in 1862 and amassed a fortune of $150,000 in Confederate currency, worth about $10,000 Federal dollars then.

The period following August 18, 1863, may be the "golden age" of Camp Douglas, a renaissance among the prisoners. However, it was not without a blemish. John M. Copley described how some gambled away their rations and became "mere skeletons and living shadows." Continuous card playing in barracks disturbed Burke.

Those who had no money found other occupations. The game of checkers was a favorite time killer. Flying kites was popular, also jumping, foot races, ball games, and playing marbles. The garrison enjoyed watching the kites soar away, not knowing that sly prisoners were posting letters out of camp. They discovered the ruse when none of the kites returned.[7] A heavy snowfall was always the signal for day-long warfare.

Morgan's men established a handwritten newspaper on March 21, 1864, called the *Prisoner Vidette.* Lappens's factory advertised, "Pipes, Pipes, Pipes, by the wholesale and retail, Block 17, three doors west of the south east corner. Give him a call you [will] not be other than satisfied." Another ad read: "Soldiers Friend. Boyd's Plus Ointment. The cry rings throughout the land, Peace, Peace, Boyd's Pills, No Humbug." It reported that John Curd was preparing a variety show with trick animals.[8] Curd had found his niche at Camp Douglas.

While prison officials censored mail, they did not restrict the *Vidette.* An unsigned editorial attacked loyalty and the American system of government: "Because we have declined to publish articles discussing the different questions of the day, we would not have our readers infer that we are loyal," the writer explains. "The word loyal expresses nothing the citizen of Dixie owes to his country; it is a damning proof of tyranny, conceit and presuming impudence; and those who use the word, in the affairs of our government, never shall have my confidence as long as our Republican form of government is not proved a fallacy, in theory and in practice." He apparently felt that no government was entitled to a pledge of allegiance. Another Southerner named Thomas Jefferson may have agreed.

Morgan's command first published the *Vidette* in Tennessee on August 15, 1862, and it then continued as a journal in various prisons such as Fort Delaware and Camp Douglas. Printed editions of the *Vidette* are considered the most interesting of the Confederate soldiers' newspapers.[9]

The *Vidette* was only a small part of the creativity. John F. Clarer of the Second Kentucky Cavalry was a silversmith with his own room fitted up as a workshop. He produced rings, breast pins, and hat ornaments inlaid with gold, silver, and pearl. About 30 ringmakers kept busy. The rings sold from 50¢ to $10. Mechanics of all kinds manufactured furniture, buggies for the officers, and a buggy for Reverend Tuttle.[10]

One problem was how to market these items. This was where the patrol guards came in. They either bought products directly from the prisoners or acted as agents and took a commission. Of course, this practice was strictly prohibited. The same system existed at Elmira, where prisoners turned out extraordinary picture frames.[11]

Burke developed a passion for writing and created a fine prison journal. He was also known as the finest chef in Prisoner's Square, if not the entire camp. A literary club met regularly, and books were available through Reverend Tuttle. He still believed, however, that, except for some of Morgan's men, "there are as many men at Camp Douglas who cannot read nor write as there are in the whole State of Illinois."[12]

Most barracks had a storyteller or humorist. The most memorable of these was a ventriloquist, famous since the beginning of the war. He had seen much action with the 42nd Tennessee Infantry. Friends called him "Pig" because of his small size. Guards at Camp Douglas heard chickens squalling in their pockets and under their caps in the winter of 1864.[13] They forced Pig to stop, and he suddenly disappeared. He had taken the oath.

Rumormongers always infested the camp to whip up false hopes and anxieties. The most cruel rumor was that ten prisoners would be shot for the alleged shooting of Union prisoners in the South. Practical jokers ran loose without a chain and often went too far. As a prisoner prepared to escape through a tunnel, one joker wrote "Secesh" in chalk on the back of his jacket.[14]

Each barracks had a "reader" of banned newspapers. The main qualification was a loud clear voice. Pickets were stationed outside to watch for patrols while readers reported what the prisoners wished to hear.[15]

Captured musicians kept their instruments under the code of chivalry. They gave concerts, and soloists or quartets often performed. Burke told how "a reb string band consisting of two violins, two guitars, and a flute furnished good music from dark till bed time." The men danced and paid musicians with thirds of bread or a chew of tobacco.[16] The "ladies" wore hats, and Copley says there was no fear of being "churched" for dancing.

Theater was in great demand, as when black prisoners planned to stage a minstrel show in barracks and four hundred patrons tried to enter. John Curd managed them. Admission was 15¢ in Federal money or three dollars Confederate, but patrols closed the show because of overcrowding. They could have earned perhaps $30 in Federal money, almost three months' pay for a Yankee soldier. Confederate dollars were good for postage or in case of exchange. The black troupe staged the show in Burke's kitchen the following week, admission 25¢ in sutler's checks.

Another diversion was going to Garrison Square to watch the changing of the guard. It was a colorful spectacle with much saluting, barking of orders, dressing the lines, and exercise in the manual of arms, all of which prisoners observed with a critical eye.[17] They left little doubt that they could do better, but the garrison did not take them up on the challenge.

While the beatings, shootings, and hunger were painful, nothing hurt more than separation from female companionship. Prisoners preferred, above all, to watch a woman walk through the camp or to look at one on the stockade. Intense excitement prevailed on April 10, 1864, when two women escorted by an officer came though Prisoner's Square. One of them kissed a prisoner, to everyone's great delight, but possibly not the officer's. The prisoners responded by clearing her path with the battle cry known to both armies: "Give way to the right and left! Let the artillery pass!" A woman standing on the platform took a liking to a prisoner named Derbis and sent him a basket of provisions and a bouquet. The monotony of prison life could not be discounted. A guard sympathized with prisoners "in their weary moving about, simply killing time."[18]

Frigid winds finally cleared the observation tower as fall came around, but it remained like a giant wooden soldier staring sightlessly at the camp. Crowds disappeared, beer gardens closed, and horses had an easier time pulling the cars to Camp Douglas. The artisans and craftsmen remained in Prisoner's Square, however. They worked through the long winter, contributing to the legend of Camp Douglas.

CHAPTER 19

Winding Down the War

Sweet urged to remove restrictions—Cruelty of the guards—High mortality continues—Prisoners offered the oath of allegiance—General exchange begins—The South sends clothing and tobacco—Hoffman refuses to pay Sweet's detectives—Jubilation at Lee's surrender—Courage of a Georgia boy—All quiet on Cottage Grove.

Security was well organized by 1865, and streets, sinks, water, and drainage were good. Officials completely filled Prisoner's Square with 16 rows of four barracks, two of them continuing as hospitals. General Sweet named Captain Shurly as special inspector. His experience as administrative officer gave him a good background for the assignment. He fired a blockbuster report right out of the gate, telling Hoffman on January 8, 1865, that "many of the prisoners are destitute of beds of any kind. Quality of food is good. Quantity, barely sufficient in this climate." He, too, urged removing restrictions on selling vegetables. Like Lieutenant Briggs, Shurly recommended that prisoners receive vegetables from home. "The Government would save largely in the cost of medicines," he sensibly pointed out. "Cooking stoves would be much cheaper to use in the kitchens than the Farmer boilers now there," he added.[1]

Shurly did not mention some new restrictions. For example, Sweet moved the deadline farther into the square, and prisoners could no longer stroll there on pain of being shot. The new rules restricted them to the streets between barracks. General Sweet had little choice. Prisoners numbered 11,702, and the army had only given him the Eighth and 15th VRC, and two companies from the Seventh and 12th VRC, about a thousand men. One ray of sunshine for prisoners broke through when Sweet booted the hated Red O'Hara out of Prisoner's Square for trading with them.

The 24th Ohio Battery still pointed its guns, but this threat could not prevent an attack from inside. Washington added about two

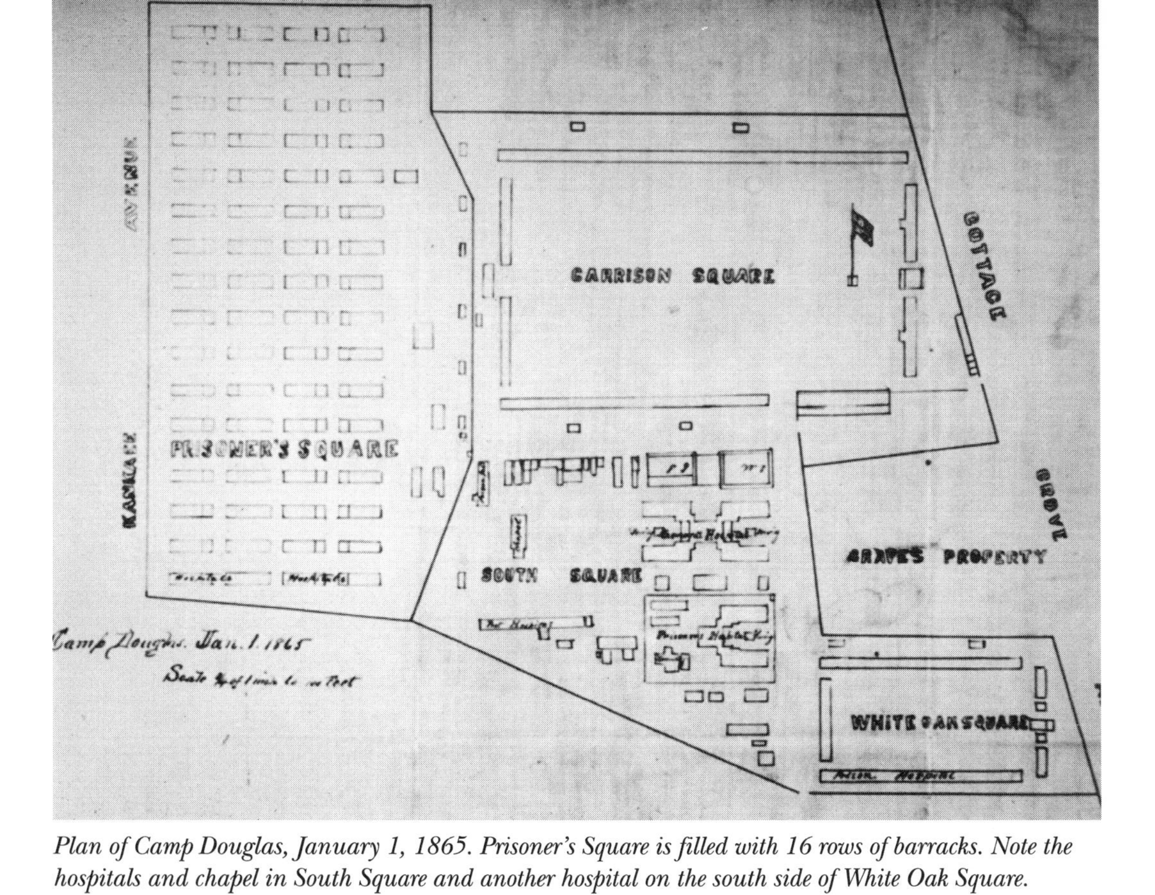

Plan of Camp Douglas, January 1, 1865. Prisoner's Square is filled with 16 rows of barracks. Note the hospitals and chapel in South Square and another hospital on the south side of White Oak Square. (Image courtesy of the National Archives.)

hundred reinforcements in February from the 48th Missouri Infantry, mostly Rebel deserters of uncertain quality. Nervous guards were shooting without hesitating.

M. J. Bradley recalled an incident that still disturbed his sleep. "A man who had just come into the prison, being very thirsty, and the water having been shut off from us, as had frequently been the case, seeing some snow lying near the fence, on the ground, attempted to pick up some and eat it, when he was shot by the guard without any warning whatever, and he fell near that infernal dead line."[2]

Sergeant T. B. Clore wrote, "These brutal guards would in the dead hours of the night, while walking around the prison, deliberately fire at random into the barracks, where the men were sleeping, just out of pure devilment. So common did this become that many built defenses against these midnight assaults."[3]

J. S. Rosamond confirmed, "Many a minnie ball went crashing through our barracks at night at some real or imaginary noise. It was dangerous even to indulge in a snore."[4]

A spent bullet hit John M. Copley in his bunk, and he claimed that guards opened fire if more than two prisoners congregated on the street. He exaggerated. No such limit was imposed until February 11, 1865. After that date, up to five prisoners could gather together. Sweet aimed to prevent a concentrated attack.[5]

One former prisoner alleged that his cousin was shot dead in the doorway of his barrack, and the guard was promoted. The fact is that guards were promoted only for shooting escapees, and the ex-prisoner was writing 63 years later. However, records do show that his cousin, John P. Hutchings, Third Kentucky Cavalry, died at camp on October 7, 1863.[6]

Garrison officers probed one shooting on January 7, 1865, and learned that Pvt. David Tolman, 15th VRC, fired at a prisoner who had stepped across the deadline. His ball passed into Ward H (Barrack 41) in Prisoner's Square and seriously wounded two patients. Officers concluded only that Tolman fired too high, "but would recommend that the sentinels be instructed to carefully fire low under such circumstances, so as not to injure others who are innocent of any offense." What offense? Tolman saw the man retrieving clothing that had blown out of Number 41 and fired anyway.[7] In justice to him, he acted according to orders. As in all wars, it comes down to an individual's own conscience. General Daniel Tyler would have told him to hold his fire.

"Smiler" Redmond (as Burke identified him) committed a worse crime on January 13, the day after the Tolman report. Tolman, at least, had the excuse that he was supposed to shoot when prisoners crossed the deadline. In Smiler's case, prisoners were supposed to use the toilets assigned to their barracks. Regulations said nothing about shooting them, but Smiler fired at one man for merely walking toward the wrong toilet. The bullet shattered his right ankle and lodged in his left foot.[8] No record of an investigation can be found, although officers would have praised Smiler, regardless.

Smiler was Joseph R. Redman, born near a small Illinois farming town in 1844, the same year as Bull McCurley. He had black hair, black eyes, and dark skin, and stood five feet seven inches tall. Redman enlisted in the 128th Illinois Infantry Regiment on July 27, 1863, but was transferred to the Invalid Corps "as unfit for field service." He arrived at Camp Douglas with Company I of the Eighth VRC in September 1863.[9] Like Bull McCurley, he found his mission there.

Another bad incident soon followed the Smiler shooting. The patrol was savagely beating and kicking a prisoner two days later for allegedly taking bones from the garbage barrel. When he grabbed one guard's foot in self-defense, another guard shot him in the side. They did not take the victim to the hospital. "He was visited by Captain Hastings [Joshua H. Hastings, Company B, 15th VRC]," according to Burke, "who consoled him by telling him that if his wound did not kill him he would, for he must behave as a prisoner of war and not strike at his men."[10] A quick trigger finger was the watchword with Hastings, and some bad shootings occurred on his watch. Colonel Strong did not intervene.

Yet, Sweet considered the patrol in Prisoner's Square an elite unit, and MPs shocked him by arresting one in a house of prostitution downtown. "Soldiers who are in the habit of visiting such places are unfit for the responsible position of members of the Provost Prison Guard, and are with this relieved from duty with such guard," Sweet said harshly. However, not all of his men were sadists or patrons of the Prairie Queen. He had the pleasure of detailing one patrol guard as sexton of the chapel.[11]

The army placed "houses of ill fame" off limits to military personnel around January 1, 1864. Officials did not state the reasons, but venereal disease would be a likely ground. About one in 40 patients at the post hospital suffered from syphilis or gonorrhea, or both, while such cases among the prisoners were almost nonexistent.[12] Putting these houses out of business as hangouts for deserters and criminals also motivated the army. The glory days of the Prairie Queen were setting below the horizon.

Nevertheless, no sooner had Sweet fired the patrol guard when MPs arrested Sgt. James Holt, Company H, 15th VRC, in a house of ill fame on January 13, 1865. Holt claimed that it was a frameup and that his accusers had seized him on the street with a valid pass. Lieutenant Colonel Martin Flood of the 15th VRC sent the matter to Sweet with his affidavit that "Sgt. Holt has heretofore been of good character that entitles his statement to credit."

Colonel Flood seemed inclined to give enlisted men a break, and probably had come up from the ranks. He once assigned a troubled private to the nearby soldier's rest home, but the soldier was sent back. "Burkheart is known to be worthless for any other position," Flood noted in the VRC ledger, "and was therefore supposed to be eminently qualified to saw wood." Sweet accepted Flood's version of what happened to Sergeant Holt and concluded that the arrest was not justified.[13]

Burke concluded that a shortage in his bank account was not justified. Fifteen dollars, worth about $1,500 in Confederate money, was missing on January 13. He saw Capt. W. H. Bushell, in charge of prisoners' funds since the departure of Colonel Mulligan, and "thru whose hands all money letters pass after they are examined," Reverend Tuttle stated. He claimed that Bushell "has been faithful to the last degree," which shows how little he knew. Burke received no satisfaction from the "faithful" Bushell.[14]

No supplies came through from the faithful General Beall either. Even General Sweet felt that he had to do something to clothe prisoners. The faithful Captain Goodman made a "special requisition" on January 13 for 8,000 blankets, 2,000 coats or jackets, 3,000 pairs of trousers, 5,000 shirts, 10,000 drawers, 12,000 pairs of stockings, and 3,000 pairs of shoes.[15] A faithful clerk mistakenly showed Sweet's approval as "Colonel," instead of General.

Sweet did not care to have any more inspection officers in Prisoner's Square like Lieutenant Briggs or Captain Shurly. He appointed Capt. Wells Sponable, his patrol commander, to do the weekly reports required by the War Department. It was Sponable who had refused to stop Red O'Hara from breaking up religious meetings in Prisoner's Square.

Sponable started right off with the ridiculous assertion on January 15, 1865, "Quality of food—good. Same as used by Federal Troops." He reported the following week that he had sufficient clothing and bedding for the prisoners, except Hood's men.[16] "Water—a great plenty; same as used in the City of Chicago," he added. Then he noted that 125 prisoners had died in the past two weeks. About 11,699 men crammed Prisoner's Square, and the camp was again on the way to record high mortality.

More gloom descended when prisoners read that Union forces had captured Fort Fisher, the main supply depot of the Confederacy. They knew that sustaining their troops would now be impossible. The sad news depressed even the hired prisoners, and a fight exploded in their barracks on January 17, with nine men suffering wounds from knives and other weapons.[17]

Meanwhile, another commission met at Camp Douglas to investigate a shooting on January 20, 1865. Private Newell Sanford, Company A, Eighth VRC, shot William A. Chance, Company A, 33rd Alabama, "who was at the time committing a nuisance (urinating) in a street of said square."[18] Chance died. The commission found that Sanford "was acting in obedience to the orders and under the command of Capt. J. H. Hastings, and was justified in shooting said prisoner of war."

Such incidents made escape more urgent. The mounting toll left bunkmates and messmates surviving as extended families, and the dead were sorely missed. Discussion of personal affairs was constant. As Copely once said, "All the property that a man owned was on record." Guards told prisoners that the oath of allegiance was available again, and many seized it as a way out. Burke and his friends called it "taking the dog." They yelled "another state's gone out!" and sang Yankee Doodle at those who took the oath.[19]

Taking the oath was good life insurance, since the sickness and lack of hospital space were as hazardous as rifle bullets. Sponable reported the death of 83 more prisoners in his January 29 report and made the incredible claim, "General health of prisoners—good." The situation was fast approaching that of 1863, when Chicago doctors labeled the prison an extermination camp. Yet, it was in good condition, but blankets and clothing were barely sufficient.

A steady 8 percent of the prison population was dying. With 208 answering the long roll in January, it would not be long before the camp extinguished a thousand more lives. It came close to that figure in the end.[20] Even Sponable gave in a bit by recommending "that the sutler be directed to keep constantly on hand and for sale to the prisoners onion and cabbage whenever they can be procured." He did not ask Hoffman to restore the vegetable ration.

Officials released only 162 prisoners in January. Some sick finally left under General Butler's plan to exchange the disabled. Then came the best news in years. The Cartel was restarting, and the two governments had scheduled a general exchange to commence on February 1, 1865. Prisoners would be hungry, meanwhile, as Captain Shurly reported an immense saving of $2,969.75 by reducing the bread ration for December 1864.[21] The new Cartel became a race against death with the lack of vegetables and reduced bread ration helping to fill the dead house.

Burke felt no pangs as he cooked another lavish dinner on January 24, 1865, to celebrate his 23rd birthday. He used a pound of butter and a pound of sugar to make dumplings, boiled beef, bean soup, bread, and delicacies such as vinegar pie. He reflected without guilt that "there are a great many who wash clothes for something to eat." He did not say where or how he obtained the life-saving beans. However, money was talking loud and clear again at Camp Douglas. He had leftover bread from his dinner to pay for washing and made a good hash on the coal stove while Henry White watched for patrols. The extra food stayed well frozen in Chicago's giant outdoor refrigerator.

The lucky dinner guests probably ate in shifts, since the kitchen measured only 20 feet by 24 feet. The sleeping dormitory was 70 feet long by 24 feet wide, and 12 feet up to the open rafters.[22] A medical inspector from the surgeon general's office counted only 165 men in "several barracks," which was normal capacity. Most barracks were crowded with up to 190 men.

The lack of ceilings permitted guards to invent a new game called the "circus," forcing prisoners to climb onto rafters and do tricks. They punished a prisoner this way on January 30 for sitting by the stove after midnight. They penalized another one caught spitting on the floor, and he replaced the first. "Soon after all had quieted down a prisoner in the barrack was caught stealing bread from the kitchen which caused a little disturbance," Burke recorded.[23] He received 22 lashes with a strap while laid across a barrel with his pants down, "making him beg considerably."

Guards terrorized prisoners with a drunken rampage the following night. "Some 200 men in barrack No. 5 were driven into the cold and made to stand on one foot," Burke raged. "Several were hung from the second bunk by their feet, and in this position they were whipped with belts by the guards just as a negro would be whipped or worse. All of the men in one whole barrack was made to stand out awhile and then bare themselves and sit on the snow and ice till they melted through to the ground. There were 10 or 12 men whipped altogether in the same manner as those in number 5."

Finally, the patrol came across one husky prisoner who "said he would die defending himself." The guards debated whether to kill him or call off the party. They decided to turn in. Adding to the misery was overcrowding, with two hundred men in barrack Number 5.

It is not clear whether the raiders were guards who manned the stockade or those who belonged to the interior patrol. It appears that they were the former, since Burke would have called them the patrol had they been the ones. Then why did the patrol not protect the prisoners against outsiders? They had no answer.

A prison committee informed authorities about the drunken raid. They made no reply, and some prisoners thought of attacking the fence. This incident caused about 40 or 50 men to take the oath against their conscience in the hope of leaving. "There has been seven men shot for various trivial offenses this month," Burke sadly noted. The respected U.S. Sanitary Commission confirmed the harsh treatment.[24]

The spitbox game was part of it. Each barracks had four. When the patrol saw a man missing the box, he had to clean it until he caught someone spitting on the floor. If that person refused to take his turn at the box, then the first man either reported him to the patrol or continued to clean the box. Neither option was pleasant. The last man on the box took his position next to it every morning at roll call.[25]

Discipline may have been easier to accept had exchange gotten underway or had General Beall's supplies come through. Letters from home urged prisoners to take the oath of allegiance because exchange seemed unlikely. The bitter siege in front of Petersburg, Virginia, seemed to nullify further cooperation in getting their men back. Meanwhile the sutler illegally sold Plantation Bitters, which helped to some extent. He guaranteed that this old "reliable remedy" would cure most of the diseases ravaging the camp, and it did succeed in making the men merry. They needed it because the mule had grown to 15 feet high and 12 feet long. "It looks like a big trestle, and is about two inches wide on top, rather too sharp to ride comfortably," Burke quipped. Some prisoners who rode it reported that from it they could see over the stockade.

General Sweet had his own mule to deal with, as General Hoffman was back in full force. He resumed his Washington office on February 1, 1865, as sole commissary of prisoners. Records gave no clue about the reasons for these changes.

Economy was the watchword with Hoffman back, and Sweet gave the prison committee working for General Beall a parole of honor on February 2, 1865, to go to Chicago and find the missing supplies.[26] Very likely, they telegraphed Beall in New York and visited railroads to verify that the goods had not been bottled up somewhere. Surprised freight clerks found four prisoners from Camp Douglas casually dropping in to ask about their consignment. The committee returned to camp pursuant to the code of chivalry, probably on the streetcar that stopped opposite the gate on Cottage Grove. They had nothing to report, however.

Help from Beall became more crucial, as Sponable's preposterous report on February 4 again stated, "General Health of Prisoners—Good," while showing that 64 had died in the past week. Only four days later, Lieutenant Fife reported to Sweet that a prisoner named Thomas P. Strickland had died of smallpox in Prisoner's Square.[27] He did not say whether this was a new case or one discharged from the hospital. Sweet felt that serious negligence had occurred and ordered Dr. Whitehill to investigate. Camp Douglas records do not confirm that anyone named Strickland died, but Fife should have known.

On that same day, General Sweet offered prisoners the oath instead of exchange, so they knew something was up. Burke was proud when only five Kentucky men applied for it, while 109 others signed for returning to the Confederate army. Sweet's February report to Hoffman told the old dreary story, with 308 men dying that month. He complained that "probably one-third of the prisoners would take the oath if they could be assured of immediate release." Reverend Tuttle was already on the lecture circuit with "Three Years Among the Rebel Prisoners."[28]

Sweet planned to make room in the hospital by first releasing patients who opted for exchange. He also began restricting prisoners from moving about the square. Prison officials now punished men for being absent from quarters. This was still a long way from locked cell blocks, since prisoners could leave barracks and accept the consequences. Sweet mainly aimed to isolate "diehards" who prevented others from taking the oath. Some men were losing faith in ever going back, Burke admitted, "altho the papers say it is a general exchange."

Authorities suddenly processed about five hundred men on February 12, the largest such group since April 1, 1863. The exchange began by signing the parole in three places at the express office.

Burke's parole probably read: "I, the undersigned Curtis R. Burke, a private of the Fourteenth Regiment of Ky. Cav. Vols., do solemnly swear that I will not bear arms against the United States of America or give any information, or do any military duty whatsoever until regularly exchanged as a prisoner of war. Description: Height, 5 ft. 8 in.; Hair, Auburn; Eyes, gray; Complexion, dark. (signed) Curtis R. Burke."

Prisoners who were staying behind used eight kitchens to cook five days' rations for their departing comrades. The rations consisted of boiled beef and crackers. Stanton attempted to sabotage the exchange by again offering the oath, and Sweet called out the entire square at once on February 17. Only 14 men from five states stepped to the front at Sweet's invitation. "They took their baggage and were moved over to the oath barracks in another part of the camp by themselves," Burke said with contempt.[29] They had the audacity to return to Prisoner's Square for their evening meal, but loyal prisoners had already eaten their share. About 1,500 men left for exchange in February, but Burke sadly conceded that 1,400 planned to take the oath.

Guards moved the prisoners who signed for exchange into special barracks in Prisoner's Square and stripped them of overcoats and blankets despite the cold trip ahead. General Grant suggested this step. Hoffman was against taking blankets, something upon which he had always insisted. Somehow, he had mellowed. The rapidly aging widower planned to cash in his army career for an "I Do," and start a new life with a new love much younger than he.

General Sweet was probably responsible for taking both coats and blankets away. Stanton suddenly lifted the ban on the sutler selling vegetables near the end of February.[30] It was too late. The January and February death toll reached 551. Sponable's reports showed about 65 deaths per week, but all the while stating, "General Health of Prisoners—Good."

Hoffman finally responded to Sweet's demand to quickly release prisoners who did not wish to be exchanged. "Arrangements will be made at the proper time for those who publicly decline the offer of exchange!" Hoffman snapped. Sweet feared that this foot-dragging left prisoners no choice but to sign for exchange, given the high mortality at camp. "When will that proper time be?" Sweet demanded.[31]

Sweet knew he would look bad if everyone preferred to return to the front. Hoffman and Stanton had seriously misread the prisoners. The new policy of requiring them publicly to declare for the oath in front of their fellows made them silent. They would rather remain prisoners. Stanton's plan to demoralize them had miscarried and filled Camp Douglas with thousands of men who would neither take the oath nor sign for exchange.

The *Tribune* claimed, on February 18, 1865, that out of 10,248 prisoners remaining, about eight thousand would not go back. The paper was seldom wrong about the camp, so when a squad of five hundred started processing out on February 20, Burke saw them as "a fine looking set of men."[32]

Burke was called out for exchange three days later. Henry White received $20 from home, and "we commenced living well again," Burke said with satisfaction. Guards got drunk that night and started abusing prisoners. Another beastly winter gripped the camp and could prove the *Tribune* wrong about the prisoners not wishing to go back. Exchange looked attractive compared with the disease and death, the cruelty and degradation gripping Camp Douglas.

However, a most astonishing event intervened. Apparently the prison committee working for General Beall had succeeded in their mission to Chicago. Substantial supplies, but no food, reached camp on February 20. Incredibly, three paroled Confederate officers accompanied the shipment: Col. M. D. Barber, 45th Arkansas Infantry, Lt. Col. William C. Clifton, 39th Alabama Infantry, and Maj. A. L. McCafee, 6th Coupee Battery. They knocked on the door and demanded entry as agents of General Beall.[33]

Imagine General Sweet's consternation when he met with the Rebel officers. He had no choice but to allow them into Prisoner's Square with their supplies. "They were not to communicate in any way with the prisoners of war except as necessary," his orders read. That was not all. The War Department directed him to give the three a parole of honor, provide them with quarters in Garrison Square, and "issue passes to the City of Chicago without guards." They, in

Camp Douglas prisoners captured at Franklin, Tennessee, wearing the new uniforms and clothing sent by General Beall. (Image courtesy of Mike Miner).

turn, promised "not to hold any conversation with any person or persons whatsoever on the subject of the rebellion, the armies engaged in it, or anything related thereto." Presumably, they could say hello and goodbye and nod their heads. No other incident so dramatically illustrated the futility of the war, except perhaps returning slaves to their owners in 1862.

General Beall made seven deliveries from February 20 to March 14, 1865. He sent 6,709 blankets, 2,204 pairs of drawers, 4,080 pairs of pants, 4,368 jackets, 5,320 shirts, 200 pantaloons, 5,120 pairs of shoes, 2,600 pairs of socks, and 411 boxes of tobacco.[34] He did not explain the lack of food, but prisoners deeply appreciated the huge supply of tobacco which had cost Beall about $1,233 in Federal money. Southern tobacco growers were happy, and Southern cotton was selling well in New York. It was not likely that the fading Confederacy could have produced enough goods for General Beall, and Northern factories may have filled some orders for him.

Richmond did not publicize the agreement for good reason. Asking for sacrifices could be difficult while a Confederate general was running around New York City like he owned the place, and Southern boys might ask why they should die for the New York Board of Trade. Likewise, Northern sailors might ask why they were blockading Southern ports while cotton flowed through New York City. As a result, little was known about Beall's activities. Southern families believed that the new uniforms in prison photos were only studio props. Beall had to defend himself against charges that he was a collaborator or worse when information about the agreement surfaced after the war.

The enormous amount of blankets, clothing, and tobacco for Camp Douglas, alone, shows how successful the venture was. Nonetheless, a dispute arose because Beall made the jackets and pants in Confederate gray, enabling the South to re-equip prisoners who returned. Halleck, accordingly, canceled the agreement, and General Beall surrendered to Federal authorities in New York City. Officials soon found that few prisoners wished to go back, and they released General Beall again to carry on with his mission.

Burke appears to have obtained a new Confederate uniform, also, from what he said in his diary. Right now, he purchased note paper from the sutler before departing, "as I suspect paper might be scarce in Dixie." The camp was in a state of tumult, and "the tailors, shoemakers, ring makers, toothpick makers, and washmen still do a very good business."[35] He began the process of leaving on February 27, and used all his sutler's checks. The fact that he did not give them to Pa was significant. He abandoned his blanket in the barrack as he checked out, "rather than give them a chance to take it from me." His failure to slip it to Pa was further evidence of the rupture of what had been a deep and loving relationship. The departing men could carry nothing except a change of underclothing and their personal belongings.

A Yankee soldier tagged their blankets and extra clothing under the pretense that they would be shipped separately. "Some of the boys comically ordered their blankets, etc. checked to the Spotswood, American, and other Richmond hotels," Burke chuckled. Meanwhile, the war continued, with guards beating, kicking, and slapping prisoners, many of whom whispered of vengeance.[36] Two men, desperate to leave, tried to slip into Burke's squad. They were caught and made to wear the barrel.

Pa received permission to see Burke before he was moved to Garrison Square. Differing emotions must have strained the meeting between father and son. Pa had not signed for exchange. Life was comfortable in the Masonic barrack, where he had plenty of food, clothing, and tobacco. Dying for Southern rights required more hard currency than he had in his bank account right then. Pa had been Burke's role model, his idol. He had quit college to join his father in the 14th Kentucky, but that was then. Now a mountain stood between them that Pa could not climb. The "Cause" was lost for Pa, but still alive for his son. Burke did not record what was said at that last meeting, and he never mentioned Pa again. He was not one to forgive a traitor.

The prisoners marched a half mile to the train in charge of their guard regiment, the 48th Missouri Infantry. The road back was doubtful as the defenses around Petersburg, Virginia, disintegrated, but right now the men thought about the place they were leaving. "We did not get to see much of the City," Burke regretted, "altho I would have liked very much to have passed through it as we were in sight of it for so long."[37] Burke and Henry White rode in "third class cars," and took one behind the locomotive. This almost cost them their hard-won lives when the train collided with another 72 miles out of Chicago.

The water tender smashed through the front of Burke's car nearly drowning everyone, and the impact ripped seats from the floor. The collision injured one guard and several railroad workers and killed the engineer of the other train. Burke was pinned under his seat but escaped injury. Water poured out of the tender all night, lapping away at the trapped men. The road back was still most difficult. Rescue workers finally got to them in the morning. They did not arrive in Richmond until March 10. Burke was hateful and malicious when he sighted black Union soldiers camped near the city.

He discovered to his dismay that General Morgan had not enrolled his regiment with Confederate authorities, and it was unknown in Richmond. It made no difference. Everyone received a 30-day furlough with vague and impossible orders to report to various commands as far away as Tennessee and North Carolina.[38]

Regardless, it appeared that exchanges would continue, and Hoffman decreed on March 1 that "guerrillas will not be forwarded until further orders, nor any who are bad characters." Two days later he ordered General Sweet to release all civilians "whose homes are within the rebel lines who are not awaiting trial on grave charges." Accordingly, prisoners from the Camp Douglas Conspiracy remained in custody. They had suffered a 15 percent death rate, about equal to that of the Confederates. Hoffman suddenly halted exchanges on March 3 without explanation.[39] Perhaps the South could no longer deliver Union prisoners to City Point.

Another reason may have been the curious incident that occurred on March 3, when five hundred Camp Douglas prisoners reached Virginia. About two hundred of them changed their minds after hearing dismal stories from Confederate deserters. They returned to Camp Douglas. The road back had become a full circle.[40]

This was not the first time that prisoners had returned voluntarily. Two escapees came back during the terrible freeze of January 1864. Two others returned after taking the oath of allegiance. One was a Cherokee Indian who found he had language problems in Chicago. The other, a private in a Tennessee regiment, decided "to stay where he felt most at home."[41]

One group of 1,492 signed paroles and departed around March 10. Nothing went well for this batch. They missed the exchange at City Point, and Robert E. Lee surrendered before another could be arranged.[42] They were stranded, as the North refused to furnish transportation. One of Morgan's men walked home to Kentucky, not an easy trek through the devastated South.

On March 13, 1865, William Hoffman was promoted from

brigadier general to major general.[43] He had come a long way from the dusty lieutenant trudging down the road to Mexico City, or the lonely captain who pursued Indians across the wastes of Nebraska. Like General Sweet, he saw his opportunity in the Civil War and made the most of it.

Then tragedy struck during what should have been a happier time for prisoners. On March 15, Sweet reported the third killing of a prisoner by another. Samuel Turner of the First Tennessee Infantry stabbed a man to death. Turner had previously knifed two other prisoners. Sweet had described him as "a desperate man" but had failed to remove him from the prison population.[44] His indifference cost a man his life. However, officials did not plan to repeat the trial of William Kilpatrick in 1862. It was the South's problem, now, according to the army. Yet, there was no just reason for not putting Turner on trial in Chicago. Instead, Hoffman ordered Sweet to deliver him to the Confederate exchange agent along with witnesses and a full report. Turner probably escaped punishment. The Confederacy also lay mortally wounded.

It did not appear that many more prisoners were willing to rush back as the second month of the Cartel ended. Sponable's report on March 29 stated that 292 Confederates enlisted in the Sixth U.S. Volunteer Infantry and in the Navy. No one was returning South. Prisoners read three newspapers each day to see how the war was going. Even discounting Northern propaganda, it was obvious that the end was near.

A sewer pipe broke, with close to ten thousand prisoners and a thousand guards still on hand. Prisoners were put to work repairing the overburdened system, but not without some incentive. Dr. Whitehill purchased 42 gallons of whiskey on March 23, costing the prison fund $147. He justified this expense "as necessary for the preservation of their health, they being constantly exposed while at work to wet and cold and consequent disease arising therefrom."[45] The men believed that it was the best prescription Dr. Whitehill ever wrote.

Sweet's detectives occupied him more than supervision of the camp, since the sewer problem was not Dr. Whitehill's responsibility. Hoffman continued to refuse payment, and Sweet again attempted to undermine him. He wrote the adjutant general of the army on March 29, 1865, for "leave to disburse $3,000 for detective salaries and expenses incurred in the Camp Douglas Conspiracy." The answer was no.[46] The adjutant was not about to cross Hoffman, whose influence increased as he soaked up more and more of the collapsing Confederate army.

Sweet did take notice of his responsibilities when the University of Chicago complained about the garrison hunting on school grounds. Its board of trustees was top-heavy with influential politicians, including men who knew President Lincoln. Sweet circulated an order on March 29 that "officers and enlisted men are prohibited from entering the grounds of the University with fire arms, or shooting birds or other game on such grounds!"[47]

Losing their hunting privileges was a blow to the garrison, as it appeared that they would be there for some time. About 9,266 prisoners still remained at the end of March. However, 99 faithful did leave for the front before the surrender in April.[48] John M. Copley was never called for exchange since he had given up that right. A kindly officer had obtained a job for him in the prison hospital because of his youth, and regulations required hospital workers to take the oath of allegiance. He was still there late in June. Those who did not sign for exchange continued as prisoners of war. Only 73 new prisoners arrived in 1865.

General Sweet continued to play the conspiracy game in hopes of getting money for his spies and detectives. He arrested a citizen in Chicago for "disloyalty" on April 3, 1865, and jailed him at Camp Douglas.[49] He had no such authority under the embalmed Constitution or from the army. Sweet wielded more power over the city than any other person in its history.

Suddenly, the cataclysmic struggle was almost over. Robert E. Lee surrendered on April 9, leaving Joseph E. Johnston's army in North Carolina as the only remaining threat. General Sweet treated the matter as finished, and so did many Confederates. Soon, they filled ten more companies of infantry for the Union army "to join in the Indian frontier warfare." They could still win some victories. These enlistees did not include two thousand who had joined the Union army and navy previously.[50]

Sweet ordered a hundred guns fired on April 12. He mounted the platform in Garrison Square and spoke "of the death of the now dying rebellion and the glorious future which now lay ahead of the nation when the white winged messenger of peace shall reign gloriously." He had forgotten the Indians. Parson Brownlow had addressed prisoners from this platform three years earlier, telling them that they were "the dupes of designing leaders." James T.

Mackey, the diarist, had been there, along with many comrades who had since answered the long roll. Reverend Tuttle got in a few words, and the garrison sang "John Brown's Body."[51]

President Abraham Lincoln's assassination two days later ruined the celebration. General Sweet attempted to lower the flag the next morning, but the lanyard came off the pulley. A soldier fell to his death attempting to free it, and no one else volunteered. Legend described how a "ragged Georgia boy" climbed the pole as thousands watched, "and in a few seconds fixed the rope; then, waving his old Confederate hat three times about his head, threw it at the crowd below. A mighty cheer went up as he started his descent. The prisoners caught it up and for the first and only time a Rebel yell was heard in a Northern Prison."[52]

Federal soldiers supposedly carried the Georgian to headquarters where he obtained his freedom and a reward. Too many prisoners mentioned such an incident for something like it not to have happened. P. H. Prince, on the other hand, accused the garrison of bayoneting a prisoner to death for applauding the news about Lincoln's death. Prince conceded that he was in the hospital when this killing allegedly took place, "but the boys told me about it when I was returned to the barracks."[53]

Prince was right about retaliation. Guards forced five prisoners to "point for grub" on April 23, "with the tip end of their four fingers on the ground." Their crime was talking after Taps. Prisoners became hopeful when Hoffman ordered 1,800 of their number shipped to New Orleans, by way of Cairo.[54] The historic exchange route of 1862 was open again, but this time they were just ex-prisoners of war without an army. The road back would be barren and desolate. No warm camp fires awaited them, no old comrades rushed to shake their hands.

Meanwhile, a beef protest jolted General Sweet. Worse, the ringleaders came from his own Eighth VRC. However, these were not his old soldiers, but a batch of replacements. Private Silas Mann, a new musician in the Eighth VRC, wrote home on April 25, 1865, that the troops were tired of receiving poor quality salt beef. "Strange as it may seem one morning when our Genl Sweet arose he discovered a cross before his dwelling (for he was a roman) and on this cross was crucified a large quantity of said salt beef," Mann giggled.

Mann mistakenly believed that Sweet was Roman Catholic because Ada attended Catholic school. Sweet's father was an elder in the

Baptist church and a missionary to Wisconsin Indians. Sweet and his wife chartered the First Church of Christ (Episcopal) in Lombard, Illinois, after the war.[55] The pranksters included a sign that read: "This poor old bull was killed in 1812 and served to the soldiers in 1865."

This incident should have ended any chance for the Eighth VRC to serve at President Lincoln's funeral procession in Chicago on May 1, but it did not. The garrison competed fiercely for this honor, and the Eighth VRC band was considered the best. General Sweet detailed four hundred men each from the Eight and the 15th VRC for the procession.[56]

Beall's three Confederate officers probably saw the funeral. Contrary to all reason, Hoffman detained them at Camp Douglas long after they had distributed supplies and completed their mission. They asked Hoffman early in April why they could not go home and await exchange there. He informed them on April 27, 1865, that their applications "cannot be favorably considered."[57] He even denied Major McCafee's request for ten days' leave. It was an unpleasant bit of spite. The officers could have escaped by simply going downtown and boarding a train, but Hoffman knew that they would not violate their parole of honor.

Lincoln's funeral did not relieve Sweet from the endless demands of his detectives, however. In what he called "a last resort," Sweet appealed to Maj. Henry L. Burnett, the prosecutor in the conspiracy trials. He had made Burnett a famous man, and Detective Thomas Keefe (called O'Keefe by Sweet) was demanding $716.82, more than a private's pay for the entire war.[58] Sweet could not take his demands lightly, since Keefe had helped fabricate the conspiracy. Burnett should have believed in it before anyone, but he did not respond.

Hoffman again demanded a report about whether Sweet had reimbursed the prison fund $531.36 in unauthorized payments to his men. Sweet astounded him when he instead applied for $358.20 to pay another agent, and $38.46 to pay an unnamed prisoner who must have been an informer. Sweet then asked Burnett for protection. He confessed that he had paid $1,614.37 to detectives from the prison fund without authority.[59] Again, there was no response. Hoffman had almost hounded Colonel Mulligan into a court-martial for this amount of money, so Sweet had something to worry about.

He exploded when Winslow Ayer demanded more money for

testifying at the conspiracy trials. Sweet denounced him for "failure to give information at the time of the maturing of the plot to attack Camp Douglas!" John T. Shanks appeared in the middle of Sweet's troubles and complained that he needed replacement coats and blankets for his men.[60] This request should have gone to the quartermaster, but Sweet was not likely to turn him down.

A historic order came on May 8, 1865, directing Sweet to release all prisoners, except those above the rank of colonel. The government would provide them transportation home upon their taking the oath of allegiance.[61] Those who did not take the oath could either walk or become homeless in Chicago. More than one prisoner chose these options.

Careful records had to be kept of each prisoner, as to name, place of residence, and date and place of capture. In other words, the prison rolls had to be verified. Prisoners numbered 6,107 according to the *Official Records*, but only 5,609 according to Captain Sponable.[62] He was probably more accurate. Sponable's reports in the National Archives show careful gathering of data. It seems that 498 men were unaccounted for. About 893 were missing in the 1862 exchange according to the *Tribune*'s count. Adding that to the 498 lends credibility to claims that at least six thousand died at Camp Douglas.

Sweet continued to censor prison mail, probably to suppress information about the high mortality. A begging letter from a Camp Douglas prisoner dated May 9, 1865, bears the approval stamp, "By order of B. J. Sweet." Deaths climbed toward eight hundred at this time. Reverend Tuttle was also paying a high price for the war and requested leave "to visit his only son, not expected to live," who was a private in Sherman's army.[63]

General Sweet continued to protect the city and the nation from treason as the camp wound down. He ordered the arrest of the H. H. Forsyth family in Chicago "for hanging a picture of John Wilkes Booth in their house." No such picture was found by the patrol during a raid on May 10. Forsyth, "an old resident of Kentucky," was too ill to travel, so the patrol arrested his two daughters and took them to Camp Douglas. Of course, Sweet had no warrant as required by the supposedly restored Constitution. The women denied the charges, and Sweet released them after a "wholesome lecture."[64]

Meanwhile, prisoners moved out of camp at five hundred per week, and some distinguished people came to visit on May 12. They celebrated the formal opening of the new chapel in Garrison Square which had been under construction since September 1864.[65] This was a homecoming for Dwight L. Moody, who talked about the origin of religious services for the prisoners. Reverend Tuttle declared the chapel open to all "Christian denominations and clergymen from the Christian Commission." The chapel only had four months to live.

Camp Douglas survived a little longer as the "great clearing off" did not come until June, when 4,090 departed. About 1,770 refused to take the oath, according to Sponable, and the War Department held them until June 25. Only one prisoner escaped in 1865. Deaths reached 867, only a hundred fewer than in 1862. It was not over, yet. The post hospital held 59 prisoners too ill to travel. The army released Ninian Edwards from duty with a eulogy by General Sweet, for his "business capacity and efficiency."[66]

All guards were withdrawn on July 5, 1865, and the war finally ended at Camp Douglas three months after Lee's surrender at Appomattox.[67] Sixteen prisoners remained in the post hospital. The name of the first prisoner to enter the camp is not known. The identity of the last one out the gate is speculative, but someone hastily scrawled "Henry Harrison, 64th Va.?" on the blank side of the final prison roll.

CHAPTER 20

An End to Chivalry

Why they fought—Theories about the sickness and death—Camp Douglas becomes a mustering-out depot—Hoffman criticizes Sweet—The property is sold—General Sweet resigns—Some relics of the camp—Cost to build and operate—Camp Douglas compared with Andersonville.

Most prisoners were honest about why they went to war. Race and slavery came to center stage. The destitute Arkansas Post prisoners were highly critical of white officers who planned to lead black troops. "But you have no business to make soldiers of niggers," they argued.[1] Curtis R. Burke wrote that "most of the prisoners would rather remain a year longer than be exchanged for negroes." Racist comments in his journal are common.

M. J. Bradley called blacks "african demons." Many prisoners said they were fighting for "Southern Rights," meaning white supremacy. Camp Douglas records show that enlisted men did own slaves. Three sergeants in the Seventh Texas Infantry each had one at Fort Donelson. One prisoner wrote home from Camp Douglas that he expected the servants "to do their duty until I return." A prisoner named John C. Lester was one of six founders of the Ku Klux Klan at Pulaski, Tennessee, in December 1865.[2]

Union soldiers were no different from Confederates in opposing political, social, and economic equality for the black race. Finding a white recruit at Camp Douglas willing to fight for social justice was unlikely. Their letters and diaries speak about making war on the rebellion, not slavery. Private Tebbets of the 45th Illinois Infantry, killed at Shiloh, enlisted "to save the best form of government."

Colonel Mulligan blamed even the war on blacks. "President's proclamation published," he recorded in his diary on January 3, 1863. "Something about freeing niggers. These niggers keep this part of the world in business. We kill our beloved white brothers to save our beloved black cousins. We endanger a Republic to save a plantation.

We have forgotten Washington to exalt Fred Douglas. Sambo is the burden of our prayers and peccadilloes. For him we issue unlimited greenbacks!"[3]

Yet, Mulligan fought hard for the Union, or did he fight for himself? Men usually go to war to preserve their place in society, whatever that society happens to be and whatever that place is. Colonel Mulligan probably saw his place threatened by a divided nation. The permanent disruption of law and commerce between the states would damage the professional class to which he belonged. Slavery was irrelevant to his place in society, and he no doubt disapproved of recruiting blacks into the army.

However, influential Chicagoans recruited a black regiment at Camp Douglas in December 1863, but it never guarded prisoners. Black soldiers did so at Point Lookout, Maryland, where one Confederate complained, "Today the negroes are again on guard and are very insolent." No prisoner at Camp Douglas ever called a white guard insolent. They did consider one black civilian employee insolent. A member of the Third Tennessee Infantry assaulted him one day to his comrades' great satisfaction.[4]

Race and slavery aside, the most devoted Confederates were alienated long ago from the government in Washington. They wanted to expel the North from what they considered their native land. William Micajah Barrow of the Fourth Louisiana Infantry, for example, saw the struggle "as a second war of independence for the South." One Confederate officer boasted about braving death by refusing to walk under the former U. S. flag as he entered Camp Douglas.[5]

Others found no precise reason for enlisting. One prisoner told De Land that he joined for the $50 bonus to pay off his debts. Some said they were drunk when they signed up. Henry Morton Stanley supposedly enlisted to please the father of a young lady with whom he was infatuated.[6]

Black prisoners left no record of why they were in the Confederate army. Some had no choice, and it is understandable that some slaves preferred soldiering to slavery. Free blacks who served the Confederacy had their own agendas.

Camp Douglas held other minorities besides black prisoners. Five women and a child came in 1862. The Arkansas Post prisoners in 1863 included "Mexicans, Spaniards, and half-blood and full blood Cherokee Indians." Union army officers were at a loss, and entered blacks as servants, contraband, or negroes. They deemed some to be soldiers, depending on how they were captured.

Prison rolls were generally inaccurate for many reasons. Handwriting was often poor or illegible. Compilers misspelled names and entered wrong data for companies and regiments. Prisoners sometimes gave false information to confuse authorities. Regional accents caused difficulty as Yanks and Rebs had trouble understanding each other.

Ironically, Camp Douglas records became important to ex-prisoners and their survivors who applied to the former Confederate states for pensions. Many did not receive discharges after the surrender, and some belonged to units whose muster rolls did not go to Richmond. Burke's regiment, the so-called 14th Kentucky Cavalry, is an example. Henry White, Burke's friend in Company B, used a false name at camp, as did many others. This proved costly. The *Confederate Veteran* magazine carried many ads in later years seeking to establish proof of military service because names did not appear on Camp Douglas rolls.[7]

Escapes were among the worst kept records, however, as the camp did not keep a separate docket. Prison rolls listed 77 escapes up to July 1862, although this is unreliable due to poor recordkeeping by Colonel Mulligan.[8] The camp reported 319 escapes from July 1862 to the end of the war, so about 425, total, would be accurate. Authorities kept no specific record of the number of escapees recaptured. It appears to have been least 50 percent, with more than two hundred retaken.

Escapes are the least important of the Camp Douglas stories from a practical standpoint. True, they were chronicles of the human will, the exploits of men who dared to challenge their fate. However, escapees numbered only 1.5 percent of the almost 27,000 prisoners. The War Department recognized this fact and did not invest in sufficient guards or effective weapons. Escaping prisoners never harmed civilians or damaged private property. Otherwise, War Department officials probably would have converted barracks into locked cell blocks.

Several factors may explain this good behavior toward civilians. First, friends in the vicinity were well known, so escaping prisoners had no reason to bother strangers. Second, friends provided money, eliminating the need to rob anyone. Third, if prisoners were heading back South, they needed to hitch rides on wagons without raising an alarm. Finally, while every army harbors its share of criminals and psychopaths, those who escaped from Camp Douglas were different.

Regardless, the absence of cell blocks allowed for frequent

attempts to climb the fence. Burke recorded eight such tries, most of them successful. Articles in the *Confederate Veteran* describe three more, one of them successful. About 25 prisoners allegedly used ladders in the 1862 conspiracy. Most escapes depended on access to the fence. The former state prison at Alton, Illinois, with high brick walls and iron-barred cell blocks, lost only 114 prisoners in three and one-half years.[9]

Imagine a prison, today, secured with only a wooden stockade between 14 and 16 feet high and lit by kerosene lanterns at night. Prisoners are housed in open dormitories with freedom to roam about and even go to the sinks at night. Guards are disabled and armed only with clumsy single-shot muzzle-loading muskets and a tricky black-powder revolver. No barrier separates visitors from inmates, and packages are allowed to pass without going through a metal detector or x-ray. Finally, prisoners are permitted to keep axes, hammers, matches, cutlery, and saws. How many inmates do you think such a prison would be able to keep confined?

Reverend Tuttle remembered two young women placing a package in the supply wagon going to camp. He investigated and found a "fine blue uniform coat." Later, he saw the women visiting Polk Johnson, a prisoner and son of the postmaster general for two presidents of the former United States.[10] Tuttle probably ruined a delightful escape. According to the Illinois adjutant general, "Fat looking turkeys were discovered to contain revolvers, knives, or other articles."

Prison officials were short of guards even to enforce the martial law decree of July 1862. It appears that Mrs. Walsh, the wife of Charles Walsh, took her small daughter to play near the camp and slip in money and letters to prisoners.

Yet, comparatively few attempted escape. Curtis R. Burke merely thought about it. Many tried because they saw little hope of survival as a long-term prisoner. Others looked upon it as a personal challenge. Devotion to the cause motivated some. The risk was evident, although most escapes were without injury. Bribery was rare under Sweet, which increased the risk.

Authorities did not compile figures of those killed and wounded in escape attempts. It may be close to 25 dead and 45 wounded. This number does not include the shooting of at least 20 others who were not escaping. The Illinois adjutant general's postwar report makes the absurd claim that only one prisoner was shot at Camp Douglas.[11]

Hospital records did not record deaths from gunshot wounds suffered at camp. They listed prisoners shot to death by guards only as "died." Besides the hospital ledgers, doctors kept medical histories on a prescribed form called a "Medical Descriptive List" showing diagnosis, treatment, and surgery, much like the patient charts used today. Too often it read, "The patient died." Surgeons did many autopsies in a desperate attempt to learn more about diseases sweeping the camp.

Camp Douglas became a major medical center, serving the entire army, with a general hospital in Chicago and one at Camp Douglas. The city hospital had four stories, with two wings and 140 beds. It even contained an eye and ear clinic. The War Department built a Marine hospital near downtown to serve seamen. General Sweet complained that the hospital at camp created a security problem, when "patients and attendants must constantly come in and go out."[12] The camp's post hospital and the prison hospital served the garrison and the prison respectively. The smallpox facility was a branch of the post hospital, which explains why Union soldiers ended up there also.

The prison hospital, completed in April 1864, continued to win compliments. Four wards in each wing were "well lighted and ventilated by cold-air shafts opening in the floor," according to Medical Inspector Coolidge. "The walls also had air shafts, with openings near the ceiling and floors. Each wing had Wards on the second floor, also well lighted and vented. Ceilings measured 12 feet high throughout." He found running water toilets in each ward connected to the sewers. Inside privies fouled the air in hospitals elsewhere, according to Coolidge.

Reports described another prison hospital in White Oak Square for skin diseases, measuring 80 by 20 feet with 30 beds. These facilities were still open late in June 1865 to the extent that the post surgeon needed 150 pounds of soap and an ice box.[13]

The Medical and Surgical History of the War of the Rebellion was dubious about Camp Douglas medical reports.[14] For example, 23,037 cases of sickness occurred in 1864, alone, according to the study. This was more than three times the number reported by the camp. It appears that post surgeons did not include many sick in barracks. For example, they listed only 407 patients, total, in December 1864, while the medical study found 577 in hospitals and 1,547 sick in barracks.

TABLE VII
CASES AND CLASSES OF DISEASE AND DEATH
CAMP DOUGLAS PRISON DEPOT
FEBRUARY 1862 TO JUNE 1865[15]

	Cases	*Deaths*
Fevers, such as smallpox and malaria	15,938	1,407
Diarrhea and dysentery	13,455	698
Anemia	585	4
Consumption	259	113
Rheumatism	3,212	37
Scurvy	3,745	39
Bronchitis	1,628	27
Pneumonia and pleurisy	4,655	1,296
Wounds, injuries, unspecified diseases	1,279	80
Other diseases	25,332	308
TOTALS	**70,088**	**4,009**

The study did not explain "wounds and injuries" or whether they occurred at camp or in the field. The worst figures related to scurvy victims. This was a noncommunicable disease, one for which doctors knew both prevention and cure.

A prisoner suffered at least two illnesses, and some as many as three, according to the figures. Smallpox caused the highest mortality among the fevers at 823, accounting for 20.5 percent of the deaths, a staggering amount. One medical investigator speculated that this mortality resulted from lack of vaccination by the South. "The eruption was reported as having broken out on some of the prisoners within a day or two after their arrival at the depot," he argued. In one case, a prisoner captured at Cumberland Gap on September 9, 1863, died of smallpox on the 26th. Another, captured near Atlanta in 1864, expired with smallpox only three weeks after reaching camp.[16]

Smallpox vaccinations caused terrible ulcers because of the prisoners' poor condition, including the scurvy they brought with them, the study claimed. It showed that earlier in the war Confederate soldiers received a full ration in the army, and scurvy was rare. Fresh beef and vegetables later diminished considerably, and scurvy set in. This must have happened earlier than thought, as it appeared among the prisoners in 1862.

Doctors theorized that "the hardships and exposures entailed on the men by the military events that ended in their capture were the main causes of the disease and mortality with which they were afflicted during their subsequent confinement." They stressed that the foul air in and around the barracks carried diseases. Modern medicine would probably agree that overcrowding helped spread bacteria and viruses.

The number of deaths at Camp Douglas remains uncertain. The official tally by the *Medical and Surgical History* is 4,039, but those who died in barracks likely escaped the notice of hospital clerks. One inspector had charged earlier that authorities were not properly reporting deaths. Regardless, the figure of 4,039 is 15 percent, almost one out of seven prisoners. Elmira, New York, was worse with a 24 percent death rate, and 2,937 out of 10,178 prisoners died in one year.

OTHER MORTALITY FIGURES FOR CAMP DOUGLAS

1862—*Chicago Tribune*	976
1863—*Official Record*	721
1864—*Official Record*	1,231
1865—*Official Record*	867
TOTAL:	3,795

The mortality in 1865 made it the worst year for such a short time. Smallpox remained very prevalent, and prisoners suffering from scurvy fell like tenpins with other diseases. Camp Douglas still ranks first among Northern prisons for the number who died, although eventually it was no longer the largest prison.

Point Lookout, Maryland, where James T. Mackey died, received 32,140 prisoners through November 30, 1864, and 1,532 of them died. From then until the end of June 1865, when the camp closed, 20,124 more arrived and 1,428 died.[17] Its total of 52,264 prisoners is double that of Camp Douglas. Yet, 2,960 perished there as compared with more than 4,000 in Chicago.

The theory that harsh conditions at Camp Douglas caused the mortality does not hold true, since Point Lookout was no vacation spa. Perhaps more died at Camp Douglas because of Chicago's sickly population, its lethal water supply, and its lack of control of milk production in the area. The organism responsible for diphtheria "grows freely in milk,"[18] and vendors simply transferred it from diseased cows to the camp. Kentuckians had the right idea in preferring "something more in keeping with the needs of a grown-up individual."

Camp Douglas was unique among the Federal prisons that eventually numbered 24 camps, because troops in training and prisoners lived in the same square for two years. Elmira remained a post for recruiting and training troops besides the prison, but prisoners were kept in a separate camp from the start. Smallpox struck there, also, only the doctors covered it up under the names "variola" or "varioloid," and the townspeople did not become alarmed as happened in Chicago.[19]

Illinois had three more prisons, Rock Island, Camp Butler near Springfield, and Alton. Rock Island did not receive prisoners until 1863, and they numbered only 8,400. Officials buried some 1,900 there. Camp Butler was too small and only held about 2,100 prisoners from Fort Donelson. Both places transferred prisoners to Camp Douglas.

Alton was the former state penitentiary. However, only between one and two thousand prisoners were on hand at any one time. About 1,354 dead lie in the North Alton Confederate Cemetery.[20] Camp Morton, at Indianapolis, Indiana, was also a parole camp and a prison, but it received only nine thousand prisoners. The site is now a residential area, and the dead are buried in a cemetery similar to Oak Woods in Chicago.

Both sides regarded prisoners as pawns. They suffered retaliation at Camp Douglas for matters beyond their control, such as Andersonville. Withholding antiscorbutic is the worst example of retaliation, and while officials fed them with one hand, they sold their rations with the other. The South was also to blame because it helped kill the Cartel with shortsighted racial policies.

When a Confederate general tried to restart exchanges in the spring of 1864, except "recaptured slaves," Richmond replied that it would not tolerate any exchange of blacks. Another 1,339 prisoners died at Camp Douglas, alone, from then until the Cartel restarted in February 1865, and Confederates were dying in 21 other Federal prisons. Meanwhile, the bureaucrats in Richmond went to church with their nicely starched families.[21]

TABLE VIII[22]

DATA ON THE 700 DAYS: AUGUST 1863 TO AUGUST 1865

Arrived	13,887
Sick	6,349
Died	2,349
Escaped	245

Official Records claim 26,781 Confederates passed through Camp Douglas: 8,962 in 1862; 3,932 from January to April 1863; 13,887 from August 1863 to the end of the war. The army later reduced the figure to 26,060. Perhaps it found duplication of names.[23]

The war did not end for General Sweet after the camp emptied. Hoffman was chewing him out like a buck private on July 20, 1865, "due to serious errors" in his hospital accounts. Sweet received another blast in August for failure to send the roll of prisoners transferred to the post hospital.[24] Hoffman's thirst for vengeance was unrelenting, and these attacks could sully Sweet's reputation.

Sweet's paperwork would not win any court cases. He showed W. H. Wright as dead on August 16, 1864, and taking the oath on April 22, 1865. Unfortunately, the first report was correct. Sweet reported another prisoner named Walter P. Key as dead on October 24, 1864. Hoffman pointed out that Key had never been listed as a prisoner, but he was there, and did die on October 27.

Sweet could not personally oversee such details, and Captain Shurly was a weak administrator. Sweet erred in not verifying the rolls with Rebel sergeant-majors before sending them to Hoffman. Smith was not the only name to cause a nervous breakdown. Incredibly, two John Cohens resided in Prisoner's Square, one in Company I, Second Kentucky Cavalry, and the other in Company A, 30th Mississippi Infantry.[25] Officials almost released the wrong Cohen once.

Sweet's burdens sharply increased as thousands of soldiers descended on the camp for discharge. It was a repeat of the parolee invasion of 1862 that stunned Colonel Tucker. Cook stoves were scarce because many had been removed to punish the prisoners. This did not deter the hardened veterans, who simply made open fires outside. Colonel Skinner complained that they were "using vast quantities of fuel" and endangering the camp.

The veterans returned none too soon. Citizens complained that many ex-prisoners remained in Chicago and were taking the jobs of Union veterans. "No true hearted man would give preference to a rebel," the *Tribune* muttered. However, the paper saw no harm "if by working the repentant rebel becomes a useful member of society which he probably never has been previously."[26]

Returning veterans may have been drinking heavily, because General Grant prohibited the sale of liquor to "troops arriving at Camp Douglas," also sale to them "along the line of travel." Soon the army discharged 28 Illinois regiments. Twenty regiments from other states processed out through the end of August 1865, but not entirely without incident. The Ninth Iowa Infantry went downtown on July 14 and tore up the red light district on Wells Street. Chicago police reported extensive property damage, but made no arrests.[27]

The *Tribune* talked of keeping the camp as a permanent installation. Its water supply was sufficient, including separate fire hydrants. Medical buildings and the smallpox facility were well established, and railroads and public transportation ran nearby. It was more modern than many residential areas. The University of Chicago, for example, suffered severe sanitary problems and requested permission to connect to the camp's sewer system. Captain Shurly granted it on July 29, 1865, according to an engineering plan submitted by the university.[28]

Nevertheless, some people wanted Camp Douglas closed. It blocked commercial, industrial, and real estate interests. John Wentworth, a powerful Chicago politician, wrote Secretary of War Stanton on August 22, 1865, "It is feared that an effort will be made to retain a portion of Camp Douglas to oblige a few officers. Our people want no camps nor garrisons here. Camp D is in a thickly settled portion of our city, near our college, churches, etc., etc."[29]

Disposing of the camp was much easier than building it. General Hoffman ordered that "all the buildings, fencing, etc., to be sold or otherwise disposed of." Ads in the *Tribune* put everything up for sale, including horses, mules, carts, buildings, and equipment. The camp was gone by the end of November 1865. This turned out to be a mistake, as the government then had to build Fort Sheridan near Chicago to suppress a militant labor movement. The Camp Douglas prison fund after the liquidation was $181,739.96.[30]

While Prisoner's Square contained more buildings, the most valuable property was in Garrison and White Oak Squares.

TABLE IX
DESCRIPTION OF BUILDINGS AT CLOSE OF WAR[31]

Buildings	*Number/Dimensions*
Headquarters	1/80x40
Officers quarters	66 rooms
Offices	14/12x12
Garrison barracks with kitchens	40/85x24
General hospital, 4 wings	1/100x80
Post hospital	1/28x204

Prison hospital, 2 wings each	1/100x28
Smallpox hospital, 2 wings each	1/204/40
Quartermaster warehouse	1/60x100
Commissary warehouse	1/40x100
Ordinance warehouse	1/20x60
Prison barracks, Prisoner's Square	64/24x90
Garrison guard house	1/20x40
Wash house	1/24x66
Guard house & court-martial hall	1/24x50
Post church	1/30x75
Water pipes	3,600
Sewerage	5,000

Prisoner's Square boasted a drug store, sutler's store, surgeon's office and dispensary, an express office, a tool shop, and a patrol office, all near the gate to Garrison Square. Behind them was the "Four of Diamonds" dungeon, and 64 barracks. This square contained nine water hydrants by the close of the war.

The location of structures in Garrison Square is uncertain. Stables inside the main gate near Cottage Grove fed and housed 44 horses. Included were sheds to cover three hundred tons of coal and eight hundred cords of wood. A bakery equipped with water pipes baked for 11,000 men. The quartermaster warehouse held sufficient equipment and gear to outfit 15,000 men. A commissary warehouse could store ten days' rations for 20,000 troops, and a butcher shop could do the same with meat.[32]

Other service structures were a guardhouse to hold 60 men; a carpenter shop for 33 carpenters, a glazier, a blacksmith, and a horseshoer; plus a tool shop. A power tool consisted of a four-horsepower steam engine operating a crosscut and rip saw. Nine latrines in Garrison Square seated 30 men each, and authorities installed 12 water hydrants and three fire plugs.

General Orme and General Sweet added an eating saloon, a barbershop, a newsroom, a photo studio, and the chapel to Garrison Square in 1864. Disputes arose earlier about ownership of the private structures. Three sutlers' stores served Garrison Square alone.[33]

Colonel Tucker told Orme, who told Hoffman, that only the chapel did not belong to the government. All other private structures became Federal property. Unfortunately, Tucker neglected to put it in writing or to inform the tradesmen of this rule. Hard feelings and substantial financial losses resulted. The War Department had no intention of returning the YMCA chapel.

General Sweet resigned from the army on September 19, 1865. He was the most successful of the commandants and ended up a hero while others were sullied. His administration succeeded because he was willing to learn from history and build on the experience of prior commanders. Moreover, he delegated authority to capable officers, such as Colonel Strong and Colonel Skinner. Also, he recognized that many of Hoffman's ideas were a threat to the orderly administration of the camp. His order to house the prisoners in tents was one example. Withholding vegetables was another.

Sweet's attempt to oust Colonel De Land showed that ambition could make him irrational. However, he steered his course with the precision of a laser beam once he came to power. His cunning orchestration of the Camp Douglas Conspiracy made believers out of those who should have known better, especially General Hooker and Governor Yates. Now he was ready to call in his chips. He never dreamed that the dark shadow hanging over Camp Douglas was drifting down upon him and that his triumphs would be short lived.

Captain Shurly succeeded General Sweet for a short time as commander but had no independent authority. The last commander of Camp Douglas was Capt. E. C. Phetteplace, who replaced Shurly around October 1, 1865.[34]

Phetteplace had personally arrested St. Leger Grenfell in his Chicago hotel room during the raids of November 7, 1864. Legends claimed that Grenfell moved toward his pistol, but Phetteplace was too fast for him. However, he did allow Grenfell to stop at the hotel desk and pay his bill. Some social graces had to be observed even in a disorderly world. General Sweet later assigned Phetteplace to the "guard of honor" over the remains of President Lincoln. Now he had the honor of presiding over the remains of a camp filled with the murmuring of so much pain, disease, and death.

A winter wind swept in under leaded skies and went moaning through the camp. Broken doors banged against the sides of shattered barracks. The abandoned stockade creaked uneasily, as though fearing another attack. Phetteplace could see where prisoners had tunneled out onto College Place the night of December 3, 1863. Over there was where they had broken through the fence in the northwest corner of the square on October 28, 1864. Here, next to this barrack, a prisoner had crumpled with a ball in his head for urinating in the street.

The tar paper had disappeared from the roof of White Oak dungeon, and rain had poured in. The hole where prisoners had been kept was filled with water, and the door on Grenfell's cell was rusted. Phetteplace shivered as his eyes fell on the dead house next to the dungeon. It was finally empty.

Another reminder of the camp was the smallpox cemetery next to the university on Douglas property. It was still well cared for and held 655 Confederates, some Federal soldiers, one sailor, and three civilians from the Camp Douglas Conspiracy. All were in carefully marked individual graves. The army planned to move them to Oak Woods by the end of 1865.

General Meigs received a dramatic telegram from Chicago at 2:00 P.M. on March 20, 1866: "The ground comprising Camp Douglas was surrendered to Mufflin & Loomis & T. Porter Jany 1st, to Douglas Estate Jany 5th to H. Graves Jany 8th. The last buildings were sold on the 24th of December. L. H. Pierce Lt. Col. U.S.Q.M."[35]

The Mufflin-Loomis-Porter group had purchased the fairgrounds west of camp before the war.[36] Whether they ever received rent from the army is doubtful. They had already removed the smallpox cemetery from the Douglas estate according to the telegram. However, that story was only beginning, and history had not closed the books on Camp Douglas. It never would.

The chapel continued an unbroken record of bad luck when the War Department sold it to a businessman hostile to religion. It had been promised to Reverend Tuttle's Saint Mark's Parish. Its new owner harshly rejected Tuttle's pleas for the building. Henry Graves is credited for saving the chapel bell. It was allegedly cast partly from coins contributed by the prisoners, the garrison, and congregations in the city, even by the Chicago Reform School. The bell finally ended up at the Chicago Historical Society, where it is kept hidden in a secret warehouse.[37] This famous relic tolled joyously at Union victories, mourned the death of President Lincoln, and clanged sadly for prisoners and soldiers whose lives were lost at Camp Douglas.

A desk that held the prisoners' records, Dunavan's sheet music, and burial records kept by Capt. Charles Goodman are also at the Historical Society. These, along with the *Prisoner Vidette* at the Chicago Public Library, are the only known relics. However, the life of the great camp did not go out completely. In 1941, historians

Andersonville, a close-up view of hell on earth. (Image courtesy of USAMHI.)

Andersonville, taken from the top of the stockade. Note the primitive sinks in the foreground and raw sewage flowing through the camp. (Image courtesy of the USAMHI.)

identified some decrepit tenements in the area as former garrison barracks.[38]

The government still did not pay Henry Graves for use of his land. A commission decided to allow him "$225 per month or $2700 per year."[39] Colonel Potter, quartermaster at Camp Douglas, reduced the award to $1,200 per year, which Graves rejected.

Estimates of the cost to build and repair the camp vary because no records exist. One figure is $400,000. Hoffman reported total expenditures of $208,230.91 from 1862 to 1865, not counting the cost of maintaining the garrison. Parolees caused $15,000 damage. De Land spent about $30,000. The new hospital and sewer system cost taxpayers about $15,000. Sweet allegedly invested $375,000 in barracks, fences, sewers, and new buildings.[40] General Hoffman's report is probably the most accurate, without counting the original cost to build the camp in 1861. That probably came to about $50,000 for 60 buildings, unless officials allowed the contractors shamelessly to overcharge.

The constant change of command hindered improvements after it became a prison camp. Commanders such as Mulligan, Cameron, and De Land believed that fighting the war was their primary mission. Colonel Tucker first saw the need for long-range planning, but authorities replaced him three times. General Ammen, an experienced administrator, was transferred. General Orme had to waste his waning strength on matters other than administration. Secretary of War Stanton did not perceive, as did Hoffman, that prison administration was a science requiring training and experience.

The location at Chicago helped prisoners despite the cold climate. Relief committees, medicine, supplies, and the services of many surgeons became available. Contractors purchased meat at local packing houses, and building materials were plentiful. Journalists and independent inspectors examined the camp constantly because of easy access to Chicago by rail and water. Continuous monitoring by the surgeon general's office, various departments of the army, and civilian doctors was not difficult. Lake Michigan made a modern sewer system possible. This caused conditions to improve steadily and enabled the prisoners to pursue social activities. By comparison, Andersonville worsened with time.

Camp Douglas is often compared with Andersonville. It was a death camp, but totally unlike Andersonville. The difference was significant in social behavior. Prisoners could maintain many of their customs at Camp Douglas. One example was the practice of convening a court and trying wrongdoers, just as done at home. Other examples were the camp newspaper, the craft workers, the artisans, and the musicians who played on. Copley's remark, about not being "churched" for dancing, showed that he related his experience in camp to what he had known at home. Prisoners were able to cook some Southern-style dishes until Hoffman removed the stoves.

Companies and regiments were recruited locally in the South, just as they were in the North, and prisoners continued to elect their sergeant-majors at camp. A useful social structure was preserved through these military organizations. Curtis R. Burke may have died but for the strong support of friends and father.

Burke mentioned that, except for card playing, visiting in barracks was just like at home. Tunneling was possible because barracks concealed what was being done, while prisoners at Andersonville had no shelter. Ministers and priests in the area provided plenty of religion. Mail service lasted until the end, but express delivery was a victim of retaliation. Hoffman and Stanton continuously closed the sutlers, but the store was open most of the time to alleviate some hardship.

D. F. Brandon's photo studio helped prisoners to maintain contact with loved ones. They had a bank to hold their money, a modern hospital, if one was lucky enough to find a bed, running water toilets, and a wash house. Fussy prisoners who could afford it went to the barber shop, and surgeons made house calls. Knowledge that the garrison would enforce the law was a deterrent to crime. Three Chicago newspapers kept the prisoners aware of what was going on.

True, some of this is too rosy a picture. The bank was risky, and the hydrants often froze. Still, Camp Douglas was not an open, running sore like Andersonville. Major Henry Wirz, the commander of Andersonville, was tried and executed for war crimes, but it appears that he too was a victim of the death camp. Wirz did not receive the money or materials to build a suitable prison, and the South had no Col. William Hoffman to alleviate conditions. The desolate swamps of southwest Georgia were the worst possible location for a prison. Essentials such as food, building materials, medical care, inspectors, and religion were out of reach.[41]

Andersonville was a garbage pit, a giant maggot that swallowed men without malice. Union prisoners lacked every support, which made social bonding difficult. It simply had no facilities to carry on the activities they had known in civilian life or in the army. In addition, the South was unable to enforce the law in that remote location. Consequently, the stockade had no patrols, which enabled criminals to prey on their fellows. Andersonville was barren of expectations because it was without hope.

Camp Douglas, however, struggled to look like a prison camp. Prisoners there had reason to feel that they were entitled to fair treatment, adequate food, shelter, clothing, and medical care. Cruelty and hunger caused most of the bitterness. Efforts to improve living conditions went almost unnoticed as prisoners were beaten, tortured, and shot, sometimes for no possible reason. Dr. Clark expressed disgust at White Oak dungeon, but did not order it closed. Soon officers saw nothing wrong in killing a prisoner for urinating in the street.

Sale of the prisoners' rations poured substantial wealth into the prison fund. It appears that the worst year was 1864. Curtis R. Burke described hunger, but not starvation. Prisoners could make a reasonable argument, however, that hunger became starvation when they were reduced to eating rats. John M. Copley charged that "the majority of the prisoners used the most rigid and strict economy in taking care of their rations, but with that were continually hungry."[42] Cash from selling rations at all camps amounted to $1,845,125.99 by the end of the war.[43] Officials rewarded spies and detectives with this money at Camp Douglas, and it paid bungling contractors who installed inadequate water pipes. Others reaped double profits in building the new prison hospital.

Survivors of Camp Douglas could not understand the institutionalized cruelty and attributed it to a "mean Yankee nature." J. S. Rosamond did not believe that the guards had ever been to the war. "Veterans would have treated prisoners like brothers," he thought.[44] He was wrong. Many guards had seen action. Rosamond did not realize that he was a casualty of modern warfare. The war continued at Camp Douglas, with the enemy being subdued by any means available. That is why Colonel De Land hanged men by their thumbs, why Colonel Strong imposed forced labor, and why Colonel Sweet used sadistic guards to keep the men in line.

Chivalry was only a dream that was passing, like a beautiful summer slipping into autumn, but this time never to return. The nature of the conflict had changed while prisoners languished in Chicago.

On November 15, 1864, Gen. William T. Sherman cut loose from Atlanta to bring total war to the South. He was too late. It had already happened at Camp Douglas.

Statistics aside, the prisoners themselves must always return as the center of interest. Most had lost the best years of their youth in this alien and deadly environment, and memories of the camp overshadowed the remainder of their lives. Yet, thousands of them forged their character and strength at Camp Douglas. For many others, weaknesses they never imagined came to the surface. Reverend Tuttle said about them that "the selfish principle generally predominates." He was sometimes right and often wrong. Men created friendships in Chicago that lasted until they answered the long roll.

The war was over for most of them when they passed through the gate on Cottage Grove. They had to create new lives, new dreams, and new hopes after the war. The old social, political, and economic orders in their homeland had been swept away. Many prisoners found the road back too difficult and started new lives elsewhere. In either case, they were forced to redefine their place in society. How they responded was influenced in large part by their Camp Douglas experience.

SOME FINAL WORDS

T. M. Page: "The survivors of that imprisonment ought to arrange for a general meeting in some Confederate reunion, for no body of men was ever more tried in any ordeal which tests human nature and proves it creditable to mankind."

J. S. Rosamond: "If there are any of those yankees alive who guarded Camp Douglas in 1865, if I were in their shoes, I would not tell that I was one of them."

B. R. Froman: "Who can say that the sudden escape of these twenty-one thousand prisoners, and their addition to the Confederate army would not have altered the result of the civil war, and the destiny of the country."

T. D. Henry: "Think of a man's mind being racked by all these punishments, for the innocent suffered as well as the guilty, and as frequently, when no one was to blame, were all punished; and it is almost a miracle that anyone should have remained there twenty months without losing their reason."

M. J. Bradley: "Thank God, there are enough pure whole-souled christians remaining in the world to keep the churches in existence.

This subject is so revolting and its recollections so sickening that I can pursue it no further—others must contribute their mite as I have done to the memory of the nineteen months of torment endured by myself and others at Camp Douglas. It brings such a crowd of horrors to my mind that I can scarcely realize its truthfulness; although I personally witnessed all, and more than I have stated. Oh, horror of horrors! sooner than undergo their repetition, gladly would I rush upon the bayonet, or force my way to the cannon's mouth. Yea, I would welcome death as a relief."

R. T. Bean: "I wondered what caused all of this fearful mortality. Before me I saw the headstones of five thousand six hundred Confederates whose lives went out in prison. Was it starvation, neglect, and cruelty? God alone knows."

Curtis R. Burke: "As we marched out the gate into the open country the boys had to give vent to their feeling, by giving three ringing cheers, singing Dixie."

Sergeant T. B. Clore: "Did Wirtz, the commandant of Andersonville prison, ever do anything as inhumanly brutal as was inflicted on Confederate prisoners in Camp Douglas and other Federal prisons, and which was paralleled only by the brutal Germans in the World War?"

E. D. Blakemore: "They might very well have given us more to eat, as I did not have a square meal for twenty-one months, and if some of those in authority at that time will come to see me I will show them what they might have given me for dinner. But it was war times and we will have to do what we can to forget its hardships and its brutalities. If some of my old comrades should happen to see this I shall be glad for them to remember me kindly."[45]

John M. Copley: "I, J. M. Copley, of the County of Dickson, State of Tennessee, do solemnly swear that I Will support, protect and defend the Constitution and Government of the United States against all enemies, whether domestic or foreign; that I will bear true faith, allegiance and loyalty to the same, any ordinance, resolution or laws of any State, convention or legislature to the contrary notwithstanding; and further, that I will faithfully perform all the duties required of me by the laws of the United States; and I take this oath freely and voluntarily, without any mental reservation or evasion whatever."

HEAD QUARTERS POST,

Camp Douglas, Chicago, Illinois.

SPECIAL ORDERS, }
No. 156 } June 10 1865.

[EXTRACT.]

~~In pursuance of General Orders No. [illegible], A. G. O., dated Washington,~~ D. C., June 6, 1865, the Quartermaster's Department will furnish transportation from Chicago, Illinois, to Shelby N. C. for the following named released Prisoners of War:

Alfred W. Biggerstaff

Q. M. Office, Chicago, June [illegible] TRANSPORTATION FURNISHED [illegible] Baltimore [illegible] BY [illegible] ELLISON

By Command of B. J. SWEET,
Brev't Brig. General Commanding Post.

True Copy,
John H. [illegible]
Col. & Chief [illegible]

Signed, E. R. P. SHURLEY,
Capt. & A. A. A. General.

Prisoner of war transportation order from Camp Douglas to Shelby County, North Carolina. (Image courtesy of the North Carolina State Archives.)

CHAPTER 21

Lost in Chicago

Search for the Confederate dead—What the army discovered—An undertaker profits—Bodies stolen and lost—Fate of smallpox victims—A Confederate monument rises at Oak Woods Cemetery.

The treatment of the Confederate dead is a shameful chapter in the Camp Douglas story. Authorities did not arrange for a cemetery when the prisoners arrived in 1862, although abundant land lay nearby. Then they closed the camp after the war without regard for more than four thousand dead. Only city of Chicago complaints about Rebel graves blocking urban development caused the army to launch a postwar investigation. By then it was too late, and a struggle to rescue the remains lasted into the next century.

This was in sharp contrast to other Northern prisons whose reputations are just as unsavory. The commander at Fort Delaware supervised burials there. Officials carefully marked coffins and headboards and identified each grave.[1] Treatment of the dead at Camp Douglas did not remotely resemble such care.

Most of the dead, about 3,384, went to "Potter's Field" in Chicago's City Cemetery, while the quartermaster buried 655 smallpox cases across from camp on the Douglas estate beginning in August 1863.[2] The potter's field, or paupers' section at City Cemetery, was the worst burial place imaginable.

It lay six miles north of camp, where the playing field in the southeast corner of Lincoln Park is today, at North Avenue and Lake Shore Drive.[3] This was the edge of Lake Michigan during the war, and the playing field was sand. Many prisoners are probably still there.

City Cemetery was a wet land. Graves contained water even in the dry season. Potter's field was to have closed in 1857. "Nor is this the worst of the case," the *Tribune* reported on February 16, 1863. "What is called the Potter's Field, where these 640 rebel corpses are buried

C. H. Jordan, the undertaker. (Image courtesy of the Chicago Historical Society.)

at the public charge, are interred, is on the very lowest land, and on the immediate borders of the slough where the lake water constantly ebbs and flows." The paper described the graves as shallow, "almost on the very surface."

Many remains were already missing if only 640 graves could be seen. The *Tribune* reported 980 dead at Camp Douglas in 1862.[4] Families returned 24 bodies home, so 956 graves should have been visible.

Most of the dead in 1863 had also disappeared according to a Chicago Public Works report for the period January 1, 1862, to April 1, 1863. "There have been buried in the public grounds during the time specified, 2,218 persons, exclusive of the rebel prisoners, which were 615 in number," the superintendent wrote.[5] However, at least seven hundred prisoners died between January and April 1863. No bodies were removed home during this time, so the superintendent should have found 1,340 graves, adding seven hundred to the *Tribune* count of 640.

The smallpox cemetery at Camp Douglas held no more than about one hundred dead at the time, reducing the number at City Cemetery to about 1,240. Therefore, at least 50 percent of the prisoners who died by April 1, 1863, had vanished.

Various explanations were put forward for this astonishing state of affairs. Many bodies were washed into the lake, according to the *Tribune,* toward the water intake crib only a mile south. The cemetery was also a favorite hunting ground for grave robbers.[6] Another likely explanation is that someone dumped the bodies into mass graves.

Colonel L. H. Pierce of the quartermaster general's office began investigating the situation at City Cemetery about December 1, 1865, on orders from Washington.[7] Pierce found that a court had decided that the city did not own the cemetery ground, which further endangered the Confederate remains. Cemetery officials led him to a Chicago undertaker named C. H. Jordan, as the one who brought in the Rebel dead.

Jordan claimed that he had a verbal contract with Captain Potter at Camp Douglas "for burying all soldiers who died at $4.75 per body." This price included "removing and interring the body and furnishing the coffin." Jordan's story about a verbal contract was probably true, because quartermaster records do not show any written agreement.

Jordan told Pierce that about 4,050 prisoners died. They were all buried at City Cemetery, except the 655 smallpox victims buried

Unidentified infantry at Camp Douglas with Jordan's hearse coming into view behind them at left. (Image courtesy of the USAMHI.)

across from Camp Douglas and about four hundred dead who were shipped home. Officials allowed prisoners to telegraph the deceased's family if it were within the Union lines. Families who could afford it then contacted Jordan to have the remains sent back. Prison rolls carry many entries, "In the vault of C. H. Jordan." Jordan shipped 143 bodies to Kentucky according to official records, and two bodies to Cincinnati. He claimed to have sent four hundred to their families, which made the number who died more uncertain.[8] Otherwise, he stored bodies in the Camp Douglas "dead house" when the ground froze, or in the morgue at City Cemetery. Their identity was soon lost in either place.

C. H. Jordan was a prominent undertaker in the city for many years.[9] He settled in Chicago as sales manager for a casket company about 1853 and started his undertaking business. It was only necessary to call oneself an undertaker to be one. Jordan continued in the business after the war and buried most of Chicago's rich and famous citizens in the best cemeteries.

He thought a pauper's grave was good enough for the prisoners, however, and purchased burial tickets for potter's field from the city clerk. It is not certain how much he paid. The *Tribune* said $1.50, but the city attorney claimed it was only one dollar. A ticket at the National Archives reads "One Dollar and Fifty Cents for an adult internment in the Chicago Cemetery." Jordan probably received a 50¢ discount for the pauper's section. Neither Jordan, nor the sexton at the cemetery, nor the city clerk considered it necessary to file burial reports for the prisoners as required by state law.[10]

Colonel Pierce learned that "on presenting this ticket at the Cemetery, the Cemetery authorities took the body and buried it in the Potter's Field." He described the place as "simply a sand waste over which the sand is continuously drifting. Some graves are now on sand ridges which are shifting positions daily," he observed. "In a short time the only traces of the graves can be procured from the fence I shall erect, unless yearly care is taken to remove the sand," he predicted. The Public Works report noted that "the east fence of the cemetery was there to protect Potter's Field, but was rotting away and almost covered by drifted sand."

The Reverend Edmund B. Tuttle wrote: "Each grave is marked; but sand which is continually being thrown up by the waves will soon cover them, to sleep on till the morning of the Resurrection." He did not attend burials, as burying prisoners without any last rites was customary. The city attorney coldly informed Pierce that Chicago "claims the right to again bury on the same ground in eight to ten years (when these bodies will probably be decomposed) should the ground be wanted."

Officials paid Jordan enough to provide a decent coffin and a proper grave in a good cemetery, leaving a fair profit of one dollar per body. Yet, he furnished rude pine boxes at little cost and tripled his profits by paying only one dollar for a pauper's grave. Ninian Edwards and his contractors were penny-ante by comparison.

Colonel Pierce reported to General Meigs that he had found only 2,968 names at City Cemetery.[11] "They state that from Feby 1862 till all the secesh had left here, nearly all of the Medical Colleges in the North West were supplied by bodies stolen from the rebel dead buried in the cemetery, and the appearance of some of the graves gives evidence of the truth of this statement."

Cemetery needs at Camp Douglas were comparable to those of the prison at Elmira, New York, where the commanding officer leased an excellent plot in the Elmira City Cemetery. A prison detail prepared bodies for burial and marked the coffins. The sexton received $2.50 to bury each body in a separate grave, keep the records, and make the headboard. A man came up from Alabama in 1905 to take his father home, but was so pleased with the cemetery that he decided to let him rest there.[12]

In Chicago, the situation was so desperate that Colonel Pierce recommended removing the remains to Rosehill Cemetery, seven miles northwest of the city. He could purchase an acre there for from five to six hundred dollars to hold two thousand dead. Meigs, still concerned with economy, rejected the idea. He ordered the ground at City Cemetery enclosed "and that yearly care be taken to remove the sand which may have drifted over the graves."[13] The city attorney had already told Pierce that the army could not put up fences.

Nothing was done, and the severe deterioration and loss of Confederate bodies continued. This brought an urgent report the following year from Gen. C. H. Hoyt, a new quartermaster officer in charge of the investigation. He found only 1,402 graves at City Cemetery on December 1, 1866. "Very little care seems to have been taken in the interment of the bodies; they are crowded together, and in some cases the numbers are confused," he warned. About two thousand bodies were now unaccounted for, amounting to at least two-thirds of the dead.

The situation became more critical when Chicago mayor J. B. Rice informed the army that it had to remove all bodies because the cemetery was closing. They did not discuss the possibility of sending them back to the former Confederacy. Costs may have been a factor. Next, the Chicago Common Council sent an urgent letter to Hoyt on December 17, 1866. They reminded him that the government did not provide a burial ground for the prisoners, and "that the City Government consented to their interment in said Cemetery." They did not know that the government had contracted with Jordan to provide decent burials.

Meigs finally agreed on January 14, 1867, to remove the remains from City Cemetery. However, Gen. J. D. Bingham, a third quartermaster officer, reported on February 26 that Rosehill Cemetery refused to allow Confederate dead inside, but "it might procure a lot outside."[14] Rosehill already contained many Union dead, including soldiers from Camp Douglas and the general hospitals, which may explain its attitude.

Bingham added that "Oak Woods Cemetery submitted a plan to inter at $2.00 for each grave and that the burials will be made at $1.00 each making the total cost of ground and burial $3.00 each. This did not include the cost of disinterring and removing the bodies from City to Oak Woods. They had received informal proposals for doing this at $2.50 and $2.00 each." City Cemetery put the number of removals at three thousand.

"I have no means of ascertaining whether or not fraud has been practiced in thus increasing the numbers from 1,402 to 3,000," Bingham claimed. The truth was that Bingham did not care. He could have ordered a squad of soldiers into Potter's Field to verify the numbers. City Cemetery authorities assured a lone inspector sent by Bingham that only 40 bodies were missing, and that these had been sent home. That ended the inquiry.[15]

Like Jack's fabled beanstalk, the number of bodies at City grew to 3,384. Bingham was referred to Joseph W. Ernst, the sexton. He could move the bodies to Oak Woods and furnish new coffins if required at $2.50 each. "Mr. Ernst would be a suitable man as he made the interments and knows the locations of the bodies," Bingham advised General Meigs. "I do not think the price is too high."

The price was not too high compared with what was paid C. H. Jordan. Ernst was familiar with the Confederate burials because he had worked at the cemetery at the time. He was now in charge of exhuming all remains as the cemetery prepared to close.

Unlike Rosehill, Oak Woods could not refuse the burials because the government already owned a plot inside, not that it objected. It was anxious for the business. The government had purchased two acres there in 1863 for Federal burials. Apparently it made the interments at Rosehill, instead, and the plot remained vacant until the Camp Douglas smallpox cemetery was emptied in 1865.

Oak Woods planned to inter the remains from City Cemetery in burial trenches adjoining those removed from the smallpox cemetery. Officials offered a pleasing design "so that each body shall occupy an exact width of two feet and then by reference to the register a ready and certain mode will be provided for finding the location of each body."[16] A drawing in the National Archives shows an oval field extending 150 feet running east and west and 250 feet from the north to south. Graceful cement walkways separate the burial trenches, with numbered stone markers in front of each grave.

Oak Woods may be the largest Confederate burial site outside the South, but subsequent events make it impossible to learn the number buried there. The rest of the story is like the Camp Douglas Conspiracy, too incredible for belief.

General Bingham reported on May 1, 1867, that the removal to Oak Woods had been completed. However, the army had awarded the contract not to Ernst, but to a M. O'Sullivan at $1.98 for each body disinterred and removed. The price was supposed to include coffins.[17] This absurdly low bid had apparently influenced Meigs, who should have known better, but did not care.

M. O'Sullivan had been a civilian storekeeper at the quartermaster warehouse in Chicago during the war. He served as alderman for the central business district in 1867, replacing James J. O'Sullivan, who resigned. M. O'Sullivan may have gotten the City Cemetery contract through his army connections. James J. O'Sullivan was a lawyer who had once served as city attorney.[18] He probably was the one who consulted with Pierce about the burials in 1865.

C. H. Jordan listed the sale by him of "15 Reb coffins plus nails to Alderman James J. O'Sullivan" on April 20, 1867, for $44.50—an extortionate price.[19] A "Reb coffin" meant a crude pine box constructed for less than one dollar. Neither O'Sullivan was in the undertaking business. They lacked the experience, equipment, and trained employees even to make a coffin, much less to properly carry out the removals.

Prosecutors charged James J. O'Sullivan with attempted rape in

August 1864.[20] He claimed that it was a frame-up by the woman to force him to get her mother out of jail. Several affidavits regarding the woman's "utter worthlessness" were presented to the grand jury, and the male panel refused to indict Alderman O'Sullivan. The *Tribune* was happy that they did not disgrace the City Council again. "There are black sheep enough on its roll already," the paper admitted.

The O'Sullivans' bid of $1.98 per body failed to consider what Jordan charged for coffins, and the cost of transporting the remains. One route was ten miles south by boat and then west by land to Oak Woods. The coffins could have been carted downtown and shipped on the Illinois Central Railroad that ran nearby the cemetery. The O'Sullivans left no clue about what was done.

An eyewitness named Albert F. Scharf claimed "that in some of the rude coffins no bodies were found, showing that the nimble grafters had imposed on Uncle Sam by getting paid for burying empty boxes." Scharf had been at Camp Douglas with the 19th Illinois Infantry. He knew Henry Graves and had visited him at Cottage Grove. One of his copper pennies had gone into the bell for the prison chapel. A reporter confirmed that "in many instances the coffins were found to be empty."[21] He described Potter's Field as "a deep ravine, which is a great portion of the time covered by water."

The move to Oak Woods began on April 13, 1867, and lasted through April 30. Oak Woods did not certify the number of coffins received or verify that it had counted or inspected the remains. This was the last thing it wanted to do. It buried whatever the O'Sullivans brought in and simply copied names and grave numbers from City Cemetery records into its own burial register. It was money in the bank. Of course, these records could not be verified because Confederate burials were never recorded with the city clerk. Regardless, the quartermaster believed that thousands of bodies were unaccounted for.

Incredibly, knowing that, the army still failed to supervise, inspect, or validate the removals. It was only the taxpayer's money. History was blindfolded, and knowing how many Confederates, or which ones, are at Oak Woods is impossible.

Cost of removals was $6,700.32 paid the O'Sullivans, based on 3,384 bodies. Oak Woods received $10,152 for reinterring the same unverified number. Add approximately $14,250 paid to C. H. Jordan during the war, and the total was $31,102 at a time when the dollar meant something.

However, this was the second, not the first phase of Confederate re-burials. The 655 smallpox victims had been at Oak Woods since around December 11, 1865. General Hoyt learned of the prior burials by accident during his investigation of City Cemetery. It appeared that someone, perhaps General Hoffman or General Meigs, had hired an unknown contractor to remove them from the former site of Camp Douglas to the government plot.[22] It must have been an oral contract because no record of it can be found.

The contractor and the army incredibly botched this operation. The Oak Woods superintendent told General Hoyt "that among the bodies removed were those of twelve U. S. soldiers—That none of the Headboards on the graves at the old Cemetery at Camp Douglas were removed with the bodies, but were thrown aside. The Secretary of Oak Woods endeavored at the time to procure the necessary information to perfect the records of the Cemetery, but was unable to do so."[23]

Who the contractor was or how much he was paid cannot be learned. Insensitive and incompetent are too mild a term to describe him. Only the most brutal of men would deliberately destroy someone's identity. Apparently, the army did not supervise or inspect these removals, either. For all it knew he could have dumped the bodies in Lake Michigan.

Oak Woods still has no record of their names. In addition, no one knew that three civilians arrested in the 1864 conspiracy were among the smallpox victims. Lewis Turner of Missouri, and Peter Stifle from Crawford, Illinois, died less than two weeks after Sweet threw them into the guardhouse. Parkerson Sherman, also of Crawford, Illinois, lived for only one month.[24]

General Hoyt confirmed that "deceased U. S. soldiers and the Rebel Prisoners of War appear to have been mixed promiscuously and sent by the wagon load from Camp Douglas without care or order." Attendants burned all uniforms at the smallpox hospital. Consequently, opening the coffins would not have mattered but in one case. Officials could have identified the remains of a 14-year-old black recruit in the 29th Regiment, U.S. Colored Infantry, named Martin Winchester.[25]

Information about "twelve U.S. soldiers" probably came from the contractor. Camp Douglas hospital records list 23 Union soldiers, and a navy recruit, who died of smallpox, and therefore had to be in that cemetery.

TABLE X
UNION DEAD BURIED IN THE CONFEDERATE CEMETERY AT OAK WOODS[26]

1. John L. Adams, Pvt. Co. C, 15th V.R.C. d. 12-9-64.
2. Warren B. Aiken, Pvt. Batt. L, 2nd Ill. Light Art d. 3-11-64
3. Robert Alexander, Pvt. Co. I, 15th V.R.C. d. 11-13-64.
4. John E. Allen, Pvt. Co. A, 196th Penn. Inf. d. 11-18-64.
5. William Buck, Pvt. Co. G, 9th Ill. Inf. d. 4-24-64.
6. Isaac J. Dennon, Cpl. Co. F, 15th V.R.C. d. 1-22-65.
7. Robert T. Dutches, Pvt. Co.__ , 11th Ill. Cav. d. 1-3-64.
8. Zachariah W. Easter, Sgt. 24th Oh. Batt. d. 11-12-64.
9. Joshua Faulkner, Pvt. Co. C, 15th V.R.C. d. 4-12-64.
10. Joseph J. Headlock, Pvt. Co. B, 15th V.R.C. d. 12-30-64
11. Charles S. Keith, Pvt. Co. D, 12th Ill. Cav. d. 1-28-64.
12. Charles T. King, Pvt. Co. F, 8th V.R.C. d. 2-22-64.
13. William King, Pvt. Co. M, 12th Ill. Cav. d. 3-15-64.
14. Stephan Little, Pvt. Co. H, 12th Ill. Cav. d. 2-2-64.
15. George W. Logan, Pvt. Co. A, 15th V.R.C. d. 4-12-64.
16. Joseph Mckay, Navy recruit. d. 2-1-64.
17. John Rhodes, Pvt. Co. F, 15th V.R.C. d. 2-3-65.
18. Noah Smetters, Pvt. Co. E, 15th V.R.C. d. 8-11-64.
19. Lockwood Southard, Pvt. 24th Oh. Batt. d. 11-17-64.
20. Thomas J. Strain, Pvt. Co. A, 48th Mo. Inf. d. 4-18-65.
21. Robert E. Surgeant, Pvt. Co. D, 12th Ill. Cav. d. 2-26-64.
22. Nelson Wantz, Pvt. Co I, 15th V.R.C. d. 12-29-64.
23. Martin Winchester, Pvt. 29th U.S. Colored Inf. d. 1-25-64.
24. Charles Wixon, Pvt. Co. H, 2nd Minn. Inf. d. 3-28-64.

The government placed 12 headstones at the site, and the legend grew that these men were guards. Those in the 48th Missouri, 196th Pennsylvania, 24th Ohio Battery, and the Eighth and 15th VRC come to 14 guards. Hit harder than any other outfit was the 15th VRC with nine dead. The presence of the child, Martin Winchester, shows that black recruits were scarce around Chicago. Almost the entire black male population had already joined the army.

Swift burials in the smallpox cemetery often left service records incomplete, and some families had difficulty securing pensions from Washington after the war. Warren B. Aiken's widow had to obtain an affidavit from her husband's commanding officer swearing that he had seen her husband's body.[27] Camp Douglas hospital records later proved invaluable in establishing these deaths.

The ordeal of the Confederate dead continued long after Camp Douglas was gone, and a third round of reburials took place. On January 25, 1882, E. R. P. Shurly, the former adjutant at Camp Douglas, wired Washington that "recently the remains of Union and Confederate soldiers have been exhumed in the vicinity of Camp Douglas. In 1864-65 the small pox hospital was located near there and about 150 bodies who died in that place were buried there," he advised.[28] Shurly was wrong about the number of dead by a wide margin, further proof that few people in the administration knew or cared about what C. H. Jordan was doing. It now appeared the contractor had not only botched the removals from the smallpox cemetery in 1865, but had left many bodies as well.

The army ordered its third inquiry since the war, and the quartermaster in Chicago reported on February 17, 1882, that "these graves are on the site of the burying ground used for those who died of smallpox at Camp Douglas. The bodies dug up are supposed to be those of prisoners. There are signs of more on the premises and the owner says unless some steps are taken for their removal he will take them up himself and bury them."[29]

A subsequent report on May 3, 1882, informed Washington that "thirteen (13) bodies have been dug up and removed to the Soldiers' Lot at Oakland [Oak Woods] Cemetery, at a cost of $7.00." Oak Woods has no record of these burials, but the "Soldiers Lot" was the Confederate cemetery, and no reason exists to doubt that the 13 were buried as reported.

More turmoil was created when the village of Hyde Park, which then contained Oak Woods, threatened to put a street through the Confederate cemetery in 1885. The quartermaster office alerted Washington, and it seemed that the troubles of the Confederate dead would never end.

However, nothing came of this incident except a quartermaster report that 4,039 Confederates and 12 Union soldiers were there. This figure was correct on its face. Oak Woods allegedly received 3,384 remains from City Cemetery; add 655 Confederates from the smallpox cemetery, including the 13 bodies found there in 1882, and the total was 4,039.

An Ex-Confederate Soldiers Association of Chicago, headed by Thomas P. Longwood, a Camp Douglas alumnus, petitioned

Congress in August 1887 to place a monument at Oak Woods. It was unlikely that Congress would give permission, but another crisis developed. The burial plot looked like the potter's field at City Cemetery, and the dead were again on the edge of extinction. Complaints caused the quartermaster to repeat the investigations of 1865-67. This was the fourth time that the government had stepped in.

On September 1, 1890, General Bingham reported that "many of the graves are sunken and many of the corner stakes are missing. There are evidences that one of the sections has been used as a road way. The ground around these lots has been raised and improved which gives them the sunken appearance." As a result of this report, Illinois congressman Frank Lawler notified the Confederate Association that it had permission to repair and improve the lot, "provided that no part of the expense therefore be made a charge against the United States."[30]

The association built the monument in the center of the two-acre tract, now sunk far below the level of the cemetery. It consisted of Georgia granite and was completed in 1893 at a cost of $10,000. Still owed was $2,000. Of the $8,000 paid, $7,500 came from sympathizers in Chicago and other parts of the North. Not everyone in Chicago was pleased. Some Union army veterans saw it is "a seeming attempt to eulogize a bad and dead cause."[31]

Nevertheless, thousands of persons attended on Memorial Day, May 30, 1895, when the association dedicated the monument. It was a chance to see President Grover Cleveland, who had dodged the Civil War by paying a substitute three hundred dollars to go in his place. Louisiana sent a magnolia tree. Five-year-old Jimmy Pope, a descendant of President Tyler, did the planting in soil sent up from Mississippi battlegrounds. Assisting were the United Daughters of the Confederacy, the Sons of Confederate Veterans, and the Oak Woods Board of Directors.[32] The tree died in the Chicago winter, and the plot continued to deteriorate. The Confederate Association did nothing to repair or improve the ground, and the weight of the monument caused more sinking of the swampy land.

The remains soon faced extinction again. Weeds, water, and debris draining down from the surrounding area submerged the plot. This calamity brought on the fifth army inquiry since the war. Only Congress could save the remains from final destruction. On May 20, 1899, Oak Woods advised Congress that the best solution was to take

Confederate monument, Oak Woods Cemetery, January 1991. (Image made by the author.)

down the monument, fill the two acres to the level of the rest of the cemetery, without removing the dead, and to reset the monument on top.[33]

Congress appropriated $3,850 for the project and $250 per year for perpetual care. Oak Woods covered the plot with about six feet of earth in 1902. Visitors to the site do not realize that they are walking over a buried cemetery. Cemetery officials had to kill it to save it.

The possibility arose four years later that they might excavate the plot and restore the original cemetery. Congress had passed a bill on March 9, 1906, creating a commission to mark the graves of all Confederate prisoners in the North. A commissioner visited Oak Woods in 1910 and "found that it would likely be possible to locate the graves of those whose remains were removed from city cemetery." However, the commission was costing ten times more than anticipated, so Congress provided only for the placing of bronze tablets to show the names and commands of the dead.[34]

Accordingly, in 1912 Oak Woods raised the monument about eight feet and inserted a sub-base of granite under it with 16 bronze tablets attached, listing 4,243 names. A concrete walk ran around the monument, completing the Confederate Mound as it appears today. The cost was $22,331.19, and the result was balanced and pleasing.

One grave marker is visible at the edge of the lot. A headstone reading "James W. Leak, 1st Alabama Infantry, February 10, 1865" supposedly shows the boundary of the burial trenches below. City Cemetery records were wrong. His name was Joseph W. Leak, and he died on February 11.[35] The army inspects the plot yearly to verify that those in charge are maintaining perpetual care.

Only two Confederates escaped the calamity of a pauper's grave at City Cemetery without going home. Symbolically, one was Jewish and one Catholic.

"Theodore Hirsch, Pvt., Holmes Light Battery, Louisiana Artillery, died December 12, 1864" and was removed to Chicago Jewish Cemetery. This was the best section of City Cemetery on high, dry ground. Hirsch later found a safe haven at the Hebrew Benevolent Society Cemetery in Chicago, when the Jewish Cemetery was closed around 1872 to make way for Lincoln Park.[36] However, his grave was lost due to a fire in the cemetery office in 1911 that destroyed some of his records.

"James Lyons, Pvt., Co. H, 15th Tennessee Infantry, died January

27, 1865" and was removed to Calvary Cemetery in Evanston, Illinois, where Colonel Mulligan is buried. Calvary has no record of receiving the body, but he undoubtedly is there, since the information on Hirsch proved accurate.

Epilogue

Reverend E. B. Tuttle: A benefactor donated a lot for him to build a chapel at 36th Street and Cottage Grove, near the former camp. This became St. Marks Episcopal Church, and it was still active in 1919 when the building was sold to a black congregation. Allan J. Fuller, the former adjutant general, and later a judge on the Illinois Supreme Court, was a member of St. Marks. Former prisoners wrote to Tuttle asking about job opportunities in Chicago. He abandoned his successful parish in 1867 and returned to the army. He quit the army to become an expatriate in Europe. Camp Douglas had left its mark on him. Later he returned to his roots in New York and wrote an Illinois history. The former chaplain died in New York in 1881, at age 65.

Curtis R. Burke: He and Henry White explored Richmond and traveled to Abbeville, South Carolina, on their furlough. Burke was in Danville, Virginia, when Lee surrendered, and witnessed the flight of the Confederate government and the arrival of President Jefferson Davis. The Confederate Commissary was issuing rations as late as May 2, and Burke even drew $32 in silver.

He and Henry White had hopes of reaching Texas to carry on the war. On May 24, however, they learned that it was truly over, with Federal troops in control of all railroads and waterways. Burke had no intention of returning to Ohio, "since he could not live North," and made his way toward Kentucky. In Memphis, a childhood sweetheart coldly and cruelly rejected his proposal of marriage, and told him to go home. "Another Lost Cause on my shoulders!" he lamented.

He could not find work and took the oath of allegiance in exchange for a steamboat ticket to Cincinnati at government expense. Another eagle had fallen. Burke met his brother in Cincinnati and learned that Pa had been released from Camp Douglas in May and was with their mother near Medina, Ohio. Pa had decided that he could live in the North, after all. Burke found a job in Lexington, Kentucky, painting houses at $1.25 per day and hurriedly reclaimed a valise that he had left as security for a hotel bill. To his great relief he found that his new Confederate uniform was "all safe."

Henry Graves: He continued to reside at Cottage Grove. The War Department settled his rent claim, and the city paved a street through former Garrison Square, naming it Graves Place. He became wealthy after selling Camp Douglas land and drove a fine team of horses along beautiful Grand Boulevard. This was formerly Kankakee Avenue, the western border of Prison Square, now named Martin Luther King Drive. He still refused to move from his Camp Douglas home. In 1907 he was dying of old age at 86, and the homestead looked as it did during the war. Both he and the historic building were gone by 1909.

The University of Chicago: It built a theological seminary in 1869 on the former smallpox cemetery. The university was bankrupt by 1882, killed off by Camp Douglas, extravagant building schemes, and inadequate financing. Officials revived it in 1892 with massive funding from John D. Rockefeller, and they began laying the foundations for a world-class institution three miles south of its Civil War site. Atomic fusion was born on campus a half-century later.

The City of Chicago: Many refugees sought shelter among the empty graves in City Cemetery when fire leveled Chicago in 1871. Post-war Chicago was a city of the poor who had less protection against the savage winters than the prisoners at Camp Douglas. They tore down outhouses and fences for fuel, and as the population grew so did the stench from excrement, sewage, and horses. Flush toilets and wash houses were unimaginable for them. Economic depression was added to the sub-zero cold of the early 1890s, and without public aid programs the penniless were more at risk than the Confederates had been. Cholera and typhoid killed thousands whose bodies were carted to a potter's field and lost for a hundred years.

Colonel Joseph H. Tucker: A second son died in the war and the third was considered for West Point. Tucker left Chicago in 1865 and went into business in New York City. He wrote to Reverend Tuttle, but never returned to the wartime scene of trouble and heartache. The man who had wielded so much power and authority was an invalid in 1887 and died in New York on October 23, 1894, at age 75. He had never been a military man, just a businessman.

General James A. Mulligan: He ordered, "Lay me down and save the flag!" while being carried off the field at Winchester, Virginia. His funeral in Chicago was a tumultuous scene in the wartime city, and his monument dominates the western entrance to Calvary Cemetery in Evanston, Illinois.

General Daniel Cameron: The 65th Illinois Infantry compiled a distinguished record after leaving Camp Douglas as exchanged prisoners. Cameron earned a division command for his performance at the Battle of Knoxville and fought through the Atlanta campaign to become a brigadier general. He became active in national politics after the war as a conservative Democrat. Cameron married a young woman from Scotland and retired to his farm near Chicago. There he fathered 12 children and died at age 51, only 12 years after the war.

General Charles V. De Land: He took his war record to the people of Michigan and was elected to the state legislature. De Land was one of those officers who caused the North to win the war, whatever his failures at Camp Douglas. He held various state posts and was still in government as late as 1895. The general died in 1903 and was buried in Jackson, Michigan.

General William Ward Orme: He resigned from the army due to poor health shortly after leaving Camp Douglas. President Lincoln then appointed him supervisor of the Treasury Department at Memphis. His illness caused him to leave in November 1865 and return home to Bloomington, Illinois, where he died on September 13, 1866.

General Benjamin J. Sweet: He was the only Camp Douglas commander who did not win his star on the battlefield. He purchased a small farm in Wheaton, Illinois, and practiced law after resigning from the army. However, he soon held positions as U.S. pension agent in Chicago, Illinois supervisor of Internal Revenue, and deputy I.R.S. commissioner in Washington. The general died suddenly of pneumonia in 1874, aged 41. He was only 33 when he commanded Camp Douglas and leaped into national prominence. His remains lie in Chicago's Rosehill Cemetery.

An investigation sullied the general's reputation in 1876 when U.S. Congressman Hurlbut of Illinois charged that Sweet had bribed a man named George W. Campbell to obtain the pension office. Hurlbut was a member of the Committee on Civil Service Reform and a former major general of the Union Army who had commanded the 16th Army Corps. Sweet's powerful political sponsor, Joseph R. Jones, denied that Sweet had bribed him. Jones did admit that a man named George W. Campbell and Sweet were the only ones considered for the appointment. Jones testified before Congress that Sweet had agreed to pay George $2,500 yearly to run the pension office while Sweet looked after his law practice. Hurlbut claimed that Sweet paid George the money as a ghost payroller to have Jones sponsor Sweet. The matter was never resolved.

Charles Walsh: His cartage business in Chicago flourished after the conspiracy trials, and he even received city contracts to haul mail and clean streets. He never strayed far from the former site of Camp Douglas where he had gained nationwide publicity. He died in his mansion less than two miles away in 1885. Eight of his ten daughters became Catholic nuns.

General William Hoffman: He reverted to his rank of colonel in the regular army in 1865 and commanded posts at St. Louis and Fort Leavenworth. He found romance at Rock Island, Illinois, where he had built a prison camp. Hoffman became a civilian for the first time in his adult life and married a woman from Rock Island upon retiring at age 64. He died on August 12, 1884, of an enlarged prostate, and rests in Rock Island. A special act of Congress raised his widow's pension to $50 per month because of Hoffman's wartime services.

Miss Ada C. Sweet: She never married, but raised her younger brother and two sisters after their mother died in a train accident. She and the general were more like brother and sister than parent and child. Her education ended around age 14 at the Catholic school in Chicago. Ada became her father's secretary at 16 when he was appointed U.S. pension agent in Chicago in 1869. In 1874, President Grant appointed her to that office after her father died, an unusual position for so young a woman then.

Miss Sweet enjoyed talking about the camp and regretted that all trace of it had disappeared since new owners tore down the landmark university. Congress sullied Ada's reputation in the 1876 investigation of the Chicago Pension Office. Congressman Hurlbut charged that she had bribed a B. H. Campbell (George W. Campbell's brother?) to cause the pension agent in Chicago to resign so that she could have the job. She made no reply, and the matter was not resolved.

Daniel F. Brandon: He could not face the likelihood of taking baby pictures and making family albums after four years at Camp Douglas. He gave up photography when the camp closed and operated an artist's studio near downtown Chicago. Brandon moved away from his house on Cottage Grove in 1867 and directly into the path of the Chicago Fire of 1871. While he and his family survived, most of his Camp Douglas work did not.

Buckner and Mary Morris: Judge Morris was ruined by the Camp Douglas trials and tried to survive with a small law office on the western boundary of the city, a place of rutted dark streets and reeking privies. He died in poverty on December 16, 1879. Mary Morris returned to Chicago for the funeral, but sub-zero weather prevented her attendance. She was not well and died two years later. Buckner's grave at Rosehill is unmarked.

Camp Douglas: The area developed into a fashionable residential district in the 1870s. Cottage Grove was a major business district from 26th to 39th Streets by 1896. Starting in 1900, the area began a sharp decline for the next 52 years and became a notorious slum.

Now cleared and redeveloped, the camp site has reappeared. White Oak Square and part of Garrison Square are grassy fields; a modern apartment building marks the location of the Graves cottage and the entrance to the camp; a child's playground is located where the university building stood; automobiles at a nearby shopping center park in the smallpox cemetery; large sections of Prison Square emerge on the east side of King Drive between 31st and 33rd Streets. Like the university, which died and was reborn, the camp is covered with ice and snow again. For the prisoners who are lost in Chicago, the winters never end. For those who reached Oak Woods, Camp Douglas is eternal.

Notes

Abbreviations After First Citation:
CHS—Chicago Historical Society
CWTI—*Civil War Times Illustrated*
GO—General Order
ISHL—Illinois State Historical Library
LOC—Library of Congress
MS—Manuscript
NA—National Archives
OR—*Official Records of the War of the Rebellion*
RG—Record Group in the National Archives
SO—Special Order
USAMHI—United States Army Military History Institute
VRC—Veteran Reserve Corps

CHAPTER ONE

1. Emmet Dedmon, *Fabulous Chicago* (New York: Random House, 1954), 70.

2. Ibid.

3. John Moses and Joseph Kirkland, *History of Chicago* (Chicago: Munsell & Co., 1895), I:119.

4. Ibid., 119-20.

5. Herman Kogan and Lloyd Wendt, *Pictorial History of Chicago* (New York: E. P. Putnam & Co., 1958), 85.

6. Harold Mayer and Richard Wade, *Chicago: Growth of a Metropolis* (Chicago: University of Chicago Press, 1969), 42. Moses and Kirkland, *History of Chicago,* I:120-21.

7. Lloyd Lewis and Henry Justin Smith, *Chicago, The History of Its Reputation* (New York: Harcourt, Brace & Co., 1929), 65-66; Common Council Proceedings, 21 Oct. 1861, File 0190, Illinois Regional Archives Depository, Northeastern Illinois University.

8. *History of Medicine and Surgery and Physicians and Surgeons of Chicago* (Chicago: Biographical Publishing Corp., 1922), 73; Diary of Robert Tarrant, Manuscript, CHS; Lewis and Smith, *Chicago,* 79.

9. Bessie Louise Pierce, *A History of Chicago* (Chicago: University of Chicago Press, 1940), 376.

10. Moses and Kirkland, *History of Chicago,* I:119, 146.

11. Lewis and Smith, *Chicago,* 95; Joseph Kirkland, *The Story of Chicago* (Chicago: Dibble Publishing Co., 1892), 255.

12. Weston A. Goodspeed and Daniel D. Healy, *History of Cook County* (Chicago: Goodspeed Historical Ass'n, 1909), I:306.

13. Ibid., 434-35.

14. Ibid., 436-37.

15. E. B. Long, "Camp Douglas: A Hellish Den," *Chicago History* (Fall 1970):94.

16. Wayne C. Temple, Ph.D, *Stephen A. Douglas, Freemason* (Bloomington: The Masonic Book Club, 1982), 52.

17. Robert W. Johannsen, *Letters of Stephen A. Douglas* (Urbana: University of Illinois Press, 1961), 437; Temple, *Stephen A. Douglas,* 49-50.

18. Edward A. Pollard, *Southern History of the War* (New York: The Fairfax Press, 1866), 58.

19. *Chicago Tribune,* 23 Apr. 1861; Goodspeed and Healy, *History of Cook County,* I:443.

20. Mulligan papers, Chicago Historical Society.

21. Harvey M. Karlen, Ph.D, "Postal History of Camp Douglas, 1861-1865," *The American Philatelist* 10 (Oct. 1979):815.

22. William Bross, "History of Camp Douglas." Paper read before the Chicago Historical Society, June 18, 1875, in *Reminiscences of Chicago During the Civil War,* Mabel McIlvaine, ed. (Chicago: Lakeside Press, R. R. Donnelley & Sons Co., 1914), 164; *Chicago Tribune,* 28 Feb. 1862.

23. Unidentified newspaper clipping, 24 Oct. 1894, CHS; Elias Colbert, *Chicago, Historical and Statistical Sketch of the Garden City* (Chicago: P. T. Sherlock, 1868), 93.

24. Prints and Photo Dept., CHS.

25. *Official Records of the War of the Rebellion* (Washington: U. S. Government

Printing Office, 1901), Series II, Volume III, 56; B. R. Froman, "An Interior View of the Camp Douglas Conspiracy," *Southern Bivouac* 1-No.2 (Oct. 1882):64.

26. Chicago Title and Trust Co., (Pre-fire records, tract book 340), 185-89, 192-95; Philip M. Hauser and Evelyn M. Kitagawa, *Local Community Fact Book for Chicago, 1950* (Chicago: University of Chicago, 1953), 146; Charles Cleaver, in *Reminiscences of Chicago During the Forties and Fifties*, 59; Record Group 92 in the National Archives.

27. Joseph L. Eisendrath, Jr., "Chicago's Camp Douglas," *Journal of the Illinois State Historical Society*, 55 (Spring 1960):37-63; Bross, "History of Camp Douglas," 163.

28. Camp Douglas newspaper file, CHS.

29. Jesse L. Rosenberger, *Through Three Centuries* (Chicago: University of Chicago Press, 1922), 83.

30. Benjamin J. Smith, 51st Illinois Infantry, Company C. "Recollections of the Late War, Private Smith's Journal," 9, MS, Illinois State Historical Library.

31. Private James Buckley, Company F, 45th Infantry Regiment, Illinois Volunteers, courtesy of Alan C. Hunt, Springfield, Illinois.

32. *Chicago Tribune*, 6 Feb. 1862; Reverend James Bassett, 30 May 1862, ISHL.

33. Letters of George Russell, Douglas Brigade, ISHL; Frank Wintersmith to his mother, Manning-Biggs family papers, University of Kentucky, Lexington.

34. Camp Douglas consolidated morning reports, Illinois State Archives, Springfield.

CHAPTER TWO

1. *Chicago Tribune*, 14 Feb. 1862.

2. General Order No. 19, Camp Douglas Order Book, 4 Dec. 1861, CHS.

3. Compiled from the records of the Commissary General of Prisoners, Microcopy 598, RG 109, Roll 58; *Chicago Tribune*, 3 Jun. 1862.

4. Camp Douglas Order Book, 2 May 1862; Howard Kenneth Story, "Camp Douglas, 1861-1865" (M.A. thesis, Northwestern University, 1943), 29-30; *Chicago Tribune*, 12 Jun. 1862.

5. RG 393, v. 245.

6. Paul M. Angle, "The Story of an Ordinary Man," *Journal of the Illinois State Historical Society,* 33 No. 1 (Mar. 1940):230.

7. Ed Gleeson, *Rebel Sons of Erin, A History of the Tenth Tennessee Infantry Regiment* (Indianapolis: Guild Press of Indiana, 1993), 14.

8. Ibid., 103; *Battles and Leaders of the Civil War* (New York: Thomas Yoseloff &. Co., 1956), I:410.

9. OR Ser. II, Vol. III, 267-301.

10. Ibid., 274; Friederike H. Lesser, *Civil War Prisons: A study of the conditions under which they operated* (Montgomery: University of Alabama, 1968); OR Ser. II, Vol. III, 277.

11. He was the author of the *Biographical Register of Officers and Graduates of the United States Military Academy at West Point* (1879), which is still considered a classic.

12. OR Ser. II, Vol. III, 282; *Chicago Tribune,* 5 Mar. 1862.

13. John F. Stover, *History of the Illinois Central Railroad* (New York: Macmillan Publishing Co., 1975), 95; *Diary of Andrew Jackson Campbell,* edited by Jill K. Garrett, Columbia, Tennessee (1965), 22-23. Special Collections, Chicago Public Library.

14. J. T. Lowery. "Experience as a Prisoner of War," MS Collection, William R. Perkins Library, Duke University; Milton A. Ryan, 14th Mississippi Infantry, "Experience of a Confederate Soldier in Camp and Prison in the Civil War," Civil War Times Illustrated Collection, United States Army Military History Institute.

15. OR Ser. II, Vol. III, 288.

16. Ibid., 297; *Chicago Tribune,* 22 Feb. 1862.

17. Microfilm Publications. Selected Records of the War Department Relating to Confederate Prisoners of War, 1861-65 (Washington: National Archives), Commissary General of Prisoners, Camp Douglas, Ill., Military Prison, Microcopy No. 598, RG 109, Roll 54.

18. Roger D. Hunt and Jack R. Brown, *Brevet Brigadier Generals in Blue* (Gaithersburg: Olde Soldier Books, Inc., 1990), 288; Cullum, *Biographical Register of Officers and Graduates of the United States Military Academy at West Point* (New York: James Miller, 1879), 347; Collection of Civil War Pension Records, NA.

19. William Best Hesseltine, *Civil War Prisons, A Study in War Psychology* (New York: Frederick Ungar Publishing Co., 1930), 35; OR Ser. II, Vol. III, 54-57;

Frank L. Byrne, "Prison Pens of Suffering," *The Images of War* (Garden City: Doubleday & Co., 1983), IV:399; OR Ser. II, Vol. III, 57.

20. Hesseltine, *Civil War Prisons,* 168; OR Ser. II, Vol. III, 122-23; Stephen Z. Starr, *Colonel Grenfell's Wars* (Baton Rouge: Louisiana State University Press, 1971), 275.

21. Microcopy 598, RG 109.

22. Diary of Charles Edwin Taylor, 20 Feb. 1862, courtesy of Medford H. Roe, Jr.

23. Milton A. Ryan, "Experience of a Confederate Soldier," CWTI Collection, USAMHI.

24. Camp Douglas Order Book, GO 26, 23 Feb. 1862, CHS; "Dear Parents," F. W. Tupper letter, 3 Mar. 1862, ISHL; Hesseltine, *Civil War Prisons,* 56-57.

25. Goodspeed and Healy, *History of Cook County,* I:453.

26. *Chicago Inter-Ocean,* 25 May 1895.

27. Camp Douglas Order Book, Special Order No. 36, Fuller to Tucker, 20 Feb. 1862; GO 26, CHS.

28. Camp Douglas Order Book, GO 1,2,3, 22 Feb. 1862.

29. Karlen, "Postal History of Camp Douglas," 926.

30. Ibid., 927.

31. "Dear Ma," letters of George A. Pope, William R. Perkins Library, Duke University; Letters of John W. Robison, Tennessee Library and Archives; Camp Douglas letter file, RG 109, Box 116.

32. OR Ser. II, Vol. III, 297.

33. Ibid.; Hesseltine, *Civil War Prisons,* 60.

34. OR Ser. II, Vol. III, 297; 312.

35. Ibid., 301.

36. Ibid., 315; Report of the Illinois Adjutant General, I:123-24.

37. *The Richmond Dispatch,* 17 Feb. 1864; Mark Grimsley, "Ulysses S. Grant," *Civil War Times* 7 (Feb. 1990):32-34; OR Ser. II, Vol. III, 316; *Chicago Tribune,* 24 Feb. 1862.

38. *Chicago Inter-Ocean,* May 25, 1895.

39. Story, "Camp Douglas, 1861-1865," 15; *Confederate Prisoners of War, 1861-65.*

40. *Chicago Daily News,* 24 Aug. 1968; *Confederate Prisoners of War, 1861-65,* Roll 56.

41. *Chicago Tribune,* 24 Feb. 1862.

42. 3 Mar. 1862. Letters of Frank W. Tupper, 53rd Illinois Infantry, ISHL.

43. *Chicago Evening Journal,* 21 Feb. 1862; *Chicago Tribune,* 24 Feb. 1862; J. W. Robison to his wife, 30 Apr., 6 Jul. 1862.

44. *Chicago Tribune,* 31 Feb. 1862.

45. *Evening Journal,* 23 Feb. 1862.

46. *Chicago Tribune,* 24 Feb. 1862.

47. OR Ser. II, Vol. III, 316-17,18.

48. *Chicago Tribune,* 26 Feb., 31 Mar. 1862; *Chicago Times,* 26 Feb. 1862.

49. *Confederate Prisoners of War, 1861-65.*

50. Arthur C. Cole, *The Era of the Civil War* (Springfield: Illinois Centennial Commission, 1919), 225-29.

51. *Chicago Tribune,* 24, 25 Feb. 1862.

52. Ibid., 25 Feb. 1862.

53. Report of the Illinois Adjutant General, I:124; Alfred T. Andreas, *History of Chicago,* (Chicago: A. T. Andreas Co., 1885), II:301; *Chicago Tribune,* 27 Feb. 1864; Mulligan papers, CHS.

54. Edmund B. Tuttle, *History of Camp Douglas* (Chicago: J. R. Walsh & Co., 1865), 8, 19; Harpel Scrap Book obituary, 8:56, CHS.

55. RG 393, v. 242.

56. RG 249, v. 2.

57. *Ottawa Free Trader,* Ottawa, Illinois, 15 Mar. 1862.

58. George A. Pope to Mrs. L. J. Pope.

59. *Life of Mary Monholland, One of the Pioneer Sisters of the Order of Mercy in the West.* By a member of the Order (Chicago: J. S. Hyland & Co., 1894), 107.

CHAPTER THREE

1. George L. Holderith, "James A. Mulligan" (M.A. thesis, Notre Dame University, 1932), 5.

2. Report of the Illinois Adjutant General, Vol. 2.

3. *Battles and Leaders of the Civil War,* I:307-13.

4. OR Ser. II, Vol. I, 182; Mulligan papers, 13 Apr. 1862; 29 Apr. 1862, CHS.

5. Frederick H. Dyer, *A Compendium of the War of the Rebellion* (Dayton: Morningside Bookshop, 1978), II:1054-55.

6. Francelia Colby, *Our Family,* 101, MS, CHS.

7. Mary A. Livermore, *My Story of the War* (Hartford: A. D. Worthington & Co., 1889), 182-83.

8. OR Ser. II, Vol. IV, 777; Hesseltine, *Civil War Prisons,* 66; Joan Marie G. Kubalanza, "A Comparative Study of Conditions at Two Civil War Prison Camps: Camp Douglas, Chicago, Illinois, and Camp Sumpter, Andersonville, Georgia" (Master's thesis, Department of History, De Paul University, 1979), 3.

9. Camp Douglas Order Book, 1 Dec. 1861, CHS; Seymour J. Currey, *Chicago, Its History and Its Builders* (Chicago: S. J. Clarke Publishing Co., 1912), II:133.

10. OR Ser. II, Vol. III, 316-17.

11. Letters of John W. Robison to his wife.

12. *Chicago Tribune,* 3 Mar. 1862; OR Ser. II, Vol. III, 361.

13. Jill K. Garrett Collection, Tennessee State Library and Archives.

14. OR Ser. II, Vol. III, 361, 604.

15. Hesseltine, *Civil War Prisons,* 43.

16. *The Medical and Surgical History of the War of the Rebellion,* 3 Vols. (Washington: Government Printing Office, 1888), 69.

17. *Chicago Tribune,* 5 Mar. 1862; OR Ser. II, Vol. III, 360.

18. OR Ser. II, Vol. III, 360.

19. Tuttle, *History of Camp Douglas,* 11.

20. *Chicago Tribune,* 3, 15 Mar. 1862.

21. Ibid., 26 Mar. 1862.

22. Mark W. Sorensen, "The Civil War Prisoner of War System" (unpublished MS, Illinois State Archives, 1978), 32.

23. Froman, "Interior View of Camp Douglas Conspiracy," 64.

24. Pierce, *A History of Chicago,* 377; William R. Moody, *The Life of Dwight L. Moody* (Chicago: Fleming R. Revell Co., 1900), 83-84.

25. OR Ser. II, Vol. III, 362.

26. Ibid., 386.

27. Ibid.

28. *Chicago Tribune,* 12 Mar. 1862.

29. James Taswell Mackey diary, 9 March 1862, MS, Eleanor S. Brockenbrough Library, Museum of the Confederacy, Richmond. James S. Hodge is buried in Chicago. *Confederate Soldiers, Sailors and Civilians Who Died as Prisoners of War at Camp Douglas, Chicago, Ill., 1862-1865.* Kalamazoo: Edgar Gray Publications.

30. OR Ser. II, Vol. III, 335.

31. OR Ser. II, Vol. I, 174.

32. OR Ser. II, Vol. III, 337, 383.

33. Ibid., 386, 389-90.

34. OR Ser.II, Vol. III, 433.

35. *Chicago Tribune,* 26 Mar. 1862.

36. OR Ser. II, Vol. III, 403, 405.

37. Ibid., 388-89; *Chicago Tribune,* 21 Mar. 1862.

38. *Confederate Veteran* 15 (May 1907):234; Mackey diary, 30 Mar. 1862.

39. OR Ser. II, Vol. IV, 323-24; J. T. Lowery, "Experiences as a Prisoner of War," MS Collection, William R. Perkins Library, Duke University; J. T. Branch, "Account of Escapes from Camp Morton," *Confederate Veteran,* 8 (Feb. 1900):71.

40. Mulligan papers, CHS; Chicago Common Council Proceedings, File No. 0339, 0003, Illinois Regional Archives Depository, Northeastern Illinois University.

41. *Chicago Tribune,* 25 Apr. 1862.

CHAPTER FOUR

1. Mackey diary, 1, 2 Apr. 1862.

2. *Chicago Tribune,* 8, 9 May 1862; Confederate Prisoners of War, 1861-65, Roll 58.

3. OR Ser. II, Vol. III, 433; Vol. VII, 898.

4. OR Ser. II, Vol. III, 459-60; Jonathan T. Dorris, *Pardon and Amnesty Under*

Lincoln and Johnson (Chapel Hill: University of North Carolina Press, 1953), 20.

5. OR Ser. II, Vol. III, 457-58; "Dear Ma," letters of George A. Pope, Perkins Library.

6. George Levy, "Prisoners in the Dust: Hostages and Pawns Under the Lincoln Administration," *The Lincoln Newsletter,* A Publication of the Lincoln College Museum, Vol. XIV, No. 2 (Summer 1995); Gleeson, *Rebel Sons of Erin,* 75-103.

7. OR Ser. II, Vol. III, 542, 632.

8. Caroline Kirkland, *Chicago Yesterdays* (Chicago: Doughaday & Co., 1919), 108-09.

9. Chicago Historical Society, MS Collection. Source unknown; Mackey diary, 10 Apr. 1862.

10. *Battles and Leaders of the Civil War,* I:504-05.

11. Fuller to Mulligan, 14 Feb. 1862, Mulligan papers, CHS; Report of the Illinois Adjutant General, I:124; Kubalanza, "A Comparative Study," 8; Goodspeed and Healy, *History of Cook County,* I:451-52.

12. W. C. Keady, "Incidents of Prison Life at Camp Douglas. Experience of Corporal J. G. Blanchard," *Southern Historical Society Papers,* 12 (1864):269-73; *Southern Bivouac* 2 (Oct. 1882):410.

13. Papers of Malcolm McNeill, 1853-1874, Folio 1359, Elizabeth Winston Collection, North Carolina State Archives, Raleigh, NC; Goodspeed and Healy, *History of Cook County,* I:466; Stephen Longstreet, *Chicago, 1860-1919* (New York: David McKay Company, Inc., 1973), 52-53.

14. Carter H. Harrison, *Growing Up With Chicago* (Chicago: Bobbs-Merrill Co., 1944), 11, 14, 17; Levi D. Boone and Buckner Morris.

15. Kogan and Wendt, *Chicago, A Pictorial History,* 97-99; Goodspeed and Healy, *History of Cook County,* I:470-71.

16. Lewis and Smith, *Chicago,* 91; Arthur Charles Cole, *The Era of the Civil War* (Springfield: Illinois Centennial Commission, 1919), 228, 262, 310-11; Bruce Grant, *Fight for a City* (Chicago: Rand McNally & Co., 1955), 13-18.

17. "Dear Sir," Samuel L. Foute to Colonel Tragg, 9 Apr. 1862, The Tragg Collection, MS Division, Library of Congress.

18. *Autobiography of Sir Henry Morton Stanley,* edited by his wife, Dorothy Stanley (Boston: Houghton Mifflin Co., 1909), 264; *Confederate Prisoners of War, 1861-65.*

19. Stanley, 209.

20. Dennis Kelly, "A History of Camp Douglas, Illinois Union Prison, 1861-65," MS, United States Department of the Interior, National Park Service, Southeast Region, 1989, 74; OR Ser. II, Vol. IV, 247; Goodspeed and Healy, *History of Cook County,* I:454; *Chicago Tribune,* 9, 19 Jul. 1862; Andreas, *History of Chicago,* II:511.

21. *Autobiography of Sir Henry Stanley,* 209-10.

22. War Department Collection of Confederate Service Records, NA.

23. Richard Hall, *Stanley, An Adventurer Explored* (Boston: Houghton Mifflin Co., 1975), 130; *Confederate Prisoners of War, 1861-65,* Roll 56; Report of the Illinois Adjutant General, Vol. 8.

24. *Confederate Veteran* 2 (Nov. 1894):332; 3 (Jan. 1895):16; 18 (May 1910):205; 37 (Mar. 1929):84.

25. *Confederate Prisoners of War, 1861-65,* Roll 54; Civil War Diary of Willie Micajah Barrow, *The Louisiana Historical Quarterly,* Vol. 17, No. 4 (Oct. 1934):722-31. Barrow's diary is presented as written; Barrow diary, 10 Apr. 1862.

26. Barrow diary, 27-28 Apr. 1862.

27. Reverend E. B. Tuttle, post chaplain; Barrow diary, 14 May 1862.

28. "Dear Emma," John L. Williams to his niece, 18 July 1862, MS Division, LOC.

29. Mackey diary, 3, 6, 24 May 1862.

30. Mulligan papers, CHS; *Chicago Tribune,* 28 Apr. 1862.

31. *Confederate Veteran* 15 (May 1907):234.

32. *Chicago Tribune,* 29 Apr. 1862.

33. Camp Douglas Order Book, 20 May 1862, CHS.

34. James M. McCaffrey, "A Short History of the Civil War Sutler," *Civil War Times* 4 (Jun. 1985):36; Kelly, "History of Camp Douglas," 94.

35. Camp Douglas Order Book, 20 May 1862; Kelly, "History of Camp Douglas," 98.

36. Hesseltine, *Civil War Prisons,* 30.

37. OR Ser. II, Vol. III, 549-50.

38. Ibid., 647; *Chicago Tribune,* 9 Jun. 1862.

CHAPTER FIVE

1. *Chicago Tribune,* 9, 16 Jun. 1862.

2. Ibid., 4 May 1862.

3. William H. Harder (undated memoir):36, Tennessee State Library and Archives.

4. *Chicago Tribune,* 16 Jun. 1862; *Battles and Leaders of the Civil War,* I:313.

5. *Confederate Prisoners of War, 1861-65.*

6. OR Ser. II, Vol. IV, 111.

7. Barrow diary, 23 Jun. 1862; Mackey diary, 23 Jun. 1862; OR Ser. II, Vol. IV, 193.

8. Microcopy 598, Roll 64, NA.

9. OR Ser. II, Vol. IV, 62.

10. *Chicago Tribune,* 30 Oct. 1862. Hudson probably worked in the Adams Express office at camp.

11. Barrow diary, 6 Sep. 1862.

12. *Chicago Tribune,* 21 Feb., 22 Sep. 1863.

13. OR Ser. II, Vol. IV, 90,93.

14. Dr. Brockholst McVickar was a pioneer Chicago physician. Thomas Neville Bonner, *Medicine in Chicago, 1850-1950* (Madison: American Research History Center, 1957), 72; OR Ser. II, Vol. IV, 107-08.

15. William Quenton Maxwell, *Lincoln's Fifth Wheel, The Political History of the United States Sanitary Commission* (New York: Longmans, Green & Co., 1956), 8; OR Ser. II, Vol. IV, 106.

16. OR Ser. II, Vol. III, 698.

17. OR Ser. II, Vol. IV, 102-03, 172.

18. Ibid., 110.

19. Ibid., 111.

20. Ibid., 129.

21. Ibid., 152-53.

22. RG 109, Box 117, Collection of Confederate Records.

23. OR Ser. II, Vol. IV, 166.

24. OR Ser. II, Vol. VIII, 986-1003; Vol. IV, 253; *Black's Medical Dictionary,* edited by C. W. H. Havard, MA, DM, FRCP, 35th edition (Totowa: Barnes & Noble, 1987), 604.

25. OR Ser. II, Vol. IV, 154-55.

26. *Confederate Prisoners of War, 1861-65*; OR Ser. II, Vol. IV, 248.

27. OR Ser. II, Vol. IV, 180.

28. Ibid., 166-67.

29. Ibid., 179; Mackey diary, 14 Jul. 1862.

30. Tuttle, *History of Camp Douglas,* 20; OR Ser. II, Vol. IV, 162.

31. OR Ser. II, Vol. IV, 166, 238; Hesseltine, *Civil War Prisons,* 126. Belle Isle in the James River is an example. So is Andersonville.

32. OR Ser. II, Vol. IV, 166, 178-79.

33. Ibid., 172-73; Mrs. Jane Bradley was the former widow of Henry Graves's brother and received 11 acres of the Cottage Grove property by will. It abutted the camp on the north, from Cottage Grove to present Vernon Street. Chicago Title and Trust Co., (Pre-Fire Records); MS, "Abstract of Title to Former Camp Douglas Land," CHS; OR Ser. II, Vol. IV, 185-86.

34. *Chicago Tribune,* 26 Nov. 1862; Letter Book of William H. Osborn, Illinois Central Archives, Newberry Library, Chicago; OR Ser. II, Vol. III, 549-50; Eugene C. Murdock, *One Million Men: The Civil War Draft in the North* (Madison: State Historical Society of Wisconsin, 1971).

35. *Chicago Tribune,* 27 Feb. 1862; Hesseltine, *Civil War Prisons,* 114.

36. OR Ser. II, Vol. IV, 188; Unidentified news clipping, 24 Oct. 1894, CHS.

CHAPTER SIX

1. RG 249, v. 2.

2. OR Ser. II, Vol. IV, 194.

3. Ibid, 194-95; 223-24.

4. Ibid., 147-48; *Dictionary of American Biography,* American Council of Learned Societies (New York: Scribner's & Sons, 1928-32), VI:298.

5. OR Ser. II, Vol. IV, 147, 154.

6. Roy D. Basler, ed., *The Collected Works of Abraham Lincoln* (New Brunswick: Rutgers University Press, 1953), VI:532; VII:66, 100, 129, 257, 430; VIII:30, 86; Dorris, *Pardon and Amnesty Under Lincoln and Johnson,* 60-61; RG 393, v. 235:291.

7. Basler, *Collected Works of Abraham Lincoln,* VII:136.

8. OR Ser. II, Vol. IV, 230; Goodspeed and Healy, *History of Cook County,* II:455; *Medical and Surgical History,* Vol. I, Part III:50.

9. OR Ser. II, Vol. IV, 228-29.

10. Ibid., 228, 247-48; Microcopy 598, Roll 56.

11. Camp Douglas Order Book, 5, 11, 19, Jul. 1862; 6 Aug. 1862, CHS.

12. OR Ser. II, Vol. IV, 247, 252.

13. Ibid., 266-69.

14. Ibid., 278.

15. Karlen, "Postal History of Camp Douglas," 928.

16. OR Ser. II, Vol. IV, 278; Currey, *Chicago: Its History and Its Builders,* II:134, 124; Karlen, "Postal History of Camp Douglas," 928.

17. *Chicago Tribune,* 25 Jul. 1862; Kirkland, *Chicago Yesterdays,* 110-11.

18. OR Ser. II, Vol. IV, 278-79; *Chicago Tribune,* 5 Aug. 1862.

19. McClelland Papers, MS Collection, CHS.

20. OR Ser. II, Vol. IV, 293-94; Letter to Tucker, 7-28-62, RG 393, v. 242.

21. OR Ser. II, Vol. IV, 229.

22. Ibid., 312-13, 335-36.

23. Mackey diary, 28 Jul. 1862; OR Ser. II, Vol. IV, 279.

24. OR Ser. II, Vol. IV, 280-81.

25. Ibid., 301. The letter referred to is Tucker's report to Hoffman on 9 July 1862 describing the shortages in detail, Ser. II, Vol. IV, 180.

26. OR Ser. II, Vol. IV, 339; Mackey diary, 19 Jul. 1862.

27. Hesseltine, *Civil War Prisons,* 65; Story, "Camp Douglas, 1861-1865," 21.

28. OR Ser. II, Vol. IV, 324-25; *Medical and Surgical History,* Vol. I, Part III:49.

29. OR Ser. II, Vol. IV, 263.

30. RG 109, Box 117, Collection of Confederate Records.

31. RG 393, IV:41.

32. OR Ser. II, Vol. IV, 112.

33. Mackey diary, 2 Aug. 1862.

34. Bonner, *Medicine in Chicago, 1850-1950,* 72. Dr. Boone invested in real estate, railroads, and commercial ventures; OR Ser. II, Vol. IV, 339-40.

35. OR Ser. II, Vol. IV, 339-40; *Biographical Sketches of Leading Men of Chicago* (Chicago: Wilson & St. Clair, 1868), 277-78.

36. OR Ser. II, Vol. IV, 347; *Halpin & Bailey's Chicago Street Directory 1862-1863*; Basler, *Collected Works of Abraham Lincoln,* III:203n; A charismatic Indian leader named Black Hawk invaded Illinois in 1832 with a force of four hundred to five hundred Sauk and Fox warriors to reclaim lands they had signed away in 1804; Bonner, *Medicine in Chicago, 1850-1950,* 72, 160.

37. RG 109, Box 117.

38. OR Ser. II, Vol. IV, 324, 353.

39. Ibid., 376.

40. Ibid., 432.

41. Ibid., 385.

42. Ibid., 758-59.

43. *Chicago Tribune,* 21 Aug. 1862.

44. Compiled from the Records of the Commissary General of Prisoners, RG 109, Roll 54.

45. OR Ser. II, Vol. IV, 414-15.

46. Ibid., 458-59.

47. Ibid., 551-52, 615.

48. Dorris, *Pardon and Amnesty Under Lincoln and Johnson,* 61.

49. Harder memoir, 40.

50. Basler, *Collected Works of Abraham Lincoln,* V:403.

51. Ibid., IV:504.

52. *Chicago Tribune,* 1 Jul. 1864.

53. *Confederate Prisoners of War, 1861-65,* Rolls 55 & 56.

54. RG 109, Roll 56; Cole, *Era of the Civil War,* 225, 233.

55. *Confederate Prisoners of War, 1861-65,* Roll 56; OR Ser. II, Vol. IV, 551-52, 892-94.

56. Microcopy 598, Roll 56, NA.

57. Currey, *Chicago: Its History and Its Builders,* II:129.

58. RG 109, Box 117.

59. Spot F. Terrell, 49th Tennessee Infantry, "A Confederate Private at Fort Donelson," *The American Historical Revue* (New York: Macmillan Co., 1926), 482-83.

60. Journal of Marion F. Baxter, 20th Mississippi Infantry, III:3, Baxter Collection, USAMHI.

61. Terrell, "A Confederate Private at Fort Donelson," 483.

62. Ibid., 484.

63. Courtesy of Tim Burgess, Hendersonville, Tennessee.

64. Chicago Tribune, 4 Oct. 1862.

65. RG 109, Roll 56; *Confederate Veteran* 15 (May 1907):234.

66. Unidentified newspaper article, 24 Oct. 1894, MS, CHS.

67. OR Ser. II, Vol. IV, 758-59.

68. Ibid., 758-59; RG 249, v. 2.

69. *Chicago Tribune,* 19 Nov. 1862.

70. *Confederate Prisoners of War, 1861-65,* Rolls 55 & 56. The *Official Records* do not provide returns from the camp before July 1862.

71. RG 108, Roll 56.

72. OR Ser. II, Vol. VII, 986-1003.

73. *Chicago Tribune,* 22 Sep. 1862; *Medical and Surgical History,* Vol. I, Part III:49.

CHAPTER SEVEN

1. *Chicago Tribune,* 23 Sep. 1862.

2. *Battles and Leaders of the Civil War,* II:604.

3. Andreas, *History of Chicago,* II:302.

4. Ezra Warner, *Generals in Blue* (Baton Rouge, Louisiana State University Press, 1964), 514-15.

5. OR Ser. II, Vol. IV, 595-96.

6. *Chicago Tribune,* 4 Oct. 1862.

7. Ibid., 1 Oct. 1862.

8. Memoirs of Pvt. Thomas Jefferson Moses, Company G, 93rd Illinois Volunteers, courtesy of Mr. Tom Gaard, Des Moines, Iowa; Harvey M. Trimble, *History of the Ninety-Third Volunteer Infantry* (Chicago, Blakely Printing Co., 1898), 11; Peter Cozzens, *The Shipwreck of Their Hopes* (Urbana: University of Illinois Press, 1994), 227, 231.

9. E. B. Sherman, "A Letter from Camp Douglas," 4 Oct. 1862, MS Division, LOC.

10. Nicholas De Graff, 115th New York Infantry, Civil War Diary, CWTI Collection, USAMHI.

11. Otto Eisenschiml, *Vermont General, The Unusual War Experiences of Edward Hastings Ripley, 1862-1865* (New York: Devin-Adair Co., 1960), 46.

12. OR Ser. II, Vol. IV, 600; Eisenschiml, *Vermont General,* 50.

13. Colbert, *Chicago, Historical and Statistical Sketch,* 93-94; OR Ser. II, Vol. V, 214-15.

14. *Medical and Surgical History,* Vol. I, Part III:49.

15. Eisenschiml, *Vermont General,* 58; De Graff diary, 16 Oct. 1862; *Chicago Tribune,* 18 Nov. 1862.

16. OR Ser. II, Vol. IV, 645; Benjamin W. Thompson, 111th New York Infantry, Civil War Diary, CWTI Collection, USAMHI; *Chicago Tribune,* 9 Oct. 1862.

17. *Medical and Surgical History,* Vol. I, Part III:49; *Chicago Tribune,* 10 Oct., 11 Nov. 1862.

18. Diary of Col. James A. Mulligan, 27 Oct. 1862, CHS.

19. Kelly, "History of Camp Douglas," 23; Hesseltine, *Civil War Prisons,* 235.

20. Charles Wesley Belknap, 125th New York Infantry, Civil War Diary, CWTI Collection, UASMHI.

21. OR Ser. II, Vol. IV, 698-99, 710-11; Kelly, "History of Camp Douglas," 95.

22. OR Ser. II, Vol. V, 106.

23. Andreas, *History of Chicago,* II:226-27.

24. OR Ser. II, Vol. V, 130.

25. RG 393, v. 233:138.

26. Belknap diary.

27. OR Ser. II, Vol. V, 105-6.

28. Eisenschiml, *Vermont General,* 66-68.

29. Story, "Camp Douglas, 1861-1865," 42.

30. *Black's Medical Dictionary.*

CHAPTER EIGHT

1. Sorensen, "Civil War Prisoner of War System"; *Chicago Tribune,* 31 Jan. 1863.

2. *Chicago Tribune,* 27 Mar. 1863; Smith, "Recollections of the Late War," 15-16.

3. OR Ser. II, Vol. V, 157; Warner, *Generals in Blue,* 6; *Battles and Leaders of the Civil War,* I:567.

4. *Chicago Tribune,* 3 Feb. 1863.

5. Ibid., 28 Jan. 1863.

6. Rossiter Johnson, *A History of the War of Secession* (New York: Wessels & Bissell Co., 1910), 277; OR Ser. II, Vol. V, 176.

7. OR Ser. II, Vol. V, 203.

8. Ibid., 344.

9. *Chicago Tribune,* 31 Jan. 1863; *Battles and Leaders of the Civil War,* III:460, 462, 471.

10. Hazel Hankenson, "Where Dixie Sleeps Farthest North," *Confederate Veteran* 33 (Aug. 1925):301; OR Ser. II, Vol. V, 214; Story, "Camp Douglas, 1861-1865," 46.

11. Eisenschiml, *Vermont General,* 74.

12. *Chicago Tribune,* 28, 31 Jan. 1863.

13. OR Ser. II, Vol. IV, 207; Vol. V, 235.

14. *Chicago Tribune,* 3 Feb. 1863.

15. Eisenschiml, *Vermont General,* 73.

16. C. G. Benedict, *Vermont in the Civil War* (Burlington: The Free Press Assoc., 1888), II:210.

17. William W. Calkins, *The History of the 104th Regiment, Illinois Volunteer Infantry, 1862-1865* (Chicago: Donohue & Henneberry, 1895), 79.

18. OR Ser. II, Vol. V, 345, 367; based upon a cost of $519.48 per day for rations, which indicates a loss of 7.60 percent per prisoner; *Chicago Tribune,* 3 Feb. 1863.

19. Tucker owned the Briggs Hotel at Randolph and Wells Streets in Chicago. *Bailey's Chicago Street Directory, 1864-65. Harpel Scrap Book Obituary,* IX:179, CHS; Albert Castel, "Black Jack Logan," *Civil War Times* 7 (Nov. 1976):6, 8. Logan sponsored the Illinois "Black Code" in 1853, excluding blacks from Illinois under threat of being fined and sold in lieu of payment of the fine.

20. *Chicago Tribune,* 10 Feb. 1863.

21. OR Ser. II, Vol. V, 265; *Chicago Tribune,* 16 Feb. 1863.

22. OR Ser. II, Vol. V, 281, 297; Vol. VI, 823.

23. *Chicago Tribune,* 28 Feb. 1863.

24. OR Ser. II, Vol. VII, 221.

25. *Chicago Tribune,* 31 Jan. 1863; OR Ser. II, Vol. V, 345.

26. OR Ser. II, Vol. V, 343-45.

27. Ibid., 344.

28. Ibid., 588.

29. RG 94, Ninth Vermont Order Book.

30. OR Ser. II, Vol. V, 346.

31. *Confederate Prisoners of War, 1861-65,* Roll 58.

32. Minutes of Special Meeting of the Trustees, 26 March 1863, The Old University of Chicago Records. Thomas Hoyne was the mayor of the city of Chicago at the time and a trustee of the university. His son was a student there.

33. *Chicago Tribune,* 21 Feb. 1862.

34. OR Ser. II, Vol. V, 344.

35. OR Ser. II, Vol. III, 604-05.

36. OR Ser. II, Vol. V, 345.

37. *Confederate Prisoners of War, 1861-65; The Chicago Sunday Record Herald,* 6 Oct. 1912, Old University of Chicago Records, Special Collections, Regenstein Library; OR Ser. II, Vol. V, 400.

38. Goodspeed and Healy, *History of Cook County,* I:469; OR Ser. II, Vol. VIII, 986-87; *Chicago Tribune,* 4 Apr. 1863; Camp Douglas Post Hospital Register 212, NA.

39. OR Ser. II, Vol. V, 415.

40. Ibid., 342; *Chicago Tribune,* 31 Mar. 1863.

41. Eisenschiml, *Vermont General,* 85-92.

42. OR Ser. II, Vol. V, 440.

43. Ibid., 449.

44. Ibid., 450.

45. Margaret Leech, *Reveille in Washington 1860-1865* (New York: Time Incorporated, 1962), 197-98; OR Ser. II, Vol. V, 444.

46. OR Ser. II, Vol. V, 548-49.

47. Ibid., 476-77, 495-97; smallpox appeared in the camp as early as 10 November 1862, Goodspeed and Healy, *History of Cook County,* I:469.

48. OR Ser. II, Vol. V, 934.

49. Tuttle, *History of Camp Douglas,* 20.

50. OR Ser. II, Vol. IV, 28-81; Vol. V, 492.

51. OR Ser. II, Vol. V, 511-13; Vol. VIII, 990.

52. OR Ser. II, Vol. VIII, 986-1003.

53. By the end of July 1864 Andersonville held 31,678 prisoners, and 12,912 Union graves were found after the war, a 40 percent death rate. Hesseltine, *Civil War Prisons,* 146, 152.

54. Bonner, *Medicine in Chicago, 1850-1950,* 34; *Medical and Surgical History,* Vol. I, Part III:67.

55. *Chicago Tribune,* 4 Feb. 1863; Story, "Camp Douglas, 1861-1865," 46.

56. Colbert, *Chicago, Historical and Statistical Sketch,* 94.

57. Sorensen, "Civil War Prisoner of War System," 6.

58. Dorris, *Pardon and Amnesty under Lincoln and Johnson,* 26.

59. OR Ser. II, Vol. VI, 175.

60. OR Ser. II, Vol. V, 686-87.

CHAPTER NINE

1. Kubalanza, "A Comparative Study," 35-36; OR Ser. II, Vol. VII, 604.

2. OR Ser. II, Vol. VI, 4.

3. *Battles and Leaders of the Civil War,* III:634.

4. J. G. Randall, *The Civil War and Reconstruction* (Chicago: D.C. Heathe & Co., 1937), 532-33.

5. OR Ser. II, Vol. VI, 200, 206.

6. *Record of Service of Michigan Volunteers in the Civil War,* Michigan State Historical Library, Lansing; *Loomis Index,* Michigan State Archives, Lansing; *Chicago Tribune,* 19 Sep. 1863; Hunt and Brown, *Brevet Brigadier Generals in Blue,* 157.

7. Kelly, "History of Camp Douglas," 51.

8. Curtis R. Burke, Civil War Journal, *Indiana Magazine of History,* Pamela J. Bennett, ed., Vol. 66 (June, 1970):121; Vol. 65 (Dec., 1969):283. Burke was 21 years of age and a thin five feet seven inches when he entered the camp. His diary is presented as written. The "14th Kentucky Cavalry" is not listed with the official regiments in Morgan's command, *Reminiscences of General Basil W. Duke, CSA* (New York: Doubleday, Page & Co., 1911), and it is not the official 14th Kentucky Cavalry in the Kentucky adjutant general's reports. Burke's unit appears to have consisted of irregulars, a step above guerrillas.

9. Burke, Civil War Journal, 120-21; Kelly, "History of Camp Douglas," 79.

10. Burke, Civil War Journal, 24 Aug. 1863; *Chicago Tribune,* 21, 24 Aug. 1863.

11. *Chicago Tribune,* 19 Aug. 1863.

12. Burke, Civil War Journal, 9 Jul. 1863.

13. *Chicago Tribune,* 1 Sep. 1863; Burke, Civil War Journal, 2 Oct. 1863.

14. OR Ser. II, Vol. VI, 434, 461; *Battles and Leaders of the Civil War,* III:62-69.

15. Gary L. Todd, "An Invalid Corps," *Civil War Times* 8 (Dec. 1985):16.

16. OR Ser. II, Vol. VI, 212; *Chicago Tribune,* 28 Oct. 1864.

17. OR Ser. II, Vol. VI, 434.

18. RG 393, v. 244:1-22.

19. RG 393, v. 233:175; Kelly, "History of Camp Douglas," 96.

20. OR Ser. II, Vol. VI, 314.

21. Burke, Civil War Journal, 14 Sep., 24 Nov. 1863.

22. Ibid., 11, 14 Sep. 1863.

23. *Pardon and Amnesty Under Lincoln and Johnson,* 25, 27; Burke, Civil War Journal, 7 Sep. 1863.

24. OR Ser. II, Vol. VI, 332, 363.

25. Ibid., 371-74.

26. Ibid.

27. Bell Irvin Wiley, *The Life of Johnny Reb* (New York: Bobbs-Merrill Co., 1962), 105.

28. RG 393, v. 237:18.

29. *Chicago Tribune,* 31 Oct. 1864; RG 393, v. 233:38-39; v. 244, GO 12; Burke, Civil War Journal, 14 Oct. 1863; OR Ser. II, Vol. VI, 390.

30. RG 393, v. 244:266; Burke, Civil War Journal, 15 Oct. 1863.

31. *Chicago Tribune,* 19 Oct. 1863.

32. Longstreet, *Chicago, 1860-1919,* 30-31.

33. *Chicago Tribune,* 25 Oct. 1863.

34. Burke, Civil War Journal, 31 Oct. 1863.

35. *Chicago Tribune,* 7 Jun. 1863.

36. OR Ser. II, Vol. VI, 417-18, 464.

37. Kelly, "History of Camp Douglas," 145.

38. RG 395, v. 244; Burke, Civil War Journal, 25 Oct., 4 Dec. 1863.

39. RG 393, v. 243:491.

40. Ibid., v. 233:172; RG 293, 243:39; RG 393, v. 422:16.

41. RG 393, v. 233:167; *Chicago Tribune,* 19 Oct. 1863.

42. *Chicago Tribune,* 30 Apr. 1862.

43. OR Ser. II, Vol. VI, 434-35.

44. Ibid., 461-64.

45. Ibid., 462.

46. OR Ser. II, Vol. VII, 605-07.

47. OR Ser. II, Vol. VI, 463.

48. Ibid., 461-64.

49. *Dictionary of American Biography,* VI:42-43.

50. OR Ser. II, Vol. VI, 461-64; Burke, Civil War Journal, 21 Oct. 1863.

51. OR Ser. II, Vol. VI, 461-64.

52. Kelly, "History of Camp Douglas," 76.

53. Ibid., 54.

54. *Confederate Veteran,* 5 (Mar. 1897):368.

CHAPTER TEN

1. RG 249, v. 3.

2. T. D. Henry in "Treatment of Prisoners During the War," *Southern Historical Society Papers* 1 (Jan.-Jun., 1876):277. Henry was in Company E, Duke's Regiment, Second Kentucky Cavalry.

3. RG 393, v. 244, GO 18.

4. RG 393, v. 240:32.

5. OR Ser. II, Vol. VI. 315; RG 393, v. 244, GO 18.

6. *Confederate Prisoners of War, 1861-65,* Roll 53; *Chicago Tribune,* 18 Dec. 1863; Story, "Camp Douglas, 1861-1865," 82.

7. *Chicago Tribune,* 9 Nov. 1863.

8. RG 393, v. 234:106, 107.

9. Alan T. Nolan, *The Iron Brigade* (New York: Macmillan, 1961), 52.

10. OR Ser. II, Vol. VI, 633; Burke, Civil War Journal, 11 Nov. 1863.

11. OR Ser. II, Vol. VI, 504; RG 393, v. 244, GO 19.

12. RG 84, Order Book, Eighth Veteran Reserve Corps, Companies B,C,E,F.

13. RG 393, v. 234:124; OR Ser. II, Vol. VI, 489-90.

14. OR Ser. II, Vol. VI, 490.

15. Burke, Civil War Journal, 14, 15 Nov. 1863; OR Ser. II, Vol. VI, 633-36.

16. OR Ser. II, Vol. VI, 525.

17. R. T. Bean, "Seventeen Months in Camp Douglas," *Confederate Veteran* 22 (Jun. 1914):269; Burke, Civil War Journal, 16 Nov. 1863.

18. R.G. 393, v. 233:187.

19. OR Ser. II, Vol. VI, 660-61; Story, "Camp Douglas, 1861-1865," 62-63.

20. Burke, Civil War Journal, 22 Nov. 1863; Bell I. Wiley, "The Common Soldier of the Civil War," *Civil War Times* 4 (Jul. 1973):50.

21. Henry, "Treatment of Prisoners," 276.

22. Kelly, "History of Camp Douglas," 56; Burke, Civil War Journal, 19-20, 24 Nov., 1 Dec 1863.

23. OR Ser. II, Vol. VI, 625, 660; Bean, "Seventeen Months in Camp Douglas," 268.

24. RG 393, v. 234:132.

25. OR Ser. II, Vol. VI, 637.

26. Ibid., 860-61.

27. Ibid., 680-82; RG 393, v. 234:47, 150.

28. *Chicago Tribune,* 18 Dec. 1863; E. R. Hopkins, "At Fort Donelson," *Confederate Veteran* 38 (Mar. 1930):85.

29. Burke, Civil War Journal, 3, 5 Dec. 1863. "Sleeper": a supporting floor beam.

30. Burke, Civil War Journal, 4 Dec. 1863.

31. Oscar A. Cliett, "Incidents and Reminiscences of Two Years of Prison Life" (MS published in *The Home Journal,* Perry, Houston County, GA, 1899), 17. Courtesy of Mr. Joseph Cliett, Jacksonville, Florida.

32. OR Ser. I, Vol. 52, Part I, 504; RG 393, v. 244:24.

33. Hoffman to Orme, 13 Jan. 1864.

34. Swett capitalized on his association with Lincoln after his death and conspired with Lincoln's son, Robert, to have his mother declared insane on 19 May 1875 in Chicago. Samuel A. Schreiner Jr., *The Trials of Mrs. Lincoln* (New York: Donald I. Fine, Inc., 1987); Warner, *Generals in Blue,* 350-51.

35. OR Ser. II, Vol. VI, 718; Peggy Robbins, "The Greatest Scoundrel," *Civil War Times* 5 (Nov.-Dec. 1992):56; OR Ser. II, Vol. VI, 778.

36. OR Ser. II, Vol. VI, 779-98.

37. Ibid., 786.

38. Ibid., 797.

39. Ibid., 785, 789.

40. Ibid., 779.

41. Ibid., 779-98, 799-812; Story, "Camp Douglas, 1861-1865," 61.

42. OR Ser. II, Vol. VI, 764-67.

43. Kelly, "History of Camp Douglas," 58.

44. OR Ser. II, Vol. VI, 778, 799-80.

45. Ibid., 800.

46. RG 109, Box 117.

47. Dorris, *Pardon and Amnesty Under Lincoln and Johnson,* 59, letter of Pvt. Nathan B. Deatherage.

48. RG 393 v. 244, GO 25.

49. Burke, Civil War Journal, 25 Dec. 1863.

50. Ibid.

51. RG 393, v. 234:162.

52. Ibid., v. 245.

53. OR Ser. II, Vol. VI, 802-03.

54. Ibid., 804-05.

CHAPTER ELEVEN

1. Burke, Civil War Journal, 1 Jan. 1864; Goodspeed and Healy, *History of Cook County,* I:309.

2. M. J. Bradley, "The Horrors of Camp Douglas as related by a prisoner," in Griffin Frost's *Camp and Prison Journal* (Quincy: Quincy Herald Book and Job Office, 1867), 277; Bean, "Seventeen Months in Camp Douglas," 270; *Chicago Tribune,* 8 Jan. 1864.

3. RG 395, v. 244; T. M. Page, "The Prisoner of War," *Confederate Veteran* 8 (Feb. 1900):63.

4. OR Ser. II, Vol. VI, 800.

5. *Chicago Tribune,* 8, 10 Jan. 1864.

6. RG 393, Part 4, v. 234, Records of the U. S. Army Continental Commands, Camp Douglas Letter Book, 175; RG 393, v. 240:68.

7. *Confederate Prisoners of War, 1861-65,* Roll 55.

8. The 15th Tennessee Cavalry on Morgan's raid is not the same Confederate unit as the 15th Tennessee Cavalry (Stewart's) or the 15th Tennessee Cavalry (Russell's). These were official units. General Marcus J. Wright, *Tennessee in the War* (New York: Ambrose Lee Publishing Co., 1908), 90; John B. Lindsley, *Military Annals of Tennessee, Confederate* (Nashville: J. M. Lindsley & Co., 1886), 733-34. The one on the raid was not known in Richmond,

although it was formed in September 1862 as part of Basil Duke's Brigade. It probably failed to file a muster-in roll.

9. OR Ser. I, Vol. XV, 556-57; Ser. II, Vol. III, 436-37; Ser. IV, Vol. I, 409, 529, 625, 1020; Charles W. Wesley, "Negroes in the Confederate Army," *The Journal of Negro History* 4 (July, 1919, No. 3):239-53; Luther P. Jackson, "Free Negroes of Petersburg, Virginia," *The Journal of Negro History* 12 (Jan. 1927, No. 1):386-88; John D. Winters, *The Civil War in Louisiana* (Baton Rouge: Louisiana State University Press, 1963), 34-35; Merle R. Eppse, *The Negro, Too, in American History* (Nashville: National Publication Co., 1943), 225-26; Ira Berlin, *Slaves Without Masters* (New York: Oxford University Press, 1975), 386-87; OR Ser. III, Vol. II, 584-85; Vol. V, 671-72.

10. RG 393, v. 244:282; OR Ser. II, Vol. VI, 354; *Confederate Veteran* 5 (Mar. 1897):368.

11. Burke, Civil War Journal, 3 Jan. 1864.

12. Kelly, "History of Camp Douglas," 103, 104.

13. *Chicago Tribune,* 1 Sep. 1863; James S. Coke, *Confederate Veteran* 14 (Oct. 1906):38; Burke, Civil War Journal, 8 Jan. 1864.

14. Cliett, "Two Years of Prison Life," 23.

15. OR Ser. II, Vol. VIII, 76-77.

16. RG 393, v. 244, GO 9.

17. Ibid., v. 418.

18. Ibid., v. 244, GO 12.

19. Burke, Civil War Journal, 19 Jan. 1864; "Doorstep Reminiscences," *Confederate Veteran* 10 (Oct. 1902):453.

20. RG 109, Box 117, Collection of Confederate Records.

21. RG 393, v. 234:362; *Halpin & Bailey's Chicago City Directory, 1862-63*; Census, 1870.

22. Burke, Civil War Journal, 15 Mar. 1864; OR Ser. II, Vol. VI, 860-61; RG 393, v. 234:232; RG 249, v. 7.

23. OR Ser. II, Vol. VI, 824.

24. Ibid., 848-51.

25. Ibid., 851; Burke, Civil War Journal, 14 Jan. 1864.

26. Burke, Civil War Journal, 29 Jan. 1864; RG 94, Plan of Camp Douglas, 1 March 1864, 8 August 1864, 1 January 1865; OR Ser. II, Vol. VII, 616.

27. RG 393, v. 234:179; *Chicago Tribune,* 30 Jan. 1864.

28. OR Ser. II, Vol. VI, 908-10.

29. Misc. MS, CHS.

30. Burke, Civil War Journal, 4 Feb. 1864. The barracks were arranged in long rows around the sides of the square.

31. Burke, Civil War Journal, 14 Feb. 1864.

32. OR Ser. II, Vol. VI, 927-29.

33. MS Original Autograph Letters, v. 49:659, CHS. Colonel Kilburn was chief commissary of the Department of the Ohio, which included Illinois.

34. Basler, *Collected Works of Abraham Lincoln,* II:188; Mark E. Neely, Jr., *The Abraham Lincoln Encyclopedia* (New York: Da Capo Press, 1982), 95.

35. Neely, *Lincoln Encyclopedia,* 95.

36. Autograph Letters, v. 49:651, CHS.

37. He was instrumental in winning over delegates to Lincoln at the nominating convention in Chicago in 1860. *Dictionary of American Biography,* III:175; *The Diary of Orville Hickman Browning,* Vol. I, Theodore Calvin Pease and James G. Randall, eds. (Springfield: Illinois State Historical Library, 1925), v. xix; Browning diary, 14 Dec. 1863, for the release of Henry N. Warfield from Camp Douglas. Warfield had escaped through the tunnel in December 1863, but later surrendered.

38. Levy, "Prisoners in the Dust."

39. Browning diary, 15 Mar. 1865.

40. Autograph Letters, v. 49:663, CHS.

41. *Chicago Tribune,* 27 January 1864; RG 393, v. 244:301.

42. RG 395, v. 244, SO 179.

43. Cliett, "Two Years of Prison Life," 26.

44. Burke, Civil War Journal, 3 Nov. 1864; Page, "Prisoner of War," 64; OR Ser. II, Vol. VI, 927-29; *Chicago Tribune,* 8 Jan. 1864.

45. OR Ser. II, Vol. VI, 929.

46. Ibid., 798-99; Burke, Civil War Journal, 2-17 Oct. 1864.

47. OR Ser. II, Vol. VI, 929.

48. Browning diary, 17 Oct. 1864.

CHAPTER TWELVE

1. Burke, Civil War Journal, 22 Feb. 1864; RG 393, v. 244, GO 21.

2. Burke, Civil War Journal, 22, 27 Feb. 1864.

3. Ibid., 29 Feb. 1864.

4. RG 393, v. 233:52,160; *Chicago Tribune,* 1 Feb. 1864.

5. John Robertson, *Michigan in the War* (Lansing: W. S. George & C., 1882).

6. *Record of Service of Michigan Volunteers in the Civil War* (Brig. Gen. George H. Brown, Adj. Gen.) 2.

7. Letters of General William Ward Orme, CHS.

8. RG 393, v. 244, GO 25.

9. Tuttle, *History of Camp Douglas,* 34.

10. RG 94, 15th VRC. Ledgers.

11. OR Ser. II, Vol. VII, 20-21; Karlen, "Postal History of Camp Douglas," 821; OR Ser. II, Vol. VII, 57.

12. Burke, Civil War Journal, 7 Mar. 1864.

13. Ibid., 14 Mar. 1864.

14. OR Ser. II, Vol. VI, 372.

15. Burke, Civil War Journal, 23-24 Mar. 1864; RG 393, v. 244, GO 20.

16. OR Ser. II, Vol. VI, 1014-15.

17. Burke, Civil War Journal, 29 Mar. 1864.

18. OR Ser. II, Vol. VI, 1036, 1073.

19. Burke, Civil War Journal, 14 Mar. 1864.

20. RG 94, Regimental Letter Book.

21. Burke, Civil War Journal, 22 Mar., 3 Apr. 1864.

22. Ibid., 27 Mar. 1864; Tuttle, *History of Camp Douglas,* 17.

23. RG 393, v. 234:244.

24. OR Ser. II, Vol. VIII, 986-1003; RG 393, v. 234:238; Burke, Civil War Journal, 30 Mar., 2 Apr. 1864.

25. RG 94, Regimental Letter Book.

26. Orme letters, CHS.

27. Burke, Civil War Journal, 25 Mar. 1864.

28. RG 393, 237:180.

29. *Medical and Surgical History,* Vol. I, Part III:49.

30. RG 249, v. 8.

31. RG 393, v. 244; *Chicago Tribune,* 15 Apr. 1864; Burke, Civil War Journal, 5 Oct. 1864; OR Ser. II, Vol. VII, 703.

32. Burke, Civil War Journal, 3 Apr. 1864.

33. Ibid., 16 Aug. 1864.

34. Ibid., 16 Apr., 4 Jul. 1864.

35. Wiley, "Common Soldier of the Civil War," 49; Burke, Civil War Journal, 12, 18 Apr., 9 Dec. 1864.

36. OR Ser. II, Vol. VII, 57.

37. Burke, Civil War Journal, 20 Apr. 1864.

38. Ibid., 23 Apr. 1864; OR Ser. II, Vol. VII, 62-63, 221.

39. OR Ser. II, Vol. VII, 57-58; Vol. VIII, 102; RG 393, v. 244, GO 334.

CHAPTER THIRTEEN

1. *Battles and Leaders of the Civil War,* III:58; Raymond Dorn, "General Benjamin J. Sweet, A Manufactured Hero" (unpublished MS), 33-34.

2. Andreas, *History of Chicago,* II:310.

3. John J. Flynn, *Handbook of Chicago Biography* (1893), 345.

4. Henry, "Treatment of Prisoners," 276.

5. Kelly, "History of Camp Douglas," 105-06.

6. Kubalanza, "A Comparative Study," 35-36.

7. Hesseltine, *Civil War Prisons,* 144; James R. Clark, "The Cost of Capture," *Civil War Times* 1 (Mar. 1992):31:26; Burke, Civil War Journal, 16 Jan., 12 Apr., 19 May 1864; Tuttle, *History of Camp Douglas,* 20.

8. MS, CHS.

9. OR Ser. II, Vol. VII, 142-43; Burke, Civil War Journal, 29 Apr. 1864.

10. Burke, Civil War Journal, 29 Apr. 1864.

11. OR Ser. II, Vol. VII, 125.

12. Burke, Civil War Journal, 13 May 1864; RG 395, v. 244.

13. SO No. 224.

14. Burke, Civil War Journal, 19 May 1864; RG 393, v. 234:325; J. J. Moore, "Camp Douglas," *Confederate Veteran* 11 (Jun. 1903):270.

15. RG 393, v. 234:384-85.

16. Burke, Civil War Journal, 24 May 1864; RG 393, v. 234.

17. RG 395, v. 244, SO 227.

18. OR Ser. II, Vol. VII, 184-85.

19. Burke, Civil War Journal, 1 Jun. 1864; OR Ser. II, Vol. VII, 187-88.

20. Original Autograph Letters, v. 49, CHS; Burke, Civil War Journal, 2 Jul. 1864; Kelly, "History of Camp Douglas," 102; *Chicago Tribune,* 26 Sep. 1863; OR Ser. II, Vol. VIII, 995-99.

21. OR Ser. II, Vol. VII, 184-85.

22. Ibid., 195, 201-02, 369.

23. Ibid., 150-51, 183-84.

24. Burke, Civil War Journal, 3 May, 5 Jun. 1864; Frank L. Klement, *Dark Lanterns, Secret Political Societies, Conspiracies, and Treason Trials in the Civil War* (Baton Rouge: Louisiana State University Press, 1984), 197.

25. Bean, "Seventeen Months in Camp Douglas," 270.

26. Bradley, "Horrors of Camp Douglas," 270.

27. John M. Copley, *A Sketch of the Battle of Franklin, Tennessee, With Reminiscences of Camp Douglas* (Austin: E. Von Boeckman, 1893), 89. Lieutenant Joel A. Fife, Eighth VRC, was wounded while fighting in the 75th Illinois Infantry.

28. J. M. Berry, "Prison Life in Camp Douglas," *Confederate Veteran* 11 (Apr. 1903):37-38.

29. Burke, Civil War Journal, 21 Jun. 1864.

30. Ibid., 26 Jun. 1864.

31. Ibid., 9 Jun. 1864; *Blanchard's Street Guide* (1866), CHS; Longstreet, *Chicago, 1860-1919,* 42.

32. RG 393, Records of U.S. Army Continental Commands, Camp Douglas Letter Book, 340; *Life of Mary Monholland,* 110-11; *Chicago Tribune,* 26 May 1895.

33. Baptismal Records of The Reverend Patrick Joseph R. Murphy, 1864-1866, St. James Catholic Church, Chicago; Rev. Clinton Locke, D.D., Rector of Grace Church, 1859-1895 (unpublished, undated MS, Rush-Presbyterian-St. Luke's Medical Center Archives, Chicago).

34. Burke, Civil War Journal, 23, 27 Jun. 1864.

35. Henry, "Treatment of Prisoners," 278; J. W. Cook, "Villainous Inspectors at Camp Douglas," *Confederate Veteran* 16 (Aug. 1908):406; Original Autograph Letters, v. 49, CHS. Major Piper was killed in action later that year.

36. Burke, Civil War Journal, 29 Jun. 1864.

37. Kelly, "History of Camp Douglas," 65; Report of the Illinois Adjutant General, I:123.

38. Burke, Civil War Journal, 170; Hesseltine, *Civil War Prisons,* 144; Sorensen, "Civil War Prisoner of War System," 38-39; Henry, "Treatment of Prisoners," 278.

39. Burke, Civil War Journal, 4 Jul. 1864.

CHAPTER FOURTEEN

1. *Chicago Tribune,* 23 Jul. 1864.

2. Ibid., 28 Dec. 1864.

3. OR Ser. II, Vol. VII, 503; Burke, Civil War Journal, 24 Mar. 1864.

4. Burke, Civil War Journal, 7 Jul. 1864.

5. Fort Jefferson military prison, about 80 miles off Key West, Florida; Burke, Civil War Journal, 22 Jul. 1864.

6. OR Ser. II, Vol. VII, 496-97; Burke, Civil War Journal, 11 May 1864.

7. Burke, Civil War Journal, 28 Jul. 1864.

8. RG 393, v. 244, GO 65.

9. Burke, Civil War Journal, 28 Jul. 1864. William Brown, Private, Barnes Georgia Battery, died 25 May 1864, and is buried in Chicago; Burke, Civil War Journal, 20 Aug. 1864.

10. RG 393, Records of the U.S. Army Continental Commands, Camp Douglas Letter Book, 462.

11. Burke, Civil War Journal, 18 Jul. 1864; 1, 6, 21 Aug. 1864.

12. Kelly, "History of Camp Douglas," 66; RG 393, v. 240:167, 244, SO 295.

13. Diary of Private Edwin Greble, 196th Pennsylvania Infantry Regiment, Greble Collection, MS Division, LOC; Greble diary, Aug. 16, 1864.

14. Burke, Civil War Journal, 19 Jul. 1864.

15. Ibid., 19 Aug. 1864.

16. OR Ser. II, Vol. VII, 573-74; Kelly, "History of Camp Douglas," 97.

17. Burke, Civil War Journal, 15, 30 Aug., 22 Sep. 1864.

18. Kelly, "History of Camp Douglas," 74; *Chicago Tribune,* 19 Oct. 1863; Burke, Civil War Journal, 17 Oct. 1863.

19. OR Ser. II, Vol. VII, 595-97; Burke, Civil War Journal, 24 Aug. 1864.

20. Tuttle, *History of Camp Douglas,* 14; E. R. Hopkins, "At Fort Donelson," *Confederate Veteran* 38 (Mar. 1930):85.

21. Tuttle, *History of Camp Douglas,* 14; Burke, Civil War Journal, 6 Dec. 1864; *Chicago Tribune,* 26 May 1895.

22. Camp Douglas newspaper file, CHS.

23. Julian Edward Buckbee papers, CHS; OR Ser. II, Vol. VII, 664.

24. Private Duckworth is listed as a member of the Ninth Kentucky Cavalry and is buried in Chicago; Private Hunter, 14th Kentucky Cavalry, was removed home.

25. Page, "Prisoner of War," 63; Tuttle, *History of Camp Douglas,* 48; Whitehill, CW Misc. Collection, USAMHI.

26. Burke, Civil War Journal, 18 Aug. 1864; Edwin Greble Diary, Greble Collection, MS Division, LOC.

27. RG 393, v. 240:209; "Doorstep Reminiscences," *Confederate Veteran* 10 (Oct. 1902):453; Henry, "Treatment of Prisoners," 278.

28. Burke, Civil War Journal, 22 Aug. 1864.

29. Ibid, 27 Aug. 1864.

30. Ibid; Cliett, "Two Years of Prison Life," 31.

31. RG 249, v. 8.

32. OR Ser. II, Vol. VII, 694, 767, 1083.

33. Greble diary, 28 Aug. 1864.

34. OR Ser. II, Vol. VII, 1067.

CHAPTER FIFTEEN

1. W. H. H. Terrell, *Indiana in the War of the Rebellion* (Indianapolis: Indiana Historical Bureau, 1960), 43-48; Burke, Civil War Journal, 15 Aug., 7 Sep. 1864; Greble diary, 6 Sep. 1864.

2. Greble diary, 16 Aug. 1864.

3. Burke, Civil War Journal, 8 Sep. 1864; Kelly, "History of Camp Douglas," 74.

4. OR Ser. II, Vol. VII, 1067.

5. Ibid., 703, 767.

6. Ibid., 615-23, 793.

7. *Battles and Leaders of the Civil War,* IV:424; William Joseph Stier, "Death of a Cavalier: The Demise of John Hunt Morgan," *North South Trader's Civil War* 22 (Jul.-Aug. 1995):22-27.

8. RG 393, v. 239; OR Ser. II, Vol. VII, 795, 809-10; RG 393, v. 246, SO 332.

9. RG 393, v. 244, GO 85.

10. Greble diary, 9 Sep. 1864.

11. OR Ser. II, Vol. VII, 840-41.

12. *Chicago Tribune,* 26 May 1895.

13. OR Ser. II, Vol. VII, 861.

14. Greble diary, 25 Aug., 20 Sep. 1864.

15. Burke, Civil War Journal, 24 Sep. 1864.

16. Ibid., 26-29 Sep.; 3 Oct. 1864.

17. Ibid., 26, 29, Sep.; 1 Oct. 1864; RG 393, v. 334:433.

18. Court Martial Records of the Office of the Judge Advocate General, RG 153, Box NN 2841.

19. Compiled Service Records of the Confederate Army, Microcopy 311, Roll 13, NA.

20. OR Ser. II, Vol. VII, 897.

21. *Chicago Tribune,* 29 Sep. 1864.

22. Burke, Civil War Journal, 28 Sep. 1864.

23. RG 393, v. 239:13.

24. Ibid, v. 244, GO 95.

25. Froman, "Interior View of Camp Douglas Conspiracy," 65.

26. Bean, "Seventeen Months in Camp Douglas," 311.

27. *Confederate Veteran* 22:311.

28. OR Ser. II, Vol. VII, 907; Greble diary, 2 Oct. 1864.

29. Burke, Civil War Journal, 2 Oct. 1864.

30. OR Ser. II, Vol. VII, 913.

31. Burke, Civil War Journal, 5 Oct. 1864; Camp Douglas Hospital Register, 215.

32. Burke, Civil War Journal, 9 Oct. 1864.

33. Ibid., 19 Oct. 1864.

34. OR Ser. II, Vol. VII, 767; Greble diary, 11 Oct. 1864.

35. Burke, Civil War Diary, 2-23 Oct. 1864; Page, "Prisoner of War," 63.

36. OR Ser. II, Vol. VII, 795; Page, "Prisoner of War," 63; *Medical and Surgical History,* Vol. I, Part III:49.

37. OR Ser. II, Vol. VII, 913.

38. Hunt and Brown, *Brevet Brigadier Generals in Blue,* 288; OR Ser. II, Vol. VII, 959-60.

39. OR Ser. II, Vol. VII, 954.

40. Ibid., 954-55.

41. RG 393, v. 234:458.

42. *Confederate Veteran* 8:63; Burke, Civil War Journal, 14 Jul. 1864.

43. Burke, Civil War Journal, 28 Aug. 1864.

44. RG 393, v. 241:2:6.

45. Greble diary, Oct. 15, 1864.

46. OR Ser. II, Vol. VII, 995.

47. Ibid., 1006, 1058-59.

48. Ibid., 1026-27; Burke, Civil War Journal, 27 Oct. 1864.

49. Burke, Civil War Journal, 6, 10 Jun., 25 Oct. 1864.

50. Bean, "Seventeen Months in Camp Douglas," 22:270.

51. Greble diary, 24 Oct. 1864; Francis B. Heitman, *Historical Register and Dictionary of U.S. Army Officers* (Washington: U.S. Government Printing Office, 1903), 885.

52. Currey, *Chicago: Its History and Its Builders,* II:139; Andreas, *History of Chicago,* II:308.

53. OR Ser. II, Vol. VII, 1083.

54. *Chicago Tribune,* 31 Oct. 1864; Burke, Civil War Journal, 29 Oct. 1864.

55. Burke, Civil War Journal, 31 Oct. 1864.

56. OR Ser. II, Vol. VII, 1067; RG 393, v. 234:439.

57. RG 393, v. 234:439.

CHAPTER SIXTEEN

1. Starr, *Colonel Grenfell's Wars,* 187-88; Klement, *Dark Lanterns,* 197.

2. Cole, *Era of the Civil War,* 260-61.

3. Ibid., 300, 305, 307.

4. Starr, *Colonel Grenfell's Wars,* 148.

5. Robbins, "The Greatest Scoundrel," 56-57; Starr, *Colonel Grenfell's Wars,* 150.

6. Grant, *Fight for a City,* 14; Starr, *Colonel Grenfell's Wars,* 155-56.

7. Klement, *Dark Lanterns,* 196.

8. Starr, *Colonel Grenfell's Wars,* 156.

9. Ibid., 157.

10. Ibid., 155, 157-58.

11. Ibid., 159.

12. Charles Walsh resided on Ellis Avenue, one block east of the camp. *Bailey's Chicago Street Directory, 1864-65.* A report received at camp on 6 May 1864 that a Mrs. Walsh who lived near Camp Douglas was aiding prisoners to escape by using her small daughter probably referred to this family. RG 393, v. 237:186; Starr, *Colonel Grenfell's Wars,* 166.

13. 39th Congress, 2d Session, House of Representatives, Executive Doc. No. 50, *The Case of George St. Leger Grenfel* (Washington: U.S. Government Printing Office, 1867), 191.

14. Starr, *Colonel Grenfell's Wars,* 173, 177.

15. Froman, "Interior View of Camp Douglas Conspiracy," 67.

16. Ibid., 68; Burke, Civil War Journal, 4 Aug. 1864. Mrs. Sarah B. Walker, a "Southern lady" in Chicago, was appointed agent by friends of the prisoners to distribute goods to them at Camp Douglas. Andreas, *History of Chicago,* II:303.

17. RG 393, v. 234:454.

18. Thomas Henry Hines, "The Northwestern Conspiracy," *Southern Bivouac,* New Series II (Jun. 1886-May 1887):573.

19. Ibid., 508, 574.

20. Ibid., 574.

21. OR Ser. I, Vol. 39, Part 3:678.

22. Ibid.

23. RG 393.

24. OR Ser. I, Vol. 39, Part 3:739.

25. Tuttle, *History of Camp Douglas,* 27; RG 393, v. 429.

26. *Confederate Prisoners of War, 1861-1865,* Roll 53; Story, "Camp Douglas, 1861-1865," 94.

27. *Chicago Tribune,* Nov. 8 1864.

28. OR Ser. I, Vol. 39, Part 3:696.

29. Klement, *Dark Lanterns,* 208. Semmes was a resident of Chicago; RG 323, v. 235:13.

30. Tuttle, *History of Camp Douglas,* 31-33.

31. Hunt and Brown, *Brevet Brigadier Generals in Blue,* 599; Tuttle, *History of Camp Douglas,* 28.

32. RG 393, v. 235:53.

33. OR Ser. I, Vol, 39, Part 3:739.

34. RG 393, v. 235:31.

35. Ibid., v. 234; OR Ser. 1, Vol. 239, Part 3:762.

36. *Chicago Tribune,* 11 Nov. 1864.

37. Ibid., 8 Nov. 1864; Charles S. Winslow, *Biographical Sketches of Chicagoans,* Vol. 4, 1770-79, MS, Chicago Public Library; A. T. Andreas, *History of Cook County* (Chicago: A. T. Andreas, Publisher, 1884), 256; Raymond H.

Hamilton, *The Epic of Chicago* (Chicago: Willett, Clark & Co., 1910), 293-94.

38. Starr, *Colonel Grenfell's Wars,* 122-23.

39. RG 393, v. 235:67; John A. Marshall, *American Bastille: A History of the Illegal Arrests and Imprisonment of American Citizens During the Late Civil War* (New York: Da Capo Press, 1970), 98-101.

40. RG 393, v. 240:117-18.

41. Mark E. Neely, Jr., *The Fate of Liberty* (New York: Oxford University Press, 1991), 168.

42. Klement, *Dark Lanterns,* 207, 233; Story, "Camp Douglas, 1861-1865," 96.

43. Starr, *Colonel Grenfell's Wars,* 187-88.

44. Ibid., 188; Klement, *Dark Lanterns,* 197; House Executive Doc. No. 50, 67-68, 396. Klement cites: "Confederate Papers Relating to Citizens or Business Firms," NA; "John T. Shanks papers in Compiled Service Records of Confederate Soldiers Who Served in Organizations from Texas," NA.

45. RG 393, v. 235:261.

46. Starr, *Colonel Grenfell's Wars,* 225.

47. Ibid., 223; House Exec. Doc. 580-81.

48. Jon L. Wakely, *Biographical Dictionary of the Confederacy* (Westport: Greenwood Press, 1977), 310-11; Dorn, "General Benjamin J. Sweet," unpublished MS.

49. Klement, *Dark Lanterns,* 208.

50. Ibid., 196, 211; Starr, *Colonel Grenfell's Wars,* 227.

51. Starr, *Colonel Grenfell's Wars,* 230; Nancy D. Baird, "The Yellow Fever Plot," *Civil War Times* 7 (Nov. 1974):16-18.

52. *Ex Parte Milligan,* 4 Wall 2, 18 L. ED. 281 (1866).

53. OR Ser. II, Vol. VIII, 688-89.

54. Froman, "Interior View of Camp Douglas Conspiracy," 69; Story, "Camp Douglas, 1861-1865," 94.

55. RG 109, Roll 53; *Chicago Tribune,* 4 Apr. 1865; Basler, *Collected Works of Abraham Lincoln,* V:437.

56. Basler, *Collected Works of Abraham Lincoln,* VIII:123; Robbins, "The Greatest Scoundrel," 90.

57. Otway B. Norvell, "The Secret Order in Camp Douglas," *Confederate*

Veteran 11 (Apr. 1903):168-71. Norvell was a member of the Supreme Council.

58. RG 393, v. 234:448.

59. Klement, *Dark Lanterns,* 213, quoting *Chicago Times* of 20 Feb. 1865; RG 323, v. 235:7; Burke, Civil War Journal, 7 Nov. 1864.

60. RG 323, v. 244:16; SO No. 96, RG 395, v. 244; Compiled Service Records, Sixth U.S. Volunteer Infantry, NA.

CHAPTER SEVENTEEN

1. OR Ser. II, Vol. VII, 1104-05; Burke, Civil War Journal, 10 Nov. 1864.

2. RG 393, v. 239:14.

3. OR Ser. II, Vol. VII, 1134-36; Long, "Camp Douglas: A Hellish Den," 94.

4. Burke, Civil War Journal, 9-20 Nov. 1864.

5. RG 393, v. 239:29.

6. OR Ser. II, Vol. VII, 1117; *Battles and Leaders of the Civil War,* IV:107.

7. Kelly, "History of Camp Douglas," 149.

8. Burke, Civil War Journal, 22 Nov., 8 Dec. 1864.

9. Ibid., 21, 22 Nov. 1864.

10. OR Ser. II, Vol. VII, 1257.

11. RG 393, v. 246, SO 361, 408.

12. OR Ser. II, Vol. VII, 834-35; Burke, Civil War Journal, 3, 30 Nov., 3 Dec. 1864.

13. Burke, Civil War Journal, 24 Nov. 1864.

14. Ibid., 30 Nov. 1864.

15. RG 109, Box 116.

16. RG 393, v. 244, GO 121.

17. *Battles and Leaders of the Civil War,* IV:435, 441, 455; Copley, *Sketch of the Battle of Franklin, Tennessee,* 76-77.

18. Copley, *Sketch of the Battle of Franklin, Tennessee,* 46-47.

19. Ibid., 59.

20. Camp Douglas Hospital Records, Register 217.

21. OR Ser. II, Vol. VII, 1187-88.

22. Copley, *Sketch of the Battle of Franklin, Tennessee,* 88.

23. RG 94, Regimental Letter Book.

24. Ibid., Eighth VRC Ledger books.

25. RG 393, v. 244, GO 121.

26. Copley, *Sketch of the Battle of Franklin, Tennessee,* 88. The sewer lines ran from north to south at the east end of Prisoner's Square.

27. Ibid., 159-60.

28. Burke, Civil War Journal, 6 Dec. 1864.

29. Copley, *Sketch of the Battle of Franklin, Tennessee,* 160-61.

30. Burke, Civil War Journal, 29 Nov. 1864.

31. Ibid., 1 Feb. 1865.

32. Cliett, "Two Years of Prison Life," 17.

33. Copley, *Sketch of the Battle of Franklin, Tennessee,* 98-99.

34. Burke, Civil War Journal, 3 Jan. 1865; Copley, *Sketch of the Battle of Franklin, Tennessee,* 120-28.

35. Burke, Civil War Journal, 3 Jan. 1865.

36. P. H. Prince, "Hardship in Camp Douglas," *Confederate Veteran* 15 (Dec. 1907):565-66. Prince arrived on 23 November 1864.

37. Copley, *Sketch of the Battle of Franklin, Tennessee,* 144.

38. OR Ser. II, Vol. VII, 986-1003.

39. Henry, "Treatment of Southern Prisoners," I:278.

40. Sergeant T. B. Clore in Cornelius Hite's, "Man's Inhumanity to Man" *Confederate Veteran* 32 (Jun. 1924):218; Copley, *Sketch of the Battle of Franklin, Tennessee,* 135.

41. J. A. Templeton, "Prison Reminiscences," *Confederate Veteran* 34 (May 1926):196-97. Templeton was a prisoner from 4 October 1863 to 4 May 1865 and was in the dungeon once for attempting to dig a tunnel.

42. Sorensen, "Civil War Prisoner of War System," 33.

43. Burke, Civil War Journal, 31 Oct., 3 Nov. 1864. Burke saw the flames from a glue factory fire in Bridgeport, 12 blocks west of camp.

44. Bradley, "Horrors of Camp Douglas," 278.

45. *Medical and Surgical History,* Vol. I, Part III:49; Burke, Civil War Journal, 26 Jul. 1864.

46. Compiled Service Records, NA.

47. Copley, *Sketch of the Battle of Franklin, Tennessee,* 109. Prairie Bull was also known as Bull McCurley; Cook, "Villainous Inspectors at Camp Douglas," 406.

48. Compiled Service Records, NA.

49. Copley, *Sketch of the Battle of Franklin, Tennessee,* 103-10.

50. *Confederate Veteran* 16:406.

51. Prince, "Hardships in Camp Douglas," 565.

52. Ibid., 565.

53. Berry, "Prison Life in Camp Douglas," 11:37-38. The First Michigan left the camp in March 1864; Cook, "Villainous Inspectors at Camp Douglas," 406.

54. Burke, Civil War Journal, 3 Apr.; 3 Dec. 1864.

55. Bean, "Seventeen Months in Camp Douglas," 310.

56. RG 94, Eighth VRC Order Book.

57. Burke, Civil War Journal, 16 Sept. 1864.

58. Bean, "Seventeen Months in Camp Douglas," 310; OR Ser. III, Vol. IV, 1037.

59. Burke, Civil War Journal, 9 Dec. 1864; Copley, *Sketch of the Battle of Franklin, Tennessee,* 143.

60. OR Ser. II, Vol. VII, 1199-1200, 1207; Burke, Civil War Journal, 12 Dec. 1864; Hesseltine, *Civil War Prisons,* 208.

61. Also on the committee were Joseph D. Hunt, Thomas J. Chambers, and W. T. Brantly; OR Ser. II, Vol. VII, 1187-88.

62. Burke, Civil War Journal, 16 Dec. 1864.

63. Ibid., 15 Dec. 1864; Karlen, "Postal History of Camp Douglas," 930.

64. Burke, Civil War Journal, 19 Dec. 1864.

65. Ibid., 23, 26 Dec. 1864.

66. RG 393, v. 239:49-55.

67. Burke, Civil War Journal, 8, 23 Dec. 1864.

68. OR Ser. II, Vol. VII, 1275.

69. Burke, Civil War Journal, 31 Dec. 1864.; *Medical and Surgical History,* Vol. I, Part III:45.

70. Andreas, *History of Chicago,* 2:303; OR Ser. II, Vol. VII, 834-35.

71. RG 393; Camp Douglas Letter Book, 282, 462, CHS; RG 92.

72. RG 393, v. 244:134; R. D. Rugeley, "Escape from Camp Douglas," *Confederate Veteran* 9 (Jan. 1901):30; RG 393, v. 244:128.

73. Burke, Civil War Journal, 1 Jan. 1865.

CHAPTER EIGHTEEN

1. Copley, *Sketch of the Battle of Franklin, Tennessee,* 184.

2. Bradley, "Horrors of Camp Douglas," 276.

3. Frederick Francis Cook, *Bygone Days in Chicago* (Chicago: A. C. McClurg & Co., 1910), 38-39; John Kaufhold, "The Elmira Observatory," *Civil War Times* 4 (Jul. 1977):31, 33; J. T. Lowry, "Experience as a Prisoner of War," MS Collection, William R. Perkins Library, Duke University.

4. Cliett, "Two Years of Prison Life," 23.

5. Compiled Service Records of Confederate Officers and Enlisted Men, NA.

6. Tuttle, *History of Camp Douglas,* 16.

7. Report of the Illinois Adjutant General, I:127; "Dear Emma," John L. Williams to his niece, 18 July 1862, MS Division, LOC; *Chicago Tribune,* 7 Mar. 1864.

8. Chicago Public Library, Special Collections.

9. Bell I. Wiley, "Soldier Newspapers of the Civil War," *Civil War Times* 4 (Jul. 1977):27.

10. Burke, Civil War Journal, 28 Mar. 1864; Tuttle, *History of Camp Douglas,* 17.

11. Diary of William Gramling, Chemung County Historical Society.

12. Tuttle, *History of Camp Douglas,* 8.

13. Copley, *Sketch of the Battle of Franklin, Tennessee,* 180.

14. Burke, Civil War Journal, 9 Jan., 27 Mar. 1864.

15. Ibid., 2 Feb. 1865.

16. Ibid., 21 Apr. 1864; Copley, *Sketch of the Battle of Franklin, Tennessee,* 172-73.

17. Burke, Civil War Journal, 5 Oct. 1863; Currey, *Chicago: Its History and Its Builders,* I:135.

18. Burke, Civil War Journal, 10 Apr. 1864; Currey, *Chicago: Its History and Its Builders,* II:135.

CHAPTER NINETEEN

1. OR Ser. II, Vol. VII, 44.

2. Bradley, "Horrors of Camp Douglas," 273.

3. *Confederate Veteran* 32 (Jun. 1924):218.

4. Ibid, 16 (Aug. 1908):421.

5. Copley, *Sketch of the Battle of Franklin, Tennessee,* 143; Burke, Civil War Journal, 11 Feb. 1865.

6. J. A. Yeager, "A Boy With Morgan," *Confederate Veteran* 34 (Aug. 1926):294; *Confederate Soldiers, Sailors and Civilians Who Died at Camp Douglas*; Burke, Civil War Journal, 3 Jun. 1864.

7. OR Ser. II, Vol. VIII, 66-67; Burke, Civil War Journal, 6 Jan. 1865.

8. Burke, Civil War Journal, 13 Jan. 1865.

9. Compiled Military Service Records, NA.

10. Burke, Civil War Journal, 15 Jan. 1865.

11. RG 94, Eighth VRC Ledger Books.

12. Camp Douglas Post Hospital Records, NA.

13. RG 94, Regimental Letters, Circulars, and Endorsement Book.

14. Burke, Civil War Journal, 13 Jan. 1865; Tuttle, *History of Camp Douglas,* 20.

15. OR Ser. II, Vol. VIII, 66.

16. RG 109, Box 116; OR Ser. II, Vol. VIII, 76.

17. *Battles and Leaders of the Civil War,* IV:642-43; Burke, Civil War Journal, 17 Jan. 1865.

18. OR Ser. II, Vol. VII, 115-16.

19. Burke, Civil War Journal, 27 Jan. 1865.

20. OR Ser. II, Vol. VIII, 144-45.

21. RG 393, v. 245:120.

22. *Medical and Surgical History,* Vol. I, Part III:49.

23. Burke, Civil War Journal, 134.

24. OR Ser. II, Vol. VIII, 337-51.

25. Burke, Civil War Journal, 9 Feb. 1865.

26. Ibid., 2 Feb. 1865.

27. RG 393, v. 239.

28. OR Ser. II, Vol. VIII, 210; *Chicago Tribune,* 16 Jan. 1865.

29. Burke, Civil War Journal, 13, 17 Feb. 1865.

30. Ibid., 20 Feb. 1865; OR Ser. II, Vol. VIII, 227, 257, 289; Kelly, "History of Camp Douglas," 119.

31. OR Ser. II, Vol. VIII, 219, 220.

32. *Chicago Tribune,* 18 Feb. 1865.

33. RG 109, Box 117, Collection of Confederate Records.

34. *Confederate Prisoners of War, 1861-65,* RG 109, Roll 58.

35. Burke, Civil War Journal, 20, 26 Feb. 1865.

36. Ibid., 2 Mar. 1865. These were favorite hotels in Richmond for those who could afford them.

37. Burke, Civil War Journal, 2 Mar. 1865.

38. Ibid., 11 Mar. 1865.

39. RG 393, v. 241:227; OR Ser. II, Vol. VIII, 360.

40. Goodspeed and Healy, *History of Cook County,* I:495.

41. Kelly, "History of Camp Douglas," 131; Report of the Illinois Adjutant General, I:127.

42. OR Ser. II, Vol. VIII, 322; Dorris, *Pardon and Amnesty Under Lincoln and Johnson,* 157.

43. Hunt and Brown, *Brevet Brigadier Generals in Blue,* 288.

44. OR Ser. II, Vol. VIII, 401.

45. RG 393, v. 242.

46. RG 323, v. 235:263.

47. RG 393, v. 244, GO 8.

48. OR Ser. II, Vol. VIII, 1001.

49. *Chicago Tribune,* 3 Apr. 1865, reporting the rearrest of a suspect in the conspiracy.

50. Ibid., 12 Apr. 1865; Goodspeed and Healy, *History of Cook County,* I:495-96.

51. *Chicago Tribune,* 12 Apr. 1865.

52. J. N. Hunter, "Courage of a Georgian in Camp Douglas," *Confederate Veteran* 15 (Sep. 1907):389

53. *Confederate Veteran* 15:566.

54. J. S. Rosamond, "In Camp Douglas in 1865," *Confederate Veteran* 16 (Aug. 1908):421

55. Civil War Letters of Silas Jasper Mann, Company G, 45th Ohio Infantry, and Company B, Eighth VRC, courtesy of Dennis Keesee, New Albany, Ohio; Raymond Dorn, "General Benjamin J. Sweet."

56. *Chicago Tribune,* 2 May 1865.

57. RG 249, v. 13.

58. RG 393, v. 235:312.

59. Ibid., v. 241:317; v. 235:344, 352.

60. Ibid., v. 235:359; v. 239:97.

61. OR Ser. II, Vol. VIII, 538.

62. Inspection reports of Captain Wells Sponable, RG 109, Box 116.

63. Karlen, "Postal History of Camp Douglas," 960; RG 393, v. 239:191.

64. RG 393, v. 235:393, 240:389; *Chicago Tribune,* 12 May 1865.

65. *Chicago Tribune,* 13 May 1865.

66. OR Ser. II, Vol. VIII, 1002; RG 393, v. 244; GO 18.

67. Ibid., 700-01.

CHAPTER TWENTY

1. *Chicago Tribune,* 4 Feb. 1863.

2. Bradley, "Horrors of Camp Douglas," 266; Wiley, "Common Soldier of the Civil War," 19; RG 109, Roll 56; "Dear Ma," George A. Pope to Mrs. L. J. Pope; *Pulaski Citizen,* 20 Jan. 1876, 8 May 1890, 12 Dec. 1901, courtesy of Gilbert D. Dickey.

3. Diary of Col. James A. Mulligan, CHS.

4. The 29th Regiment, U. S. Colored Troops, Report of the Illinois Adjutant General, VIII:777; "In Vinculis: A Prisoner of War," *Civil War Times* 9 (Jan. 1985):26-33; *Confederate Veteran* 23:26; Lowry, "Experience as a Prisoner of War."

5. Harder memoir.

6. RG 393, v. 234:82; *Autobiography of Henry Morton Stanley,* 166.

7. *Confederate Veteran* 23 (Apr. 1915):188.

8. *Confederate Prisoners of War, 1861-65;* RG 109, Roll 56.

9. Burke, Civil War Journal, 27 Feb. 1864; 17 Jun. 1864; M. L. Vesey, "Camp Douglas in 1862," *Confederate Veteran* 38 (Mar. 1930):300; RG 393, v. 243:186; OR Ser. II, Vol. VIII, 987-1003.

10. Tuttle, *History of Camp Douglas,* 11-12.

11. Report of the Illinois Adjutant General, 13 Jul. 1865.

12. *Halpin and Bailey's Chicago Street Directory, 1864-65*; RG 393, v. 238.

13. *Medical and Surgical History,* Vol. I, Part III:49; RG 393, v. 239.

14. *Medical and Surgical History,* Vol. I, Part III:49.

15. Ibid., I:46.

16. Ibid., I:67; RG 109, Roll 58.

17. OR Ser. II, Vol. VII, 1243; Vol. VIII, 999-1003.

18. *Black's Medical Dictionary,* 199.

19. Elmira Military and Prisoner of War Cemetery file, Box 4, RG 92.

20. National Cemetery Data Book, 129-131.

21. Sorensen, "Civil War Prisoner of War System," 24, 25; OR Ser. II, Vol. VII, 995-1000; Burke, Civil War Journal, 12 Mar. 1865, attending church in Richmond. "The ladies and citizens were generally dressed fine."

22. OR Ser. II, Vol. VIII, 986-1003.

23. *Medical and Surgical History,* Vol. I, Part III:63.

24. RG 393, v. 241:358, 380.

25. RG 249, v. 7.

26. *Chicago Tribune,* 19 May 1865.

27. Story, "Camp Douglas, 1861-1865," 112; *Chicago Tribune,* 10 July 1865; RG 393, v. 235:397; v. 239:276.

28. Minutes of the Executive Committee of the Board of Trustees, 11 June 1864, The Old University of Chicago Records; Box 2, Folder 7.

29. RG 92.

30. OR Ser. II, Vol. VIII, 714; *Chicago Tribune,* 3 Oct. 1865; Kelly, "History of Camp Douglas," 109.

31. Report of Illinois Adjutant General, I:121-22.

32. Kelly, "History of Camp Douglas," 79, 82.

33. Ibid., 86; RG 393, v. 234:282.

34. RG 393, v. 233; Karlen, "Postal History of Camp Douglas," 822.

35. *Chicago Tribune,* 4 Dec. 1865; RG 92.

36. Chicago Title & Trust Co., (Pre-fire Records), Book 340:192-95.

37. RG 92; Camp Douglas newspaper file, CHS; Camp Douglas, Inventory No. 1919.33, CHS.

38. Chicago Historical Society, Camp Douglas Newspaper File.

39. RG 92.

40. Story, "Camp Douglas, 1861-1865," 115; RG 249, William Hoffman Papers; Colbert, *Chicago Historical and Statistical Sketch,* II:95, Tuttle, *History of Camp Douglas,* 15; *Chicago Tribune,* 28 Jan. 1863; Kelly, "History of Camp Douglas," 107.

41. Hesseltine, *Civil War Prisons,* 140, 243; Kubalanza, "A Comparative Study," 53.

42. Copley, *Sketch of the Battle of Franklin, Tennessee,* 166.

43. OR Ser. III, Vol. V, 147.

44. Rosamond, "In Camp Douglas," 421.

45. Mamie Yeary, ed., *Reminiscences of the Boys in Gray, 1861-1865* (Dallas: Smith & Lamar, 1912), 88.

CHAPTER TWENTY-ONE

1. OR Ser. II, Vol. VI, 525.

2. RG 92, Cemeterial Files, Box 141.

3. I. J. Bryan, *History of Lincoln Park* (Chicago: The Commissioners, 1899);

"Historical Register of the Twenty-Two Superseded Park Districts" (Chicago Park District, MS, 1941), 132; *Guide Map to Chicago* (Chicago: Chas. Shober & Co., 1868) shows "Rebel Graves" near the shore line 150 yards north of North Avenue and State Streets.

4. *Chicago Tribune,* 11 Dec. 1862; 16 Feb. 1863.

5. "Report of the Superintendent of Cemetery Grounds and Public Parks," CHS (10 April, 1863), 70.

6. RG 92, Cemeterial Files, Box 141.

7. Ibid.

8. Page, "The Prisoners of War," 8:63; *Confederate Prisoners of War, 1861-65,* Roll 58.

9. Andreas, *History of Chicago,* II:450

10. RG 92, Cemeterial Files, Box 141; Common Council Proceedings, 1861-65, Illinois Regional Archives Depository, Northeastern University.

11. The Quartermaster count of bodies sent home was 143 soldiers and 39 civilians. *Confederate Soldiers Sailors and Civilians Who Died at Camp Douglas.*

12. Clay W. Holmes, *The Elmira Prison Camp* (New York: G. Putnam's Sons, 1912), 130, 134.

13. RG 92, Cemeterial Files, Box 141.

14. Ibid.

15. Ibid.

16. 56th Congress, 1st Session, House of Representatives, Report No. 1077. *Confederate Mound in Oak Woods Cemetery,* Chicago, Ill., (17 April 1900):2. Each section consisted of five burial trenches with four walkways, RG 92, Cemeterial Files, Box 141.

17. RG 92, Cemeterial Files, Box 141.

18. *Halpin & Bailey Chicago Street Directory, 1861-65*; Andreas, *History of Chicago,* II:49-50.

19. Day Book of Burials, C. H. Jordan, 1866, MS Collection, CHS.

20. *Chicago Tribune,* 16 Sep. 1864.

21. *Chicago Messenger,* 16 Apr. 1914, interview with Mr. Scharf, Sr; MS Collection, CHS; *Chicago Times,* 15 Apr. 1867.

22. Oak Woods Cemetery Archives, Confederate Register, 36-203; Chicago Common Council Proceedings, 1861-65.

23. RG 92, Cemeterial Files, Box 141.

24. Camp Douglas Hospital Records, RG 94, Entry 544, Field Record of Hospitals. Illinois, Register 215; 15th VRC Ledger Books, Companies A to F.

25. RG 92, Cemeterial Files, Box 141; Compiled Service Records of United States Colored Troops, M589.

26. Camp Douglas Hospital Records, RG 94, Entry 544. Field Record of Hospitals, Illinois, Register 215.

27. Compiled Pension Records, NA.

28. Office of the Quartermaster General, RG 92, Cemeterial Files, Box 41.

29. Ibid.

30. Ibid.

31. John P. Hickman, "Confederate Monument in Chicago," *Confederate Veteran* 1 (Nov. 1893):346; *Chicago Daily News,* 24 Aug. 1968.

32. Camp Douglas Newspaper file, Chicago Municipal Reference Library; John M. Taylor, "Grover Cleveland and the Rebel Banners," *Civil War Times* 4 (Sep./Oct. 1993):22-24; Oak Woods Cemetery publication, *Chicago as We Remember Her* (1951), 18-19.

33. House of Representatives, Report No. 1077:2,4.

34. Ibid., Document No. 1105:3,4.

35. RG 92, Cemeterial Files, Box 141; *Confederate Soldiers, Sailors and Civilians Who Died as Prisoners of War at Camp Douglas.*

36. *The Israelite, A Weekly Periodical,* Cincinnati, Ohio, 28 Feb. 1862; *Confederate Soldiers, Sailors and Civilians Who Died at Camp Douglas.* Hebrew Benevolent Society Cemetery Records, Register of the Range of Adults, 25, Grave 17, "Theodore Hirsh. Dec. 15 1864 Prisoner of Camp Douglas."

Bibliography

I. PRIMARY SOURCES

1. Manuscript Materials

Baptism Records. St. James Catholic Church, Chicago.

Calvary Cemetery Archives, Evanston.

Camp Douglas Newspaper File, Autograph Letters, Vol. 49.

Chicago Historical Society, Miscellaneous Manuscripts.

Chicago Park District.

City of Chicago Municipal Reference Library.

Hebrew Benevolent Society Archives, Chicago.

Illinois State Historical Library, Springfield.

Illinois State Archives, Springfield.

Illinois Regional Archives Depository, Northeastern Illinois University, Chicago.

Kentucky State Archives, Louisville.

Library of Congress.

Louisiana State University, Baton Rouge.

Michigan State Archives, Lansing.

National Archives. Record Groups 92, 109, 249, 393.

Newberry Library, Chicago.

Museum of the Confederacy, Richmond.

Oak Woods Cemetery Archives, Chicago.

Pre-fire Records. Chicago Title & Trust Co.

Regenstein Library, University of Chicago.

Rush-Presbyterian-St. Luke's Medical Center Archives, Chicago.

Tennessee State Archives, Nashville.

United States Army Military History Institute.

2. Government Publications

Historical Register and Dictionary of the U.S. Army. Government Printing Office, Washington, 1903.

House of Representatives, Executive Document 50. 39th Congress, 2nd Session. *The Case of George St. Leger Grenfel.*

House of Representatives, Report No. 1077, 56th Congress, 1st Session. *Confederate Mound in Oak Woods Cemetery.* National Archives. Selected Records of the War Department Relating to Confederate Prisoners of War, 1861-1865, Microcopy 598, Record Group 109.

The Medical and Surgical History of the War of the Rebellion, 3 Vols. Government Printing Office, Washington, 1888.

The War of the Rebellion: A Compilation of the Official Records of the Union and Confederate Armies, 70 Vols., 128 books. Government Printing Office, Washington, 1901.

3. State Publications

State of Illinois. Illinois State Historical Library, *Report of the Adjutant General, 1861-66.* Springfield.

State of Michigan. Michigan State Historical Library, Report of the Adjutant General, *Record of Service of Michigan Volunteers in the Civil War.* Lansing.

4. City of Chicago Publications

Proceedings of the Common Council, 1861-1865. Illinois Regional Archives Depository.

Reports of the Department of Public Works, 1861-1867. Chicago Historical Society.

5. Newspapers

Chicago Tribune

Chicago Times

Chicago Inter-Ocean

Chicago Evening Journal

Chicago Daily News

Chicago Messenger

Chicago Times

Christian Times

Greenville Advocate

Pulaski Citizen

The Israelite, Cincinnati, Ohio

Sunday Record Herald

Ottawa Free Trader

6. Diaries, Letters, Memoirs, Personal Narratives and Recollections

Barrow, Willie M. Civil War Diary in *Louisiana Historical Quarterly*. Edited by Wendell H. Stephenson and Edwin A. Davis. 17 (1934):436-51, 712-31.

Baxter, Marion F. 20th Miss. Inf. Regt., Diary. Lionel F. Baxter Collection, United States Army Military History Institute.

Bean, R. T. "Seventeen Months in Camp Douglas." *Confederate Veteran*. 22 (Jun. 1914):270.

Belknap, Charles W. 125th N.Y. Inf. Regt., Diary. Civil War Times Illustrated Collection, United States Army Military History Institute.

Benedict, C. G. *Vermont in the Civil War.* 2 Vols. Burlington: The Free Press Association, 1888.

Berry, J. M. "Prison Life in Camp Douglas." *Confederate Veteran*. 11 (Apr. 1903):37-38.

Bradley, M. J. "The Horrors of Camp Douglas as related by a prisoner," in Griffin Frost's *Camp and Prison Journal,* Quincy Herald Book and Job Office, Quincy, 1867.

Branch, J. T. "Account of Escapes from Camp Morton." *Confederate Veteran*. 8 (Feb. 1900):71.

Bross, William. "History of Camp Douglas," in *Reminiscences of Chicago During the Civil War.* Mabel McIlvaine, ed. Chicago: Lakeside Press, R. R. Donnelley & Sons, 1914. (First published in "Biographical Sketch of the Late Gen. B. J. Sweet." *History of Camp Douglas*. A paper read before the Chicago Historical Society. Chicago: Jansen, McClurg & Co., 1878.)

Buckley, James. Co. F. 45th Ill. Inf. Regt. Letter dated 19 December 1861 reporting mutiny of the Mechanic Fusileers. Original letter owned by Alan C. Hunt, Springfield, Illinois.

Burke, Curtis R. Civil War Journal in *Indiana Magazine of History*. Edited by Pamela J. Bennett. 65 (Dec. 1969):283-327; 66 (June 1970):110-72; (Dec. 1970):318-61; 67 (June 1971):129-70.

Campbell, Andrew Jackson. Civil War Diary. Edited by Jill K. Garrett. Special Collections, Chicago Public Library.

Cliett, Oscar A. "Incidents and Reminiscences of Two Years of Prison Life." Manuscript. Published in *The Home Journal,* Perry, Houston County, Georgia, 1899.

Clore, T. B. in Cornelius Hite's "Man's Inhumanity to Man." *Confederate Veteran*. 32 (Jun. 1924):218.

Coke, James S. *Confederate Veteran*. 14 (Oct. 1906):38.

Cook, Frederick Francis. *Bygone Days in Chicago, Recollections of the "Garden City" of the Sixties*. Chicago: A. C. McClurg & Co., 1910.

Cook, J. W. "Villainous Inspectors at Camp Douglas." *Confederate Veteran*. 16 (Aug. 1908):406.

Copley, John M. *A Sketch of the Battle of Franklin, Tennessee, With Reminiscences of Camp Douglas*. Austin: E. Von Boeckman, 1893.

De Graff, Nicholas. 115th N. Y. Inf. Regt., Diary. Civil War Times Illustrated Collection, United States Army Military History Institute.

Duke, Basil W. *Reminiscences of General Basil W. Duke, CSA*. New York: Doubleday, Page & Co., 1911.

Duke, Basil W. *A History of Morgan's Cavalry*. Edited by Cecil F. Holland. Bloomington: Indiana University Press, 1960.

Foute, Samuel L. "Dear Sir." Letter about life as a prisoner of war at Camp Douglas in 1862. Tragg Collection, Manuscript Division, Library of Congress.

Froman, B. R. "An Interior View of the Camp Douglas Conspiracy." *Southern Bivouac.* 1-No.2 (Oct. 1882):63-69.

Garrett, Jill K. Collection, ca. 1800-1969. Tennessee State Library and Archives, Nashville.

Hankenson, Hazel. "Where Dixie Sleeps Farthest North." *Confederate Veteran.* 33 (Aug. 1925):301.

Greble, Edwin. 196th Pennsylvania Inf. Regt., Diary. Manuscript Division, Library of Congress.

Harris, W. T. *Confederate Veteran.* 33 (Nov. 1925):429.

Harrison, Carter H. *Growing Up With Chicago.* Chicago: Bobbs-Merrill Co., 1944.

Henry, T. D. "Treatment of Prisoners During the War." *Southern Historical Society Papers.* 1 (Jan.-Jun. 1876):278.

Hickman, John P. "The Confederate Monument in Chicago." *Confederate Veteran.* 1 (Nov. 1893):346.

Hines, Thomas Henry. "The Northwestern Conspiracy." *Southern Bivouac.* New Series II (Jun. 1866-Mar. 1887):437-45, 500-10, 567-74.

Hopkins, E. R. "At Fort Donelson." *Confederate Veteran.* 38 (Mar. 1930):85.

Hunter, J. N. "Courage of a Georgian in Camp Douglas." *Confederate Veteran.* 15 (Sep. 1907):389.

Kirk, Edmund [Gilmore, J. R.]. "Three Days at Camp Douglas" in *Our Young Folks.* 1 (Apr.-Jun. 1865):252-60, 291-98, 357-60.

Lamons, J. T. *Confederate Veteran.* 7 (Jan. 1899):28.

Livermore, Mary A. *My Story of the War.* Hartford: A. D. Worthington & Co., 1889.

Lowry, J. T. "Experience as a Prisoner of War." Manuscript Collection, William R. Perkins Library, Duke University. (First published in *Confederate Veteran.* 18 (Jul. 1910):334-35.)

Mackey, James T. Diary. Eleanor S. Brockenbrough Library, Museum of the Confederacy, Richmond.

McNeill, Malcolm. Papers. North Carolina State Archives, Raleigh.

Moore, J. J. "Camp Douglas." *Confederate Veteran.* 11 (Jun. 1903):270-71.

Norvell, Otway B. "The Secret Order in Camp Douglas." *Confederate Veteran.* 11 (Apr. 1903):168-71.

Page, T. M. "The Prisoner of War." *Confederate Veteran.* 8 (Feb. 1900):64.

Pope, George A., "Dear Ma," Letters from Camp Douglas, 1862. William R. Perkins Library, Duke University.

Prince, P. H. "Hardship in Camp Douglas." *Confederate Veteran.* 15 (Dec. 1907):565-66.

Robison, John W. Papers, 1861-1863. Tennessee State Library and Archives.

Rosamond, J. S. "In Camp Douglas in 1865." *Confederate Veteran.* 16 (Aug. 1908):421.

Rugeley, J. T. "Escape from Camp Douglas." *Confederate Veteran.* 9 (Jan. 1901):30.

Ryan, Milton A. 14th Miss. Inf. Regt. "Experiences of a Confederate Soldier in the Civil War." Civil War Times Illustrated Collection, United States Army Military History Institute.

Smith, Benjamin T. *Recollections of the Late War, Private Smith's Journal.* Edited by Clyde C. Walton. Chicago: Lakeside Press, R. R. Donnelley & Sons, 1963. (Manuscript is in the Illinois State Historical Library, Springfield.)

Stanley, Dorothy, ed. *Autobiography of Sir Henry Morton Stanley.* New York: Houghton Mifflin Co., 1909.

Taylor, Charles E. 20th Miss. Inf. Regt. Diary. (Manuscript is owned by Medford H. Roe, Jr., Mobile, Alabama.)

Templeton, J. A. "Prison Reminiscences." *Confederate Veteran.* 34 (May 1926):196-97.

Terrell, Spot F. "A Confederate Private at Fort Donelson." *The American Historical Review.* 31:477-484. New York: Macmillan Co., 1926.

Thompson, Benjamin W. 111th N.Y. Inf. Regt., Diary. Civil War Times Illustrated Collection, United States Army Military History Institute.

Tuttle, Rev. E. B. *The History of Camp Douglas; Including Official Report of Gen. B. J. Sweet; With Anecdotes of the Rebel Prisoners.* Chicago: J. R. Walsh & Co., 1865.

Vesey, M. L. "Camp Douglas in 1862." *Confederate Veteran.* 38 (Mar. 1930):299-300.

Williams, John L. "Dear Niece." Letter about life as a prisoner at Camp Douglas in 1862. Manuscript Division, Library of Congress.

Yeager, J. A. "A Boy With Morgan." *Confederate Veteran.* 34 (Aug. 1926):294-98.

Yeary, Mamie., ed. *Reminiscences of the Boys in Gray, 1861-1865.* Dallas: Smith & Lamar, 1885.

II. SECONDARY SOURCES

1. Histories

A. General Accounts

Battles and Leaders of the Civil War. 4 Vols. New York: Thomas Yoseloff, & Co., 1956.

Calkins, William W. *The History of the 104th Regiment, Illinois Volunteer Infantry, 1862-1865.* Chicago: Donahue & Henneberry, 1895.

Johnson, Rossiter. *A History of the War of Secession.* New York: Wessels & Bissell Co., 1910.

Leech, Margaret. *Reveille in Washington, 1860-1865.* New York: Time, Inc., 1962.

Pollard, Edward A. *Southern History of the War.* New York: Fairfax Press, 1866.

Randall, J. G. *The Civil War and Reconstruction.* Chicago: D. C. Heathe & Co., 1937.

Trimble, Harvey M. *History of the Ninety-Third Volunteer Infantry.* Chicago: Blakely Printing Co., 1898.

B. Illinois Histories

Cole, Arthur, C. *The Era of the Civil War, 1848-1870.* Vol. 3. Springfield: Illinois Centennial Commission, 1919.

C. Chicago Histories

Andreas, A. T. *History of Chicago.* 3 Vols. Chicago: A. T. Andreas Co., 1885.

Colbert, Elias A. *Chicago, Historical and Statistical Sketch of the Garden City.* Chicago: P. T. Sherlock, 1868.

Currey, J. Seymour. *Chicago, Its History and Its Builders.* 5 Vols. Chicago: S. J. Clarke Publishing Co., 1912.

Dedmon, Emmet. *Fabulous Chicago.* New York: Random House, 1954.

Gilbert, Paul and Charles Lee Bryson. *Chicago and Its Makers.* Chicago: Felix Mendelsohn, 1929.

Hamilton, Raymond H. *The Epic of Chicago.* Chicago: Willett, Clark & Co, 1910.

Kirkland, Caroline., ed. *Chicago Yesterdays.* Chicago: Doughaday & Co., 1919.

Kirkland, Joseph. *The Story of Chicago.* Chicago: Dibble Publishing Co., 1892.

Kogan, Herman and Lloyd Wendt. *Pictorial History of Chicago.* New York: E. P. Putnam & Co., 1958.

Lewis, Lloyd and Henry Justin Smith. *Chicago, the History of Its Reputation.* New York: Harcourt, Brace & Co., 1929.

Longstreet, Stephen. *Chicago, 1860-1919.* New York: David McKay Co., Inc., 1973.

McIlvaine, Mabel, ed. *Reminiscences of Chicago During the Forties and Fifties.* Chicago: The Lakeside Press, R. R. Donnelley & Sons, 1913.

Moses, John and Joseph Kirkland. *The History of Chicago, Illinois.* 2 Vols. Chicago: Munsell & Co., 1895.

Pierce, Bessie Louise. *A History of Chicago.* Chicago: University of Chicago Press, 1940.

"The Chicago Conspiracy." *Atlantic Monthly.* 16 (Jul. 1865):108-20.

D. Histories of Cook County

Andreas, A. T. *History of Cook County.* 1 Vol. Chicago: A. T. Andreas, Publisher, 1884.

Goodspeed, Weston A. and Daniel D. Healy. *History of Cook County.* 2 Vols. Chicago: Goodspeed Historical Association, 1909.

2. Biographies

Biographical Sketches of Leading Men of Chicago. Chicago: Wilson & St. Clair, 1868.

Cullum, General George W. *Biographical Register of Officers and Graduates of the United States Military Academy at West Point.* New York: James Miller, 1879.

Dictionary of American Biography. American Council of Learned Societies. New York: Scribner & Sons, 1928-33.

Eisenschiml, Otto. *Vermont General, The Unusual War Experiences of Edward Hastings Ripley, 1862-1865.* New York: Devin Adair Co., 1960.

Flynn, John J. *Hand Book of Chicago Biography.* 1893.

Hall, Richard. *Stanley, An Adventurer Explored.* Boston: Houghton Mifflin Co., 1975.

Harpel, Charles. Obituary notices, 11 Vols. Chicago Historical Society.

History of Medicine and Surgery and Physicians and Surgeons of Chicago. Chicago: Biographical Publishing Corp., 1922.

Hunt, Roger D., and Jack R. Brown. *Brevet Brigadier Generals in Blue.* Gaithersburg: Olde Soldier Books Inc., 1990.

Life of Mary Monholland, One of the Pioneer Sisters of the Order of Mercy in the West. By a Member of the Order. Chicago: J. S. Hyland & Co., 1894.

Moody, William R. *The Life of Dwight L. Moody*. Chicago: Fleming R. Revell Co., 1900.

Starr, Stephen Z. *Colonel Grenfell's Wars*. Baton Rouge: Louisiana State University Press, 1971.

Temple, Wayne C., *Stephen A. Douglas, Freemason*. Bloomington: The Masonic Book Club, 1982.

Wakelyn, Jon L. *Biographical Dictionary of the Confederacy*. Westport: Greenwood Press, 1977.

Warner, Ezra. *Generals in Blue*. Baton Rouge: Louisiana State University Press, 1964.

Winslow, Charles S., *Biographical Sketches of Chicagoans*. 10 Vols. Chicago Public Library, 1948.

3. Special Monographs

Basler, Roy P. ed. *The Collected Works of Abraham Lincoln*. New Brunswick: Rutgers University Press, 1953.

Berlin, Ira. *Slaves Without Masters*. New York: Oxford University Press, 1975.

Bonner, Thomas Neville. *Medicine in Chicago, 1850-1950*. Madison: American Research History Center, 1957.

Bryan, I. J. *History of Lincoln Park*. Chicago: The Commissioners, 1899.

Byrne, Frank L. "Prisons Pens of Suffering." *The Images of War*. 4 Vols. Garden City: Doubleday & Co., 1983.

Clingman, Lewis B. Jr. "History of Camp Douglas." Master's thesis, De Paul University, 1942.

Cozzens, Peter. *The Shipwreck of Their Hopes*. Urbana: University of Illinois Press, 1994.

Dorris, Jonathan T. *Pardon and Amnesty Under Lincoln and Johnson*. Westport: Greenwood Press, 1953.

Dyer, Frederick H. *A Compendium of the War of the Rebellion*. 2 Vols. Dayton: Morningside Bookshop, 1978.

Eppse, Merle R. *The Negro, Too, in American History.* Nashville: National Publication Co., 1943.

Gleeson, Ed. *Rebel Sons of Erin, A History of the Tenth Tennessee Infantry Regiment.* Indianapolis: Guild Press of Indiana, 1993.

Grant, Bruce. *Fight for a City, The Story of the Union League Club of Chicago.* Chicago: Rand McNally, 1955.

Hauser, Philip M., and Evelyn M. Kitagawa. *Local Community Fact Book for Chicago, 1950.* Chicago: Chicago Community Inventory, University of Chicago, 1953.

Hesseltine, William B. *Civil War Prisons: A Study in War Psychology.* Unger, NY: American Classics, 1971. (First published by Ohio State University Press, Columbus, 1930.)

Holderith, George L. "James A. Mulligan." Master's thesis, Notre Dame University, 1932.

Holmes, Clay W. *The Elmira Prison Camp.* New York: G. P. Putnam & Sons, 1912.

Johannsen, Robert W. *Letters of Stephen A. Douglas.* Urbana: University of Illinois Press, 1961.

Kelly, Dennis. "A History of Camp Douglas Illinois, Union Prison, 1861-1865." Manuscript, United States Department of the Interior, National Park Service, Southeast Region, 1989.

Klement, Frank L. *Dark Lanterns: Secret Political Societies, Conspiracies, and Treason Trials in the Civil War.* Baton Rouge: Louisiana State University Press, 1984.

Kubalanza, Joan Marie G. "A Comparative Study of Conditions at Two Civil War Prison Camps: Camp Douglas, Chicago, Illinois and Camp Sumpter, Andersonville, Georgia." Master's thesis, De Paul University, 1979.

Lesser, Hedwig F. *Civil War Prisons: A study of the conditions under which they operated.* Montgomery: University of Alabama Press, 1968.

Lindsley, John B. *Military Annals of Tennessee, Confederate.* Nashville: J. M. Lindsley & Co., 1886.

Locke, Rev. Clinton, D.D. "Grace Church." Rush-Presbyterian-St. Lukes's Medical Center Archives, Chicago.

Marshall, John A. *American Bastille: A History of the Illegal Arrests and Imprisonment of American Citizens During the Late Civil War.* New York: Da Capo Press, 1970.

Maxwell, William Quenton. *Lincoln's Fifth Wheel, The Political History of the United States Sanitary Commission.* New York: Longmans, Green & Co., 1956.

Moss, Rev. Lemuel. *Annals of the United States Christian Commission.* Philadelphia: J. B. Lippencott & Co., 1868.

Murdock, Eugene C. *One Million Men: The Civil War Draft in the North.* Madison: State Historical Society of Wisconsin, 1971.

Neely, Mark E., Jr. *The Abraham Lincoln Encyclopedia.* New York: Da Capo Press, 1982.

Neely, Mark E., Jr. *The Fate of Liberty.* New York: Oxford University Press, 1991.

Nolan, Alan T. *The Iron Brigade.* New York: Macmillan Publishing Co., 1961.

Robertson, John. *Michigan in the War.* Lansing: W. S. George & Co., 1882.

Rosenberger, Jesse L. *Through Three Centuries.* Chicago: University of Chicago Press, 1922.

Schreiner, Samuel A. Jr. *The Trials of Mrs. Lincoln.* New York: Donald I. Fine, Inc., 1987.

Sorensen, Mark W. "The Civil War Prisoner of War System." Manuscript, Illinois State Archives, 1978.

Story, Howard Kenneth. "Camp Douglas, 1861-1865." Master's thesis, Northwestern University, 1942.

Stover, John F. *History of the Illinois Central Railroad.* New York: Macmillan Publishing Co., 1975.

Terrell, W. H. H. *Indiana in the War of the Rebellion.* Indianapolis: Indiana Historical Bureau, 1960.

Wiley, Bell I. *The Life of Johnny Reb.* New York: Bobbs-Merrill Co., 1962.

Winters, John D. *The Civil War in Louisiana.* Baton Rouge: Louisiana State University Press, 1963.

Wright, Marcus J. *Tennessee in the War.* New York: Ambrose Lee Publishing Co., 1908.

4. **Articles and Essays in Periodicals, Annuals, and Publications of Learned Societies**

Angle, Paul M. "The Story of an Ordinary Man." *Journal of the Illinois State Historical Society.* 33 (Mar. 1940):229-32.

Baird, Nancy D. "The Yellow Fever Plot." *Civil War Times.* 7 (Nov. 1974):16-23.

Cabeen, Richard McP. "Camp Douglas and Its Prisoner of War Letters." *Seventeenth American Philatelic Congress Year Book.* (1951):76-100.

Castel, Albert. "Black Jack Logan." *Civil War Times.* 7 (Nov. 1976):4-10, 40-45.

Clark, James R. "The Cost of Capture." *Civil War Times.* 1 (Mar. 1992):26-30.

Eisendrath, Joseph L. "Chicago's Camp Douglas, 1861-1865." *Journal of the Illinois State Historical Society.* 55 (Spring 1960):37-63.

Grimsley, Mark. "Ulysses S. Grant." *Civil War Times.* 7 (Feb. 1990):32-34.

Jackson, Luther P. "Free Negroes of Petersburg, Virginia." *The Journal of Negro History.* 12 (Jan. 1927):386-88.

Karlen, Harvey M., "Postal History of Camp Douglas, 1861-1865." *The American Philatelist,* Journal of the American Philatelic Society. (Sep. 1979):815-24; (Oct. 1979):920-29, 960.

Kaufhold, John. "The Elmira Observatory." *Civil War Times.* 4 (Jul. 1977):30-35.

Levy, George D. "Prisoners in the Dust: Hostages and Pawns Under the Lincoln Administration." *The Lincoln Newsletter.* Vol. XIV, No. 2 (Summer 1995).

Long, E. B. "Camp Douglas: A Hellish Den." *Chicago History.* 1 (Fall 1970):83-95.

McCaffrey, James. "A Short History of the Civil War Sutler." *Civil War Times.* 4 (Jun. 1985):36-39.

Meketa, Jacqueline. "A Poetic Plea From Prison." *Civil War Times.* 30 (Mar. 1991):28-32.

Pearson, Priscilla and Robert D. Hoffsommer, eds. "In Vinculis: A Prisoner of War, Part II." *Civil War Times.* 9 (Jan. 1985):26-33.

Robbins, Peggy. "The Greatest Scoundrel." *Civil War Times.* 5 (Nov.-Dec. 1992):54-57, 89-90.

Sabine, David B. "The Fifth Wheel." *Civil War Times.* 2 (May 1980):14-23.

Stier, William Joseph. "Death of a Cavalier: The Demise of John Hunt Morgan." *North South Trader's Civil War.* 22 (Jul.-Aug. 1995):22-27.

Taylor, John M. "Grover Cleveland and the Rebel Banners." *Civil War Times.* 4 (Sep./Oct. 1993):22-24.

Todd, Gary T. "An Invalid Corps." *Civil War Times.* 8 (Dec. 1985):10-19.

Wesley, Charles W. "Negroes in the Confederate Army." *The Journal of Negro History.* 4 (Jul. 1919):239-53.

Wiley, Bell I. "The Common Soldier of the Civil War." *Civil War Times.* 4 (Jul. 1973).

Wiley, Bell I. "Soldier Newspapers of the Civil War." *Civil War Times.* 4 (Jul. 1977):20-29.

5. Miscellaneous

Black's Medical Dictionary. Edited by C. W. H. Havard. 35th Edition. Totowa: Barnes & Noble, 1987.

Confederate Soldiers, Sailors and Civilians Who Died As Prisoners of War at Camp Douglas, Chicago, Ill., 1862-1865. Kalamazoo: Edgar Gray Publications.

Halpin & Bailey's Chicago Street Directories, 1861-1867.

Index